D0513773

About the editors

Dale Hay was awarded her PhD in developmental psychology from the University of North Carolina, USA. She has taught in Canada, the USA and the UK. Until recently Dr Hay was a scientist at the MRC Unit in Child Psychiatry, London, UK, and she is now a lecturer in the Faculty of Social and Political Sciences, University of Cambridge, UK.

Adrian Angold trained in medicine at the London Hospital Medical College and specialized in psychiatry at the Maudsley Hospital, London. He is currently Assistant Professor, Child and Adolescent Psychiatry at Duke University Medical School, North Carolina, USA.

*Precursors and Causes
in Development and
Psychopathology*

Precursors and Causes in Development and Psychopathology

Edited by

Dale F. Hay
University of Cambridge, UK

and

Adrian Angold
Duke University, North Carolina, USA

JOHN WILEY & SONS
Chichester · New York · Brisbane · Toronto · Singapore

Other Wiley Editorial Offices

John Wiley & Sons, Inc., 605 Third Avenue,
New York, NY 10158–0012, USA

Jacaranda Wiley Ltd, G.P.O. Box 859, Brisbane,
Queensland 4001, Australia

John Wiley & Sons (Canada) Ltd, 22 Worcester Road,
Rexdale, Ontario M9W 1L1, Canada

John Wiley & Sons (SEA) Pte Ltd, 37 Jalan Pemimpin #05–04,
Block B, Union Industrial Building, Singapore 2057

Library of Congress Cataloging-in-Publication Data

Precursors and causes in development and psychopathology / edited by
    Dale F. Hay and Adrian Angold.
        p.   cm. — (Wiley series on studies in child psychiatry)
    Includes bibliographical references and index.
    ISBN 0-471-92211-0 (ppc)
    1. Child psychopathology—Etiology.   2. Child psychology.
    I. Hay, Dale F.   II. Angold, Adrian.   III. Series.
    [DNLM: 1. Child Behavior Disorders—etiology.   2. Child
Development.   3. Child Development Disorders—etiology.   4. Mental
Disorders—etiology.   5. Mental Disorders—in infancy & childhood.
WS 350.6   P923]
RJ499.P697   1993
618.92′89071—dc20
DNLM/DLC
for Library of Congress   92–49875
                                                                      CIP

British Library Cataloguing in Publication Data

A catalogue record for this book is available from the British Library

ISBN 0-471-92211-0

Typeset in 10/12pt Times from author's disks by Photo·graphics, Honiton
Printed and bound in Great Britain by Biddles Ltd, Guildford and King's Lynn

Contents

List of Contributors

ADRIAN ANGOLD

Developmental Epidemiology Program, Department of Psychiatry, Duke University, Durham, North Carolina, USA

ROBERT CAIRNS

Department of Psychology, University of North Carolina, Chapel Hill, North Carolina, USA

MARLENE CAPLAN

Thomas Coram Research Unit, Institute of Education, London, UK

DOUGLAS FRYE

Department of Computer Science, Yale University, New Haven, Connecticut, USA

JEAN-LOUIS GARIEPY

Department of Psychology, University of North Carolina, Chapel Hill, NC, USA

ROBERT GOODMAN

Department of Child and Adolescent Psychiatry, Institute of Psychiatry, London, UK

DALE F. HAY

University of Cambridge, UK

MARC LE BLANC

School of Psycho-Education, University of Montreal, Montreal, Quebec, Canada

ROLF LOEBER

Western Psychiatric Institute and Clinic, School of Medicine, University of Pittsburgh, Pittsburgh, PA, USA

ANNE M. MCGUIRE

Department of Psychology, University of North Carolina, Chapel Hill, NC, USA

PETER MUNDY

Departments of Psychiatry and
Psychology, University of California at
Los Angeles, Los Angeles, CA, USA

ALISON NASH

Department of Psychology, State
University of New York at New Paltz,
New Paltz, NY, USA

ANDREW PICKLES

MRC Child Psychiatry Unit, London, UK

MARIAN SIGMAN

Departments of Psychiatry and
Psychology, University of California at
Los Angeles, Los Angeles, CA, USA

Series Preface

During recent years there has been a tremendous growth of research in both child development and child psychiatry. Research findings are beginning to modify clinical practice but to a considerable extent the fields of child development and child psychiatry have remained surprisingly separate, with regrettably little cross-fertilization. Much developmental research has not concerned itself with clinical issues and studies of clinical syndromes have all too often been made within the narrow confines of a pathological condition approach with scant regard to developmental matters. This situation is rapidly changing, but the results of clinical-developmental studies are often reported only by means of scattered papers and scientific journals. This series aims to bridge the gap between child development and clinical psychiatry by presenting reports of new findings, new ideas, and new approaches in a book form that may be available to a wider readership.

The series includes reviews of specific topics, multi-authored volumes on a common theme, and accounts of specific pieces of research. However, in all cases, the aim is to provide a clear, readable, and interesting account of scientific findings in a style that makes explicit their relevance to clinical practice or social policy. It is hoped that the series will be of interest to both clinicians and researchers in the fields of child psychiatry, child psychology, psychiatric social work, social paediatric, and education—in short, all concerned with growing children and their problems.

This seventh volume in the series tackles an issue that is of central improtance for both clinical psychiatry and child development; namely, what is meant by the concept of "cause" and how the mechanisms involved in causation can be studied and delineated. At first sight this might seem a very straightforward question, but as the essays in this volume bring out the considerations are far from simple and straightforward. The complexity arises both from the fact that most causation is multifactorially determined and from the fact that many causal processes involve several steps or stages. There is an essential need to differentiate between features that tend to occur before some important outcome, but which are not involved directly in causation, and those that are an intrinsic part of the causal mechanisms. Thus, children tend to crawl before they walk (and in that sense crawling is a precursor of walking), but it is obvious that crawling does not "cause" walking. The distinction is far from an esoteric academic one. Rather, it is central to our understanding of the processes involved in normal and abnormal development.This volume provides a thoughtful, and interesting, review of the concepts and findings that apply to the differentiation of precursors and causes in relation to some key features of normal and abnormal development. The findings give rise to some provocative, and sometimes surprising, conclusions and have important implications for policy and practice as well as research.

MICHAEL RUTTER

Preface

The conclusions we come to in this book owe much to the fact that Adrian Angold and I have both worked at the Institute of Psychiatry, London, and in the Piedmont region of North Carolina, in counterbalanced order. We have therefore been exposed to the methods and traditions of both medical and developmental science, in Britain and the US, and feel compelled to seek some sort of synthesis across academically and geographically distinct cultures. We share this goal with others who, in the last decade, have defined the new field of developmental psychopathology. Perhaps our effort is most distinguished by an attempt to think about development in the interactionist Carolina tradition, i.e. with an eye to the complexities of what the organism might be really doing in any given social situation. My own thinking about development has been greatly influenced by Harriet Rheingold, Robert Cairns, and Gilbert Gottlieb, with whom I studied as a graduate student; Adrian has been latterly influenced by that tradition.

Our particular struggles with the concept of precursor and its relationship to causality stem from our empirical studies, supported by the Medical Research Council, on early precursors to prosocial behaviour and conflict and on childhood depression. In both cases, we defended the phenomena in question as worthy of study on the grounds of resemblance to things other people were studying in older individuals. Yet we know well the pitfalls of using resemblance as a criterion for conceptual relatedness—our first collaborative effort was an analysis of the concept of validity, and we were persuaded by those psychometricians who have criticised the use of face validity as a criterion for anything. So obviously a search for precursors must move beyond their face validity—but that in turn flung us into the whirlpool of causal analysis. This book represents our attempt to sort out our ideas about precursors and causes by asking some of the scholars whose work we most respect to think about these issues with us. We are extremely pleased with the seriousness with which they have taken up this charge, and are most grateful to them all. Additionally, however, we must thank some other individuals who have participated in symposia on these issues, at the Institute of Psychiatry and at the Society for Research in Child Development meetings in Seattle, in 1991. They are: E. J. Costello, Catherine Lord, Barbara Maughan, and David Quinton.

We are grateful to our editors for help with the mauscript. The series editor, Michael Rutter, read the book carefully and offered many helpful suggestions; although I suspect he does not completely agree with our recommendations to abandon conventional causal analysis, his comments have helped us sharpen our arguments. Wendy Hudlass and Lewis Derrick of John Wiley & Sons have been most helpful as well. And, finally, I should like to thank my son, who was born about the same time as the idea for this project and is now older than I would like to admit (delays in bringing this project to conclusion are probably not unrelated to this parallel development). He has reminded me daily of the complexities of individual development and, surprisingly, has made me more sympathetic to stage theory as a description if not an explanation of developmental progressions. My efforts in editing this book are dedicated to him.

DALE HAY
University of Cambridge
February 1993

Chapter 1

Introduction: Precursors and Causes in Development and Pathogenesis

Dale F. Hay and Adrian Angold

> Veniente occurrite morbo . . . discite,
> o miseri, et causa cognoscite rerum.
> (Meet the morbus at its onset.
> Learn, you unfortunates, and understand
> the causes of things.)
> <div align="right">Persius, <i>Satires</i> III. 64, 68
(cited in Kraupl-Taylor, 1979)</div>

OBJECTIVES

What causes one body to become diseased, while another remains whole and healthy? What causes one adolescent boy to become studious but depressed, while the boy across the street plays truant and steals hubcaps? What causes one child of alcoholic parents to succumb to alcoholism, while a sibling evinces no signs of problem drinking or any other psychiatric disorder? Will we get any purchase on these questions if we follow Persius's advice, and attempt to "meet the morbus at its onset"—in other words, if we take a developmental perspective, and try to identify the earliest manifestations of a disorder or disease? Within the realm of psychopathology can we find precursors of adult disorders, and, if we do, does that improve our chances of understanding what causes the disorders to occur?

Our aim in this book is to examine ways in which the concepts of "precursor" and "cause" have been applied to normal and abnormal development. In doing so, we had to confront the age-old problem of defining what a cause might be. Causality is crucial, but there is by no means agreement on how to find causes in a living, developing system. In this chapter we shall summarize some traditional approaches to the concept of causation, and then illustrate some ways in which medical researchers and developmentalists have tried to search for causes. Finally, we shall examine some definitions of the term "precursor" and consider whether a

Precursors and Causes in Development and Psychopathology.
Edited by D. F. Hay and A. Angold © 1993 John Wiley & Son Ltd

search for precursors might take us some steps forward in "understanding the causes of things."

ATTEMPTS AT DEFINING THE CONCEPT OF CAUSE

Both the developmentalist and the clinician continue to partake in the centuries-old philosophical debate about causality (e.g. Butterworth & Bryant, 1990; Gottlieb, 1991; Oyama, 1985). Current discussions return again and again to four definitions set forth thousands of years ago, namely, Aristotle's distinctions between four different types of causes: *material, efficient, formal,* and *final* causes. As discussed by contemporary developmental scholars (Hopkins & Butterworth, 1990), these four different types of causes correspond to four basic questions about events in the natural world: "(1) What matter was involved? (2) What was responsible for the presence of the object of investigation? (3) What forms did it possess? (4) What was it striving for?"

To illustrate these four types of causation, consider first a physical event: the case of a snowball rolling down a hill. What caused it to do so? The sources of information used in answering this question might include the following:

(1) Its material composition (i.e. the snowball's molecular structure and its temporary status as a solid);
(2) The forces acting efficiently upon it to propel it down the hill (gravitational forces and the action of the child who was rolling it);
(3) Its form, in the sense that its approximation to a spherical shape befits it for rolling;
(4) The object of its rolling down the hill.

With respect to the latter question, in some cases, the object of the roll might be stated in terms of a description of its eventual outcome: the snowball rolled down in order to rest at the bottom of the hill. In other cases, however, consideration of final causation addresses the issue of purpose: for example, the child's aim to increase the size of the snowball, in order to build a snowman, or, alternatively, to stockpile an array of snowballs for use as weaponry. Note that, in the case of a physical object, final causation refers to an external agent's purpose, not necessarily the snowball's own striving. With conscious, or at least animate, organisms, discussions of final causation become embedded in a cluster of distinctions about function as opposed to purpose (see Hay, 1980).

Another basic distinction between different types of causes overlies the Aristotelian scheme. In our attempts at "understanding the causes of things", do we look within the thing itself or at the external forces impinging upon it? If we undertake a search for endogenous cauuses, we almost immediately run up against issues of material, formal, and final causation.

Let us now consider how the four Aristotelian categories, as well as the basic distinction between endogenous and exogenous causation, continue to loom large in the medical and developmental perspectives on the origins of psychopathology. We begin with an examination of some of the causal concepts employed in the medical approach to the understanding of disease.

THE MEDICAL MODEL

Aetiology and pathogenesis

The aetiology of a disease is the cluster of factors that lead to and promote the development of that disease. These factors may exist at a number of levels, ranging from the nature of social organizations to the structure of individual molecules. Classical infectious disease epidemiology has often been primarily concerned with aetiology—with predicting the presence of disease, often in the absence of a clear understanding of the processes by which the disease is actually generated. The famous work of John Snow provides a good illustration. Snow first observed that an outbreak of cholera had a geographical distribution that suggested a water-borne source. He then disabled the water pump that seemed to be responsible, and the epidemic abated. Therefore, it appeared that tainted water was an aetiological factor in the transmission of cholera. However, at that time the bacterial origin of cholera was still unknown, and it remained possible that water-borne epidemics resulted from the spread of "miasmas" with tainted water as their vehicle.

A more recent example of an aetiological hypothesis proving correct in the absence of any understanding of the mechanism concerns the relationship between asbestos and mesothelioma. In the 1950s it was observed that mesothelioma was much more prevalent than expected downwind of a particular asbestos plant in London, leading to a hypothesis that asbestos was an aetiological factor for mesothelioma. However, exactly how asbestos leads to the formation of this particular tumour remains uncertain to this day.

Many other examples could be cited, and it is perhaps not unfair to say that for most diseases a good deal may be known about aetiology, while the link between aetiological factors and the disease process remains unclear, or, at least, imperfectly described. At the cellular level, most genetic disorders are in this position. Even when a single Mendelian genetic abnormality is known to be responsible for a disease, it is rarely the case that all the steps in the causal pathway are known. For instance, neurofibromatosis has long been known to be caused by a dominant gene, but how that gene leads to the appearance of tumours, and why in some cases only skin pigmentation changes occur, while in others multiple tumours with a wide distribution appear, is unclear. Even when a genetically determined biochemical lesion has been clearly described, as in phenylketonuria, we do not know why the pathophysiological manifestations of that lesion take the particular form they do.

In general, then, aetiology cannot be equated with pathogenesis. The pathogenesis of a disease is the process whereby that disease is generated. To return to the example of phenylketonuria, the pathogenesis of a disease involves a failure in the production of the enzyme phenylalanine hydroxylase, which leads to a build-up of phenylalanine in the body. Thus, part of the pathogenetic mechanism is clear, although, as we have already noted, beyond this point the pathogenesis of the disorder remains to be worked out.

Risk and vulnerability

Both aetiology and pathogenesis are theoretical concepts about the causes of disease. The notion of risk occupies a rather different position in that it is a purely statistical concept. The demonstration that X is a risk factor for Y simply means that, if X is present, Y is more likely to occur. The dangers of making causal inferences from measures of risk (such as odds ratios or correlation coefficients) are pointed out in every introductory statistics textbook. However, the demonstration that X is a risk factor for Y is often the first step in demonstrating an aetiological relationship between X and Y. In fact, the work of John Snow in showing that a factor such as a particular water source was a risk factor for cholera was a vital step in the discovery of the aetiology of that disease.

The point at which a risk factor comes to be regarded as an established aetiological agent is difficult to define with any precision. In general, it relies upon scientists' consensus that the weight of evidence points to a specific link that can be incorporated into a coherent pathogenetic theory. Experimental studies are obviously important here, in so far as experimental manipulations of a particular risk factor, with everything else kept as constant as possible, provide strong evidence of a specific causal link. Consider how much more convincing John Snow's geographical observations became when he disabled the pump. However, the experimental approach is most easily deployed when the risk factor is an exogenous, efficient cause. Hypotheses about endogenous risk factors and about formal and final causation yield much less easily to experimentation. Thus, for example, the important concept of individual vulnerability to disease is much more difficult to address in this way.

A common pathway for the accumulation of knowledge about diseases runs as follows:

$$Risk \longrightarrow Aetiology \longrightarrow Pathogenesis$$

However, it should not be supposed that this is a necessary progression. The direction of the arrows may be reversed, or, more commonly, simultaneous progress may be made at each level. The original hypothesis that there was a relationship between smoking and lung cancer sprang from clinical observations, and the aetiological hypothesis that cigarette smoke contained carcinogens predated Dolls's epidemiological demonstration that smoking was indeed a risk factor for lung cancer. Similarly, the study of risk factors for coronary artery disease has proceeded hand in hand with laboratory investigations of the aetiology and pathogenesis of atheroma. It is therefore more appropriate to see these three links in the chain of causation as being interdependent, and often circular, with progress in one domain stimulating further research in the others.

Prevention and treatment

Prevention refers to the situation in which some action reduces the later occurrence of an undesired outcome. Thus prevention is a major aim of pathologists of all sorts, whether of the mind, body, or body politic. Epidemiologists have distinguished between three modes of prevention. Primary prevention refers to situations where the undesired outcome is prevented from occurring at all. That is, the incidence of a disorder (the occurrence of new cases) is reduced. Here the aim is to prevent exposure to risk factors, or to build host resistance to them. Secondary prevention involves reducing the prevalence of a disease (the number of cases in the population at any one time, and so is directed towards those in the early stages, with the aim of compensating for their inadequate resources for coping with the disease. Identifying precursor conditions may be critical for secondary prevention. Tertiary prevention aims at reducing disabilities resulting from a disorder and at rehabilitating or improving the functioning of those who are chronically affected. Thus secondary and tertiary prevention efforts will often represent what is more commonly referred to as "treatment".

Prevention and treatment have an important place in causal analyses of disease. In developing causal theories, in the absence of knowledge about pathogenesis, it seems sensible to work backwards from what we know about the mechanism of action of the effective preventative agents or treatment strategies. The dopamine theory of schizophrenia is a case in point. It was observed that drugs that were effective in schizophrenia had effects on dopaminergic pathways in the brain, so it seemed reasonable to investigate the possibility that dopaminergic abnormalities are responsible for schizophrenia. However, there are also dangers inherent in this line of reasoning, since a treatment may operate through a mechanism quite different from that which causes the disorder in the first place. Thus the disease state resulting from a malignant tumour may be cured by its removal, but it is ridiculous to say that it was caused by the lack of earlier operations! The onset, maintenance, and termination of a disease may have quite different causes.

The effectiveness of a new treatment is usually tested by means of double-blind clinical trials, in which some individuals experience the new treatment while others experience conventional care. This application of the experimental method, in common with Snow's disabling of the water pump, focuses the pathologist's attention on efficient causes whose influence can be detected under controlled conditions. One contribution of a developmental perspective on pathogenesis lies in its renewed attention to endogenous influences, and in its willingness to grapple with the difficult concepts of final and formal causation.

THE DEVELOPMENTAL PERSPECTIVE VS THE MEDICAL ONE

In contrast to the experimental approach to pathogenesis, the developmental theorist usually cannot concentrate only on efficient causation. Rather, the definition of development itself invokes images of final and formal causation. In one of the most frequently cited definitions, Nagel (1957) noted; p. 17; that

> The concept of development . . . involves two essential components: The notion of a system possessing a definite structure and a definite set of pre-existing capacities; and the notion of a sequential set of changes in the system, yielding relatively permanent but novel increments not only its structure but in its modes of operation as well.

Thus, with respect to final causation, Nagel is concerned in the first instance to distinguish development from other sorts of change. Development means going somewhere in particular, not just oscillating back and forth. Furthermore, what it is that is developing is a structure, and its formal as well as material properties shape what comes next. We now highlight a few issues about final and formal causation that are currently being debated by developmental theorists, and start by considering how one defines normal and abnormal outcomes of development.

"Teleonomic" progressions in development and disease

Mayr (1961) coined the term "teleonomy" to describe the unfolding of a programme of individual development towards some end. That end is not a mystical notion, but simply the appropriate end-product of the programme, which has resulted from the process of natural selection. The existence of an end-point in development does not necessarily imply that the route to that end-point is fixed in one's genetic inheritance. Rather, Mayr (1974) noted that some developmental programmes are relatively "open", others relatively "closed"—i.e. more or less influenced by environmental input along the way.

Most developmental studies rely on the identification of some satisfactory end-point, even if they do not define it clearly. Studies of pathogenesis often do as well. Consider, for instance, the case of carcinoma of the cervix. Investigations of this process began from the observation that there was a class of cancers that appeared to arise from the cervix and spread both locally and sometimes to other regions of the body. In other words an end-point was first observed. The question then became: How is this end-point reached?

We now know that certain factors are associated with the appearance of pre-malignant atypical cells in the cervix (a precursor condition), which may progress through further degrees of cellular transformation to "malignant" lesions that are capable of invading and damaging normal tissues. This process only continues if the tumour achieves an adequate blood supply and survives the inflammatory response that such an invasion will often precipitate. At a later stage, spread of abnormal tissue may occur, with the appearance of independent tumours in other parts of the body.

Thus the process of disease progression has much in common with development. It is "programmed" by the nature of cellular transformation that begins the process, and in general follows a reasonably regular course, though with wide variations in rate. Furthermore, there is hierarchical integration as diseases develop. Cell transformation is required before local invasion occurs, and metastasis is usually a feature of an advanced invasive tumour. Each step, therefore, builds on the preceding stage, and the "achievements" of the preceding stage are "integrated" into that which succeeds it. Thus, metastatic tumours consist of invasive groups of transformed cells which may, in turn, metastasize themselves.

Just as there are relatively "open" programmes for certain aspects of normal development (Mayr, 1974), pathology is similarly constrained by context and shaped by experience. All possible abnormalities do not occur, and there are tremendous differences in the frequencies of occurrence of different disorders. Thus, when examining the role of particular aetiological influences, it is possible to use experimentation to test possible efficient causes in the context of a "teleonomic" disease process.

The enchantments of teleology

So far we have been considering the matter of end-points in development and disease at a purely descriptive level. More difficult conceptual problems arise when description of an apparently teleonomic process merges into teleological causal reasoning—when one begins to suggest that the cause of the outcome lies in a striving towards that end. At this point concepts such as "end-point", "goal", "function", and "purpose" get badly confused.

Many scholars have pointed out that developmentalists will inevitably become entangled in the problem of teleology, simply because they are studying living systems: "Thinkers from Aristotle to the present have been challenged by the apparent contradiction between a mechanistic interpretation of natural processes and the seemingly purposive sequence of events in organic growth, in reproduction, and in animal behaviour"; teleological notions arise again and again in reaction to "Descartes' grossly mechanistic interpretation of life" (Mayr, 1961, p. 1501). Goodwin (1990) notes that Descartes recognized the creative quality of human development, yet proceeded to ignore it, by insisting on applying the same analytic principles to living and non-living systems: "For him, the organism was a machine, an automaton. Our scientific culture has tried hard to validate this proposition. But the organism has resisted, just as the mind has resisted" (Goodwin, 1990, p. 60). This resistance is seen in contemporary studies of cognitive development, where it becomes clear that human thinking cannot always be described on an algorithmic basis (Johnson-Laird, 1990).

It is thus not surprising that alternatives to mechanical explanations of development are repeatedly raised. Yet vitalistic theories themselves soon move into the realms of the mystical. And some contemporary critics, such as contextualist and dialectical theorists (see e.g. Kramer & Bopp, 1989; Moshman, 1982) and life-span developmental theorists (e.g. Uttal & Perlmutter, 1989), consider a predetermined end-point to be a highly restrictive concept. They believe it places limits on a full understanding of the complexities of development.

What contemporary theorists are struggling with is the way in which teleological questions can be investigated in a scientifically rigorous manner. Ignoring goal-directedness in development seems naïve; but finding the appropriate methods to incorporate some aspects of final causation into developmental theory is by no means an easy task. Various issues have come up again and again in such discussions, and are still a matter of lively debate (see Hopkins & Butterworth, 1990). For example, does goal-directedness require consciousness? Do teleological systems have to be error-free—that is, if the process does not reach its logical conclusion, how do we know it was directed to a particular goal? How do we map the various routes to a single goal that might be undertaken? The contemporary developmentalist seems to want to know the actual mechanics of final causation. This quest reveals the difficulty twentieth-century post-positivists have in going beyond efficient causation.

Some of these issues, notably that of consciousness, seem less relevant when considering teleonomic disease processes. No one would see a diseased organism as consciously striving to reach the end state of renal failure, but it is far from foolish to see renal failure as the result of unfolding and organized pathological processes. The pathological examples point up the fact that one might wish to distinguish *descriptive* from *explanatory* teleonomy. In other words, noting a particular end-point in a developmental pathway or a disease does not necessarily equate that end-point with the purpose of the progression (consider again the snowball example raised earlier).

O'Connor (1987) has noted that Aristotle himself used the concept of final causation in both a descriptive and an explanatory sense: "For if a thing undergoes a continuous change and there is a stage which is last, this stage is the end" (*Physics*, **194A**, 25–30, cited in O'Connor, 1987, p. 146). O'Connor notes that some developmental theorists (e.g. Lerner & Kaufman, 1985) reject the descriptive meaning of final cause, arguing that development is context-dependent and no single outcome could ever be spotted. O'Connor goes on to claim that the other sense of final causation, the purposive one, is defensible and an important component of developmental and evolutionary thinking.

In contrast, we would argue the opposite position. We agree that, from both the developmental and pathological perspective, one cannot usually specify single outcomes. It does seem to be a multivariate world. However, if one can specify a probable, species- or disease-characteristic outcome or two, the scientist has a place to go, in the same way that claims about a possible precursor provide a place to begin. This aids proper description of the progression, if not ultimately providing a single explanation.

Identifying a probable outcome also helps us discover the forces operating on the developing organism that help it get there. For example, some theorists have claimed that genetic programming is largely responsible for an organism's reaching a species-specific end-point. In such caases, development is assumed to be *canalized*, rolling along a predefined trajectory towards a specified end-point, and relatively buffered against environmental interference (as in Waddington's famous landscape metaphor). However, Gottlieb (1991) argues that organisms must reside in species-appropriate environments for such species-appropriate end-points to be reached (see also Scarr, 1992). It is by focusing on precisely measurable developmental attainments (such as a mallard chick's recognition of an adult mallard's call) that Gottlieb and others have discovered the importance of the usual social environment for the flowering of species-characteristic behaviour.

Getting to grips with form

As we have seen, it is virtually impossible for the developmental theorist to shy away entirely from concepts like end-point, goal, and purpose and to restrict causal analysis to efficient causation. It is also quite likely that the developmentalist will at some point come face to face with the concept of formal causation. In Nagel's (1957, p. 17) words, the second essential component of the concept of development is the idea of "a system possessing a definite structure and a definite set of pre-existing capacities". In contemporary terminology, formal causation reasserts itself in the developmentalist's attention to mental and social structures and systems. At an even more basic level, cross-sectional comparisons of children at different developmental levels on the same task raise issues of formal causation; abstract concepts such as "age" or "stage" are implicitly being used as explanations of the children's behaviour (for a contemporary critique of misuses of the concept of age, see Rutter, 1989).

Issues about formal causation arise in structuralist approaches to development, such as those represented by Levi-Strauss, Piaget, and Chomsky (Flavell, 1982). Such theories address final causation as well:

Each of these scholars . . . focuses particularly on Man, seeing him as a constructive organism, with generative capacities, who nonetheless is preordained to follow certain paths in his intellectual development and achievement because of the structure of his own brain and the regulating forces in the human environment (Gardner, 1973, cited in Flavell, 1982, p. 4).

However, structural theories of development do not concentrate on material structures in the brain; rather, they also invoke more abstract psychological structures that themselves hold explanatory power.

Psychological structures are not single things, but relational systems:

the really central and essential meaning of "cognitive structure" ought to be a set of cognitive items that are somehow interrelated to constitute an organized whole or totality; to apply the term "structure" correctly . . . there must be, at minimum, an ensemble of two or more elements together with one or more *relationships* interlinking these elements (Flavell, 1971, cited in Flavell, 1982, p. 3).

Such unseen abstractions map very well on to the concept of "latent variable" used in contemporary statistical approaches to causal inference (see Pickles, Chapter 2 this volume).

Within a developmental framework, the concept of structure leads quite directly to the related concept of "stage". A child's way of thinking about many different sorts of problems may be viewed as a stage of cognitive development. The concept of stage is used in many different biological contexts, such as morphogenesis, embryological development, and disease processes (see Pickles, Chapter 2 this volume). Within Piaget's theory of intellectual development, the concept of stage has been discussed in detail, and its defining properties defined. These include *hierarchization, integration, consolidation, structuring,* and *equilibration* (see Pinard & Laurendeau, 1969).

Hierarchization refers to the fixed, intransitive order of stages; integration refers to the fact that a new stage integrates what has gone before, and does not just substitute for an earlier form. In other words, there is formal continuity across stages. More specifically, the property of consolidation specifies that "a period (or stage) must always involve at once an aspect of achievement of the recently acquired behaviour and an aspect of preparation for the behaviour of the following level" (Pinard & Laurendeau, 1969). The concept of consolidation thus alludes to notions of final causation, in terms of the goal-directedness of psychological development. It is hard to operationalize, and is often discussed in terms of issues relating to horizontal *décalage* (Pinard & Laurendeau, 1969).

The criterion of structuring simply re-emphasizes the systematic nature of intellectual development at a given stage—various domains of competence are interconnected into *structures d'ensemble*. More importantly the concept of equilibration provides a causal mechanism for the progression through a sequence of stages, in that there is a balance between assimilation of experience into existing structures and change in the structures in the face of new experience. To the extent that existing structures dictate the interpretation of experience, a formal causal hypothesis is set forth.

Stages of pathogenesis are identified in some areas of medicine, such as cancer research (see Pickles, Chapter 2 this volume), but are more rarely applied to psychopathology. However, issues about form, structure, and formal causation become particularly acute when considering how to diagnose pathological conditions. The descriptive question of how signs and symptoms are themselves hierarchically organized into syndromes and disorders, and how disorders covary within the same individuals, is of primary importance in the study of psychopathology from a developmental point of view (see Angold, Chapter 10 this volume). Close attention to diagnostic and measurement issues is likely to raise issues about the role of endogenous determinants of disorder and ultimately formal causation in psychopathological development.

An emphasis on endogenous determinants of subsequent development, and on formal causation in particular, soon leads to the problem of tracing change and continuity in form over time. One must ask whether early forms of a disorder or disease (as in the case of pre-cancerous cervical cells) are meaningfully related to full-blown pathological outcomes. Thus the developmental perspective on psychopathology inevitably leads to the problem of specifying early precursors of later disorders. In tackling this, we may have to confront the issue of stages in pathological development (see Pickles, Chapter 2 this volume).

A concern with form and formal causation extends beyond Piagetian approaches to psychological development; it also encompasses recent attempts to extend principles of systems theory to developmental problems. It is now frequently acknowledged that the developmentalist must attempt to identify and understand the workings of developing systems, and many are the flow charts that have been drawn up in an effort to do so (e.g. Lerner, 1991). However, it is not always easy for systems theories to move beyond systems descriptions (or rather, idealizations). Organisms themselves are described as multifaceted systems living within multifaceted systems. Thus, to the extent that there is mutual influence among system components, the form of the organism itself seems to take on causal status. Yet, if one wishes to find formal causes, how can one characterize the form of a developing entity? By definition, is that form not constantly changing?

Again, it is Descartes's mechanistic view of the animate as well as inanimate world that the contemporary developmental theorists are bent on challenging. Goodwin (1990) argues that Descartes's reliance on mechanistic explanation runs up against three hard-to-explain biological phenomena: neural activity, development, and speciation. Goodwin (1990, pp. 51–54) notes that these

> areas of difficulty . . . have something in common: they all involve the generation of complex, organized forms. . . . Behaviour and cognition also involve the generation of ordered forms in space and time, whether it be in play, ritualized courtship, pattern recognition or speech. . . . No matter how much we learn about genes and molecules, ontogeny and phylogeny will not be understood until we have an exact description of the type of dynamic organization that characterizes the living state; just as the behavior of liquids could not be understood in a generative sense until there was a theory of the dynamic space-time order that characterizes the liquid state of matter.

Goodwin goes on to argue that we must expect living systems to be in flux; what requires explanation is any discernible stasis, in terms of form and structure.

To what extent does a concern with the nature of form and a search for formal causes lead to acute scientific questions? It is easier to draw box diagrams of mutually influencing systems than to chart their workings in the flesh, in real time. Describing a system does not address the issue of how a system operates, and what efficient causes impinge upon the system to induce change. Again, as in the case of final causation, an emphasis on form and structure seems necessary at the descriptive level, but does not in itself constitute explanation. In particular, we still need to understand how efficient causes create forms that then have their own emergent properties.

A good example of this is provided by Thelen & Ulrich's (1991) application of dynamic systems theory to human motor development. These scholars state at the outset that they are neither structuralists nor are they reductionists focused on material causation. Further, in contrast to some neuroscientists, they do not believe that the motor milestones occur at the times they do because of some mechanism being switched on in the brain. At the same time they are not vitalists, in that they do not believe living systems are necessarily completely unique. Rather, they extrapolated thermodynamic principles from physical systems (such as water pouring out of a tap or through a pipe) and applied them to developmental issues.

Thelen and Ulrich note that complex physical patterns that change over time may arise in response to rather minor applications of an efficient cause, such as heat or pressure. Out of a seemingly infinite set of possibilities, only a few stable forms emerge, such as the absolutely rhythmic dripping of water from a tap at a certain level of pressure. Given their emphasis on dynamics, the predictable form is viewed not as a rigid structure but as a stable attractor. When the efficient cause—or what they refer to as a control parameter—changes, there is a temporary return to wide fluctuation in form and then perhaps a new attractor. For example, this is seen when one turns on taps at full blast.

Using this line of reasoning, Thelen and Ulrich demonstrate that the hallmark of mature human locomotion—coordinated, alternating steps with each leg—is neither genetically encoded nor switched on by a central neural mechanism at a particular age. Rather, mature stepping is a predictable form that is created through the application of a number of control parameters, including muscular maturation. A precocious version of this stable attractor can be seen in the early months of life when infants are held upright on a treadmill, long before they are able to walk on their own. This example from the domain of motor development underscores the fact that quite complicated developmental outcomes may arise predictably from a finite set of straightforward influences. This is a lesson that can be quite directly applied to psychopathological development.

PRECURSORS

Where does the concept of precursor fit into current thinking about causality? Certainly the concept of stages and sequences in a developmental progression raises the possibility that there are functional relations between early and later behaviours and structures. Let us start by considering some different meanings of the term.

The dictionary definition of precursor simply refers, in the first instance, to "a person or thing that precedes". At most, the denotative meaning of the term is one of harbinger, not prerequisite or precondition; a precursor is secondarily defined as "a person or thing that goes before and indicates the approach of someone or something else" (*Random House Dictionary*, 1980). But, as used by most developmentalists and pathologists, precursor implies some continuity of function or morbidity. A precursor does not simply precede or even simply predict a later state or behaviour, but rather is structurally, functionally, or mechanistically related to it.

Yet it is not clear what evidence is required to support a claim that an early condition is a precursor of a later one. To begin with, would we require surface similarity in features—do precursors need to look like the later condition? And, conversely, does a resemblance between an earlier state and a later outcome necessarily imply that the former is a precursor of the latter? Problems with using a criterion of surface resemblance have been noted by scholars in two quite different areas of inquiry, psychometrics and biological taxonomy. For example, in the literature on the validity of tests and measures, it has been shown that "face validity" is an inadequate criterion for attaining confidence in a measure (Messick, 1975; Mosier, 1947). The addition of a developmental perspective undermines confidence in the resemblance criterion even further, in that we know that externally similar behaviours may have different meanings at different points in development. For instance, repeated crying is normal in babies, but the same amount of crying would be cause for concern in a 15-year-old (see Angold, Chapter 10 this volume, for a detailed discussion of the application of various criteria when examining links between childhood and adult psychopathology).

These problems in equating resemblance and functional relatedness have long plagued biological classification (e.g. Eldredge & Cracraft, 1980; Wiley, 1981). On the one hand the numerical taxonomists attempt to set objective criteria of resemblance, using computer-generated algorithms to cluster "operational taxonomic units", based on very fine descriptions of morphological characteristics. In opposition to them are the cladists, who attempt to classify organisms on the basis of their evolutionary history, as determined by inferred resemblances to mutual ancestors. The cladists distinguish different levels of "true" (evolutionarily based) as opposed to surface similarity. In their terminology, characters that resemble each other might either be *homologues*, in that one is derived directly from the other, or, alternatively, *homoplasies*, having structural similarities and showing a similar course of development, but having arisen in independent lines of evolution. Yet again, the two characters might only be *analogues*, sharing a functional similarity but being structurally and ontogenetically quite different (Wiley, 1981).

In general, both the biological taxonomists and psychometricians recognize the fact that even almost perfect resemblance does not imply developmental or evolutionary links. Noting that two things are similar does not necessarily explain why either occurs or predict from one to the other, either on an evolutionary or an ontogenetic time line.

If surface resemblance is not enough, what criteria should we use? Would we require common determinants or functions at two different points in time? Stability of individual differences over time, even if the form of the behaviour or trait changed considerably? Evidence, as through Guttman scaling techniques, that a later outcome critically depends on the occurrence of an earlier condition? What if some of these criteria are met, but not others? What if the experimental method is attempted, but interventions directed to the alleged precursor fail to prevent the mature attainment or pathology? Does that discredit the precursor or the intervention?

To illustrate some of these issues, let us again turn to the realm of normal motor development to see how the question of precursors has been addressed. One of the puzzling features of newborn behaviour is its apparent precocity— newborns seem briefly able to do some things, notably stepping and swimming, that they then forget how to do for about a year. What happens to the newborn reflexes? Are they indeed precursors of mature walking and swimming—i.e. are they early occurring, necessary stages in a continuous developmental process? Or are they the ontogenetic equivalent of evolutionary analogues, bearing a surface resemblance in function (like the things called "wings" in both birds and butterflies) but being structurally and developmentally quite different (Wiley, 1981)?

The rise and fall of the stepping reflex have been examined in careful detail (Thelen, 1985; Thelen & Fisher, 1982). A critical advance was made when these investigators literally turned the question on its side, noticing, in terms of single-frame photographs and electromyographic (EMG) records, that the so-called stepping reflex was structurally and functionally almost exactly equivalent to kicking in the supine position. Furthermore, the alternation of flexion and extension and extended pausing in newborn kicking was analogous to the "swing" and "stance" phases in walking. Newborns could speed up their stepping or their kicking in the same way that adults turn walking into running—by decreasing the inter-movement interval. For the first month or so of life, stepping and kicking look almost the same. After a while, however, the behaviour disappears in the vertical but continues in the horizontal plane. Why might this be?

Thelen (1985) noted that there is a period after 6 weeks of age when motor activity and in particular inter-joint coordination becomes disorganized. Thelen (1985, p. 16) noted as well that 'The same period . . .

is also characterized by especially rapid physical growth and dramatic changes in body composition, primarily a disproportionate increase in body fat over muscle tissue.' Basically, infants become too heavy to kick successfully while standing up, and the so-called "stepping reflex" disappears. This maturational hypothesis was corroborated by experimental data. Infants younger than 6 weeks of age were unable to step if they were fitted with miniature leg weights; older infants, whose stepping reflex had disappeared, were able to step once again if their legs were placed in water.

So is the stepping reflex a precursor to mature walking or not? In form and patterning, reflexive stepping is almost exactly equivalent to walking. But the occurrence of the early manifestation is inhibited by physical growth and weight gain; thus the operation of a causal influence obscures the links between the early and the mature form of the behaviour (see Caplan, Chapter 7 this volume, for a discussion of inhibitory influences on precursors in another domain of development, prosocial behaviour).

Research on motor development also highlights ways in which activities that on the surface look very different may qualify as precursors of specified outcomes. For example, what are the precursors of crawling? Goldfield (1989, p. 917) claims that there are three—visual orientation, reaching for objects, and kicking: "Orienting the eye–head system to objects and persons in the environment motivates the infant to locomote . . . , reaching promotes steering the body, and kicking propels the body forward." Goldfield goes on to argue that the emergence of crawling follows closely on the development of a marked preference for use of one hand rather than another to reach for objects. Earlier in infancy, when hand preference is still ambilateral, infants rock back and forth; when hand preference emerges, infants who are trying to crawl tend to fall from an upright posture into a prone position on their non-preferred hand. In this example, which is the precursor condition? Is it rocking (which in many ways resembles crawling without forward propulsion into space) or hand preference (which looks quite unrelated, but may be the prerequisite attainment)?

Thelen & Ulrich's (1991) attempt to apply dynamic systems principles to motor development illustrate how one may need to use experimental procedures to uncover "cryptic precursors" of the outcome in question. Their surprising discovery that young infants held upright with their feet placed on a treadmill start to step in a mature manner provided a paradigm for the identification of a "hidden skill" and the opportunity for a detailed, longitudinal analysis of the transition from the precursor condition to mature locomotion.

In this book, we are asking whether the identification of precursors conditions helps us to find causes of development and psychopathology. Where, then, do precursors fit into concepts of causation discussed by pathologists and developmental theorists? For example, when we talk about precursor conditions as having their own causal status, are we actually making claims about formal causation? And are we setting up a scheme for the analysis of a stage-like progression towards a specified end-point?

At the very least, it seems better to start with something than with nothing. Bryant (1990) argues that, if we fail to pay attention to possible precursors, we close off our chances for accurate causal reasoning. He cites (1990, p. 38) the example of Piaget's theory of cognitive development:

> Piaget always defined the early developmental stages negatively. The inevitable Genevan claim about anything that develops was always "il y a trois stades," and in the first of these three stages the children were always completely at sea with whatever it is that they were being asked to do. Their behavior was described in negative terms, and that immediately removes a possible theoretical move. . . . You cannot say the child's early skills provide the basis for later development, because you are in effect denying that he has, at first, any such skills. You are forced into the position of arguing that his very lack of skill leads him into such a muddle that he has to be rescued or rescue himself with the help of some external factor—either a Deus ex machina or a deus in some other part of the machine.

Bryant argues strongly that understanding of children's cognitive development has been much aided by looking at what very young children know how to do, not what they cannot do.

Thus, in Bryant's view, identification of precursors permits the articulation of formal causal hypotheses. By extrapolation, in this book, we claim that similar advances can be made in the realm of psychopathology if we start not with the proposition that "all young children are psychologically healthy" but with a search for specific precursor conditions, at quite early points in development.

ARE DIFFERENT SORTS OF PRECURSORS AND CAUSES MUTUALLY DISTINGUISHABLE?

Our brief review of current thinking suggests that developmental theorists have returned to a preoccupation with structure and function, i.e. with formal and final causation. This coincides with an acknowledgement of the ethical and practical limitations of the experimental method (so good for examining issues regarding efficient causation) and with the introduction of mathematical techniques for examining causal influences among underlying abstract structures (see Pickles, Chapter 2 this volume). Thus current theories are open to hypotheses about different sorts of causes and use different sorts of decision rules, beyond experimental evidence.

At this point, when contemporary theorists are moving beyond efficient causation, we should ask: How well do the Aristotelian distinctions actually hold up under scrutiny? Are these distinctions perhaps just a matter of insufficient evidence or the level of analysis that is being used? For example, consider a situation where a woman was exposed to hazardous levels of radiation (i.e. experienced an exogenous force that may have influenced her subsequent development). Suppose that she manifested no overt ill effects, but nonetheless experienced a mutation at the level of the germ cells. Early symptoms of pathology in her own children might be explained by a second generation of scientists in terms of material or formal causation, as something emanating within the children. Here the efficient cause is not only buried within the past but has perhaps set off a series of reproductive and developmental events that themselves take on independent causal status.

These complex issues and possibilities have not been resolved by contemporary investigators. However, a number of different scholars, working in different domains, are independently searching for precursors and making inferences about causal processes. The aim of our book is to bring their ideas together, in a common forum. The chapters that follow illustrate some work in various areas of normal and pathological development.

We start with a chapter on general conceptual issues and methodology, in which Andrew Pickles describes some statistical considerations in the search for precursors and causes. In particular, he focuses on the ways in which the choice of an overall developmental or pathogenetic model constrains possibilities for statistical analysis of causal hypotheses. As an example, he illustrates ways in which stage models used in developmental psychology and psychopathology may be used to elucidate questions about precursors and causes.

We next present two theoretical chapters that address two of the most familiar causal dilemmas in developmental theory: the nature–nurture issues and the mind–body problem. Firstly, Robert Cairns and his colleagues discuss developmental behaviour genetics from a perspective that treats gene action as a phenomenon to be explained as well as a putative causal agent. They argue strongly that gene action is itself a developmental phenomenon and needs to be studied as such. They note the complementary contributions of behavioural genetic and comparative psychological strategies in tackling the complex interrelationships between gene action and development.

Next, Robert Goodman examines the relationship between brain abnormalities and psychological development. In Aristotelian terms, Goodman is at pains to go beyond the notion of "brain damage" as a simple, efficient cause of psychological difficulties. Rather, he undertakes an analysis of the more difficult issues regarding material, formal and final causation, in terms of a variety of abnormalities in the developing brain that are signs of, and possible causal influences on, psychiatric disorder.

These two theoretical chapters are followed by a series of investigations into the roles of precursors and causes in various domains of development. Each of these chapters provides a summary of the empirical research in the topic area, and, perhaps most usefully, sums up what is known about possible precursors to psychopathological conditions, with respect to the domain in question.

Thus, Marian Sigman and Peter Mundy present a careful consideration of the extent to which early cognitive processes and attainments predict a child's eventual level of intelligence and specific deficits shown in two pathological conditions, Down's syndrome and autism. More generally, Sigman and Mundy provide a clear summary of some different ways in which the concept of precursor has been investigated in the domain of intellectual development.

Next, Douglas Frye provides an incisive summary of the conceptual issues in the influential work on children's "theories of mind", which is currently providing the major developmental perspective on the origins of autism. Of particular concern in his chapter is the extent to which early precursors of a theory of mind can be discerned in infancy; this question obviously is of critical importance for the early detection of autism. A comparison with the claims made by Sigman and Mundy is instructive.

The next two chapters consider the progression of normal social relations, with attention to pathogenesis within that realm. Marlene Caplan examines prosocial development, asking what happens to very early occurring prosocial behaviours as children grow older. She emphasizes the important principle that there are losses as well as gains in normal development (see Uttal & Perlmutter, 1989), and that a causal analysis of any developmental phenomenon must examine inhibitory as well as facilitatory influences.

Next, Alison Nash and Dale Hay provide an update on Freud's classic assertion that the infant–mother relationship is a fundamental precursor of mature social relations. They take the more modern view that multiple relationships are formed in infancy, all of which may influence an individual's subsequent social adjustment and, eventually, choice of mates. They set forth five basic propositions about the links between early social relations and mating choices that may eventually throw some light on inter-generational continuities in social difficulties and personality disorder.

Two additional chapters focus on the issues of precursors and causes with respect to two forms of childhood psychopathology. First, Marc Le Blanc and Rolf Loeber provide a developmental framework in which to examine the emergence and determinants of conduct disorder and criminal offending. They outline a variety of developmental research designs in which potential causes of offending are examined. They then summarize some illustrative findings emerging from each line of inquiry. Le Blanc and Loeber are at pains to note that different sorts of causal variables (e.g. unchanging background factors as opposed to variation in state) call for different sorts of research designs.

Next, Adrian Angold asks the question: why do we not know what causes depression in childhood? He summarizes a number of definitional and measurement problems that arise when studying depression at any point in time, as well as seeking functional continuity between the childhood and adult conditions. He emphasizes the fact that, throughout the life span, depression occurs simultaneously with a number of other psychiatric conditions. The substantial co-morbidity of disorder and covariation of putative risk factors places limits on possible causal analysis.

The final chapter provides some reflection on what has gone before. We evaluate the ways in which the authors have attempted to identify precursors and causes in various realms of development and, in light of the information presented in these chapters, make some recommendations for developmental and psychopathological research in the next decade.

REFERENCES

Bryant, P. (1990). Empirical evidence for causes in development. In G. Butterworth & P. Bryant (eds), *Causes of Development: Interdisciplinary Perspectives*, Harvester Wheatsheaf, Hemel Hempstead; pp. 33–45.

Butterworth, G. & Bryant, P. (eds) (1990). *Causes of Development: Interdisciplinary Perspectives*, Harvester Wheatsheaf, Hemel Hempstead.

Eldredge, N. & Cracraft, J. (1980). *Phylogenetic Patterns and the Evolutionary Process: Method and Theory in Comparative Biology.* Columbia University Press, Guildford.

Flavell, J. (1982). Structures, stages, and sequences in cognitive development. In W.A. Collins (ed.), *The Concept of Development. The Minnesota Symposia on Child Psychology*, vol. 15, Erlbaum, Hillsdale, NJ, pp. 1–28.

Goldfield, E. C. (1989). Transition from rocking to crawling: Postural constraints on infant movement. *Developmental Psychology*, **25**, 913–919.

Goodwin, B. (1990). The causes of biological form. In G. Butterworth & P. Bryant (eds), *Causes of Development: Interdisciplinary Perspectives*, Harvester Wheatsheaf, Hemel Hempstead, pp. 49–63.

Gottlieb, G. (1991). Experiential canalization of behavioural development: I. Theory. *Developmental Psychology*, **27**, 4–13.

Hay, D. F. (1980). Multiple functions of proximity-seeking in infancy. *Child Development*, **51**, 636–645.

Hopkins, B. & Butterworth, G. (1990). Concepts of causality in explanations of development. In G. Butterworth & P. Bryant (eds), *Causes of Development: Interdisciplinary Perspectives.* Harvester Wheatsheaf, Hemel Hempstead, pp. 3–32.

Johnson–Laird, P. M. (1990). The development of reasoning ability. In G. Butterworth & P. Bryant (eds), *Causes of Development: Interdisciplinary Perspectives.* Harvester Wheatsheaf, Hemel Hempstead, pp. 85–110.

Kramer, D. A. & Bopp, M. J. (eds) (1989). *Transformation in Clinical and Developmental Psychology*, Springer-Verlag, New York.

Kraupl-Taylor, F. (1979). *The Concept of Illness, Disease and Morbus.* Cambridge University Press, London.

Lerner, R. (1991). Changing organism–context relations as the basic process of development: a developmental contextual perspective. *Developmental Psychology*, **27** (1), 27–32.

Lerner, R. M. & Kaufman, M. B. (1985). The concept of development in contextualism. *Developmental Review*, **5**, 309–333.

Mayr, E. (1961). Cause and effect in biology. *Science*, **134**, 1501–1506.

Mayr, E. (1974). Behavior programs and evolutionary strategies. *American Scientist*, **62**, 650–659.

Messick, S. (1975). The standard problem: meaning and values in measurement and evaluation. *American Psychologist*, **30**, 955–966.

Moshman, D. (1982). Exogenous, endogenous, and dialectical constructivism. *Developmental Review*, **2**, 371–384.

Mosier, C. I. (1947). A critical examination of the concepts of face validity. *Educational and Psychological Measurement*, **7**, 191–205.

Nagel, E. (1957). Determinism and development. In D. B. Harris (ed), *The Concept of Development*, University of Minnesota Press, Minneapolis, pp. 15–24.

O'Connor, B. (1987). A note on final causes and their role in contextualism. *Developmental Review*, **7**, 145–148.

Oyama, S. (1985). *The Ontogeny of Information: Developmental Systems and Evolution*. Cambridge University Press, Cambridge.

Pinard, A. & Laurendeau, M. (1969). "Stage" in Piaget's cognitive–developmental theory: exegesis of a concept. In D. Elkind & J. Flavell (eds), *Studies in Cognitive Development: Essays in Honor of Jean Piaget*, Oxford University Press, London, pp. 121–170.

Rutter, M. (1989). Age as an ambiguous variable in developmental research: some epidemiological considerations from developmental psychopathology. *International Journal of Behavioural Development*, **12**, 1–34.

Scarr, S. (1992). Developmental theories for the 1990s: development and individual differences. *Child Development*, **63**, 1–19.

Thelen, E. (1985). Developmental origins in motor coordination: Leg movements in human infants. *Developmental Psychobiology*, **18**, 1–22.

Thelen, E. & Fisher, D. M. (1982). Newborn stepping: an explanation for a "disappearing reflex". *Developmental Psychology*, **18**, 760–775.

Thelen, E. & Ulrich, B. D. (1991). Hidden skills: a dynamic systems analysis of treadmill stepping during the first year. *Monographs of the Society for Research in Child Development*, Serial No. 223, Vol. 56, No. 1, pp. 1–106.

Uttal, D. H. & Perlmutter, M. (1989). Toward a broader conceptualization of development: the role of gains and losses across the life span. *Developmental Review*, **9**, 101–132.

Wiley, E. O. (1981). *Phylogenetics: The Theory and Practice of Phylogenetic Systematics*, John Wiley, New York.

Chapter 2

Stages, Precursors and Causes in Development

Andrew Pickles

What has the workaday researcher to learn from the literature on causal analysis? In answering this question for himself, Leamer (1988) concluded "not much". He argued that, in relation to the more philosophical contributions, a simple-minded ("my") understanding of the word "cause" has not, in practice, led to incorrect inferences that a deep understanding ("anything I don't understand") would have prevented. Nor have the numerous special languages for causal analysis (e.g. Holland, 1988) offered anything that could not be adequately expressed in the traditional language of applied statistics. What of the more technical contributions? In recent years this literature has become dominated by "causal modelling", a phrase almost synonymous with the fitting of linear structural equation models of one form or another using such programs as LISREL (Joreskog & Sorbum, 1984). The relevance of this work is obscured by a mass of Greek letters, of which LISREL devotees (the Lisrelites of Hayduk, 1987) are so fond, but which few of us can even pronounce. Moreover, the structure that is represented in these models, a structure that assumes continuous variables linearly interrelated in such a way as to generate multivariate normal (or near normal) data, often appears to have little to do with our intuitive understanding of processes as involving mechanisms. Psychopathogenic mechanisms are likely to involve discrete events, transitions and interactions that are not properly conceptualized in this fashion.

This is not to say that either literature is wrong or misguided, but rather to suggest that, as a means of conveying or emphasizing some more general points about causal analysis, each has chosen a language or form of presentation that does not exploit the often well-developed intuition and vocabulary of the applied researcher. This chapter attempts to explain and illustrate one of these more general points, namely that causal inference is model dependent, through a rather informal exploration of one particular

Precursors and Causes in Development and Psychopathology.
Edited by D. F. Hay and A. Angold © 1993 John Wiley & Son Ltd

form of model—a stage model (cf. Marini & Singer, 1988). Stage models provide a clear example of a type of model with quite unexpected richness in terms of the complexity of the consequences that follow from its apparently quite simple structure. These complexities include some interesting interpretations of nonadditivity in the effects of risk factors, delineation of the difference between risk factors and precursors, and an explanation of the distinctions and relationships between development or ageing and the passage of time.

Stage models themselves have been posited as models of ordinary development, for example in the largely theoretical arguments of Piagetian cognitive development and also for the process of learning to read (e.g. Frith, 1985). They have also been useful in descriptive psychopathology, for example in their largely empirical application by Farrington (1986) in describing the criminal careers of delinquents, and Kandel (1982) in describing drug abuse "careers". In many other studies, empirical findings have suggested a stage structure for specific elements of a process. For example, precocious maturation in girls has been found to be one of many factors associated with poor educational attainment. However, the link here does not appear to be a direct one, but is mediated by a stage during which the girls associate with an older peer group and then leave education early as that peer group completes its own schooling (Magnusson, Stattin & Allen, 1986).

A markedly contrasting consideration of multistage models for human pathology is seen in the work of epidemiologists studying carcinogenesis (Armitage & Doll, 1954, 1961), where the motivation was the ability of stage models to explain age of onset distributions and synergy among risk factors at a time when techniques for observing and describing the intermediate cellular transformations were unavailable. Illustrations both of statistical models to indicate that certain previously undescribed stages may be present in a developmental or psychopathological process, and to assign status to measured variables in relation to a staged process will be described in this chapter.

Rothman (1976) has suggested a way of decomposing causes that helps in understanding that synergy among causal factors is likely to be more common than we might expect and that its occurrence is informative about causal structure. He showed that synergy can arise through there being an intermediate outcome that separates the point of action of one risk factor from that of a second risk factor. The existence of such a staged process in the development of an outcome has implications for the way it is analyzed and for the way in which statistical interaction terms are interpreted. Intermediate stages would also appear to be natural contenders for the role of precursors, and their introduction allows the simplest of transition processes to explain the basic features of a variety of distributions that are typical of the age of onset of pathologies and also the age of attainment of normal developmental milestones. Furthermore, a stage structure has fundamental implications for the timing and duration of risk factor exposure and rates of occurrence. Overall, the importance of model structure for causal analysis is thus made clear.

Enthusiasm for stage models engendered by such clear theoretical richness must, however, be tempered by empirical difficulties in their detailed operationalization. This is illustrated by the experience in the study of carcinogenesis, particularly in attempts to identify the individual stages empirically (as opposed to statistically). This chapter describes some of the current criteria and techniques used in psychology and behavioral studies to identify stages in normal and abnormal development and discusses some general statistical criteria for this purpose. It is clear, however, that further work is required to aid empirical investigation, for example, in reformulating the structural equation modelling approach so successful with continuous variables, to deal with the latent categorical variables and the progressive selection process that stage models imply. Some consideration is also given to how stage models of normal development and of the development of psychopathology might be interrelated.

DEFINITION OF CAUSE

Most scientists rightly hesitate before saying, unconditionally, that X causes Y. This is because such simple causation rarely, if ever, exists—some sort of qualification is almost always necessary. Typically a variety of conditions have to be met before, during or after the occurrence of the causative event for its full consequences to be observed. Sometimes these conditions are mere logical necessities; for example, there must be surviving subjects with the phenylketonuria gene to observe the outcome of phenylketonuric mental retardation. Such conditions can be appropriately considered as restricting the scope of the causal statement. Extending this approach of scope restriction to everything else but the particular cause in question does not however, appear sensible. Often a condition can only reasonably be considered as an essential and integral component of a larger and more complicated causal process. Thus to say that the phenylketonuria gene causes phenylketonuric mental retardation is misleading, in that it gives no hint that an essential element of the causal process is a diet containing phenylalanine. Rothman (1976) suggests that both the phenylketonuria gene and phenylalanine should be conceptualized as "component causes" that when present together form a "sufficient cause". Recognition of the fact that, most of the time, we investigate component causes is valuable for at least two interrelated reasons. Firstly, it makes clear that we should not be daunted by thinking that we need explain all occurrences of the event in question. The correct model of the part of the process in which our component cause is involved might account for only a fraction of cases. Secondly, it is a prerequisite for an understanding of synergy.

SYNERGY AND COMPONENT CAUSATION

In Figure 2.1(a) a process is illustrated in which an outcome may occur as the result of either of two specific risk factors $B1$ and $B2$ (the term "risk factor" will be used even where referring to a factor whose presence reduces the rate of outcome, i.e. is "good"). Both $B1$ and $B2$ thus constitute a sufficient cause of the outcome. However, occurrence of an outcome is rarely a deterministic or necessary consequence of mere exposure to a risk factor. More commonly only a small proportion are "hit" (develop the outcome), even when exposed. We also need to consider the fact that there

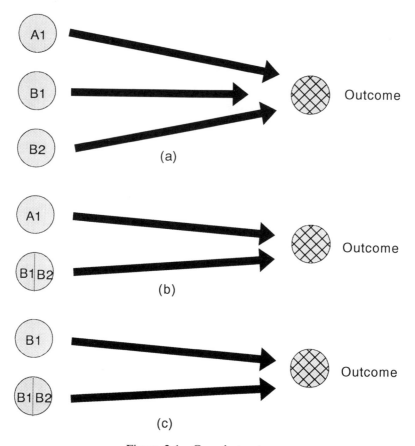

Figure 2.1 Causal structures

may be other causes of the outcome of interest that we have not measured (i.e. are neither $B1$ nor $B2$) and that we may not even know exist. We will call such causes "background factors" (A1). Figures 2.2(a)–(d) (1 stage) illustrate typical rates of occurrence when a population is exposed to three different combinations of background factors, $B1$ and $B2$: background factors but not $B1$ or $B2$ lead to an occurrence rate of 4% (2.2(a)); background factors plus $B1$ lead to an occurrence rate of 8%, of which $B1$ must account for 8%−4%=4% (2.2(b)); and background factors plus $B2$, which also lead to an occurrence rate of 8% (of which $B2$ must account for 4%) (2.2(c)). What should we expect when a population is exposed to both risk factors? If, as here, the "hit" rate from each risk is quite low and the risk mechanisms are independent of each other, then the chances of being "hit" by more than one risk factor during the time of exposure will be very small. As a result all the "hits" from background, $B1$ or $B2$ risk factors will be received by different individuals and the outcome rate will be just the sum of the component rates, i.e. 4%+4%+4%=12% (2.2 (d)). (A more exact derivation, that takes into account the chance of multiple "hits", results in the effects of risk factors combining according to a complentary log-log scale: see McCullagh & Nelder, 1983; Rutter & Pickles, 1991.) This simple addition of rates forms a benchmark against which "synergy" may be detected.

Now consider the case represented in Figure 2.1(b) where two risk factors $B1$ and $B2$ are components of a sufficient cause of an outcome, but neither is in itself alone a sufficient cause. The rate of occurrence remains at the background level when either $B1$ or $B2$ are present alone, for neither one is a sufficient cause. Only where both are present will the rate of occurrence increase above that due to the background factors. This is a clear example of synergy and more generally suggests the conclusion that risk factors that are synergistic are component causes of a sufficient cause. Now consider the case represented in Figure 2.1(c). The fact that $B1$ and $B2$ occur together in a sufficient cause would suggest that they are synergistic. However, the fact that $B1$ also has an effect in the absence of $B2$, means that it alone is also a sufficient cause. Their synergy is now only partial. The fact that $B1$ occurs as a component within every sufficient cause will also give it the additional status of a "necessary" cause. Thus partial synergy indicates a factor being involved in more than one sufficient cause, while a necessary cause must be at least partially synergistic with all other component causes.

SYNERGY, STAGES AND STATISTICAL ANALYSIS

The previous section does not directly relate to possible mechanisms nor to routine methods of analysis of data. On these issues two commonly held misconceptions must be banished from the start. Firstly, synergy need not arise out of any highlighting or masking of effects occurring in the "chemistry

28

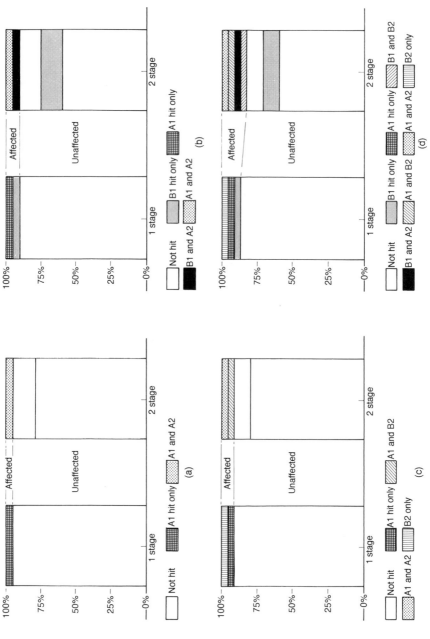

Figure 2.2 (a) Background risk factors only; (b) background and risk factor *B1*; (c) background and risk factor *B2*; (d) background and both risk factors

of the moment". Secondly, synergy need not correspond to a statistical interaction effect (Blot & Day, 1979). Both of these points can be illustrated by consideration of two-stage models. For instance, we have already noted that the effect of early maturation on educational outcome in girls seems to operate through an intermediate stage involving associating with older peers, while the use of illegal drugs is almost always preceded by a stage involving the use of legal drugs, notably alcohol and tobacco (Yagamuchi & Kandel, 1984a,b).

Let us now turn to the situation in which the appearance of the outcome of interest depends upon two "hits" having occurred (Figures 2.2(a)–(d) 2 stage) with the first hit resulting in a transition from stage 0 to an intermediate stage 1, and the second producing a transition from the intermediate stage to the final pathology. For each stage there is a background risk and a single specific risk factor and these are assumed to be independent sufficient causes with effects that combine additively at each stage, just as in the single-hit single-stage model of the previous section. However, a risk factor for the first transition can potentially operate on all subjects that are exposed to it. A risk factor for the second transition can operate only upon those who have already made that first transition and has no effect on those still in stage 1. In Figure 2.2(a) background transition rates $A1$ and $A2$ of 20% at each stage, give a base rate for the final outcome of $A1$ times $A2 = 0.20 \times 0.20 = 0.04$ or 4%. In Figure 2.2(b) the presence of $B1$, the specific risk factor for stage 1, increases the first transition rate to $(A1+B1) = 20\%+20\% = 40\%$, but getting to the final outcome relies on just the background rate $A2$, giving an overall rate of $(A1+B1)$ times $A2 = 8\%$. This can be broken down into the additive components $A1A2+B1A2 = 4\%+4\%$. Similarly, in Figure 2.2(c), the presence of risk factor $B2$ elevates the second stage transition rate to 40%, giving an overall rate $A1$ times $(A2+B2)$ or additive components $A1A2+A1B2 = 4\%+4\% = 8\%$. Finally when both are present in Figure 2.2(d), the final outcome rate will be $(A1+B2)$ times $(A2+B2)$ giving four additive components

$$A1A2+B1A2+A2B2+B1B2 \;=\; 4\%+4\%+4\%+4\% \;=\; 16\%$$

This represents an increase in the rate over the sum of the effects of background rates and each risk factor alone $(A1A2+B1A2+A1B2)$ by the amount $B1B2$ or 4%.

Thus some form of synergy is implied between $B1$ and $B2$ even though the transitions may have been separated by months or years and thus cannot be understood in terms of the chemistry of the moment. In the first example of school drop-out, recognizing the two-stage structure would suggest a likely synergy between early maturity in girls, as a risk factor for associating with older peers, and parental lack of interest in education, as a risk factor for allowing girls to leave school early. Such synergy would be rather harder to explain within the constraints of a one-stage process.

How might such a two-stage structure be represented in any statistical analysis? Where the intermediate stage is known and observable the key to the design of the analysis is to recognize that the population at risk at stage 2 is smaller than the population at the earlier stage (Robins, Davis & Wish, 1977; Kandel, 1982). In the simplest statistical approach, separate additive models with no interaction among risk factors might be fitted to the sample after breaking it down into groups defined by their degree of risk for potential involvement in the next stage. Such models can be fitted using the Grizzle–Starmer–Koch weighted least squares approach to the analysis of categorical data implemented; for example, within the SAS CATMOD procedure (SAS Institute, 1987) and the additive variants of generalized linear models with generalized relative risk functions (Breslow & Storer, 1985; Rutter & Pickles, 1991). The model structure and design of the analysis assume synergy between risk factors for different stages but no formal test is undertaken. Moreover, to allocate individuals to the appropriate groups we have to know in advance what the stage structure is. What statistical analysis is appropriate where we have just an initial stage and a final outcome and unknown intermediate stages, with our ignorance precluding the decomposition of the sample? The outcome for the whole sample could be analyzed directly in terms of the additive components described above with

$$\text{Rate} = a + b1X1 + b2X2 + b3X1X2$$

where $X1$ and $X2$ are simple dummy variables describing the presence or absence of the risk factors and $a, b1, b2$ and $b3$ are parameters to be estimated. The parameter for the interaction ($b3$ in this instance) does estimate the degree of synergy, and such synergy might be due either to "chemistry of the moment" effects or to risk factors operating on different stages (though were the data to correspond exactly to the simple stage structure with low rates then $b3$ should be equal to $b1$ times $b2$). An alternative approach would be to fit a log-linear model or linear logistic regression model as implemented in numerous programs (e.g. SAS v5 procedure GLM, 1985; SPSS-PC v3 logistic regression and hiloglinear, 1989; GLIM, 1985). Such models are nonadditive, but for low rates of outcome occurrence can be approximated by models that have additive effects on the logarithm of the outcome rate. Consider the simple "main effects" model

$$\log(\text{rate}) = a^* + b1^*X1 + b2^*X2$$

where $X1$ and $X2$ are defined as above and only three parameters $a^*, b1^*$

and $b2^*$ are to be estimated (the $*$ are to distinguish them from the parameters of the previous additive model). If the rate in the absence of both risk factors is 4%, then a^* will be equal to $\log(0.04) = -3.22$. If the rates in the presence of $X1$ and $X2$ separately are both 8% then $b1^*$ and $b2^*$ will both equal 0.69 [$\log(0.08) = -2.53$ and $-2.53 - (-3.22) = 0.69$].

Having values for a, $b1$ and $b2$ we can now calculate the rate (predicted by the model) when both $X1$ and $X2$ are present, namely antilog or

$$\exp(a1^* + b1^* + b2^*) = \exp(-3.22 + 0.69 + 0.69) = 16\%$$

This was the rate occurring for our illustrative two-stage process, a process that involved synergy between risk factors for different stages. Thus, in general, logistic or log-linear models without interaction effects for risk factors, may often imply synergy. Moreover, one obvious interpretation of the occurrence of such multiplicative effects between risk factors is to postulate a multistage process with the risk factors operating on different stages.

Another approach would be to fit a generalized relative risk model (Breslow & Storer, 1985; Rutter & Pickles, 1991). That is a model that estimates a parameter that relates directly to the extent to which the effects of two risk factors are additive or multiplicative.

RISK FACTORS, STAGES AND PRECURSORS

The previous discussion helps to resolve a long-standing debate about the onset of depression in women as a process involving vulnerability factors and provoking agents (Brown & Harris, 1978; Tennant & Bebbington, 1978). Brown and Harris used an additive model and identified an interaction effect between a vulnerability factor (having three children at home) and a provoking agent (occurrence of a life event) and found that life events had little effect unless the woman was vulnerable. Tennant and Bebbington, using a log-linear model, found no interaction effect and questioned the distinction between vulnerability and provoking factors. Postulating a two-stage process with an intermediate stage of vulnerability explains both of these findings (see also Rutter & Pickles, 1991).

This example raises another important point, for it is tempting to equate the intermediate vulnerable stage with the risk factor of having three children at home. This would be wrong, however, since it involves confusing a risk factor for entering the intermediate stage with the stage itself.

The presence in the stage model of "background" risks for entering the intermediate stage implies that having children at home is just one of the sufficient causes operating on this transition and it is not a necessary one.

There are other routes to vulnerability other than having three young children at home (as Brown and Harris found). Thus the intermediate stage more properly reflects some more generalized, perhaps more internal, form of vulnerability.

As yet the term "precursor" has not been used in this chapter, but the concept of a precursor clearly involves some notion of an early or immature form of some end-point pathology and thus would seem to correspond closely with that of stage (see also Hay and Angold, Chapter 1 this volume). The previous paragraph therefore suggests a distinction between a precursor and a risk factor, in that, while the presence of a risk factor may raise the probability of pathology occurring, the presence of a precursor marks actual progress toward it. In many instances a precursor stage may "look like" a mild form of the eventual pathology, such as the tobacco and alcohol stage of Kandel's (1982) model of the progression to hard drug abuse. However, as several of the other examples have shown, this is not a necessary element of the concept. Some precursors may be quite unlike what follows (as can be seen in many examples throughout this book; see, for instance, Sigman's Chapter 5, or Loeber and Le Blanc, Chapter 9).

QUESTIONS OF TIMING

The notion of an ordered sequence of changes in real time would seem to be fundamental to any notion of development, with skills or pathologies generally appearing within a certain age period, being delayed or advanced according to genetic endowment and social experience, and being preceded and followed by specific precursors and sequelae. Although the obvious complexity of what we see might suggest a complex underlying process, our intuitive grasp of the power of relatively simple models to describe complex processes is not well developed, and we are at risk of rejecting out of hand very straightforward models that are capable of offering considerable insight, without ignoring the complexity of the phenomenology. Some further implications of stage models spring from their ability to suggest the structure of the processes underlying age-dependent changes in rates of disorder (or the achievement of skills). Figure 2.3 shows some typical distributions for the age of onset of disorders. The first curve is typical of degenerative-type diseases, for example, Alzheimer's disease. The second curve is that for schizophrenia. In both these cases, the onset is the disorder itself and, in fact, most individuals die before showing any onset of the disorder (that is, most people never suffer from schizophrenia or Alzheimer's disease). The third curve is typical of a normal developmental milestone. In this case nearly all individuals have an onset and pathology is represented by late achievement of nonachievement of the milestone. What mechanisms might give rise to these various age patterns for development?

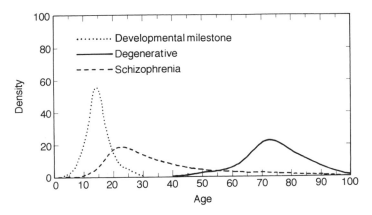

Figure 2.3   Age of onset distributions

Although development clearly occurs in continuous time, the mathematics of models in discrete time, that is where time is cut up into fixed intervals, and change examined only between intervals, is considerably more transparent. This is not a major restriction, however, since as the intervals become very short, such models typically closely approximate their continuous time equivalents. The simplest possible process involves individuals making a transition from one state or level to another with the probability of making this transition, denoted by p, being equal for all individuals and constant over time. Table 2.1 gives, from time $t=0$ onwards, the expected proportions remaining in the first state, the proportion achieving the new state in the last interval of time (the product of the transition rate p and the proportion remaining in the original state during the previous interval), and the cumulative proportion who have achieved the new state since $t=0$. Figure 2.4 displays these data and gives at the bottom the expected distribution of

Table 2.1   Proportions arriving and remaining in each state

Time	Proportion in original state	Proportion achieving final state	Total proportion in final state
0	1	0	0
1	$1-p$	p	p
2	$(1-p)(1-p)=(1-p)^2$	$(1-p)p$	$2p-p^2$
3	$(1-p)^3$	$(1-p)^2 p$	$3p-2p^2+p^3$
4	$(1-p)^4$	$(1-p)^3 p$	$4p...$

the ages at which the new state is achieved. It is clear that this bears little relationship to any of our empirical age of onset distributions.

How might we modify the model to bring it more closely into conformity with the data? Several possibilities present themselves. In the first instance, we may postulate heterogeneity in the transition probability between individuals. In the extreme, some individuals, perhaps the majority, may have a transition rate of zero. In other words, they are not liable to the outcome in question (as some researchers have suggested is the case for schizophrenia). However, no pattern of variation between subjects in time-constant transition rates can alone give rise to anything other than an age of onset distribution that is always declining with age (Heckman & Singer,

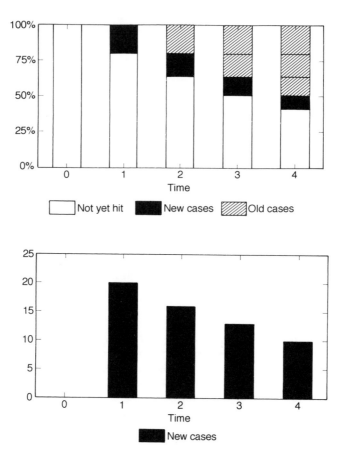

Figure 2.4 The accumulation of cases and the age of onset for a simple 1-stage model

1984). This is not to say that such heterogeneity, arising from differential exposure to risk factors or more intrinsic "frailty" or "liability" does not exist, for it clearly does. Rather, we observe that it is not a sufficient explanation by itself.

Another way to modify the model is to allow the transition rate, p, to vary with age; for example, to start with a low value and then increase. However, without postulating a formal mechanism that determines the value of p at each interval, we would be simply allowing p to vary to fit the data, describing its variation, rather than making much progress in explaining development. One possible mechanism for age dependence in p is that a build-up or degradation of some system or capacity to a threshold level must occur before an onset is observed. Such a mechanism gives rise to an inverse Gaussian distribution, with occurrences commonly grouped around the average time for that threshold to be reached (see e.g. Pickles & Crouchley, 1991). Another possible mechanism involves onsets that occur only after the breakdown of all of several parallel components, with normal behaviour being maintained as long as any one component is still working. Such a mechanism gives rise to an age of onset with a form known as a gamma distribution. A third possibility involves time variation in the environment, specifically variation in exposure to risk factors. However, such changes in exposure arise at least in part through individuals (or others around them) making or selecting environments appropriate (or inappropriate) to their current developmental capacities. Thus, change in the exposure to risk factors may be as much a consequence as an explanation of development. Something else, in addition to the foregoing, seems to be necessary to explain the underlying process.

Perhaps rather surprisingly, a possible mechanism is the device already explored of introducing intermediate stages to be traversed before the final stage can be achieved. Table 2.2 gives the proportions in various stages of the process from time $t=0$ and for each transition of a two-stage process.

Table 2.2   Proportions arriving and remaining in each state

Time	Stage 0 remaining	Stage 1 In	Stage 1 Remaining	Stage 2 In
0	1	0	0	0
1	$1-p$	p	0	0
2	$(1-p)^2$	$p(1-p)$	$p(1-p)$	p^2
3	$(1-p)^3$	$p(1-p)^2$	$2p(1-p)^2$	$2p^2-p^3$
4	$(1-p)^4$	$p(1-p)^3$	$3p(1-p)^3$	$3p^2-6p^3+3p^4$

As Figure 2.5 shows for $p=0.3$, this simple modification has brought the hypothetical age of onset distribution far closer into line with what we need, with there being some individuals who achieve the final state early, some late, but a clear clustering of cases around some middle value.

A more precise relationship between the age of onset distribution and the number of stages can be found. Consider the case where the time intervals are short such that the transition probability p is small, so making p much larger than p-squared, which, in turn, is much larger than p-cubed and so on. For the one-stage model in Table 2.1 this leads to the number of new cases expected (column 3) all being roughly equal to p and constant over time. For the two-stage model of Table 2.2 the number of cases

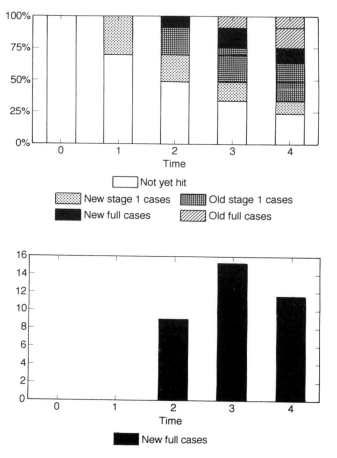

Figure 2.5　The accumulation of cases and the age of onset for a simple 2-stage model

essentially increases linearly (p^2 at time 1, $2p^2$ at time 2, $3p^2$ at time 3 and so on). These illustrate a more general relationship for stage models that in the earlier part of the age of onset distribution the number of cases increases in proportion to t^{k-1}, where k is the number of stages.

Thus, even where the intermediate stages are unobserved, analysis of the age of onset curve can give some indication as to the number of stages. For most epithelial cancers this turned out to be around five or six, understood in that context as the number of changes that an initially healthy cell must suffer before it was capable of the characteristic uncontrolled replication of a malignant cancer cell. In addition, where an intermediate stage can be observed, the relationship between its age of onset distribution and that for the final pathology is determined by its position in the sequence of stages.

THE TIMING AND DURATION OF RISK FACTORS IN MULTISTAGE MODELS

Before examining more critically the value of a multistage model, it is worth summarizing the wide-ranging implications the model has for our causal understanding. Firstly, the fact that some behaviour, skill or pathology generally occurs at a certain age is seen to be simply a function of time and the structure of the process; we explain the process of "ageing" (see also Rutter, 1989a) rather than having to use it as an explanatory factor. Secondly, as we have seen already, the identification of synergy between two risk factors suggests that they act on transitions between different stages, whereas the absence of synergy suggests they act on the same transition, and partial synergy (where a model somewhere between additive and multiplicative is suggested—see Rutter & Pickles, 1991) indicates that the two act on one transition but one of them also acts upon another. Thirdly, the impact of exposure to a risk factor that operates on a stage near the start of the process will not be seen for some time (since several subsequent transitions must first occur), while those affecting later transitions will have more immediate effects. Finally, the removal or reduction of an early-stage risk factor after initial exposure to it may have no effect on eventual outcome if the subjects under study are already past the stage upon which that risk factor acts, while the early removal or reduction of a risk factor for the final stage will always immediately reduce the eventual outcome rate. A corollary of this is that a risk factor that produces an effect that is only weakly related to the duration of exposure is likely to be influencing an earlier, rather than a later, stage.

For such a simple model these are sophisticated implications indeed, ones that in the context of developmental psychopathology would be able to explain various duration of exposure/dose response relationships (e.g. parental marital discord, Rutter & Quinton, 1984), "sensitive periods" (e.g.

separation experience, Rutter, 1987), "sleeper effects" (e.g. effects of Head Start program, Lazard & Darlington, 1982) patterns of age of onset, age dependency in risk factors and much more.

This also convincingly illustrates that what risk factors are identified as important and how they are so identified, can depend upon the structure of the model used in the analysis. Thus it is fundamental to any attempt at resolving questions about causality to identify the correct structure of the model. For a stage model, this involves determining the number of stages, the points of action of the relevant risk factors, and also the nature of the precursor stages. This requires the bringing together of epidemiological, experimental and clinical methods.

ELUCIDATING A STAGE MODEL: THE EXPERIENCE FROM RESEARCH ON CARCINOGENESIS

And there's the rub! Although the basic ideas of the multistage model have proved enormously valuable as organizing principles in cancer research (Peto, 1977; Day, 1990), detailed empirical confirmation has been difficult. For example, using epidemiological data, evidence can be found for multiplicative effects of asbestos exposure and smoking on lung cancer (Saracci, 1977), and in an ambitious attempt to apply the multistage model directly, Thomas (1983) concluded that the data were most consistent with asbestos acting on the fourth stage and smoking on the sixth and final stage. However, other studies have come to conclusions that contradict these findings or their implications (e.g. Berry, Newhouse & Antonio, 1985), and minor modifications to the model, such as allowing differing transition rates between stages or biologically plausible complications, such as persistence of asbestos fibres in the lung, prevent any firm conclusion. In part this may be simply a question of power, for the number of deaths among nonsmoking asbestos workers has been so small (14 in the 5 major cohort studies, Kaldor & Day, 1987) that little could be reasonably concluded.

The Armitage–Doll model of carcinogenesis was proposed to explain epidemiological data, and the specification of the biological meaning of a stage was not pressing when the ability to detect cells in intermediate stages was not available. Subsequent attempts to do so, based on recent advances in cell and molecular biology, have proved very difficult. A few examples of stages now exist, as in carcinomas of the colon that are preceded by adenomatous polyps. For most individuals the polyps arise sporadically but in individuals with familial polyposis they are extensive (Bussey, 1975). These individuals show a pattern of inheritance that suggests this first transition to be due to an autosomal dominant mutation, and the almost inevitable second-stage transition, that of somatic mutation of just one of their cells, explains their lifetime risk of almost 100% for cancer of the colon.

Such apparently phenotypically clear precursor stages are not common and the more general experience has been one of confusion with, for example, conflict between *in vivo* and *in vitro* results. Thus, in practice, while epidemiological and early experimental evidence of some risk factors separately influencing an early stage (initiation) and a late stage (promotion) is strong (with other risk factors appearing to do both) the detailed structure of the Armitage–Doll model with several stages and age-constant transition rates is probably not tenable (Day, 1990). Other models may apply with rather fewer stages (e.g. Moolgavkar & Knudson, 1981) but with some of the other forms of complication described earlier, for example heterogeneity and time-varying risk factors. Nevertheless, even though empirical verification is not proving straightforward, the basic structure remains intact (see Weinberg, 1989 for an intriguing summary of the recent state of play).

STAGES AND RISK FACTORS, IN NORMAL, DELAYED AND ARRESTED DEVELOPMENT

The point of the previous section is not that carcinogenesis should in any way be used as an analogy for psychological development or that of psychopathology, but to emphasize that bringing together the conceptual and the empirical notion of stages is far from trivial. If stage models have anything to offer this may only be gained where stage definition is undertaken with great caution. Some further informal consideration of what should characterize a stage may be useful. A more formal analysis remains to be done.

The concept of stages is, of course, far from being new to thinking on psychological development. And yet, the manner in which the stage concept has been arrived at, and used to guide scientific investigation, could hardly be more different from that found in cancer research. The stages of Piagetian normal cognitive development were individually defined after observation of a very limited number of subjects, whereas in cancer research stages have been inferred, to explain population or large sample data, without individual stage description. Although Piagetian stages have achieved considerable theoretical status, their empirical identification has received less attention (Fischer & Silvern, 1985). Qualitative change in behaviour or cognitive skills can be easily identified but which of these represent criteria for stages or just "substages" is unclear. Discontinuity as a criterion, both specific qualitative change and coincident and rapid change in a range of behaviors and cognitive skills, has occasionally been used with some success (e.g. McCall, Eichorn & Hogarty, 1977). The invariance in the sequence of stages is reasonably replicable as a predominant type (e.g. Wohwill, 1973), at least at the level of the group if not the individual, and such techniques as scalograms are used to determine empirically what sequences obtain.

Although supposedly synchronous in age of onset, interest has been slight in the actual location of stages in time. For example, the task of constructing age norms and distributions for stage achievement has usually been replaced by the much less demanding task of showing that success at a stage-dependent task increases with age. This lack of specific interest in issues of timing, coupled with the inevitability of the normal sequence as a logical necessity of the theory, left little scope for research in individual differences in rates of progression, their relationship to risk factors or their continuity into later developmental stages and transitions.

These last are the kinds of concerns that are at the core of a view of psychopathology as normal development "gone wrong", either slowed, arrested at some intermediate stage or having switched to some alternative pathological path. Such a view is not an uncommon one in relation to some reading difficulties. Several authors have suggested stage models of normal reading development that involve a stage of logographic reading (the recognition of individual familiar words) followed later by a stage of phonological encoding (constructing the sound of an unfamiliar word from its parts). An obvious hypothesis to explain the occurrence of some poor readers would be that they were stuck in the logographic stage (Frith, 1985), exhibiting problems specific to new or pseudowords for which phonological encoding is required. Some longitudinal studies of reading have found evidence consistent with this view. For example, Klicpera's (1989) classroom study of German children found increased errors in familiar words as children were apparently making the transition to the phonological stage, and a small group who though continuing to slowly expand their reading vocabulary of familiar words, never mastered pseudowords.

However, it is always necessary to consider the counter-evidence against rigidly sequenced stages. In this instance, there is evidence that phonological awareness, such as interest in rhyming, begins very early and that letter–sound training appears to improve reading even of those still supposedly in the logographic stage (Stuart & Coltheart, 1988). These phenomena suggest parallel rather than sequential development of skills, with each reinforcing the other with respect to progress in reading. For such a process, the temporal ordering of stages representing predominant use of logographic or phonological strategies need not be a psychological invariant and it might even be subject to environmental manipulation.

This suggests that further consideration needs to be given to both models and methods of analysis of progression through stages in which uniform sequences (e.g. Aebli, 1978) and rates of progress are not assumed. Bentler (1980) and Henning & Rudinger (1985) review some of the possibilities.

RISK FACTORS AND STAGES IN THE DEVELOPMENT OF PSYCHOPATHOLOGY

In the models for carcinogenesis a large number of cells are making their way through the multistage process but whatever the stage that the most advanced cell has reached, there are always other cells that remain still in each of the less advanced stages. Thus an individual accumulates cells from an increasingly wide range of stages over time. This accumulation process is similar to the process of the accumulation of behaviours and symptoms suggested in some models of psychopathology. For example, Loeber (1991) refers to the process of retention of behaviors typical of conduct disorder in young children by delinquent adolescents. In other situations transitions from one stage to another may involve not just the gaining of new features but the loss of previous ones. In still others, some form of reversibility may be possible; for example, Le Blanc & Loeber (Chapter 9, this volume) describe the possibility of so-called de-escalation and even desistance in the development of delinquent and criminal careers. For simplicity, the discussion below that is concerned with distinguishing risk factors from precursor stages, is set in the context of a nonreversible stage process involving accumulation. What follows may differ in important ways for the other model variants.

A typical empirical starting point is the situation in which we have a collection of apparent risk factors for some outcome. Among these "risk factors" will be some that might correspond closely with the defining criteria of a precursor stage and others that are simple risk factors. But many, for example the role of hyperactivity in the onset of conduct disorder (Taylor, 1991), could be either. The first aspect that distinguishes a risk factor from a precursor or stage is the very simple one that a precursor will usually vary over time (since it must onset at some point), while a simple risk factor can remain fixed over time (though this criterion has its exceptions, as in the example of familial polyposis where progression to an intermediate stage has been inherited). What distinguishes a precursor from a simple, but time varying, risk factor is that a precursor stage will be, statistically speaking, endogenous to the process under study whereas a simple risk factor should be exogenous. This does not refer to something being internal or external to the individual, but to an endogenous variable being one that is both caused by the process of interest and may causally affect its later development. Although there are specialized statistical tests for the endogeneity of a variable appropriate to particular processes (e.g. Chamberlain, 1985; Crouchley & Pickles, 1989), a consideration of a simpler approach may be more useful here.

In Figure 2.6 the variables, in addition to the outcome variable Y, that define a two-stage process have been divided up into a stage 1 risk factor,

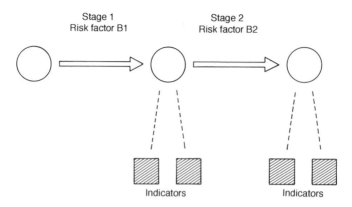

Figure 2.6 Two-stage model

$B1$, a stage 2 risk factor, $B2$, and a criterion variable, S, that defines the precursor stage. Loeber (1990) points out that Y should never precede S and that the occurrence of S must elevate the probability of Y. The fact that there are no other routes to Y not passing through S means that S is necessary for the occurrence of Y. Since the effect of $B1$ occurs entirely through the achievement of S then, where the risks $B1$ and $B2$ are independent, the value of $B1$ is irrelevant to the probability of the outcome pathology once the intermediate stage has been reached or

$$\Pr[Y=1 \mid S2=1, B1] = \Pr[Y=1 \mid S2=1]$$

This relationship will not be true for $S2$ and $B2$, or $B1$ and $B2$ and thus allows the two risk factors and the stage variable to be distinguished and located in the stage sequence. Unfortunately, where the risk factors $B1$ and $B2$ are correlated, or the variables are subject to measurement error, this simple pattern of equalities and inequalities of conditional and marginal probabilities no longer applies.

An approach that exploits the endogeneity of precursor variables is the examination of the effects of experimental manipulation of other risk factors, in particular, treatment variables in studies that use randomization (Caron & Rutter, 1991). Treatment effects can be expected to influence all stage variables beyond their point of action in the process and those effects should be relatively larger than any effect they might have on corresponding risk factors.

Another feature that might be exploited in resolving the structure is that while it is possible for a stage to separate two transitions that share identical risk factors and sensitivity to them, a stage is almost always a point at which there is a shift among risk factors in their relative importance, with the introduction or increasing effect of some risks and the elimination or reduction of others. Thus a detailed investigation of the pattern of interactions among variables would seem necessary.

The complications introduced by measurement error in the observed variables may also need to be considered. Figure 2.6 illustrates that occupation of the intermediate stage might not be observed directly but instead might be observed only by means of a set of indicator variables. Such indicator variables will be associated with some margin of error, so the stage occupied by an individual cannot be determined with certainty. It then becomes necessary to consider probabilities of occupation and nonoccupation of a latent stage. This sounds complicated, but the use of latent variables to tackle causal analysis with continuous variables has achieved great success, so here too they might help resolve many problems.

Models involving latent states of conduct disorder and adult social dysfunction have already been investigated (Pickles & Rutter, 1991) with measurement equations describing the relationships between indicators and latent states, and structural equations describing the prevalence and transitions between latent states. In that analysis, correcting for the substantial measurement error that the indicators were shown to possess, allowed a much clearer picture of the level of continuity of disorder to be seen. A similar approach applied to stage models would enable the use of a range of indicators for each stage, with the estimated performance of the indicators being used to help define the latent stage. The Pickles and Rutter study also indicated that the relative performance of the indicators varied within the population. For example, the absence of adult crime was a much better indicator of good functioning in men than in women. Similar differences in the performance of indicators have been identified in the items that identify conduct-disordered girls and boys (Robins, 1991; Taylor, 1991). Allowance for subgroup differences in the performance of the indicators is parsimonious, in that it allows the same structural model to fit all subgroups of the population. Such parsimony is valuable but we should be cautious before assuming that all such differences are measurement artifacts rather than real differences between groups in the way the pathology develops.

The above suggest that many of the concepts and findings of ordinary structural equation modelling would be relevant to the application of a latent variable approach to stage models. However, as yet the question of timing and causal ordering has not been considered and, in particular, it has been implicitly assumed that data on the occurrence of risk events and on stage occupation are consistent with the pattern required by the sequential nature of the stage model. Measurement error means that the observed data may not be so obliging. An imperfectly reliable indicator of a later stage may indicate its occupation while those from earlier stages may suggest that passage through them has not occurred. Similarly, the occurrence of a risk factor may have been recorded as occurring before the relevant stage upon which it acts has been reached. For example, a life event of causal importance may, through imperfect recall, appear to have occurred before the stage of vulnerability had been reached, rather than after it. These possibilities require that a formal latent stage model for the development of a psychopathology over time must be conceptualized in terms of latent histories, there being various possible histories that may be more or less consistent with the observed data. This aspect of the problem has little of direct parallel in more familiar structural equation modelling. The next section expands upon the need for greater conceptual precision in thinking about a multistage model for psychopathology and how it would differ from the Armitage–Doll type of structure.

INTERDEPENDENCE OF NORMAL DEVELOPMENT AND PSYCHOPATHOGY

The relationship between the processes of normal development, whether progressing normally or abnormally, and the process of the development of psychopathology ought to be profound. Such a relationship is explicit in the view of psychopathology as normal development "gone wrong", as in the example of delayed or arrested progress in reading. However, more often analyses and models appear to view psychopathology in isolation, almost as an independent outcome.

The concept of an interdependent stage process allows for a variety of possible linking mechanisms. One mechanism for interdependence would be to regard the parallel process of normal development as a source of time variation in risk variables. For example, in the development of aggressive behaviour in males, normal changes in hormonal levels around puberty would constitute a direct source of risk (Olweus, 186). Another example would be the shift of focus in relationships from parent to peers that would create new opportunities for the effects of deviant subcultures (Cohen, 1955; Sutherland & Cressey, 1974).

In the mechanism just described, the impact of development is seen even in the absence of inter-individual differences. The existence of inter-individual differences in levels, for example of hormones influencing stress inhibition and their consequent link to recidivist crime (Magnusson, 1991), provides other possible linking mechanisms. Similarly, inter-individual differences in timing of normal development may be important, as in delayed moral development on delinquency or precocious physical maturation on educational achievement. Yet another possibility is that the psychopathology arises directly out of the switching of a process of normal development onto an abnormal path.

The considerable extent of comorbidity that appears to occur among different psychopathologies strongly suggests interdependence among the mechanisms involved (Caron & Rutter, 1991; see also Angold, Chapter 10 this volume). Though not in a stage framework, Ferguson & Horwood (1992) illustrate the value of the structural modelling approach for investigating this question, finding strong evidence for the effect of attention deficit on reading problems, rather than vice versa.

Finally, insight into the relationships between different areas of normal development can be gained from the study of subjects with pathology in one or other area. The relationship between cognitive and affective development is an example, with both the efffective development of Down's subjects with a cognitive deficit (Cicchetti & Ganiban, 1990) and the social cognitive development of autistic subjects with an affective deficit being used (Rutter & Garmezy, 1983).

CONCLUSIONS

It has been argued that stage models have much to offer those engaged in studies of the development of psychopathology. However, it has also been made clear that the considerable potential of such models is unlikely to be reaped by their uncritical and insensitive application. Careful use of stage models may well achieve success but the discussion of them here has been primarily concerned to use them to illustrate a more general point. Specifically, stage models have been used to illustrate that attempts to identify risk factors and precursors are made in the context of an implicit structure or model of the process. Although no particular alternative model has been discussed, implicit has been one in which all we see is essentially the unfolding into the future of age-appropriate behaviours and symptoms that reflect largely stable inter-individual differences in some latent trait. Such "single factor" models, in emphasizing continuity, are unable to account for the numerous discontinuities that are also much in evidence as a part of development (Hinde & Bateson, 1984). Examining different models, their relative performance and conclusions, is at least as important as the causal analysis undertaken within a given model.

As has been shown, even a simple model can generate remarkably sophisticated predictions when these are followed through in terms of both inter-individual differences and the onset or unfolding of development. Such a wealth of detail should allow numerous different models of the process to be distinguished. However, causal models using continuous variables do not lend themselves easily to consideration of matters of timing. In addition, many theoretical models of development have been little concerned with inter-individual differences. For these reasons, little research into inter-individual variation in the timing of development and its relationship to psychopathology appears to have been done. Thus many longitudinal studies of psychopathology have failed to collect or to exploit data of potential value in discriminating among causal hypotheses.

Stage models have considerable appeal as a means of describing a developmental process. However, their theoretical richness cuts both ways. In implying a complex range of relationships among data they offer numerous possible testable predictions. It is probably unreasonable to expect any real data to be consistent with the full range of the predictions from the simple stage model, for example invariant sequence, age of stage attainment distributions of known form, stage-specific risk factors with appropriate additive or synergistic effects and so on. But carefully combined with other components of these model-builder's kit, to allow for various forms of measurement error, heterogeneity and time variation, obtaining such consistency will be more likely. The optimist would then hope to have achieved a convergence between the stage as a conceptual device within a model of data, the stage as an independently empirically identifiable form and the stage as a concept in developmental theory.

ACKNOWLEDGEMENTS

I would like to thank Dale Hay and Barbara Maughan for their useful comments and discussion.

REFERENCES

Aebli, H. (1978). A dual model of cognitive development. *Journal of Behavioral Development*, **3**, 221–229.

Armitage, P. & Doll, R. (1954). The age distribution of cancer and a multi-stage theory of carcinogenesis. *British Journal of Cancer* **8**, 1–15.

Armitage, P. & Doll, R. (1961). Stochastic models for carcinogenesis. In *Proceedings of the 4th Berkeley Symposium on Mathematical Statistics and Probability: Biology and Problems of Health*, University of California, Berkeley, pp. 19–27.

Bentler, P. M. (1980). The study of cognitive development through modelling with qualitative data. In R. H. Kluwe & H. Spada (eds), *Developmental Models of Thinking*, Academic Press, New York.

Bentler, P. M. (1989). *EQS: Structural Equations Program Manual*, BMDP Statistical Software, Los Angeles, Calif.

Berry, G., Newhouse, M. L. & Antonis, P. (1985). Combined effects of asbestos and smoking on mortality from lung cancer and mesothelioma in factory workers. *British Journal of Industrial Medicine*, **42**, 12–000.

Blot, W. J. & Day, N. E. (1979). Synergism and interaction: are they equivalent? *American Journal of Epidemiology*, **10**, 99–100.

Breslow, N. & Storer, B. E. (1985). General relative risk functions for case-control studies. *American Journal of Epidemiology* **122**, 149–162.

Brown, G. W. & Harris, T. O. (1978). *Social Origins of Depression*, Tavistock, London.

Bussey, H. J. R. (1975). *Familial Polyposis Coli*, Johns Hopkins University Press, Baltimore, Md.

Caron, C. & Rutter, M. (1991). Comorbidity in child psychopathology: concepts, issues and research strategies. *Journal of Child Psychology and Psychiatry*, **32**, 1063–1080.

Chamberlain, G. (1985). Heterogeneity, omitted variance bias and duration dependence. In J. J. Heckman & B. Singer, (eds), *Longitudinal Analysis of Labor Market Data*, CUP, Cambridge, pp. 3–38.

Cicchetti, D. & Ganiban, J. (1990). The organization and coherence of developmental processes in infants and children with Down syndrome. In R. Hodapp, J. Burack & M. Zigler, (eds), *Issues in the Developmental Approach to Mental Retardation*, CUP, Cambridge, pp. 169–225.

Cohen, A. K. (1955). *Delinquent Boys*, Free Press, Glencoe.

Crouchley, R. & Pickles, A. R. (1989). An empirical comparison of conditional and marginal likelihood methods in a longitudinal study. *Sociological Methodology*, **19**, 161–183.

Cudeck, R. & Browne, M. W. (1983). Cross-validation of covariance structures. *Multivariate Behavioral Research*, **18**, 147–167.

Day, N. E. (1990). The Armitage–Doll multistage model of carcinogenesis. *Statistics in Medicine*, **9**, 677–679.

Farrington, D. P. (1986). Stepping stones to adult criminal careers. In D. Olweus, J. Block & M. R. Yarrow (eds), *Development of Antisocial and Prosocial Behavior*, Academic Press, New York, pp. 359–384.

Ferguson, D. M. & Horwood, L. J. (1992). Attention deficit and reading achievement. *Journal of Child Psychology and Psychiatry*, **33**, 375–386.

Fischer, K. W. & Silvern, L. (1985). Stages and individual differences in cognitive development. *Annual Review of Psychology*, **36**, 613–648.

Frith, U. (1985). Beneath the surface of developmental dyslexia. In K. E. Patterson, J. C. Marshall & M. Coltheart (eds), *Surface Dyslexia: Neuropsychological and Cognitive Studies of Phonological Reading*, Erlbaum, London, pp. 301–330.

GLIM (1985). *The GLIM System Release 3.77 Manual*, Numerical Algorithms Group, Oxford.

Hayduk, P. (1987). *Structural Equation Modelling in LISREL*, Johns Hopkins University Press, Baltimore, MD.

Heckman, J. J. & Singer, B. (1984). A method for minimizing the impact of distributional assumptions in econometric models of duration. *Econometrica*, **52**, 271–320.

Henning, H. J. & Rudinger, G. (1985). Analysis of qualitative data in developmental psychology. In J. R. Nesselroade & A. von Eye (eds), *Individual Development and Social Change: Explanatory Analysis*, Academic Press, Orlando; pp. 295–342.

Hinde, R. A. & Bateson, P. (1984). Discontinuities versus continuities in behavioral development and the neglect of process. *International Journal of Behavioral Development*, **7**, 129–143.

Holland, P. W. (1988). Causal inference, path analysis and recursive structural equation models. In *Sociological Methodology*, C. C. Clogg (ed), American Sociological Association, Washington, DC, pp. 449–484.

Joreskog, K. G. & Sorbum, D. (1984). *LISREL VI: Analysis of Linear Structural Relationships by Maximum Likelihood, Instrumental Variables and Least Squares*, 3rd ed, Scientific Software, Mooresville, Ind.

Kaldor, J. M. & Day, N. E. (1987). Interpretation of epidemiological studies in the context of the multistage model of carcinogenesis. In J. C. Barrett (ed), *Mechanisms of Environmental Carcinogenesis*: Vol. II. *Multistep Models of Carcinogenesis*, CRC Press, Boca Raton, FL, pp. 21–57.

Kandel, D. B. (1982). Epidemiological and psychosocial perspectives on adolescent drug use. *Journal of Child Psychiatry*, **21**, 328–347.

Klicpera, C. (1989). The reading development of normal and poor readers in the first grade: how helpful is the concept of developmental stages for the understanding of reading acquisition in German-speaking children? In M. Brambring, F. Losel & H. Skowronck. (eds), *Children at Risk: Assessment, Longitudinal Research and Intervention*, Walter de Gruyter, New York; pp. 97–118.

Lazard, I. & Darlington, R. (1982). Lasting effects of early education: a report from the consortium for longitudinal studies. *SRCD Monograph 195*, **47**, nos 2–3.

Leamer, E. E. (1988). Discussion. *Sociological Methodology*, **18**, 485–493. C. C. Clogg (ed.), American Sociological Association, Washington, DC.

Loeber, R. (1990). Development and risk factors of juvenile antisocial behavior and delinquency. *Child Psychology Review*, **10**, 1–141.

Loeber, R. (1991). Natural histories of conduct problems, delinquency and associated substance abuse: evidence from developmental progressions. *Advances in Clinical Psychology*, **11**, 73–124.

McCall, R. B., Eichorn, D. H. & Hogarty, P. S. (1977). Transitions in early mental development. *Monographs of the Society for Research in Child Development*, **24**, 3rd Ser., no. 171, 108pp.

McCullagh, P. & Nelder, J. A. (1983). *Generalized Linear Models*, Chapman and Hall, London.

Magnusson, D. (1991). The patterning of antisocial behaviors in adolescence: results from Sweden. Paper presented at SRCD Seattle Meeting, April 1991.

Magnusson, D., Stattin, H. & Allen, V. L. (1986). Differential maturation among girls and its relations to social adjustment: a longitudinal perspective. In P. B. Baltes, D. L. Featherman & R. M. Lerner (eds), *Life-span Development and Behavior*, vol. 7, Erlbaum, Hillsdale, N.J., pp. 136–172.

Marini, M. M. & Singer, B. (1988). Causality in the social sciences. *Sociological Methodology*, **1988**, 347–410.

Moolgavkar, S. H. & Knudson, A. G. (1981). Mutation and cancer: a model for human carcinogenesis. *Journal of the National Cancer Institute*, **66**, 1037–1052.

Olweus, D. (1986). Aggression and hormones: behavioral relationship with testosterone and adrenaline. In D. Olweus, J. Block & M. Radke-Yarrow, *Development of Antisocial and Prosocial Behavior: Research, Theories and Issues*. Academic Press, New York, pp. 51–74.

Peto, R. (1977). Epidemiology, multistage models and short-term mutagenicity tests. In H. H. Hiatt, J. P. Watson & J. A. Winsten (eds), *Origins of Human Cancer*, Cold Spring Harbor Laboratory, Cold Spring Harbor, N.Y., pp. 1403–1430.

Pickles, A. R. & Crouchley, R. (1991). Applications of stochastic process models in clinical psychology and psychiatry. In F. Dunstan & J. Pickles (eds), *Statistics in Medicine*, Oxford University Press, Oxford, pp. 125–148.

Pickles, A. R. and Rutter, M. (1991). Statistical and conceptual models of "turning points" in developmental processes. In D. Magnusson, L. Bergman, G. Rudinger & B. Torestad (eds), *Problems and Methods in Longitudinal Research: Stability and Change*, Cambridge University Press, Cambridge, pp. 32–57.

Robins, L. (1991). Conduct disorder. *Journal of Child Psychology and Psychiatry Annual Review of Research*, **23**, 193–212.

Robins, L., Davis, D. H. & Wish, E. (1977). Detecting predictors of rare events: demographic, family, and personal deviance as predictor stages in the progression toward narcotic addiction. In J. S. Strauss & H. M. Babigan (eds), *The Origins and Course of Psychopathology*, Plenum Press, New York. pp. 379–406.

Rosenthal, R. & Rubin, D. B. (1982). A simple general purpose display of magnitude of experimental effect. *Journal of Educational Psychology*, **74**, 166–169.

Rothman, K. J. (1976). Causes. *American Journal of Epidemiology*, **104**, 587–592.

Rutter, M. (1987). Continuities and discontinuities from infancy. In J. Osofsky (ed.), *Handbook of Infant Development*, 2nd edn, Wiley, New York, pp. 1256–1298.

Rutter, M. (1989a). Age as an ambiguous variable in developmental research. *International Journal of Behavioral Development*, **12**, 1–34.

Rutter, M. (1989b). Pathways from childhood to adulthood. *Journal of Child Psychology and Psychiatry*, **30**, 23–52.

Rutter, M. & Garmezy, N. (1983). Developmental Psychology. In E. M. Henderson (ed.), *Socialization, Personality and Social Development, Volume 4, Mussen's Handbook of Child Psychology*, 4th edn, Wiley, New York, pp. 775–911.

Rutter, M. & Pickles, A. R. (1991). Person–environment interactions: concepts, mechanisms and implications for data analysis. In T. D. Wachs & R. Plomin (eds), *Conceptualization and Measurement of Organism–Environment Interaction*, American Psychological Association, Washington, DC, pp. 105–136.

Rutter, M. & Quinton, D. (1984). Parental psychiatric disorder: effects on children. *Psychological Medicine*, **14**, 853–880.

Saracci, R. (1977). Asbestos and lung cancer: an analysis of epidemiological evidence on the asbestos–smoking interaction. *International Journal of Cancer*, **20**, 323–331.

SAS Institute (1987). *SAS Manual Version 5*, SAS Institute, Cary, NC.

SPSS (1989). *SPSS/PC V3 Manual*, SPSS Inc., Chicago.

Stuart, M. & Coltheart, M. (1988). Does reading develop in a sequence of stages? *Cognition*, **30**, 139–181.

Sutherland, E. H. & Cressey, D. R. (1974). *Criminology*, Lippincott, Philadelphia.

Taylor, E. (1991). *Epidemiological Study of Hyperactivity in Girls*. Final Report of Wellcome Trust. London.

Tennant, C. & Bebbington, P. (1978). The social causation of depression: a critique of the work of Brown and his colleagues. *Psychological Medicine*, **8**, 565–575.

Thomas, D. C. (1983). Statistical methods for analyzing effects of temporal patterns of exposure on cancer risks. *Scandinavian Journal of Work Environment Health*, **9**, 353–366.

Weinberg, R. A. (1989). Oncogenes, antioncogenes and the molecular bases of multistep carcinogenesis. *Cancer Research*, **49**, 3713–3721.

Wohlwill, J. F. (1973). *The Study of Behavioral Development*, Academic Press, New York.

Yagamuchi, K. & Kandel, D. B. (1984a). Patterns of drug use from adolescence to young adulthood: 2. Sequences of progression. *American Journal of Public Health*, **74**, 668–672.

Yagamuchi, K. & Kandel, D. B. (1984b). Patterns of drug use from adolescence to young adulthood: 3. Predictors of progression. *American Journal of Public Health*, **74**, 673–681.

Chapter 3

Brain Abnormalities and Psychological Development

Robert Goodman

INTRODUCTION

This chapter examines the notion that abnormalities of the developing brain can affect behavioural and emotional development, leading to psychiatric disorders in childhood and sometimes adulthood as well. As a necessary preliminary, the first section of the chapter asks how we can recognize whether or not a brain is abnormal. The following section reviews the evidence that indisputable abnormalities of the developing brain are associated with an increased risk of psychiatric disorders, and considers the ways in which neurological and non-neurological risk factors may interact to determine the rate and type of psychiatric disorder. The next section considers mediating processes, discussing plausible routes from brain to behavioural abnormalities, and examining the research strategies that can be used to investigate the causal processes underlying brain–behaviour links. Though most of the chapter is devoted to the effects of unequivocal brain abnormalities, the final section turns to one of the many theories ascribing abnormal psychological development to putative brain abnormalities. Do birth complications commonly cause covert brain damage manifesting purely in the psychological domain? This controversy raises many theoretical issues and research strategies of wider relevance. Although the chapter's focus is on emotional and behavioural problems, it is important to remember that brain abnormalities are potentially relevant to many other aspects of psychological development as well. The impact of brain abnormalities on cognitive skills and academic attainments is a subsidiary theme throughout the chapter, and the effect of brain damage on language development has been reviewed elsewhere (Goodman, 1987).

Precursors and Causes in Development and Psychopathology.
Edited by D. F. Hay and A. Angold © 1993 John Wiley & Son Ltd

IDENTIFYING BRAIN ABNORMALITIES

In a society that considers the brain to be the organ of the mind, it is not surprising that there are many scientific and lay theories attributing disorders of psychological development to brain abnormalities. Since many of these theories refer to "brain damage", it is worth noting that potentially relevant brain abnormalities extend well beyond a narrowly defined notion of brain damage, if this term is taken to refer to the effects of injurious events or processes on a brain that had previously been developing normally. Other causes of brain abnormalities include genetic disorders transmitted by parents, new mutations, and chromosomal aberrations acquired around the time of conception. In these instances, brain development may have been abnormal from the beginning, rather than proceeding normally prior to some insult. Consequently, it can be misleading to label individuals with severe mental retardation or cerebral palsy as "brain damaged", since this focuses attention away from intrinsic lesions, and also diverts attention from the extent to which the origin and nature of the underlying brain abnormalities are frequently unknown. Another advantage of using the term "brain abnormality" rather than "brain damage" is that the former encompasses the delays in brain development that have been postulated to underlie some developmental disorders.

How to recognize an abnormal brain

Before examining the evidence that brain abnormalities lead to emotional and behavioural disorders in childhood, it is important to reflect on the inferential processes that lead to brain abnormalities being suspected in the first instance. Unless these suspicions are well founded, the whole enterprise collapses. Psychologists and psychiatrists have often accepted neurobiological assertions relatively uncritically, influenced perhaps by the high status of neurobiological knowledge as well as by the obvious difficulties in evaluating the claims of any unfamiliar discipline. It is important that psychologists and psychiatrists adopt a more critical stance, including an appreciation of the limits as well as the strengths of the different ways of recognizing an abnormal brain. Since the brain cannot be directly inspected in life, assertions about brain abnormalities are characteristically based on indirect (and sometimes tenuous) inferences. Some lines of evidence are more convincing than others, and it is useful to distinguish, in a rough and ready way, between four different levels of inferential certainty.

(1) Brain abnormalities are most convincingly inferred from the sorts of evidence acquired in a standard neurological assessment. Examples of relevant evidence include: a history of epileptic seizures; microcephaly and spastic quadriplegia on physical examination; unequivocal seizure discharges

on an electroencephalogram (EEG); and gross structural lesions of the brain demonstrated by computed tomography (CT) or magnetic resonance imaging (MRI) scanning. These sorts of findings are particularly convincing because they have often been validated against the "gold standard" of neuropathology, with clinical features being highly predictive of structural brain abnormalities, both macroscopic and microscopic, found on *post mortem* studies. For example, "hard" neurological signs, such as abnormal reflexes or sensory losses, are good predictors of focal structural abnormalities of the nervous system, as confirmed by neuropathology or neuro-imaging. Though some forms of epilepsy (e.g. classical "petit mal" absences) are not typically associated with structural brain abnormalities, the seizures themselves indicate functional brain abnormalities.

Despite these strengths, however, the reliability and validity of neurological assessments should not be exaggerated. Clinicians hold widely divergent views, for example, on the significance of slight reflex asymmetries, minor EEG changes, mild ventricular dilatation on CT scanning, or small numbers of ectopic neurones on microscopy. In each of these instances, some clinicians would conclude that there is subtle but definite evidence for brain abnormality, while other equally experienced clinicians would interpret the same findings as insignificant normal variants. In other words, clinical inferences of brain abnormalities may be very reliable in some instances but are much less reliable in "grey" areas. It is noteworthy that many of the neurobiological findings in children with psychiatric or psychological disorders fall into these grey areas.

(2) Brain abnormalities can also be inferred, with a lower degree of certainty, from "soft" neurological signs, neuropsychological investigations and derived neurophysiological measures. "Soft signs" are, by and large, levels of performance on sensory or motor tasks that are abnormal for the child's age, but would be normal for a younger child (see Shaffer et al. 1984). Unlike "hard" neurological signs, "soft signs" are not good predictors of focal brain abnormalities. The view that "soft signs" reflect diffuse, subtle or maturational abnormalities of the brain should, for the present, be regarded as a hypothesis to be investigated, and not as a conclusion to be taken for granted.

Inferences from neuropsychological tests are suspect for two rather different reasons. Firstly, even when focal or diffuse brain abnormalities can result in a particular profile of impaired psychological performance, the presence of that profile does not necessarily reflect brain abnormalities (just as a stroke typically produces a limp, but a limp is not typically due to a stroke). For example, although neurologically impaired children often have large discrepancies between their verbal and performance IQs, most children with large verbal-performance discrepancies appear neurologically intact (Rutter, Graham & Yule, 1970). Without further evidence, it is no more reasonable to assume that these children have subclinical brain abnormalities than to assume that most people who limp have subclinical strokes. A second problem with neuropsychological tests arises only in children who have psychological or psychiatric disorders. In these instances, abnormalities on neuropsychological testing may simply be one manifestation of the child's psychological disorder, without casting any additional light on whether that disorder arises from underlying brain abnormalities.

Similar problems affect the interpretation of neurophysiological measures derived from EEGs and evoked potentials. "Neurometrics" is one particularly sophisticated battery of age-normed quantitative measures derived from EEGs and multimodal evoked potentials (Prichep et al, 1983). Although abnormalities on these measures are particularly common in children with attentional or learning problems, it is possible that some neurophysiological abnormalities are consequences of psychological disorders rather than markers for brain abnormalities underlying the psychological disorders. For example, frequent shifts in attention may lead to excessive theta activity in the EEG (Prichep et al., 1983) so the presence of this EEG abnormality provides no independent evidence that distractibility is neurological in origin.

(3) Brain abnormalities can also be inferred from a history of exposure to the sorts of insults that can damage the brain. Such high-risk groups may be defined, for example, by a history of encephalitis or high-dose cranial irradiation. Although some members of a high-risk group may escape unscathed, this does not invalidate group comparisons of high-risk and low-risk individuals. In some cases, however, it is questionable how relevant purported risk factors are—as discussed later in this chapter for "birth complications". Even when risk factors for brain injury are associated with psychological or psychiatric problems, the attribution of causality may still be problematic. For example, it is equally plausible a priori that head injury leads to hyperactivity, that hyperactivity and impulsiveness lead to head injury or that some third factor, such as psychosocial disadvantage, independently predisposes a child to both head injury and hyperactivity.

(4) The presence of a specific psychological or psychiatric symptom or syndrome is sometimes taken as sufficient evidence in itself that the child has an abnormal brain. By and large, this sort of conclusion is unwarranted on the basis of existing evidence. Relatively few behavioural symptoms or syndromes have been shown to be predictably associated with *independent* evidence of underlying brain abnormalities. Even in the case of severe mental retardation, which is known to be associated with a high rate of abnormal neurological and neuropathological findings (Broman et al. 1987; Crome & Stern, 1972), it is not possible to infer underlying brain abnormalities with absolute certainty. For example, it is not uncommon to find no detectable *post mortem* brain abnormalities (Crome & Stern, 1972). Even in such apparently "organic" syndromes as non-progressive

distintegrative disorder (involving profound regression at about the age of 4, followed by severe retardation with autistic features), there is often no independent clinical or neuroradiological evidence that affected individuals have an abnormal brain (Hill & Rosenbloom, 1986). Though future investigations may yet reveal brain abnormalities that have escaped detection to date, it is currently unjustified to extrapolate from the evidence that *most* severe retardation is associated with independent evidence of brain abnormalities to the conclusion that *all* severe retardation must be due to brain abnormalities. If this is true for severe retardation, similar considerations apply with even greater force to most other behavioural symptoms and syndromes. There is little justification, for example, for using hyperactivity or learning disorders as evidence for so-called "minimal brain damage" or "minimal cerebral dysfunction".

Although it is true, as described in a later section of this chapter, that neurologically impaired children have a high rate of attentional and learning problems, most children with these problems appear neurologically intact. To assume, without further evidence, that neurologically intact children with hyperactivity have minimal brain damage is rather like assuming that neurologically intact children with a limp have a minimal stroke. Future research may show that all hyperactivity is due to a specific brain abnormality, but this is currently just one plausible hypothesis among many others. It is just as plausible, for instance, that children who grow up in unusual circumstances sometimes learn maladaptive strategies for regulating their attention and activity (as suggested by links between hyperactivity and maternal depression or institutional rearing (Breznitz & Friedman, 1988; Hodges & Tizard, 1989)). Pending further evidence, underlying brain abnormalities should not be inferred from any of the common behavioural symptoms or syndromes.

Given these reservations about the inferential processes implicating brain abnormalities, it seems prudent to rely on the best authenticated cases when examining the effects of brain abnormalities on psychological development. The following sections of this chapter do just this, examining the evidence that children with abnormal brains have an unusually high rate of emotional and behavioural problems, and then considering some of the possible mechanisms that may mediate these brain–behaviour links.

Whereas unequivocal brain abnormalities are relatively rare, and only account for a small proportion of children with psychiatric and learning problems, some theories attribute a high proportion of these common problems to underlying brain damage. The "continuum of reproductive casualty" is probably the best known of these theories, attributing a high proportion of behavioural and learning problems to relatively minor obstetric and neonatal complications (Knobloch & Pasamanick, 1959). Although this theory is no longer generally accepted by researchers and clinicians, it lives on in the minds of many parents (and some clinicians) and variants of the theory continue to provoke controversy in the research literature. In view of this continuing interest, the final section of this chapter focuses on "birth damage" hypotheses. Many of the methodological issues raised in the section apply equally to other theories that seek to explain a high proportion of common behavioural and educational disorders on the basis of questionable inferences of underlying brain abnormalities.

PSYCHOLOGICAL CONSEQUENCES OF UNEQUIVOCAL BRAIN ABNORMALITIES

Clinicians have, for many years, noted a high rate of psychiatric and learning problems in children with cerebral palsy, epilepsy or other neurological disorders (e.g. Still, 1902; Ounsted, 1955). This sort of clinic-based evidence, with its emphasis on children with well-authenticated brain abnormalities, provides suggestive but not convincing evidence for specific brain–behaviour links. The evidence is not conclusive because clinic series typically leave three key questions unanswered. Firstly, how common are comparable behavioural and learning disorders in the general population? Secondly, even if the rates of behavioural and learning disorders are higher in the clinic population than in the general population, does this simply reflect a referral bias, with children who have both neurological and psychological problems being referred for specialist advice more often than children with neurological problems alone? Thirdly, even if behavioural and learning disorders are commoner in representative samples of neurologically impaired children than in representative samples of the general population, does this reflect specific brain–behaviour links, or does it simply reflect the impact of any disabling or stigmatizing disorder, whether affecting the brain, the lungs, the skin or any other organ?

These key questions have most satisfactorily been answered by the neuropsychiatric study in childhood that was carried out on the Isle of Wight (Rutter, Graham & Yule, 1970) as part of a wider epidemiological survey involving a discrete geographical area, multiple ascertainment techniques and well-standardized assessment procedures (Rutter, Tizard & Whitmore, 1970). The rates of psychiatric and learning disorders were determined for four groups of children on the Isle of Wight:

(1) A total population sample of over 2000 children aged 10 and 11. After an initial screening phase, selected and random groups of children were intensively assessed for psychiatric and learning disorders.

(2) A group of 63 children, aged 5–14 years, had a history of epileptic seizures without any other known brain disease, disorder or injury. These children with "uncomplicated epilepsy" were assessed individually.

By definition, all of these epileptic children had functional brain abnormalities. It is reasonable to assume that some of these children would also have had structural brain abnormalities that could be demonstrated by neuro-imaging or neuropathology (e.g. Ounsted, Lindsay & Norman, 1966, for temporal lobe epilepsy).

(3)   A group of 36 children, aged 5–14 years, had cerebral palsy or related disorders. These children with "structural brain disorders" were individually assessed. One-third of this group also had epileptic seizures, but no children with severe mental handicap were included.

(4)   A group of 138 children had other chronic currently handicapping physical disorders, including asthma, diabetes, eczema, deafness, blindness and polio. None of these children were known to have structural or functional brain abnormalities, apart from the small minority with polio or some other disorder affecting the brain stem but sparing the "higher" brain structures.

The rates of psychiatric disorders in the four groups, as summarized in Table 3.1, provide answers to the three key questions that clinic series do not address. Psychiatric disorders were indeed common in the general population, but similarly defined disorders were many times commoner in children with structural and functional brain abnormalities. Much the same was true for "specific reading retardation", i.e. reading substantially below the level predicted from chronological age and IQ. Because the study involved epidemiological rather than clinic samples, the association between brain abnormalities and both psychiatric and reading disorders cannot be attributed to clinic referral biases. Finally, children with brain disorders had much higher rates of psychiatric and reading disorders than children with non-brain disorders, suggesting that brain–behaviour links cannot simply be explained in terms of the stresses imposed by any physical disorder.

Before accepting this last conclusion, however, it is important to consider the possible objection that brain disorders are typically more handicapping and stigmatizing than non-brain disorders, and that this alone accounts for the higher rates of psychiatric and learning problems. Several lines of

Table 3.1   Prevalence on the Isle of Wight of psychiatric disorder in children with and without brain disorder (data from Rutter, Graham & Yule, 1970)

Group	Prevalence of psychiatric disorder (%)
Population sample	7
Non-brain disorder	12
Uncomplicated epilepsy	29
Structural brain disorder(IQ>50)	44

evidence suggest that this is not so. Firstly, brain disorders are not necessarily more disabling or stigmatizing than non-brain disorders. Many of the Isle of Wight children with brain disorders experienced relatively little incapacity or stigmatization (e.g. children whose seizures only occurred at night). Conversely, some of the non-brain disorders (including deafness, blindness and polio) caused marked disability and may well have been seriously stigmatizing—yet the rate of psychiatric disorders among these deaf, blind or polio-affected children was only half that found in uncomplicated epilepsy, and only a third of that found in structural brain disorders. Secondly, among the Isle of Wight children with cerebral palsy and related disorders, there was no significant association between the likelihood of psychiatric disorder and the severity of physical handicap. Finally, a separate study by Seidel, Chadwick & Rutter (1975) compared children disabled by brain disorders (above the brain stem) with a matched group of children disabled by other disorders primarily affecting the musculoskeletal system. Children with an IQ under 70 were excluded, and the two groups were well matched for social background and degree of physical incapacity. Despite this close matching, psychiatric disorders were twice as common among the children with brain disorders. To summarize, the evidence suggests that brain disorders do lead to an excess of behavioural and learning problems, and that this excess cannot simply be attributed to the adverse consequences of physical illness or disability of any cause. The stigma associated with brain disorders may contribute to the high rate of associated psychiatric disorder, but as discussed in greater detail later in the chapter, this is most unlikely to be the whole story.

Although the evidence for brain–behaviour links is persuasive, it is important to remember not only that many children with brain disorders are free from psychiatric problems, but also that the great majority of children with psychiatric problems are free from overt brain disorders. On the Isle of Wight, 65% of the neuro-epileptic children had no psychiatric disorder, and fewer than 10% of the children with psychiatric disorders also had brain disorders (as indexed by epilepsy, severe mental retardation, cerebral palsy or related disorders).

Why should brain disorders result in emotional and behavioural problems in some children but not in others? Both neurological and non-neurological explanations need to be considered. From a neurological perspective, it is conceivable that some types of brain abnormalities commonly induce psychiatric disorder, while other neural abnormalities rarely do so. For example, damage to limbic structures may frequently result in behavioural abnormalities, while damage restricted to the primary sensory cortex may seldom do so. This sort of neurological explanation can be contrasted with non-neurological explanations that emphasize the importance of coexisting psychosocial or genetic risk factors. For example, brain abnormalities may result in little or no psychiatric disorder in individuals at low psychosocial and genetic risk, but the same abnormalities may greatly amplify the impact of other adverse psychosocial and genetic factors. In its most extreme form, this sort of "vulnerability" explanation assumes that the exact type of brain abnormality is irrelevant, with any type of brain abnormality acting as a risk multiplier.

Neurological and non-neurological explanations of variable psychiatric outcome lead to different predictions. If the neurological explanation were correct, the rate and type of psychiatric disorder in neurologically impaired populations would be determined by the nature of the brain abnormalities, whether or not the child was also exposed to additional environmental or genetic risk factors. Conversely, if the vulnerability explanation were correct, the occurrence and type of psychiatric disorder would be determined by coexistent psychosocial and genetic risk factors, irrespective of the nature of the underlying neurological abnormality (with the result that each sort of neurological abnormality would be associated with an increased incidence of the whole range of child psychiatric disorders). As described below, there seems to be some truth in both the neurological and non-neurological predictions, demanding some sort of combined model. To make matters yet more complicated, chance may also affect which neurologically impaired children develop emotional or behavioural problems. Since brain development is governed by probabilistic rather than deterministic processes, children who are otherwise similar (in terms of brain insult, genotype and psychosocial circumstances) may follow divergent pathways of brain development, leading to heterogeneity in psychiatric outcome (Goodman, 1991a).

Among neurologically impaired children, the rate of psychiatric disorder is influenced by the type of neurological abnormality. As shown in Table 3.1, the Isle of Wight study showed that psychiatric disorders more commonly accompanied structural brain disorders than uncomplicated epilepsy (Rutter, Graham & Yule, 1970). In this study, psychiatric disorder was commoner among children with structural brain disorders and epilepsy (58% affected) than among children with structural brain disorders and no epilepsy (38% affected). Among children with uncomplicated epilepsy, the rate of accompanying psychopathology was related to the type of seizure, though numbers were small. Psychiatric disorders were present in 75% of the 8 children with psychomotor seizures but only in 22% of the 55 children with other sorts of seizure. Since the classification of seizures has changed many times over recent years, it is important to know that psychomotor seizures are roughly equivalent to complex partial seizures, limbic seizures and temporal lobe epilepsy.

Though variously labelled, several studies have linked this sort of seizure with particularly high rates of psychiatric disorder. For example, in one intensive longitudinal study of 100 consecutively referred children with temporal lobe epilepsy, only 15 were wholly free of psychological problems during childhood (Ounsted, Lindsay & Richards, 1987). On the other hand, another study of children referred to a specialist centre found that temporal lobe epilepsy and primary generalized epilepsy were associated with comparable levels of psychopathology, once allowance had been made for confounding variables such as age at onset of seizures and degree of seizure control (Whitman et al, 1982). The conflicting evidence about the effect of type of seizure on psychopathology is unlikely to be resolved without large epidemiological studies that use a diversity of measures of psychopathology, and take adequate account of a wide range of possible confounding covariates.

Although the Isle of Wight study reported high rates of psychiatric disorder among the children with structural brain disorders, there were no cases of psychiatric disorder among the seven children whose brain abnormalities were believed to be confined to just one cerebral hemisphere, whether the left or the right. This could obviously have been a sampling artefact, given the small numbers involved, but the finding raises the possibility that bilateral brain abnormalities are particularly associated with psychiatric disorder, either because bilateral lesions are typically more extensive, or because the developing brain is less able to compensate for bilateral than for unilateral brain damage (Goodman, 1991b). It remains uncertain, however, whether truly unilateral damage is behaviourally innocuous since high rates of behavioural disturbance have been reported in children with hemiplegic cerebral palsy, typically affecting just one hemisphere (Ingram, 1955, 1956; Ounsted, 1955).

In the case of mental handicap, Gillberg et al. (1986) found the rate of psychiatric disorder in a representative sample of adolescents with severe mental handicap to be significantly lower among individuals with Down's syndrome (39% affected) than among the remainder (64% affected). Once again, this suggests that the type of underlying biological (and presumably neurological) abnormality does influence the likelihood of concomitant psychiatric disorder.

Neurological factors evidently can affect the risk of psychiatric disorder. On occasions, these neurological risk factors may override or suppress the effect of "ordinary risk factors"—those psychosocial or genetic factors that normally influence the rate of psychiatric disorder in neurologically intact children. This sort of overriding effect could account for data on sex ratios. Among pre-pubertal children without neurological problems, boys are undoubtedly the weaker sex from a psychiatric point of view. Epidemiological studies demonstrate that psychiatrically disordered boys are roughly twice as common as similarly disordered girls (e.g. Rutter et al., 1975). By contrast, psychiatric disorder was equally common in the two sexes in the Isle of Wight sample of children with neuro-epileptic disorders (Rutter,

Graham & Yule, 1970), and in a sample of children followed prospectively after a severe head injury (Rutter, Chadwick & Shaffer, 1984). One interpretation of these findings is that neurological factors overrode whichever biological or social factors normally serve to render boys more vulnerable and girls less vulnerable to psychiatric disorder. An alternative interpretation is that neurologically abnormal girls are more susceptible to psychiatric disorders than neurologically abnormal boys, with this greater susceptibility evening up what would otherwise be an unequal sex ratio. This second interpretation seems less likely since although neurological impairments commonly attenuate or eliminate the male excess of psychiatric disorders, they do not reverse the sex ratio—and if girls were more susceptible to neurological abnormalities, girls should be at greater overall risk in at least some series.

Despite the suggestive evidence that neurological abnormalities may sometimes override ordinary gender effects, it is not the case that neurologically impaired children are immune to "ordinary risk factors". In many instances, "ordinary risk factors" do increase the likelihood of psychiatric disorder in neurologically impaired children as well as in neurologically intact children. In the Isle of Wight study, for example, emotional disturbance in mothers and "broken homes" were both associated with psychiatric disorder in the neuro-epileptic children, just as they were in other children. Of course, this cross-sectional association might reflect the impact of neurologically determined behavioural problems on the parents' marriage and mental state.

The role of non-neurological factors was more convincingly demonstrated in Rutter, Chadwick & Shaffer's (1984) prospective study of childhood head injuries. The most powerful single predictor of cognitive and behavioural outcome was the severity of the head injury. Compared with children who had experienced a mild head injury or severe physical trauma not affecting the head, children with severe head injuries were much more likely to have persistent cognitive impairments and to develop psychiatric disorders. Despite this major impact of brain damage, non-neurological factors also influenced which children developed a psychiatric disorder. Thus in the severe head injury group, new psychiatric disorders developed in 14% of the children who experienced low levels of psychosocial adversity, but in 60% of children who also experienced high levels of psychosocial adversity. Similarly, the rate of new psychiatric disorders among the severely head injured was 29% when the children's pre-accident behaviour had been normal, but 55% when the children had previously shown minor emotional or behavioural problems that were not sufficient to warrant a rating of psychiatric disorder, i.e. the psychiatric impact of the neurological insult was affected by the environmental or genetic factors that resulted in slight emotional or behavioural problems prior to the insult.

Since neurological and non-neurological factors both affect the rate of psychiatric disorder, it is important to consider whether these two groups of factors act independently or interactively. For clarity, it is helpful to contrast two alternative models—a "separate paths" model and a "vulnerability" model—though hybrid models are certainly plausible. According to the separate paths model, brain abnormalities are a distinctive route into psychiatric disorder, and this neurological route is quite separate from psychosocial or genetic routes into psychiatric disorder. Following this line of argument, neurologically impaired children who do not develop psychiatric disorders for neurological reasons are just as likely as ordinary children to become psychiatrically disordered via a non-neurological route. Statistically, the separate paths model predicts that both neurological and non-neurological variables will have significant "main effects" on psychiatric outcome, without any significant additive interaction between neurological and non-neurological factors.

In contrast to the separate paths model, the vulnerability model proposes that neurological and non-neurological factors act synergistically on a shared route into psychiatric disorder. Following this line of reasoning, neurological abnormalities are relatively or totally innocuous on their own, but they amplify the effects of any coexistent non-neurological risk factors. Statistically, the vulnerability model predicts a significant additive interaction between neurological and non-neurological factors, with the combination of the two resulting in a much higher psychiatric risk than would be predicted from summing the effect of each acting in isolation. It is worth noting that even if neurological factors have no impact on psychiatric risk in the absence of coexistent non-neurological risk factors, statistical analyses may still show an apparent "main effect" of neurological factors on psychiatric outcome (see Rutter, 1985 and Rutter & Pickles, 1990, for a further discussion of this sort of statistical effect).

Many clinicians and researchers have found the vulnerability model attractive. For example, Rutter, Graham & Yule (1970, pp. 208–209) concluded from their Isle of Wight neuropsychiatric study that "the effect of brain dysfunction is largely to render the child more liable to react adversely to the stresses and strains which may impair the development of any child". As Breslau (1990) has pointed out, however, the evidence for a vulnerability model rather than a separate paths model is lacking. Her own analyses of the combined effects of brain abnormalities and an adverse family environment did not support the vulnerability model. The study, which compared neurologically normal and impaired children on interview-based dimensional measures of psychopathology, found the neurologically impaired children to be significantly more likely to have symptoms of depression and inattention. Of the measures of family and environment employed, low family cohesion was the most powerful predictor of psychiatric symptomatology. In the case of depressive symptoms, neurological abnormality and low family cohesion had separate main effects with no interaction, supporting the separate paths model. The situation was more complex in the case of inattention. In neurologically impaired children, the level of inattention was unrelated to the degree of family cohesion. In neurologically normal children, by contrast, low cohesion was associated with more inattention. The interaction was significant but negative, running counter to any notion that brain abnormality renders children more liable to become inattentive in response to family stresses. The negative interaction could be interpreted as neurological factors overriding family effects, paralleling the possible overriding of gender effects described above. There are alternative explanations, however, including the possibility that families expect and tolerate inattention in neurologically impaired children, but respond negatively to inattention in non-disabled children.

Though these results lend no support to the vulnerability model, it would be premature to abandon the model. The demonstration of statistically and clinically significant interactions may await a large enough study examining the right set of non-neurological variables. Existing studies have largely ignored two potentially relevant sorts of environmental risk factors. Firstly, the focus to date has largely been on the sorts of risk factors that impinge on all the children in the same family, though twin and adoption data suggest that the impact of these shared environmental factors may be dwarfed by non-shared environmental factors that impinge differently on different children in the same family (see Plomin & Daniels, 1987, and Goodman, 1991a, for an alternative view). Secondly, existing studies concentrate on psychosocial risk factors that are also relevant to non-handicapped children, rather than on those risk factors that may be of particular importance to neurologically impaired children. Overprotective-ness, for example, seems to be a particularly common and potent risk factor for head-injured children (Hjern & Nylander, 1964; Rutter, Chadwick & Shaffer, 1984), but it is probably less relevant (and certainly less studied) as a risk factor for non-handicapped children. It would be rash to dismiss vulnerability models until adequate studies have searched for interactions between neurological variables and environmental measures that tap within-family differences and the sorts of psychosocial factors that impinge particularly on neurologically impaired children. Arguments from analogy are necessarily weak, but it is interesting to note that behavioural geneticists searching for intuitively plausible gene–environment interactions (in the statistical sense) have found these interactions to be the exception rather than the rule (e.g. Cloninger et al., 1982; Plomin & DeFries, 1985).

Just as neurological and non-neurological factors can both affect *whether* a particular child develops a psychiatric disorder, so both neurological and non-neurological factors affect *which sort* of psychiatric disorder arises.

Table 3.2 summarizes the Isle of Wight findings on the type of psychiatric disorder in neuro-epileptic and neurologically intact children. Among the neurologically intact children with a psychiatric disorder, over 98% had either a conduct or an emotional disorder, or a mixture of the two. These were the commonest disorders among the neuro-epileptic children as well, providing the basis for the assertion that the "varieties of psychiatric problems in neuro-epileptic children were similar on the whole to those found in any group of children with psychiatric disorder" (Rutter, Graham & Yule, 1970, p. 188). This assertion was an important rebuttal of the widely held view that "brain damaged" children manifested a uniform and recognizable behavioural syndrome, the "brain-damage syndrome", that was distinct from run-of-the-mill psychiatric disorders. At the same time, however, it is important to note that certain rare disorders, including severe and pervasive hyperactivity (hyperkinesis), do seem to be particularly over-represented in the neuro-epileptic group (see Table 3.2). While the overall prevalence of psychiatric disorder was about 7 times higher in the neuro-epileptic group than in the neurologically intact group, the prevalence of hyperkinesis was almost 90 times greater in the neuro-epileptic group.

Neurological factors, then, do seem to have some influence on the type of psychiatric disorder. This conclusion is reinforced by numerous studies reporting associations between particular brain abnormalities and specific psychiatric disorders. Although the associated psychiatric disorders are sometimes referred to as the "behavioural phenotypes" of the underlying brain abnormalities, this term is misleading if it is taken to refer to invariable links rather than statistical associations. Reported associations between neurological and psychiatric disorders include: a link between hemiplegic (but not diplegic) cerebral palsy and hyperkinesis (Ingram, 1955); a link

Table 3.2 Diagnostic breakdown of psychiatrically disordered children on the Isle of Wight with and without brain disorder (data from Rutter, Graham & Yule, 1970)

Psychiatrically disordered children with	Diagnosis (%)				
	Conduct disorder	Emotional disorder	Mixed disorder	Hyperkinesis	PDD and other
No neurological disorder ($N=111$)	37	38	23	1	1
Uncomplicated epilepsy ($N=18$)	33	44	17	6	0
Structural brain abnormality IQ>50 ($N=16$)	19	25	25	19	12

PDD=pervasive developmental disorder, e.g. autism.

between developmental abnormalities of the left temporal lobe and adult-onset schizophrenia (Ounsted, Lindsay & Richards, 1987; Taylor, 1975); a link between infantile spasms due to tuberous sclerosis and autistic disorders (Hunt & Dennis, 1987); and a link between Sydenham's chorea and obsessive–compulsive disorder (Swedo, 1989).

As already mentioned, the Isle of Wight study showed that neuro-epileptic disorders were associated with an increased rate of the whole gamut of child psychiatric disorders (though hyperkinesis was particularly over-represented) (Rutter, Graham & Yule, 1970). Studies of children with head injuries have also shown increases in a broad range of psychiatric disorders (though a significant minority of children with severe closed head injuries displayed a relatively characteristic pattern of social disinhibition, reminiscent of the adult "frontal lobe syndrome") (Rutter, Chadwick & Shaffer, 1984). How can one interpret the broad range of psychopathology associated with neuro-epileptic disorders or head injury? The "vulnerability model" provides an appealing explanation, suggesting that the neurological abnormalities simply amplify non-neurological risk factors, with the latter determining the type of disorder. As described above, however, the evidence for the vulnerability model is weak (mainly reflecting a lack of relevant studies rather than an accumulation of negative studies).

Alternatively, the heterogeneity of psychiatric outcome could potentially be explained by neurological variables. Cerebral palsy, epilepsy and head injury are themselves very heterogeneous. For instance, there are wide variations in underlying neuropathology even within a single subtype of cerebral palsy (e.g. Uvebrant, 1988). It would not be surprising, therefore, if cerebral palsy rendered some children particularly prone to conduct disorder (perhaps by damaging structures normally involved in anger control), while rendering other children particularly prone to emotional disorders (perhaps by damaging structures normally involved in the regulation of affect). If this were so, examination of more homogeneous neurological groups would increase the distinctiveness of the associated psychiatric morbidity. There are some hints that this is indeed true. For example, Sollee & Kindlon (1987) used parent questionnaires to examine the pattern of psychiatric symptomatology among children with unilateral brain injuries, and found that children with lesions of the dominant hemisphere were more prone to externalizing (conduct) rather than internalizing (emotional) symptomatology, while the situation was reversed for children with lesions of the non-dominant hemisphere. These and somewhat similar findings from other studies (Stores, 1977; Weintraub & Mesulam, 1983; Voeller 1986) are suggestive but not conclusive, being based on relatively crude measures of psychopathology applied to small samples of clinically rather than epidemiologically ascertained children.

Putting together the various findings discussed in this section, it is evident that neurological and non-neurological factors can both influence the occurrence and type of psychiatric disorder. The relationship between neurological and non-neurological factors is complex, with the conclusion of any one study depending on which neurological and non-neurological factors are studied, and on which outcome measures are chosen. In some instances, multifactorial routes into psychiatric disorder seem to include major contributions from both neurological and non-neurological sources. In other instances, neurological factors seem to be the key determinant of the likelihood and type of psychiatric disorder. In these cases, the role of non-neurological factors is unclear. Consider the reported link between childhood hemiplegia and hyperkinesis (Ounsted, 1955; Ingram, 1955, 1956). Why is it that most hemiplegic children do not seem to be hyperkinetic? Does the underlying neurological damage only sometimes involve whichever brain centres normally control attention and activity? Is it a reflection of the role of chance in brain and behavioural development? Or is it the absence of other (as yet unmeasurable) genetic or environmental risk factors for hyeractivity? It may not be possible to answer some of these questions without developing novel neuropsychiatric research strategies. For example, in order to investigate the interaction of acquired brain damage and genotype, it would be helpful to investigate identical twins discordant for brain damage, though this would obviously require a national or international study in order to acquire a sufficiently large sample.

MEDIATING MECHANISMS

What are the mediating processes that result in neurologically impaired children having such high rates of associated psychopathology? The question is of obvious practical interest, and also provides a unique window on the nature of physical causation in psychological development.

When a neurologically impaired child develops an emotional or behavioural problem, it seems reasonable to enquire how the neurological disorder led to a psychiatric disorder. Before attempting to answer this question, it is important to acknowledge that coincidence does not necessarily imply causation. Even when the neurological disorder comes first, the subsequent emergence of psychiatric problems may be entirely unrelated to the neurological disorder. As described above, neurological and non-neurological risk factors may represent separate paths into psychiatric disorder. For instance, Breslau's (1990) results suggest that low family cohesion predisposes a child to develop depressive symptoms, with this effect being equally strong in neurologically impaired and normal children. Apart from coincidence, there is another non-causal link between neurological and psychiatric disorder that deserves consideration, namely the operation of third factors. For example, adverse psychosocial factors such as inadequate parental supervision may predispose a child both to neurological insults and, independently, to psychiatric disorder. It is also possible that some of the genetic causes of brain abnormalities independently contribute to psychiatric risk. To put this rather differently, brain abnormalities may sometimes be markers for the real causes of psychiatric disorder, and not those causes themselves.

Despite these various reservations, it does seem likely that psychiatric disorders in neurologically impaired children are commonly due to the brain abnormalities, and not just coincidences or products of a common antecedent. There are many possible pathways from brain abnormalities to psychiatric disorder, but it is helpful to distinguish, in a rough and ready way, between the organic and psychosocial consequences of neurological impairments (see Figure 3.1), acknowledging that the two are intimately interrelated, and that the distinction is often difficult in practice, and sometimes impossible. In principle, though, the distinction is straightforward enough. Organic consequences flow from the nature of the neurological impairment itself, or from the effects of anticonvulsant or other medication, whereas psychosocial consequences are mediated by the individual's, the family's and society's responses to the impairment and its direct consequences.

Effects on self-image are categorized as psychosocial rather than organic consequences in the belief that abnormalities of self-image largely arise from

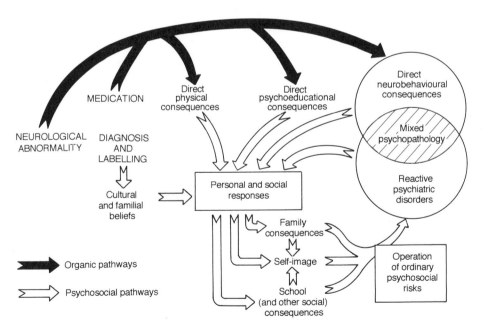

Figure 3.1   A simplified representation of organic and psychosocial pathways from brain to behavioural abnormalities

internalization of society's negative views of handicap. It is important to acknowledge, however, that an abnormal self-image may sometimes arise from organic abnormalities in the neural systems that underlie the capacity to generate self-constructs—a possibility that may be particularly relevant to abnormalities of self-image in autistic individuals that could be due to defective development of meta-representational capacity (cf. Baron-Cohen, 1988).

The underlying neurobiological abnormalities—whether structural, bio-chemical or electrophysiological—can have organic consequences in the physical, psycho-educational and neurobehavioural domains. Physical consequences include a variety of possible disabilities, ranging from easy fatiguability to lack of independent mobility, and from poor hand control to restricted visual fields. Another direct physical consequence of cerebral palsy and some related disorders is a liability to muscle contractures and other deformities, with the result that these children often have to spend many hours each week in physical therapy, and may have to undergo repeated hospital admissions for operative treatment.

Reduced IQ and specific learning problems are common psycho-educational consequences of brain abnormalities. Although idiopathic epilepsy may not be associated with any reduction in mean IQ (Bourgeois et al., 1983; Ellenberg, Hirtz & Nelson, 1986), the other common neurological syndromes in childhood are associated with a downward shift in the IQ distribution, though many of the affected children still have IQs within the normal range (e.g. Rutter, Graham & Yule, 1970). Even allowing for lower mean IQs neurologically impaired children are particularly prone to specific learning problems. On the Isle of Wight, for example, specific reading retardation (as defined by a reading ability at least two standard deviations below that predicted from chronological age and IQ) affected 26% of children with brain disorders, as compared with 14% of children with physical disorders not involving the brain, and 5% of physically normal children. In so far as neurological variables, such as type of cerebral palsy or duration of post-traumatic amnesia, predict the degree of cognitive impairment in neurologically abnormal children (Rutter, Graham & Yule, 1970; Rutter, Chadwick & Shaffer, 1984), and since brain lesions can cause specific learning problems in experimental animals (e.g. Goldman-Rakic et al., 1983), it seems very likely that neurological abnormalities lead directly to reduced IQ and specific learning problems, though this direct effect may well be compounded by the indirect effects of neurological abnormalities on expectations, educational opportunities and school attendance. In epilepsy, information processing and scholastic skill can be affected not only by clinical and subclinical seizures (e.g. Kasteleijn-Nolst Trenite et al. 1988; Mirsky, 1989), but also by the effects of anticonvulsant medication (see Cull & Trimble, 1989).

It is eminently plausible that brain abnormalities can lead directly to psychiatric symptomatology. Thus damage to the neural "centres" regulating attention could be the cause of hyperactivity; irritability and aggression could arise from amygdalar overactivity, whether driven by epilepsy or due to loss of normal inhibition from "higher centres"; and many bizarre psychiatric symptoms could potentially arise on the basis of neuronal misconnections. Plausibility is not enough, however, and the evidence that brain abnormalities lead directly to psychopathology is largely circumstantial at present. There are some relevant animal models, but these are few and far between (e.g. Delgado, 1969; Robinson, 1979). Adult neuropsychiatric disorders, such as the "frontal lobe syndrome" (see Lishman, 1987), provide further evidence for organic brain–behaviour links. Extrapolating from animals to humans, and from adults to children, is an uncertain business. The most convincing evidence for organic brain–behaviour links in childhood comes from studies of children themselves. The behavioural problems seen in children treated with particular anticonvulsant drugs (e.g. Ounsted, 1955) certainly support the notion of organic psychopathology. The existence of a wide variety of neuropsychiatric associations in childhood also suggest the existence of organic brain–behaviour links. Such links seem to provide the best explanation for the high rate of autistic symptomatology among children with tuberous sclerosis (Hunt & Dennis, 1987), for the characteristic pattern of sleep and appetite problems among children with the Prader–Willli syndrome (Cassidy, 1984), and for the severe self-injury associated with the Lesch–Nyhan syndrome (Christie et al. 1982), to name but a few instances.

To follow Jaspers's (1974) distinction, we cannot find a meaningful or understandable connection between each syndrome and its specific behavioural consequences, and this makes us more willing to accept that the links are explained by physiological rather than psychosocial processes. Though intuitively appealing, this line of argument is clearly not conclusive. The existence of underlying physiological mechanisms still needs to be demonstrated in practice, rather than simply being inferred from the absence of any plausible alternative. At the moment it remains an attractive hypothesis rather than established fact that brain abnormalities lead directly to non-understandable psychiatric disorders such as autism, hyperkinesis, schizophrenia and obsessive–compulsive disorder.

Though some brain–behaviour links are not understandable, many potentially are. It is not difficult to think of meaningful connections between neurological and psychiatric disorders (remembering, once again, that plausibility is not proof, and that humans are well able to generate meaningful connections where none exist). Physical disabilities could lead to teasing, a poor self-image, and reduced opportunities for peer interaction. Repeated hospitalizations could also disrupt friendships, and may predispose to behavioural disorders, perhaps as a result of repeated separations from family (Douglas, 1975; Quinton & Rutter, 1976). Low intelligence and specific learning problems increase the likelihood that school will be an unrewarding and frustrating experience, and this could well damage the individual's self-image and contribute to disruptive and defiant (acting-out) behaviours.

If brain abnormalities do have organic neurobehavioural consequences, such as hyperactivity or an impaired ability to decipher social and emotional cues, these organic consequences may have adverse effects on family relationships and friendship patterns. In addition, it seems likely that friends, family and teachers will modify their responses to a neurologically impaired child in the light of their beliefs and prejudices about "brain damaged" children. These beliefs will influence the likelihood of overprotection, peer rejection and unrealistic expectations. Beliefs can also interfere with parents' disciplinary techniques, either because they believe that all negative behaviour is beyond their child's control, being driven by the brain abnormality, or because they fear that discipline will trigger off a seizure or some other negative consequence. Internalization of familial and cultural beliefs may also have an adverse effect on the child's self-image. Many of the understandable paths from brain disorder to child psychiatric disorder are graphically described, with a wealth of case histories, in Taylor's (1989) account of the psychosocial consequences of childhood epilepsy.

The social and personal responses to a child's neurological disorder may expose that child to many "ordinary risk factors" for emotional and behavioural disorders. In the family domain, the extra stresses of looking after a disabled child could lead to more psychiatric problems in parents, or an increase in marital discord and breakdown. Sibling rivalry may be fuelled by the resentment of disabled children who see themselves being overtaken by younger siblings, or by the resentment of non-disabled siblings who feel they are missing out on parental attention. Parental responses to having a disabled child range from overprotection to withdrawal, and from unrealistically high expectations to the abandonment of all expectations. As already mentioned, parental beliefs can stand in the way of exerting effective and consistent discipline. Beyond the family, the neurologically impaired child may face yet more "ordinary risk factors", including rejection by schoolmates and a lack of success at school. Self-concepts are increasingly thought to play a part in resilience or vulnerability to psychiatric disorders in childhood (e.g. Rutter, 1985), and it is eminently plausible that the consequences of a neurological disorder frequently weaken a child's sense of self-esteem and self-efficacy. Taken together, these understandable responses to neurological disorder could account for a substantial level of "reactive psychopathology" mostly taking the form of the common emotional and conduct disorders. Though organically and psychosocially driven psychopathology can be distinguished in theory, they may overlap considerably in practice. For example, defiance and disruptive behaviours may commonly reflect maladaptive parental responses to organically driven hyperactivity or "difficult temperament".

It is one thing to describe reactive brain–behaviour pathways that are plausible in principle, and quite another thing to establish whether and to what extent they operate in practice. Studies evaluating putative mediating pathways have been limited in quantity and quality, so rather than attempting a comprehensive overview, it seems more appropriate to focus on those findings that illustrate the available research strategies. Some of these findings refer to neurologically impaired children and others refer to children with other physical illnesses.

The obvious first step is to establish, for any putative mediating factor, whether that factor is truly commoner in a representative sample of children with a specific physical disorder than in a control sample. For example, if having a physically ill child leads to marital breakdown, and thereby to higher rates of psychopathology in the child, the rate of "broken homes" should be higher for children with chronic physical disorders than for controls. Since this is probably not true (e.g. Sabbeth & Leventhal, 1984), it seems unlikely that marital breakdown in response to a child's handicap is a major mediator of brain–behaviour links. There may be cases where a child's handicap leads directly to parental divorce, but if so these cases are relatively rare or are balanced by cases where the child's handicap brings the parents closer together, thereby averting a divorce that would otherwise have occurred. The finding that marital breakdown is not unusually common does not mean that broken homes are innocuous for neurologically impaired children. On the contrary, children with cerebral palsy resemble non-handicapped children in manifesting more psychiatric disorder when they come from broken rather than intact homes (Rutter, Graham & Yule, 1970). Marital breakdown (or the preceding marital discord) does seem to contribute to psychopathology in disabled and non-disabled children, but the *higher rate* of psychopathology among disabled children is not due to a higher rate of marital breakdown. We must look elsewhere for the brain–behaviour links, whether psychosocial or organic, that account for the *excess* psychopathology of neurologically impaired children.

Findings on social support networks are rather similar. Kazak, Reber & Carter (1988) compared the families of children with and without a chronic physical illness (phenylketonuria). The social networks of the two groups of families were broadly similar, and in both groups lower psychological stresses were associated with larger, less dense, parental networks. Family isolation may contribute to behavioural problems both in disabled and non-disabled children, but this study suggests that the excess of problems in disabled children is not due to their parents retreating from, or being rebuffed by, the wider social world. In a similar vein, Spaulding & Morgan

(1986) found no evidence that a chronically disabled child (with spina bifida but normal intelligence) affected family functioning, marital adjustment, parental attitudes or perceptions of child behaviour. These negative results are cited here because they challenge the widely held belief that the presence of a disabled child is bound to disturb family relationships and thereby put the child at psychiatric risk. That belief is clearly wrong. It is not the case that any disability leads to an increased likelihood of any sort of family disturbance. This does not rule out the possibility that *particular* neurological disorders are liable to affect *specific* aspects of family functioning. Indeed, there are hints that this is the case. Childhood epilepsy, for instance, may lead parents to adopt a more controlling style (Ritchie, 1981), and may lead children to seek or accept a more dependent relationship with their parents (Hoare, 1984).

Demonstrating that a putative mediating factor does occur more commonly among neurologically impaired than normal children is only a first step. It is also important to demonstrate that the putative mediator is associated with psychiatric disorder *within* the neurologically impaired group. This point is nicely illustrated by considering the possible role of degree of physical disability. Neurologically impaired children are obviously more disabled as a group than ordinary children. Does this account for their high rate of psychiatric disorder, perhaps as a result of frustration or isolation? If so, the likelihood of psychiatric disorder should be related to the degree of disability—a prediction that has not generally been borne out. Neither the Isle of Wight study (Rutter, Graham & Yule, 1970) nor Breslau's (1985) clinic-based study found a significant association between degree of disability and likelihood of psychiatric disorder. Seidel, Chadwick & Rutter (1975) did find a significant association between level of disability (as judged from the mother's account) and likelihood of psychiatric disorder, but the direction of this association was contrary to expectations, with less psychiatric disorder in more disabled children. This may well have been a spurious finding, however, since the same study found no such association when the level of disability was assessed from the child's rather than the mother's account. Overall, it seems reasonable to conclude that although physical disability is common in neurologically impaired children, this cannot account for their high rate of psychiatric disorder.

The importance of community prejudice can be questioned for somewhat different reasons. There can be little doubt that neurological disorders commonly arouse powerful feelings of distaste in the general public. For instance, one survey found that a third of respondents would not knowingly permit their child to play with an epileptic child (British Office of Health Economics, 1971). Though common sense dictates that this high level of prejudice is bound to have serious adverse consequences for children with epilepsy, the case is not yet proven. For instance, the prejudices of strangers will probably have less impact on a child than the actual behaviour of schoolmates, and it is still controversial whether prejudice commonly leads to neurologically impaired children being shunned by their peers. Breslau (1985) did find that neurologically impaired children were significantly more isolated than children with cystic fibrosis. On the Isle of Wight, by contrast, children with neurological disorders were not significantly less popular than children with other physical disorders, and although there was a non-significant trend for the neuro-epileptic children to have poorer peer relationships, this trend may have been the *result* rather than the *cause* of the high rate of psychiatric disorder in the neuro-epileptic group (Rutter, Graham & Yule, 1970). Thus when children with psychiatric disorders were excluded from the analysis, the neuro-epileptic children were slightly more popular than asthmatic children. This example brings out the important point that an association is not proof of causation. Causal interpretations are tenuous without longitudinal and intervention studies.

In the hunt for key mediators of brain–behaviour links in childhood, cognitive deficits must be prime suspects. The list of cognitive impairments that could lead on to psychiatric disorders is potentially a long one, including deficits in language, attention, visuospatial skill and non-verbal communication (e.g. Weintraub & Mesulam, 1983; Vargha-Khadem, O'Gorman & Watters, 1985). The best studied cognitive problems are low IQ and specific reading problems. As described above, these problems are greatly over-represented among neurologically impaired children. Furthermore, these cognitive deficits are relatively good predictors of which neurologically impaired children develop psychiatric disorders. In the Isle of Wight study, for instance, neuro-epileptic children were more than twice as likely to develop a psychiatric disorder if their IQ was 85 or less (Rutter, Graham & Yule, 1970). After allowing for IQ, the same study also found that the presence of specific reading retardation more than doubled the psychiatric risk of neuro-epileptic chidren.

Multivariate techniques can also be used to estimate how important the mediating role of cognitive deficits might be. This can be illustrated by considering one aspect of Breslau's (1985) study comparing the psychiatric problems of children with cystic fibrosis and children with a variety of brain disorders (even though it is uncertain whether these illustrative changes were statistically significant). The association between neurological impairment (the independent variable) and social isolation (the dependent variable) was examined in the first step of a hierarchical regression analysis, using age, sex, race and socio-economic status as covariates to control for their effects. The regression coefficient of isolation on neurological impairment was 0.25 (accounting for 6.2% of the variance). When mental retardation was entered as an additional independent variable in the second step of the analysis, the regression coefficient of isolation on neurological impairment fell to 0.19 (accounting for 3.6% of the variance), representing a 42% fall in variance explained. In other words, almost half of the association between neurological abnormalities and social isolation could *potentially* be explained as a consequence of the high rate of mental retardation among the neurologically impaired children. This does not prove that mental retardation was in fact a mediator. It is possible, for instance, that mental retardation was simply a good marker for the sort of brain abnormalities that were particularly likely to result in social isolation. Even strong associations are not proof of causation.

The association between cognitive deficits and psychiatric disorder could reflect one or more of several sorts of underlying causal connections. Firstly, cognitive deficits may cause psychiatric disorders, perhaps as a result of the frustration engendered by the deficits. An alternative causal explanation is that psychiatric problems lead to cognitive deficits. For example, severe hyperactivity could disrupt a child's attention in the classroom and thereby lead to specific problems with reading and other academic skills. A third causal explanation is that cognitive and psychiatric problems arise independently from a common cause, such as damage to neural systems involved in "higher functions". If this were so, cognitive deficits would be markers for, rather than either causes or effects of, psychiatric disorder. Finally, the association between cognitive deficits and psychiatric disorders may arise simply because we use two different but overlapping terminologies. In some instances, the same problem can be described both as a cognitive deficit and as a psychiatric disorder. In other instances, closely related and highly intercorrelated problems fall on different sides of the arbitrary cognitive/psychiatric divide. Both of these considerations seem particularly germane to children whose off-task activities can be described in terms of attention deficits, suggesting a cognitive disorder, or in terms of hyperactivity, suggesting a psychiatric disorder. There is little point in asking if hyperactivity is secondary to attention deficits if the two terms are synonyms, or if the two terms refer to closely related aspects of the same underlying disorder.

Longitudinal studies can potentially help us unravel which causal processes underlie cross-sectional associations. For example, if a cognitive deficit causes a psychiatric disorder, the onset of the cognitive disorder should precede the onset of the psychiatric disorder. Conversely, the psychiatric disorder should come first if it is the cause of the cognitive deficit. Yet again, if the cognitive and psychiatric disorders are either one and the same thing, or intimately related aspects of the same underlying problem, they should emerge at the same point in development. Unfortunately, all three of these developmental sequences—cognitive deficit first, psychiatric disorder first, or both together—could also be due to the operation of some "third factor" that independently caused both the cognitive deficit and the psychiatric disorder, though not necessarily at the same time. For instance, the manifestations of an early-acquired brain abnormality can change as the brain matures, with the individual growing into some symptoms as development proceeds (Goldman-Rakic et al. 1983). As a result, even when the same underlying brain abnormality accounts for both a cognitive deficit and a psychiatric disorder, it is not inevitable that the two problems will emerge at the same developmental stage; the affected individual may grow into some problems early in development and not grow into others until later. When this is so, it will be easy to jump to the erroneous conclusion that the early manifestations caused the later manifestations (see Pickles, Chapter 2 this volume, for further discussion of ways to analyse the implications of the timing of causal factors).

Though longitudinal studies clearly cannot resolve all questions of causality, they are obviously of immense value in teasing out the origins of cross-sectional associations, and they are also particularly suitable for investigating whether events that occur during one developmental epoch have consequences at a later developmental stage. Given the many advantages of longitudinal studies, it is disappointing that so few neuropsychiatric studies in childhood have employed this approach. The Oxford study, following children with temporal lobe epilepsy into adulthood, is a notable exception that has revealed some surprising connections across time (Ounsted, Lindsay & Richards, 1987). For example, boys who experienced frequent temporal lobe seizures during adolescence were commonly sexually indifferent in adulthood, perhaps reflecting the disruption of amygdalar and hippocampal function during a key developmental epoch. The same series is also noteworthy for failing to demonstrate some expected continuities. For instance, the presence or absence of severe psychosocial adversity in childhood did not predict which individuals manifested psychiatric illnesses or personality disorders in adult life.

Intervention studies provide another powerful tool for investigating causal processes. For instance, if a cognitive deficit causes a psychiatric disorder, an intervention that cures the cognitive disorder at an early stage should prevent the subsequent emergence of the psychiatric disorder. Once the psychiatric disorder has emerged, remediation of the cognitive deficit may also cure the associated psychiatric disorder. This is not necessarily the case, however, since a psychiatric disorder could potentially be self-perpetuating even when its original cause was removed (e.g. if the child's initial behavioural problems evoke maladaptive family reactions, leading to more behavioural problems in the child, and so on). It hardly needs stressing that successful early remediation of a cognitive deficit should not prevent the emergence of a psychiatric disorder if the latter is a cause rather than an effect of the former, or if both sets of problems are due to a "third factor". This being the case, successful intervention studies can furnish convincing evidence about the direction of causality. There is one important proviso, however. Interventions may have powerful non-specific (or "placebo") effects on children's psychiatric disorders. When administered with conviction and care, almost any treatment may help, perhaps by giving the family hope, or by uniting the parents on a consistent course of action, or by providing the child with extra attention. Ideally, therefore, if we want to show that variable X is a key mediator, we need to demonstrate that an intervention targeted on X is more effective than an equally convincing and time-consuming intervention targeted on variable Y.

There have been few intervention studies in the field of developmental neuropsychiatry. The scope for such studies can be indicated by one instance each of physical and psychological inverventions. Anecdotally, switching a child from phenobarbitone to another anticonvulsant may reduce hyperactivity (Ounsted, 1955), suggesting that the administration of phenobarbitone can be an important mediating link between childhood epilepsy and hyperactivity. Hjern & Nylander (1964) found that children with acute head injuries were less likely to develop psychiatric problems if their parents had been counselled that sequelae of head injury are likely to be transient, and that head-injured children benefit from a graded reintroduction to all normal activities. The benefits of this psychological intervention strongly support the notion that some of the psychiatric problems seen after childhood head injury occur because misplaced parental concerns lead to anxiety, overprotection, lax or inconsistent discipline, or unrealistically low expectations.

In conclusion, there are many plausible pathways from brain abnormalities to behavioural disorders, and there are many research strategies for investigating which of these pathways are important in practice—but this investigation has hardly begun. There is still considerable scope for cross-sectional descriptive studies, and the potential of longitudinal and intervention approaches is almost entirely untapped.

BIRTH DAMAGE

Do birth complications account for a high proportion of common childhood problems such as hyperactivity or reading difficulties? This question raises a variety of theoretical and methodological issues that warrant careful consideration, not only because "birth damage" theories were and remain influential, but also because similar considerations apply to comparable theories attributing children's behavioural or learning problems to other biological insults, such as low-level lead or food additives.

There is nothing intrinsically implausible about the notion that mild birth complications cause common psychological problems. The underlying hypothesis can be formulated as a series of postulates. Firstly, birth is a perilous process, with death being the worst outcome of birth complications.

Secondly, there is a continuum of perinatal casualty, with sublethal complications resulting in brain damage but not death. Generations of doctors have been taught that cerebral palsy and severe mental retardation commonly result from severe birth complications that do not kill the child. Thirdly, since overt neurological disorders are accompanied by a high rate of learning and behavioural problems (as described earlier in the chapter), it is at least plausible that brain damage can sometimes result in learning or behavioural problems without any other symptoms and signs of neurological disorder. Fourthly, this sort of "covert" brain damage with purely psychological sequelae is often due to mild birth complications, and accounts for a high proportion of common emotional, behavioural and educational problems in childhood. This is a "tip of the iceberg" theory, arguing that for every child with overt brain damage due to severe birth complications, there are many more children with psychological problems due to covert brain damage inflicted by common but mild birth complications.

Of these four postulates, the first is the least controversial. That birth complications can be fatal is best demonstrated by the dramatic reduction in perinatal mortality associated with obstetric advances in the prevention or treatment of these complications. If birth complications were simply markers for intrinsically doomed foetuses, attempts to reduce perinatal death rates by treating the complications would have been ineffective.

Turning to the second postulate, it is important to consider whether birth complications exert a proportionate or an all-or-nothing effect. The notion of a continuum of perinatal casualty implies a proportionate effect, with severe complications causing death, with moderately severe complications causing cerebral palsy or mental retardation, and with mild complications causing psychological problems alone. Recent evidence is more in keeping with an all-or-nothing effect, with severe birth complications causing death, and with lesser complications generally doing no harm at all (e.g. Ounsted, 1987). Contrary to traditional teaching, cerebral palsy and mental retardation are probably not commonly due to birth complications. Although cerebral palsy is weakly associated with birth asphyxia, this may largely be due to a tendency for abnormal foetuses to develop birth asphyxia as well (Nelson & Ellenberg, 1986; Miller, 1989). If birth complications are generally markers for, rather than causes of, the neurological abnormalities underlying cerebral palsy, this would explain why the prevalence of cerebral palsy has hardly altered over recent decades despite major advances in obstetric care (Paneth & Kiely, 1984). In mental handicap too, perinatal complications may often be markers for abnormalities that preceded birth (Rantakallio & Von Wendt, 1985). In a minority of cases, however, birth complications may result in neurological damage. For example, birth asphyxia may account for up to 10% of cerebral palsy (Nelson & Ellenberg, 1986). If the foetal brain is so resilient that severe birth complications rarely result in overt brain damage, it seems implausible that mild birth complications commonly result in psychological problems due to covert brain damage. Though it is potentially perilous to extrapolate from one developmental stage to another, it is also worth noting the evidence for a threshold effect in childhood head injury, with severe head injuries resulting in cognitive and behavioural sequelae, but with mild injuries having no such sequelae (Rutter, Chadwick & Shaffer, 1984).

As regards the third postulate, there is every reason to suppose that some children with unequivocal brain abnormalities have no demonstrable neurological signs on clinical examination (see Rutter, 1983). For example, in a series of children with penetrating injuries of the brain, only a third had definite neurological signs at follow-up a few years later, and a third showed no sign whatever of neurological abnormality, dubious or definite (Rutter, 1983; Shaffer, Chadwick & Rutter, 1975). Since the rate of psychiatric disorder in this series of children was 62%, far exceeding the proportion of children with definite neurological signs, it is difficult to avoid the conclusion that behavioural symptoms are sometimes the only outward manifestations of brain damage that is undetectable by the normal neurological examination.

Turning to the final postulate, the main issue is quantitative. Birth complications probably do cause cerebral palsy, albeit rarely. If birth complications sometimes result in overt brain damage, it would be rash to assert that they never cause covert brain damage. And if covert damage due to childhood head injury can have behavioural manifestations, there is no reason to suppose that covert birth damage will not do the same. Putting these conclusions together, it does seem possible that birth complications sometimes result in learning or behavioural problems in children who have no neurological signs on clinical examination. The key issue, however, is whether such children are common or rare. On the Isle of Wight, structural brain disorders affected about six children per thousand (Rutter, Graham & Yule, 1970). If one assumes, for the sake of argument, that birth complications accounted for only 10% of these disorders, that covert damage is as common as overt damage, and that half of the affected children develop psychological problems, then children with psychological problems due to covert birth damage would amount to 0.03% of the population—accounting for well under 1% of all behavioural and educational problems. This would certainly be very different from "tip of the iceberg" predictions that birth complications were often responsible for the common behavioural and educational problems occurring in children with no demonstrable neurological signs.

It is practically impossible to rule out covert birth damage as a rare cause of psychological problems. It is possible, however, to assess whether birth complications are likely to be common causes of these problems. For any particular psychiatric or educational problem, it is important to ask three questions. Is the problem more commonly preceded by birth complications than would be expected by chance? If so, can the link be explained by a third factor, such as marked psychosocial adversity, that independently increases the likelihood of birth complications on the one hand, and educational or behavioural problems on the other? If not, what is cause and what is effect? It is possible that birth complications cause the neurological abnormalities that manifest as psychological problems in childhood. It is equally possible, however, that the causal arrow runs in the reverse direction. A foetus with a subtly abnormal nervous system, perhaps for genetic reasons, may be destined from before birth to develop learning or behavioural problems during childhood. These same neurological abnormalities may also increase the chance of a complicated birth, as suggested by the data on cerebral palsy and mental retardation described above. Since the foetus is an active participant in birth, and not simply a passive passenger who is expelled when his or her time is up, it is not too difficult to imagine that an abnormal foetus is unusually liable to an abnormal birth.

Is a psychiatric or educational problem more commonly preceded by birth complications than would be exected by chance? Though many studies have addressed this sort of question, it is hard to interpret the answers when a study is clinic-based, retrospective or uncontrolled. Only epidemiological studies can avoid the referral biases that may operate on clinic samples. For example, it is possible that the parents of a hyperactive child are more likely to seek medical help when the birth was difficult precisely because they have heard about "minimal brain damage" and believe that doctors can only help hyperactivity that is linked to birth damage. Retrospective studies can introduce a different bias. The parents of a child with a psychiatric disorder will often have reflected for many years on the likely cause of their child's problems. Such parents may well remember (and perhaps even exaggerate) minor difficulties with the birth that would have been forgotten by the parents of normal children. Consequently, retrospective accounts of birth complications are far less convincing than evidence gathered from contemporary records. The need for a control group should be obvious, but is underlined by the finding of one Scandinavian study, based on contemporary records, that over half of the control group had experienced at least one complication of pregnancy or birth (Jacobsen & Kinney, 1980). It is not hard to see how clinicians, unaware of this high base rate, could wrongly conclude that their patients had experienced an excess of birth complications. Allowing for all these pitfalls, birth complications may genuinely be over-represented in a number of psychiatric disorders, including hyperactivity (Nichols & Chen, 1981), infantile autism (Goodman, 1990) and schizophrenia (Goodman, 1988).

Once an association is established, can the link be explained in terms of a third factor, such as marked psychosocial adversity, that independently increases the likelihood of birth complications and psychological problems? One way to answer this question is to measure likely "third factors" and control for them. This is what Nichols and Chen (1981) did in their study of hyperactivity. Controlling for covariates, the links between hyperactivity and birth complications were weak but statistically significant. It is always possible, however, that even this weak link would have disappeared altogether if only the authors had included more (or better measured) covariates.

One possible way round this problem is to investigate the impact of a birth complication that strikes more or less at random. Twin pregnancies approach this "ideal", since they occur almost at random and carry a high risk of birth complications (Bryan, 1983). As in singletons, low birthweight is a good predictor of perinatal mortality (Butler & Alberman, 1968). Consequently, if hyperactivity were commonly due to perinatal adversity, low birthweight twins should be at much greater risk of subsequent hyperactivity than heavier twins. Goodman & Stevenson (1989) found no such effect in their twin study, suggesting that the weak link in singletons between hyperactivity and low birthweight may be due to unknown confounders. In singletons, for example, the weak association between low birthweight and hyperactivity may be due to conditions such as the foetal alcohol syndrome that can result both in foetal growth retardation and in subsequent hyperactivity (Spohr & Steinhausen, 1987). In twins, by contrast, where low birthweight is overwhelmingly due to the twinness itself, the effect of confounders may well be swamped.

Though the association between birth complications and hyperactivity may be spurious, this is unlikely to be true for the links between birth complications and some other psychiatric disorders. In the case of schizophrenia, for instance, there is no evidence that the unexpectedly high rate of antecedent birth complications can be explained by confounding factors such as social class or maternal mental illness (Goodman, 1988). A causal link may well be present, at least in a substantial minority of individuals with schizophrenia, but the direction of causality remains controversial.

What is cause and what is effect? For example, do birth complications convert previously normal foetuses into pre-schizophrenic children? Or are pre-schizophrenic foetuses particularly prone to experience a high rate of birth complications that are innocuous in themselves? The obvious way forward is to examine whether improved obstetric care reduces the rate of schizophrenia. If it does, it would be hard to dispute the inference that birth complications are causes rather than effects of a schizophrenic liability. An experiment that randomized pregnant women to good and bad obstetric care, and thereby to fewer and more birth complications, is clearly unthinkable. As the next best thing, it is possible to test causal hypotheses on epidemiological data, acknowledging that the lack of randomization in "natural experiments" increases the chance of spurious findings. There have been marked improvements over recent decades in the prevention and treatment of birth complications, accompanied by a dramatic fall in perinatal mortality. Has the rate of schizophrenia fallen in parallel? There are striking international differences in obstetric care and perinatal mortality. Are there equivalent international differences in the rate of schizophrenia? In the UK, higher perinatal mortality is linked to low parental social class. Is the risk of schizophrenia related to parental social class? Finally, twins experience far more birth complications than singletons. Is schizophrenia particularly common among twins? The questions are easy to pose, but the short answer to them all is that existing epidemiological data are probably inadequate to prove the case one way or the other (Goodman, 1988). Much the same is true if comparable questions are asked of infantile autism (Goodman, 1990). Without better epidemiological data, we must remain agnostic for the present.

In conclusion, the notion that birth complications commonly cause covert brain damage manifesting solely in the psychological domain is unproven. Recent studies of overt brain damage make some of the underlying assumptions seem implausible. Judging from methodologically sound studies, associations between birth complications and psychological disorders are weak. Furthermore, some of these associations may be spurious, and others may reflect reverse causality.

ENVOI

Developmental neuropsychiatry is an exciting area, spanning the brain and behavioural sciences, incorporating elements of developmental biology and developmental psychology, and examining the relationship between the normal and the pathological. Studies of the causal and non-causal relationships between brain and behavioural abnormalities in childhood have much to contribute, not only to our theoretical knowledge of the biological underpinnings of normal and abnormal development, but also to the practical care of children who are severely disadvantaged by a combination of physical and psychological handicaps. At present, developmental neuropsychiatry is still in its infancy. Though the description of developmental brain–behaviour links is well under way, the unravelling of causal mechanisms has hardly begun. Hopefully, the coming decades will see major advances as existing and innovative research strategies are brought to bear on the many fascinating questions in this area.

REFERENCES

Baron-Cohen, S. (1988). Social and pragmatic deficits in autism: cognitive or affective? *Journal of Autism and Developmental Disorders*, **18**, 379–402.

Bourgeois, B. F. D., Prensky, A. L., Palkes, H. S., Talent, B. K. & Busch, S. G. (1983). Intelligence in epilepsy: prospective study in children. *Annals of Neurology*, **14**, 438–444.

Breslau, N. (1985). Psychiatric disorder in children with physical disabilities. *Journal of American Academy of Child Psychiatry*, **24**, 87–94.

Breslau, N. (1990). Does brain dysfunction increase children's vulnerability to environmental stress? *Archives of General Psychiatry*, **47**, 15–20.

Breznitz, Z. & Friedman, S. L. (1988). Toddlers' concentration: does maternal depression make a difference? *Journal of Child Psychology and Psychiatry*, **29**, 267–279.

British Office of Health Economics (1971). *Epilepsy in Society*, Office of Health Economics, London.

Broman, S., Nichols, P. L., Shaughnessy, P., Kennedy, W. (1987). *Retardation in Young Children: A Developmental Study*. Erlbaum, Hillsdale, NJ.

Bryan, E. M. (1983). *The Nature and Nurture of Twins*, Ballière Tindall, London.

Butler, N. R. & Alberman, E. D. (1968). The multiple births. In N. R. Butler & E. D. Alberman (eds), *Perinatal Problems*, Livingstone, Edinburgh, pp. 122–140.

Cassidy, S. B. (1984). Prader–Willi syndrome. *Current Problems in Pediatrics*, **14**, 1–55.

Christie, R., Bay, C., Kaufman, I. A., Bakay, B., Borden, M. & Nyhan, W. L. (1982). Lesch–Nyhan disease: clinical experience with 19 patients. *Developmental Medicine and Child Neurology*, **24**, 293–306.

Cloninger, C. R., Sigvardsson, S., Bohman, M., & von Knorring, A. -L. (1982). Predisposition to petty criminality in Swedish adoptees. II. Cross-fostering analysis of gene-environment interaction. *Archives of General Psychiatry*, **39**, 1242–1247.

Crome, L. & Stern, J. (1972). *Pathology of Mental Retardation*, Churchill Livingstone, Edinburgh.

Cull, C. A. & Trimble, M. R. (1989). Effects of anticonvulsant medications on cognitive functioning in children with epilepsy. In B. P. Hermann & M. Seidenberg (eds), *Childhood Epilepsies: Neuropsychological, Psychosocial and Intervention Aspects*, John Wiley, Chichester, pp. 83–103.

Delgado, J. M. R. (1969). Offensive–defensive behaviour in free monkeys and chimpanzees induced by radio stimulation of the brain. In S. Garattini & E. B. Sigg (eds), *Aggressive Behaviour. Proceedings of the International Symposium on the Biology of Aggressive Behaviour*, Exerpta Medica, Amsterdam, pp. 109–119.

Douglas, J. W. B. (1975). Early hospital admissions and later disturbances of behaviour and learning. *Developmental Medicine and Child Neurology*, **17**, 456–480.

Ellenberg, J. H., Hirtz, D. G. & Nelson, K. B. (1986). Do seizures in children cause intellectual deterioration? *New England Journal of Medicine*, **314**, 1085–1088.

Gillberg, C., Persson, E., Grufman, M. & Themner, U. (1986). Psychiatric disorders in mildly and severely mentally retarded urban children and adolescents: epidemiological aspects. *British Journal of Psychiatry*, **149**, 68–74.

Goldman-Rakic, P. S., Isseroff, A., Schwartz, M. L. & Bugbee, N. M. (1983). The neurobiology of cognitive development. In M. M. Haith & J. J. Campos (eds), *Mussen's Handbook of Child Psychology*, 4th edn, vol. II, *Infancy and Developmental Psychobiology*, John Wiley, New York, pp. 281–344.

Goodman, R. (1987). The developmental neurobiology of language. In W. Yule & M. Rutter (eds), *Language Development and Disorders. Clinics in Developmental Medicine*, nos 101/102, MacKeith Press/Blackwell, London, pp. 129–145.

Goodman, R. (1988). Are complications of pregnancy and birth causes of schizophrenia? *Developmental Medicine and Child Neurology*, **30**, 391–395.

Goodman, R. (1990). Technical note: are perinatal complications causes or consequences of autism? *Journal of Child Psychology and Psychiatry*, **31**, 809–812.

Goodman, R. (1991a). Growing together and growing apart: the non-genetic forces on children in the same family. In P. McGuffin & R. Murray (eds), *The New Genetics of Mental Illness*, Butterworth/Heinemann, Oxford, pp. 212–224.

Goodman, R. (1991b). Developmental disorders and structural brain development. In: M. Rutter & P. Casaer (eds), *Biological Risk Factors for Psychosocial Development*, Cambridge University Press, Cambridge, pp. 20–49.

Goodman, R. & Stevenson, J. (1989). A twin study of hyperactivity: II. The aetiological role of genes, family relationships, and perinatal adversity. *Journal of Child Psychology and Psychiatry*, **30**, 691–709.

Hill, A. E. & Rosenbloom, L. (1986). Disintegrative psychosis of childhood: teenage follow-up. *Developmental Medicine and Child Neurology*, **28**, 34–40.

Hjern, B. & Nylander, I. (1964). Acute head injuries in children: traumatology, therapy and prognosis. *Acta Paediatrica Scandinavica*, Suppl. 152.

Hoare, P. (1984). Does illness foster dependency? A study of epileptic and diabetic children. *Developmental Medicine and Child Neurology*, **26**, 20–24.

Hodges, J. & Tizard, B. (1989). IQ and behavioural adjustment of ex-institutional adolescents. *Journal of Child Psychology and Psychiatry*, **30**, 53–75.

Hunt, A. & Dennis, J. (1987). Psychiatric disorder among children with tuberous sclerosis. *Developmental Medicine and Child Neurology*, **29**, 190–198.

Ingram, T. T. S. (1955). A study of cerebral palsy in the childhood population of Edinburgh. *Archives of Disease in Childhood*, **30**, 85–98.

Ingram, T. T. S. (1956). A characteristic form of overactive behaviour in brain damaged children. *Journal of Mental Science*, **102**, 550–558.

Jacobsen, B. & Kinney, D. K. (1980). Perinatal complications in adopted and non-adopted schizophrenics and their controls: preliminary results. *Acta Psychiatrica Scandinavica*, Suppl. 285, 337–346.

Jaspers, K. (1974). Causal and "meaningful" connexions between life history and psychosis. In S. R. Hirsch & M. Shepherd (eds), *Themes and Variations in European Psychiatry*, John Wright, Bristol, First published in 1913, pp. 81–93.

Kasteleijn-Nolst Trenite, D. G. A., Bakker, D. J., Binnie, C. D., Buerman, A. & Van Raay, M. (1988). Psychological effects of epileptiform EEG discharges. I. Scholastic skills. *Epilepsy Research*, **2**, 111–116.

Kazak, A. E., Reber, M. & Carter, A. (1988). Structural and qualitative aspects of social networks in families with young chronically ill children. *Journal of Pediatric Psychology*, **13**, 171–182.

Knobloch, H. & Pasamanick, B. (1959). Syndrome of minimal cerebral damage in infancy. *Journal of the American Medical Association*, **170**, 1384–1387.

Lishman, W. A. (1987). *Organic Psychiatry: The Psychological Consequences of Cerebral Disorder*, 2nd edn, Blackwell Scientific Publications, Oxford.

Miller, G. (1989). Minor congenital anomalies and ataxic cerebral palsy. *Archives of Disease in Childhood*, **64**, 557–562.

Mirsky, A. F. (1989). Information processing in petit mal epilepsy. In B. P. Hermann & M. Seidenberg (eds), *Childhood Epilepsies: Neuropsychological, Psychosocial and Intervention Aspects*, John Wiley, Chichester, pp. 71–81.

Nelson, K. B. & Ellenberg, J. H. (1986). Antecedents of cerebral palsy: multivariate analysis of risk. *New England Journal of Medicine*, **315**, 81–86.

Nichols, P. L. & Chen, T. C. (1981). *Minimal Brain Dysfunction: A Prospective Study*, Erlbaum, Hillsdale, NJ.

Ounsted, C. (1955). The hyperkinetic syndrome in epileptic children. *Lancet*, **ii**, 303–311.

Ounsted, C., Lindsay, J. & Norman, R. (1966). Biological factors in temporal lobe epilepsy. *Clinics in Developmental Medicine*, no. 22, SIMP/Heinemann, London.

Ounsted, C., Lindsay, J. & Richards, P. (1987). Temporal lobe epilepsy 1948–1986: a biographical study. *Clinics in Developmental Medicine*, no. 103, Blackwell Scientific Publications, Oxford.

Ounsted, M. (1987). Causes, continua and other concepts: I—The "continuum of reproductive casualty". *Paediatric and Perinatal Epidemiology*, **1**, 4–7.

Paneth, N. & Kiely, P. (1984). The frequency of cerebral palsy: a review of population studies in industrialised nations since 1950. In: F. Stanley & E. Alberman (eds), *The Epidemiology of the Cerebral Palsies, Clinics in Developmental Medicine*, no. 87. Blackwell, Oxford; Lippincott, Philadelphia, pp. 46–57.

Plomin, R. & Daniels, D. (1987). Why are children in the same family so different from one another? *Behavioral and Brain Sciences*, **10**, 1–60.

Plomin, R. & DeFries, J. C. (1985). *Origins of Individual Differences in Infancy: The Colorado Adoption Project*, Academic Press, New York.

Prichep, L., John, E. R., Ahn, H. & Kaye, H. (1983). Neurometrics: quantitative evaluation of brain dysfunction in children. In M. Rutter (ed.), *Developmental Neuropsychiatry*, Churchill Livingstone, Edinburgh, pp. 213–238.

Quinton, D. & Rutter, M. (1976). Early hospital admissions and later disturbances of behaviour: an attempted replication of Douglas's findings. *Developmental Medicine and Child Neurology*, **18**, 447–459.

Rantakallio, P. & Von Wendt, L. (1985). Risk factors for mental retardation. *Archives of Disease in Childhood*, **60**, 946–952.

Richie, K. (1981). Research note: interaction in the families of epileptic children. *Journal of Child Psychology and Psychiatry*, **22**, 65–71.

Robinson, R. G. (1979). Differential behavioral and biochemical effects of right and left hemispheric cerebral infarction in the rat. *Science*, **205**, 707–710.

Rutter, M. (1983). Concepts of brain dysfunction syndromes. In M. Rutter (ed.), *Developmental Neuropsychiatry*, Churchill Livingstone, Edinburgh, pp. 1–11.

Rutter, M. (1985). Resilience in the face of adversity: protective factors and resistance to psychiatric disorder. *British Journal of Psychiatry*, **147**, 598–611.

Rutter, M., Chadwick, O. & Shaffer, D. (1984). Head injury. In M. Rutter (ed.), *Developmental Neuropsychiatry*, Churchill Livingstone, Edinburgh, pp. 577–598.

Rutter, M., Cox, A., Tupling, C., Berger, M. & Yule, W. (1975). Attainment and adjustment in two geographical areas. I—The prevalence of psychiatric disorder. *British Journal of Psychiatry*, **126**, 493–509.

Rutter, M., Graham, P. & Yule, W. (1970). A neuropsychiatric study in childhood. *Clinics in Developmental Medicine*, nos 35/36. SIMP/Heinemann, London; Lippincott, Philadelphia.

Rutter, M. & Pickles, A. (1990). Person–environment interactions: concepts, mechanisms and implications for data analysis. In T. D. Wachs & R. Plomin (eds), *Conceptualizations and Measurement of Organism–Environment Interactions*, American Psychological Association, Washington, DC, pp. 105–141.

Rutter, M., Tizard, J. & Whitmore, K. (eds) (1970). *Education, Health and Behaviour*, Longman, London.

Sabbeth, B. F. & Leventhal, J. M. (1984). Marital adjustment to chronic childhood illness: a critique of the literature. *Pediatrics*, **73**, 762–768.

Seidel, U. P., Chadwick, O. F. D. & Rutter, M. (1975). Psychological disorders in crippled children. A comparative study of children with and without brain damage. *Developmental Medicine and Child Neurology*, **17**, 563–573.

Shaffer, D., Chadwick, O. & Rutter, M. (1975). Psychiatric outcome of localized head injury in children. In R. Porter & D. Fitzsimons (eds), *Outcome of Severe Damage to the Central Nervous System*, CIBA Foundation Symposium no. 34. Elsevier, Amsterdam, pp. 191–213.

Shaffer, D., O'Connor, P. A., Shafer, S. Q. & Prupis, S. (1984). Neurological "soft signs": their origins and significance for behaviour. In M. Rutter (ed), *Developmental Neuropsychiatry*, Churchill Livingstone, Edinburgh, pp. 144–164.

Sollee, N. D. & Kindlon, D. J. (1987). Lateralized brain injury and behavior problems in children. *Journal of Abnormal Child Psychology*, **15**, 479–490.

Spaulding, B. R. & Morgan, S. B. (1986). Spina bifida children and their parents: a population prone to family dysfunction? *Journal of Pediatric Psychology*, **11**, 359–374.

Spohr, H. L. & Steinhausen, H. C. (1987). Follow-up studies of children with fetal alcohol syndrome. *Neuropediatrics*, **18**, 13–17.

Still, G. F. (1902). Some abnormal psychical conditions in children. *Lancet*, **i**, 1008–1012, 1077–1082, 1163–1168.

Stores, G. (1977). Behavior disturbance and type of epilepsy in children attending ordinary school. In J. K. Penry (ed.), *Epilepsy: The Eighth International Symposium*, Raven Press, New York, 245–249.

Swedo, S. E., Rapoport, J. L., Cheslow, D. L., Leonard, H. L., Ayoub, E. M., Hosier, D. M. & Wald, E. R. (1989). High prevalence of obsessive–compulsive symptoms in patients with Sydenham's chorea. *American Journal of Psychiatry*, **146**, 246–249.

Taylor, D. C. (1975). Factors influencing the occurrence of schizophrenia-like psychosis in patients with temporal lobe epilepsy. *Psychological Medicine*, **5**, 249–254.

Taylor, D. C. (1989). Psychosocial components of childhood epilepsy. In B. P. Hermann & M. Seidenberg (eds), *Childhood Epilepsies: Neuropsychological, Psychosocial and Intervention Aspects*, John Wiley, Chichester, pp. 119–142.

Uvebrant, P. (1988). Hemiplegic cerebral palsy: aetiology and outcome. *Acta Paediatrica Scandinavica*, Suppl. 345.

Vargha-Khadem, F., O'Gorman, A. M. & Watters, G. V. (1985). Aphasia and handedness in relation to hemispheric side, age at injury and severity of cerebral lesion during childhood. *Brain*, **108**, 677–696.

Voeller, K. K. S. (1986). Right-hemisphere deficit syndrome in children. *American Journal of Psychiatry*, **143**, 1004–1009.

Weintraub, S. & Mesulam, M–M. (1983). Developmental learning disabilities of the right hemisphere: emotional, interpersonal and cognitive components. *Archives of Neurology*, **40**, 463–468.

Whitman, S., Hermann, B. P., Black, R. B. & Chhabria, S. (1982). Psychopathology and seizure type in children with epilepsy. *Psychological Medicine*, **12**, 843–853.

Chapter 4

Developmental Behavior Genetics: Fusion, Correlated Constraints, and Timing

Robert B. Cairns, Anne M. McGuire and Jean-Louis Gariépy

The nature of genetic influence on human behavior has been a scientific minefield over the past century. Yet no serious discussions of behavioral development can long avoid the issue of genetic involvement in behavior. The relations between genes and behavior were early recognized to be as fundamental for theories of biology as for theories of behavior (Whitney, 1990).

In this chapter we propose that genetic influences vary with time, behavioral organization, and adaptational context, and they may be rapidly modified in ontogeny and microevolution. Individual differences attributable to genetic biases that are observed early in development are not necessarily more basic or more enduring than later ones for behavioral organization; rather, the influences are continuously melded with contextual and organismic events throughout development. The development agenda addresses the problem of believing that any influence, whether genetic or early experience, has the ability to fix behavior. Accordingly, a focus upon organizational processes should be the first step for any analysis of behavior, whether the aim is to elucidate the effects of genes or the effects of culture. Genetic effects cannot be divorced from the behavioral system as a whole without distorting their role in the organization and expression of behavior. Analytic procedures that purport to unravel the role of genes in behavior without a precise analysis of the multiple determinants of the phenomena to be explained are doomed.

That complexities are encountered in this area of investigation cannot be gainsaid. Indeed, four of the proposals that we offer in this chapter may themselves seem antithetical with the developmental perspective that stimulated our work. First, we propose that genetic factors play a significant role in all behavioral adaptations. In experimental studies in nonhumans, genetic effects are more robust and more rapidly established and changed

Precursors and Causes in Development and Psychopathology.
Edited by D. F. Hay and A. Angold © 1993 John Wiley & Son Ltd

than has generally been acknowledged in the social and behavioral sciences (see Fuller & Thompson, 1978, for an excellent review). Similar but less direct information has been observed in studies of children (Corley & Fulker, 1990; Matheny, 1990; Scarr & McCartney, 1983).

Second, we propose that changes in the developmental trajectory initiated by experience are more difficult to sustain than has been generally appreciated. When observations are extended over the life course rather than over short-term intervals, slower-acting yet powerful biological–maturational influences tend to cancel out short-term and context-bound effects of early learning (e.g. Breland & Breland, 1961; Cairns, Gariépy & Hood, 1990).

Third, we propose that if normative behaviors are not fixed by early experiences, neither are they fixed by genes. To the extent that any behavioral system is frozen, its unique adaptive functions are sharply diminished or lost. The developmental perspective holds that genetic influences on behavior are dynamic, modifiable, and organized within the person in context.

Our fourth proposal calls for a reorganization of research strategies. The revised strategy requires the longitudinal study of behavioral organization in persons *in the initial stages of investigation.* Accordingly, the first steps of behavior–genetic analysis would be concerned with the detailed longitudinal description and experimental analysis of the specific behavior patterns to be explained. Appropriate quantitative and molecular methods may then be productively employed in the identification of mediational pathways. Why does a methodological shift seem in order? Although the change may be justified on theoretical and methodological grounds, perhaps the most compelling reason is that the field continues to be handicapped by controversy and legitimate questions about the replication of fundamental empirical findings.

SCIENTIFIC PERSPECTIVES

Investigators concerned with genetic influences on behavior may be classified on at least three dimensions: whether they study human or nonhuman subjects, whether they employ quantitative or proximal analyses, and whether they adopt a developmental or nondevelopmental orientation. These dimensions, though separable, are not independent.

There has been a strong tendency for researchers in behavior genetics, like other investigators of behavior, to focus either on humans or on nonhumans. This difference in focus speaks not only to the nature of the subject but to the nature of research designs, methods, and measures that may be employed in genetic analysis (Henderson, 1990). Most information available on behavioral-genetic effects in humans are based upon "experiments of nature", whereby children with known genetic backgrounds are compared to others who differ systematically from them (e.g. monozygotic twins, dizygotic twins, adopted siblings). Nonhuman investigations can employ experimental analyses including selective breeding, single-gene mutants, genetic cloning, and the creation of genetic mosaics (Hall et al., 1990).

There has been an equally large division between researchers who rely upon quantitative analyses and researchers who are involved in the direct analysis of the multiple ways in which genetic influences affect specific behavior patterns. The aim of biometric procedures is, roughly stated, to construct statistical models to evaluate the nature and source of genetic influence upon particular units of behavior. The quantitative models are based upon the statistical methods of R. A. Fisher (1930), Wright (1923), and D. S. Falconer (1960), and represented in the modern studies of J. C. DeFries, L. J. Eaves, H. J. Eysenck, D. W. Fulker, J. K. Hewitt, J. L. Jinks, R. Plomin, S. Scarr, and their colleagues. The quantitative strategy has progressed beyond the employment of statistics which purport to demonstrate the proportion of heritable variance to the sophisticated fitting of structural equation models which make explicit assumptions on the role of particular sources of internal and external variance (Corley & Fulker, 1990; Hewitt, 1990).

The alternative strategy is to focus on the ways in which genetic influences are mediated in the life course of individuals. Accordingly, efforts are made to analyze the mediational linkages between the action of genetic factors upon the mediational hormonal and physiological systems and the effects on behavior. Such investigations have elucidated the organizational links from the patterning of DNA to courtship patterns and brain architecture (e.g. Hall et al., 1990; Wimer, 1990). Investigators of humans have employed microanalyses of behavior to elucidate specific mediational influences. Such investigations have focused on how the direction of effects of socialization can be reinterpreted (e.g. children may affect adults as much as vice versa) and how similarities across generations may be mediated by shared genetic influences upon interactions rather than shared experiences (e.g. Bell, 1968; Lytton, 1980; Scarr & Kidd, 1983).

Finally, differences exist among investigators in whether they employ a holistic, developmental analysis in understanding these influences or whether age-related differences and developmental considerations are viewed as noise that obfuscates the research task. In this regard, Eaves et al. (1990, p. 266) observed:

> In spite of the obvious importance of age-related changes for our understanding of human biology and disease, geneticists have given scant attention to how such changes might be modeled. . . . The effects of age . . . have usually been treated as nuisance effects that have to be removed from family resemblance for continuous traits by more-or-less arbitrary regression techniques, or by

corrections for penetrance of major loci based on age-of-onset distributions in the case of disease. None of these methods begins to address the basic question of why age changes occur in the way they do or whether the changes are under genetic control and themselves variable between individuals.

The effect of differences in orientation cannot be overestimated. Depending upon the researcher's aims, methods, and assumptions, radically different conclusions have been reached on interpretations, generalizations, and implications (Henderson, 1990).

BIOMETRIC AND DEVELOPMENTAL ANALYSES OF HUMAN BEHAVIOR

Modern genetic studies of human behavior have relied heavily upon the study of persons who share varying degrees of similarity in genetic background. The primary contrasts have been made between the similarities of monozygotic and dizygotic twins, between adoptive and biological siblings, and between children with their biological parents and with adopted parents. Over the past 20 years, centers for such analyses have been established in North America at the University of Louisville, Calgary University, University of Southern California, University of Minnesota, University of Colorado, Pennsylvania State University, University of Virginia, and University of Richmond. These centers have often published in collaboration with other international groups in London, Stockholm, and Copenhagen.

It is beyond the scope or aims of the present chapter to detail the findings and accomplishments of these centers. Any brief summary is likely to be misleading, especially since the findings themselves are sometimes in conflict (see references in Goldsmith, 1983; Plomin, 1986; Rowe, 1987). It should be useful, nonetheless, to illustrate some of the primary outcomes from two exemplary investigations in order to bring attention to central issues.

The Louisville Twin Study

The Louisville Twin Study as been described as "a classic in developmental behavior genetics" (Hahn et al., 1990, p. 5). The study was begun in 1958–1959 by pediatrician Frank Falkner as a longitudinal examination of same-sex monozygotic (MZ) and dizygotic (DZ) twins, including patterns of their physical and behavioral development. The behavioral work was under the direction, successively, of Steven Vandenberg (1964–1967), Ronald Wilson (1967–1986), and Adam Matheny, Jr. (1986 to present). By studying the twins over time, it has been possible to investigate two key issues. One is the question of whether there are age-related changes in the degree to which MZ and DZ resemble each other. In this regard, the investigators have focused on the possibility that, with increasing age, MZ twins should resemble each other more and more, and DZ twins should resemble each other less and less. A second issue concerns the extent to which MZ twins tend to share growth spurts and growth lags. The proposition was simply that patterns of developmental change should be more similar among MZ than DZ pairs. These matters were investigated in three domains: physical development, intellectual development and social–emotional development. A summary of the findings reported in Matheny (1990) indicates the following in these domains.

Physical development

The similarity between the physical and intellectual development in MZ twins has been consistently shown to be higher than that of DZ twins. The Louisville Twin Study of same-sex twins over the first 15 years of life and into adulthood suggest that the degree of similarity in MZ twins increases rather than decreases as a function of age. The pair concordances for weight and intelligence test scores across different ages are shown in Figure 4.1. After the first year of life, the twin-pair correlations (i.e. intraclass correlations for the MZ or DZ twins) are quite similar through childhood and adolescence. Implicit in the similarity is the other important finding that growth spurts tend to occur at the same time in MZ twins, and the slight dip in the 15-year DZ correlation may reflect the additional variance associated with different adolescent growth changes (see Matheny, 1990). Figure 4.1 provides only modest support for the generalization that the MZ twin similarity relative to DZ similarity increases as a function of age. The effects obtained prior to the first birthday show such an effect, but thereafter the similarities are relatively stable over time as are the MZ–DZ similarities. Rather the same effect was observed in the Louisville Twin Study for height, although there is more marginal support for the proposition of increasing within MZ similarity and decreasing DZ similarity over time.

Intellectual development

The IQ findings shown in Figure 4.1 are startling on three counts. First, the sheer magnitude of the twin similarity on this psychological function matches the similarity observed in weight. Indeed, the DZ similarity on IQ is at some points in development greater than in weight. In terms of sheer magnitude of the twin correlations, the MZ IQ similarities appear to be at the limits of the reliability of the tests that were employed (i.e. Stanford-Binet, Bayley Scales of Mental Development, Wechsler Preschool and Primary Scale of Intelligence, Wechsler Intelligence Scale for Children, and the McCarthy Scales of Children's Abilities). The intraclass correlations for

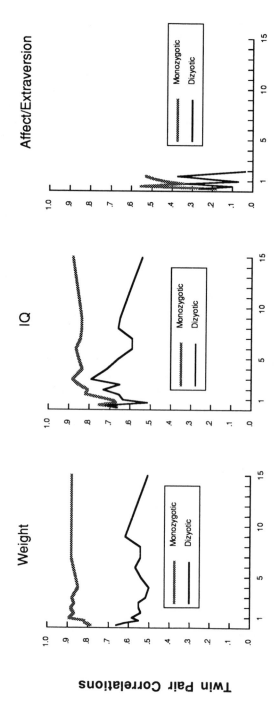

Figure 4.1 Monozygotic (MZ) and same-sex dizygotic (DZ) Twin pair correlations for Weight, IQ, and Affect/Extraversion across successive ages (adapted from Matheny, 1990)

MZ similarities remained $r' \geq 0.80$ from 18 months through 15 years. Second, the differences between MZ and DZ twin correlations in IQ are as great as the differences between MZ and DZ twin correlations in physical characteristics. Moreover, the differences are in the same direction as might be expected by an assumed genetic contribution to IQ. Third, the MZ–DZ differences appear to increase as a function of age. Support for this generalization must be tempered, however, by the finding that the DZ twin correlations fluctuate between $r' = 0.50$ and $r' = 0.80$ from 1 to 15 years of age, and the fluctuation is nonlinear.

Social–emotional development

The information of social–emotional development from the Louisville Twin Study is considerably less complete than that for measures of physical and intellectual development. The problem was in part that the methods for assessment of these characteristics were less refined. Nonetheless, measures of extraversion and affect could be derived from the infant behavior record which was obtained during the early testing periods. The results shown in Figure 4.1, though deficient in terms of the age span covered and the psychometric properties of the measures, suggest a couple of generalizations. First, the correlations are markedly lower for twin pairs of both types for the affect/extraversion measure. Second, there is considerably greater fluctuation over time among these social–emotional measures than among the physical and intelligence measures. Third, no sufficient information is available to indicate whether there is increasing similarity among the MZ twins as a function of age. On this count, the diminution of the DZ correlation to nonsignificance suggests that there is a modest or negligible genetic contribution to the characteristics that are being measured. These data, however, must be viewed with caution. As Matheny (1990) points out, the generalizations are limited by the measures that are employed. The limitations in age span studied is also problematic, in that no information was reported on the subsequent social–emotional adaptations of persons in the longitudinal sample. Here again one encounters inevitable problems of assessment, and unclarity as to whether the same constructs are being measured from infancy through adolescence and adulthood.

The Calgary Study of Twin and Singleton Families

The Calgary Study of Twin and Singleton Families was initiated in the early 1970s to study the genetic and biological factors involved in the socialization of children (Lytton, 1980). Under the direction of Hugh Lytton, the primary investigator since the inception of the work, this project identified all twins (MZ and DZ) born in the Calgary metropolitan area for over a two-year period (1969–1970). Lytton undertook the most intensive analysis of social, emotional, and parent–child relationships that had yet to be reported. In terms of sophistication of measures and interpretations, this work has yet to be matched. Modern assessments were made of parent–child interactions in DZ and MZ male pairs, and this information was compared with singleton families. The data collection provided measures of direct observation in the home, experimental assessments, test data, and ratings made when the boys were 2–3 years of age. Advanced statistical models were used to determine whether specific variance could be accounted for by effects of the parents, effects of twins upon each other, or effects that must be attributable to other environmental or genetic sources. The characteristics studied were parent–infant attachment, parent–child compliance, communication patterns, independence, physical activity levels, and cognitive patterns. In all, an average of 31 hours was required to gather and process the data for a singleton and 36 hours for every twin pair. If the Louisville Twin Study may be described as "classic", the Calgary Study of Twin and Singleton Families is just as accurately described as "heroic" (Lytton, 1980). Lytton adopted a developmental–ethological perspective to understanding genetic influences, and his analyses included proximal measures of mediation as well as advanced quantitative genetic models.

In the light of the detail and precision of Lytton's measures, certain discrepancies between his findings and those of the Louisville investigation invite scrutiny. In the various measures that pertain to intellectual and language development, there is only modest evidence for differential MZ–DZ similarity among the Calgary twin pairs at 2–3 years of age. This is shown in the measure of IQ adopted (i.e. Peabody Picture Vocabulary Test (PPVT)), direct observations of the children's speech, and speech maturity. The MZ and DZ twin pair correlations for these measures are shown in Table 4.1. A comparison of the twin correlations shown in the right-hand column of Table 4.1 indicates (a) high levels of twin correspondence, regardless of MZ–DZ status, and (b) no striking differences between MZ and DZ pairs in the level of similarity. The first finding is wholly consistent with the Louisville Twin Study; the second is not. Why the difference in findings, particularly because the comparisons were made at an average of 32 months of age (by which age the Louisville comparisons had stabilized)? It should be noted that the PPVT has been criticized as being unreliable for this age group (Lytton, 1980) and the other measures of verbal behavior were sampled in both naturalistic and experimental conditions. Nonetheless, both sets of measures have been shown in other investigations to be substantially associated with the intelligence measures employed in the Louisville investigation. Whatever the reason, there is substantial similarity between the twins in the Calgary investigation on verbal measures, and the

Table 4.1 Monozygotic (MZ) and same-sex Dizygotic (DZ) twin pair correlations means from the Calgary study of twin and singleton families at 2–3 years of age (adapted from Lytton, 1980)

Variables/measures	Means		Intraclass correlations	
	MZ	DZ	MZ	DZ
Intelligence–verbal				
IQ–PPVT	78.27	87.93	0.22	0.29
Child speech	1.24	1.52	0.79	0.69
Speech maturity	2.44	2.97	0.86	0.91
Social development				
Attachment	2.74	2.74	0.43	0.51
Compliance	2.78	3.03	0.68	0.65
Positive action	0.63	0.62	0.90	0.85
Negative action	0.71	0.77	0.51	0.53
Instrumental independence	2.94	3.13	0.90	0.59
Internalized standards	3.02	2.84	0.78	0.64

levels of verbal/communication similarity did not differ as a function of differences in the twins' genetic similarity.

Virtually the same conclusions hold for the measures of social behavior as for cognitive behaviors. As shown in Table 4.1, there were substantial similarities among the twins in the various measures of social behavior, including positive actions, independence, and internalization. Other domains of social behavior showed strong similarities, including attachment behavior, compliance, and negative actions. There was not, however, much support for the proposition that these social behavior similarities differed as a function of genetic similarities. The question may again be raised as to why the difference with the results of the Louisville investigation which collected information over the same age range. On this score, it should be noted that social behaviors were a special focus on the Calgary work, and it is in this domain that the methods and findings are especially robust. There was, however, an attempt to obtain precise measures in natural as well as experimental settings. The measures permitted the twins to influence each other in the assessments as in other aspects of everyday life. The very high correlations in both MZ and DZ thus reflect the simultaneous influence of immediate dyadic effects along with whatever constitution/genetic factors might have contributed to these effects in both children. When the total impact of these influences are considered on behavior, there is remarkable correspondence with twin pairs regardless of MZ or DZ status. The Calgary findings underscore that twins influence each other, and that this influence seems to be no greater in MZ twins than in DZ twins.[1]

Toward a resolution

A comparison between the results of these two investigations of MZ or DZ twins underscores some of the problems that beset investigators of genetic influences in human development. Replication and confirmation are the first major problem. On the one hand, the Louisville investigators have emphasized the sharp differences that appear among MZ and DZ twins in both early intellectual and social–emotional development, and that these differences in similarity increase with age. The similarities appear, on the whole, to be greater for intellectual than for social–emotional factors. On the other hand, the Calgary investigators have shown only modest differences between MZ and DZ twin correlations in social development and cognitive development. The differences persist across several measurement domains and operational definitions of the constructs.

Why do investigations of presumably the same phenomena emerge with such different findings? Why did the Calgary project show such modest differences between MZ and DZ twins and the Louisville project show such strong differences at the same ages? It cannot be that either set of investigators did not anticipate that genetic influences would emerge as important. On the contrary, both research teams must have been heavily committed to the assumption of genetic influence in order to become engaged in such a careful and programmatic study of development and genetic background. Lytton did not appear to expect such a modest yield on the MZ–DZ comparison, although his research design was clearly sensitive to the possibility of negative or counter-intuitive findings.

The reasons for such discrepancies range from a concern with sampling, statistical power, measurement, or analytic differences. The problems of empirical design have been coupled with problems of conceptualization and quantitative analysis (Oyama, 1985). In one of the more sympathetic and informed analyses, Henderson (1990, p. 283) has argued that "even rather subtle aspects of a chosen neurobehavioral phenotype can alter the outcome of a genetic study and its interpretation". Accordingly, the "phenotype" used in genetic behavioral research should be operationally defined in terms of a "measurement–environment–history" or "MEH" composite. On this count, "insecurity" may be defined quite specifically in such terms as "latency of 11-day-old cage-reared housemice to return to their home nest when placed 12 cm from the nest during the dark cycle".

The broader point that is made by Henderson is that one should understand the features of behavior being employed as the anchor in genetic studies, and it is insufficient to employ broad constructs that ignore the context in which the organism is observed and the life history of the individual. By tackling the issue of how the behaviors to be explained are organized, Henderson touches upon a most important difference between biometric–quantitative genetic analyzes and developmental–genetic analyses. But is this not too narrow a definition to be useful? In this regard, Henderson (1990, p. 284) comments: "Such specificity may seem uncomfortably narrow, but a change in any variable in the definition may result in a predictable difference in the genetic architecture of the new phenotype."

In brief, *the analysis of genetic effects on social and cognitive behaviors of humans should not be divorced from a concern with an understanding of the proximal controls, developmental functions, and experiential determinants of the behaviors.* Unfortunately, quantitative genetic studies have typically viewed behavior as a stable phenotype, much as a physical character of the organism. Indeed, the assumption seems to have been the more static the behavior, the more suitable it was for genetic analysis (Whitney, 1990). This accounts in part for the reliance upon certain reified behavior systems, such as "intelligence".[2] A broader concern with the dynamics of the behaviors under investigation has been exemplified in only a few studies of human behaviors, such as the work of the Calgary group. The concern was with the details of the ontogeny of behavior and an assessment of its determinants in parental actions, in social interchange, and in contextual evaluations. When this thoroughgoing analysis was undertaken, the precise point of entry of genetic influences could be tracked. Lytton discovered, for instance, that the variance attributable to differences in child–mother communications could be attributed not to their effects upon their mother but, instead, to the effects of maternal vocalization upon the twins. This disentangling of the bidirectional effects begins to provide a logical analysis of the bidirectional proposition that children affect adults as much as vice versa. In Lytton's analysis, special weight must be given to maternal structuring and control in the bidirectional relationship.

Such developmental–proximal analyses, that attend to the details of behavior are necessary in order to evaluate the developmental propositions on genetic influence that have been offered by Scarr (Scarr & McCartney, 1983), Bell (Bell, 1968; Bell & Harper, 1977), and others. Summary behavior variables such as "intelligence" can provide hints about the nature of influence, but they are unlikely to advance our understanding of mediational influences and precisely how genetic effects are melded into the behavior system. For instance, it can hardly be argued that the variance in scholastic aptitude test (SAT) test scores is attributable to genetic factors when "enrichment" programs reliably produce large shifts in the individual's test performance. What seems required is the painstaking study to determine precisely what aspects of SAT performance are most susceptible to modification and under what conditions, and how this susceptibility may be buffered by heritable factors. A similar concern is seen in the recent controversy about whether there is greater within-family than between-family variance in accounts of children's behavior. When concrete measures are employed, and specific families are compared, say, in terms of similarity in high school graduation or arrest, strong effects are obtained in normal samples. Different genetic/contextual effects may be observed, depending upon the nature of the sample (normal population sample or samples of adopted children), the nature of the measures (ratings or concrete behaviors), and the statistical models employed. Precision in genetic analysis presupposes an understanding of the multiple levels of organization of the behavior to be explained.

The methodological–measurement–design steps required to go beyond the nature–nurture issue may be summarized in five points. In brief, the research strategy calls for investigators to:

(1)   Define in concrete operations the behavior pattern that is to be explained;
(2)   Track the natural development of this behavior pattern in explicitly defined conditions and contexts;
(3)   Identify the primary short-term events (e.g. interactional, contextual, circadian) and long-term conditions (e.g. maturational change, social role, subcultural) that contribute to changes in the pattern through experimental–longitudinal and cross-cultural analysis;
(4)   Locate the possible pathways by which physiological and/or neurobiological effects may operate upon the behavior pattern. The pathways might operate directly upon the individual, or indirectly upon the context or reactions given to the individual and the opportunities that are afforded to him/her (Scarr & McCartney, 1983; Scarr, 1986);
(5)   Examine through convergent biometric–genetic and neurobiological–genetic research designs the extent to which genetic effects are expressed in both the behavior pattern and the relevant physiological or neurobiological pathways.

This research strategy assumes that the first requirement of behavioral science is to understand the development and organization of specific behaviors to be explained. An essential feature of this inquiry is to identify the ways in which biological factors are woven into the behavior pattern.

The problem historically has been that the field has been too modest in its research methods. By remaining committed to single-stage research designs, the discipline has become trapped by a limited vision of what is required to solve the enormous questions it has chosen to address. Completion of a single stage of the research program is almost guaranteed to yield incomplete and misleading results. Yet that has been the normative standard for research. Typically the task has been to complete research at a single stage, or part of a stage. Even elegant research designs on "nurture" have stopped halfway through step 3, and the equally elegant "nature" designs have typically begun at steps 4 or 5. The critical links between the first and second halves of the research program have been given short shrift in studies of normal human behavior systems.[3] The few success stories of behavior–genetic analysis in humans—such as phenylketonuria (PKU) and trisomy-21—owe their achievement to the fact that the most critical steps of behavioral analysis (1–3) were solved prior to the genetic analysis.

Is this task so complex that it is beyond the design and research capabilities of behavioral science? Clearly not, if progress in nonhuman investigations is taken seriously. Convincing models have already been established for at least two basic behavior systems— sexual courtship and aggression. Although illustrative, the research models described in Hall et al. (1990) and Cairns, Gariépy & Hood (1990) have taken all five of the methodological steps. Such work demonstrates how genetic, behavioral, contextual, interactional, and developmental events can be woven together to achieve behavioral adaptation. While these models have been established in models of nonhuman animal behavior (i.e. drosophila and mice), there are no compelling conceptual or methodological reasons why they cannot be extended to important behavior patterns of human beings. The behavior patterns in humans could include, for instance, meaningful adaptations such as reading, cooperation, and interpersonal violence. It would require more precision in the specification of behavior and behavior mediators than has been the case in studies of human behavior genetics. Rather than relying upon greater sophistication in mathematical modeling of genetic influence, greater attention would be given to specific phenomena and how they are mediated and organized in development.

In sum, a holistic approach to behavior development in human beings does not preclude precise genetic and ontogenetic analysis. To the contrary, it encourages such study albeit with a new set of requirements. It places even greater demands on the science by highlighting variables that have been ignored or eliminated as "nuisance variables". By shifting the level of analysis to the concrete adaptations of individuals over time, it may be possible to identify the elegant parsimony that underlies the organization of seemingly chaotic and multidetermined patterns. It should be helpful at this juncture to turn to recent efforts to complete such an integrated research program in nonhuman animals.

POPULATION AND DEVELOPMENTAL BEHAVIOR GENETICS IN ANIMAL BEHAVIOR

Genetic–behavioral interactions have been systematically explored in two domains of animal behavior. One has employed the perspectives of population biology and evolutionary biology (Lorenz, 1965; Tinbergen, 1974; Trivers, 1971, 1985; Wilson, 1975). The second has adopted the perspectives of behavioral zoology (Fuller & Thompson, 1960, 1978; Ginsberg & Allee, 1942; Lagerspetz, 1964; Scott, 1977; Scott & Fuller, 1965) and developmental psychobiology (Gottlieb, 1983; Kuo, 1967; Schneirla, 1966).

In *Sociobiology*, Wilson noted that these strategies represented a broader schism in biology between investigations in population biology and molecular biology. Population biology addresses issues of "ultimate causation" while molecular biology addresses questions of "proximal causation".[4] Although the two scientific frameworks have similar general goals—understanding the relations between genes and behavior—their aims are quite different. The distinction between "ultimate" and "proximal" causation seems to be less a matter of primacy of causation than of mechanisms that operate in vastly different dimensions of time. The task is approached from radically different perspectives and with radically different tools. Investigators from the two areas sometimes behave as if they lived in different lands. Although these two approaches to the study of behavioral genetics have similar goals—to better understand the relations between biology and behavior—they have adopted different research methodologies, employed different constructs, and, unfortunately, have often reached different conclusions.

A central issue concerns methodology. Wilson (1975) explicitly rejected the proposal that developmental study would be able to add to our understanding of genetic effects of behavior in the foreseeable future. The problem was the sheer difficulty of tracking the multiple pathways from gene to social behavior; that is, from protein syntheses to cell growth to metabolic function to physiological organization to hormonal influence to behavior ontogeny to social exchange to society. The tasks of creating an inclusive science that could encompass the several levels of analysis seemed overwhelming.

The alternative Wilson offered was to view societal organization as one endpoint and genetic transmission as the other. Such a combination of biology and sociology (i.e. *socio-biology*) could be accomplished by the application of quantitative models of population biology. Such a leap presupposes that genetic effects are conservative and reflected in societies in ways that are more reliable than in individuals. The study of genetic effects in populations would obviate the need for painstaking tracking of developmental mediation. The key assumption here, however, does not seem to be the level of analysis and whether it is the population, the person, or the system that is investigated. Rather, the most important assumption seems to be that one can gain important information about the role of genes without the detailed analysis of how the effects are produced in individuals.

The developmental analysis of genetic influences on behavior addresses issues of proximal causation. The major research task of this approach is to identify when, where, and how biological developmental, and experiential events are melded in behavioral organization. Since nonhuman subjects are more accessible than humans for experimental analysis, much of the proximal developmental research has been conducted with nonhuman animals.

One of the pitfalls of many biologically based approaches to the study of behavior and psychological processes is the belief that they can be reduced to a unitary neural–physiological pathway or genotype. Wilson (1975) dismisses variations in behavioral development as ontogenetic noise; classical ethologists claim that behavioral development is preprogrammed (Lorenz, 1965); Waddington's (1957) "epigenetic landscape" metaphor emphasizes the unitary influence of genetic factors. In contrast, developmental analyses aim to integrate the organisim's behaviors and psychological processes in the light of broader issues of individual adaptation and species evolution.

Behavioral actions, emotions, and cognitions—the stuff of psychology—have a special status for organismic adaptation. Behavior and psychological processes can be reduced to genetic or physiological structures only in a trivial and misleading sense. The accommodations of humans throughout their development to the actions and responses of their environments, particularly their social environments, constitute major extra-organismic forces of behavioral organization. Thus, detailed longitudinal investigations of social behavior patterns are crucial for understanding behavior in context. Ironically, the importance of these research strategies is more clearly appreciated by population biologists undertaking long-term field studies of animal behavior (e.g. Fossey, 1983; Goodall, 1986; Smuts, 1985). Evolutionary biology appreciates the primacy of social behavior as a major force in the evolution of humans (Alexander, 1979; Wrangham, 1979; Byrne & Whiten, 1988), perhaps even more so than do many in psychology.

In contrast, modern developmental investigators take a holistic view of behavior. Within this perspective, single traits or behaviors do not develop or function in isolation, and should not be divorced from the totality in analysis. More generally,

> The study of development requires a holistic, synthetic science. Maturational, experiential, and cultural contributions are inseparably coalesced in ontogeny. Hence developmental studies should be multi-level, concerned with ontogenetic integration, and employ person-oriented as well as variable-oriented analyses (Cairns, 1990, p. 42).

The holistic view of development was formulated in response to the question of whether ontogeny is guided by immanent forces within the organism or by external conditions that prevail during periods of growth. Von Bertalanffy (1962) suggested that neither alternative alone was sufficient to understand ontogeny because the organism contributes to the direction of its own development because it is a partial creator of the constraints that were established during preceding stages of its own growth. Schneirla (1966) extended the notion of a fusion of forces in behavioral development, proposing that developmental, biological, maturational, and experiential events all coalesce, so that any account of behavioral processes must incorporate the developmental status and current functioning of the organism. More recently, an emphasis on the holistic view of the organism in its environment has been adopted explicitly by researchers in psychology, psychobiology, and sociology (Bronfenbrenner, in press; Cairns, 1979; Cole & Cole, 1989; Gariépy, Hood & Cairns, 1988; Gottlieb, 1983, 1991; Elder, Caspi & Burton, 1988; Magnusson, 1988; Sameroff, 1983; Scott, 1977; Valsiner, 1987).

At first blush, the holistic assumption may seem to imply a research agenda of overwhelming complexity and beyond the scope of current research design and analysis. Will any empirical design that attempts to account for the multiple biological, social, and developmental contributions to behavior overload investigators and create a state of data tyranny? Paradoxically, viewing the organism as a whole facilitates identification of behavioral systems within the individual, and investigation of the development and operation of behavioral systems should sharpen our understanding. The analytic search for mechanisms is enhanced, rather than abandoned, by a concern with the adapting organism in its living, adaptive context. A major concern in contemporary developmental work has been that multiple levels of investigation, addressing both experience and ontogeny, are required to elucidate mediational processes. Studies of behavioral systems may employ various time frames, address many levels of analysis individually or simultaneously, and adopt any of a wide range of research designs and strategies. An explicit concern with development extends psychological methodologies rather than discarding them.

The developmental orientation is concerned with tracking the development of behavior patterns over the life history of individuals or groups who differ in genetic background. Such research requires that the investigator first achieve an adequate understanding of how the behavior of interest is established, maintained, and changed over time. Once that is accomplished, then attention can be given to identifying whether there is a distinctive genetic contribution to the behavior organization by appropriate comparisons that extend over the life history of individuals or groups who differ in genetic background. The aim is to identify precisely when, how, and where the key genetic effects appear in the organization of the relevant behavior. The mediation can be analyzed directly, say, upon specific actions or heightened reactivity, or indirectly, say, through differential provoked reactions and opportunities. Once the basis for difference in behavior organization is identified, it may be used as an anchor to map the domain between the gene and the behavior. This strategy presupposes that there is no direct line between DNA–RNA activity and specific action patterns. On the contrary, the genetic influence must be transmuted through neurobiological and physiological pathways, each of which has its own organizational properties.

Pervasiveness, rapidity, and reversibility of genetic influences

Consider first the elementary question of whether or not there exists conclusive evidence for the influence of genetic factors on behavior. Fuller & Thompson (1960, 1978) report that virtually every investigation that has attempted to demonstrate through selective breeding that social and nonsocial behavior patterns are directly influenced by genetic makeup has been successful. Their review of the literature indicates a genetic basis for behavior in all of the mammalian species that have been studied, from mice to monkeys. Genetic effects have been demonstrated for learning, aggressive behavior, sexual behavior, group organization, maternal activity, maturation rate, seizures, brain size and brain pathology, and life expectancy; in short, for the major features of behavior and behavioral adaptation.

Genetic effects on behavior are not only pervasive, they are readily manipulated from generation to generation. For example, the differentiation of lines of aggressive animals typically occurs within one to four generations (Lagerspetz, 1964; Cairns, MacCombie & Hood, 1983; Ebert & Hyde, 1976; Ebert & Sawyer, 1980; van Oortmerssen & Bakker, 1981). As Fuller and Thompson (1960, 1978) observed, rapid selection outcomes are not limited to aggressive behavior. Reliable selection effects for high and low levels of open-field activity have been obtained on the second generation of selective breeding (DeFries & Hegmann, 1970). Selection for emotionality in rats showed reliable effects in the first generation (Hall, 1951) and a line differentiation was reported in the second generation (Broadhurst, 1960).

As rapid as these genetic effects can be, they are rapidly reversible. Once a selection outcome has been obtained through breeding, the initial phenotypic profile can ordinarily be retrieved rapidly if the selection (or crossing) procedure is reversed (Cairns, Gariépy & Hood, 1990; Michard & Carlier, 1985). A cross between two inbred lines that differed in preference for alcohol consumption produced mice in the first generation that performed like the low parental line, possibly an example of full genetic dominance (Whitney, McClearn & DeFries, 1970). Dobzhansky (1967) provided a compelling case of reversibility in microevolution in an experiment involving selection for positive and negative geotaxis in the fruit fly, showing that 6 generations of "reverse selection" were sufficient to wipe out the differences achieved in 18 generations. Even without selection (i.e. within-line inter-breeding without regard to geotaxis scores), a similar effect was obtained in nine generations. Dobzhansky explains the results with the principle of "genetic homeostasis" (Lerner, 1954), according to which measurable characters in populations naturally tend to a near-optimal level for the species-typical environment while retaining a high adaptability to environmental change (see also Ginsburg, 1971). Thus, when a short-term environmental pressure is removed, there is a rapid return to the previously established level. Although rapidity and reversibility in selection processes have not been given much attention in the discussions of evolutionary biology or behavior genetics, they are of highest relevance for both areas, illustrating effectively the sensitivity of complex social behaviors to genetic manipulations such as selective breeding or back-crossing.

Experience and the Modification of behavioral trajectories

There is now ample evidence from studies of nonhuman mammals to indicate that behavioral trajectories resist permanent modifications by early experience. In their classic paper on "The misbehavior of organisms", Breland & Breland (1961) observed the ontogenetic course of response associations that had been firmly established through operant conditioning procedures. Even when conditioning had been successfully achieved at one stage of development, and reinforcement maintained undiminished into subsequent stages, there was a strong propensity for previously conditioned response sequences which are incompatible with species-typical patterns to become displaced. They observed (p. 00) that there was a "drift toward instinctive behavior" across development.

Buffering mechanisms exist in ontogeny which bias the organism toward species-typical trajectories even before environmental pressures are removed. In ontogenesis as in phylogenesis, there is a strong tendency toward the conservation of species-typical development patterns. This occurs despite an extraordinary ability among mammmals to adapt to local and temporal perturbations, both in the physical environment and in the social ecology. Individual "social learning" experiences and adaptational shifts tend to be context-specific, time-constrained, and age-dependent. It is hard to improve upon developmental trajectories which, by prior selection, are near optimal. This phenomenon has been called "developmental homeostasis" (Cairns, Gariépy & Hood, 1990).

Just as behaviors are not fixed by early experience, they are also not fixed by genotype. Rosenblum & Kaufman (1968) have shown that the effects of maternal separation varied for the pigtail and bonnet monkey; Seay, Schlottmann & Gandolfo (1972) have shown that separation in the patas monkey facilitates social adaptations rather than retards them (see also Sackett, 1967). Different breeds of dogs also show breed-typical responses to social rearing conditions. In a comparison between wirehaired terriers and beagles, Fuller (1967, p.1648) reports that "isolation magnifies the breed differences in activity seen in dogs reared in a standard fashion"; he argued that procedures (such as pre-test exposure to complex environments) that reduce the "stress of emergence" should reduce differences in learning and behavior among breeds of dogs which have been reared in isolation.

These findings are consistent with the outcomes of experimental studies of social attachment formation which indicate that novel attachments can be readily established in mammalian development. "Neophenotypes" (Kuo, 1967) in social attachment emerge very rapidly, typically within hours of initial cohabitation with an alien species when the animals are young and separated from their mothers (Cairns, 1966a; Cairns & Werboff, 1967; Kuo, 1930; Mason & Kinney, 1974). Despite the robustness of early attachment phenomena, they are readily reversed as the animal enters the juvenile period and early adulthood. Moreover, the reversibility is biased toward the establishment of special-typical preferences, even though the earlier cross-specific attachment had been robust and had successfully competed with "normal" same-species affiliations (Kuo, 1967). For example, lambs which have formed strong cross-specific attachments readily shift in adulthood to a preference for same-species affiliations when they are placed with other adult sheep (Cairns, 1966b).

Parallel genotype–experience interactions have been demonstrated under conditions where prior experience, genetic background, developmental status, and context and duration of assessment have been systematically manipulated. The appearance of differences in aggressive behaviors among lines or strains of mice varies with rearing condition of isolation versus group housing (Valzelli & Bernasconi, 1979; Cairns & Scholz, 1973). However, when rearing conditions are kept constant, the magnitude of genetically based differences in social behavior may be canceled out by repeated experience.

In an experiment designed to disentangle experiential and genetic effects these investigators showed that the magnitude of the difference in latency to attack between their selected lines was systematically reduced as a result of repeated testing (Cairns, Gariépy & Hood, 1990). Their design was unusual in that animals from the same family (i.e. the same litter) were assigned at random to one of four initial test conditions. One brother was first tested prior to sexual maturity (28 days of age), and another immediately after sexual maturity (day 45). Two other males in the litter (i.e. same-sex twins) were assessed in early and late maturity (days 72 and 210, respectively). After the initial test, each member of each litter then was tested on the same days as the other members of the litter. This procedure was duplicated for three selectively bred lines of animals: high aggressive, low aggressive, and mid-aggressive. By combining the features of a cross-sectional and longitudinal design, the design permitted the researchers to assess the roles of experience, development, genetic background, and the interaction among these effects.

Figure 4.2 shows that in the earlier tests (at days 28–30, prior to the onset of sexual maturation), the genetic line differences in aggressive behavior were negligible and nonsignificant. Two weeks later, however, very strong line differences emerge. But the slope of the curves indicates that the magnitude of the differences depends upon experience. On this score, a mere 10 minutes of experience in 6 months was sufficient to sharply diminish the role of genetic background. Note that the combined influence of development and experience is sufficient to equate animals in the two genetic lines in terms of aggressive measures by mid-maturity. The family of longitudinal studies shown in Figure 4.3 highlights the combined effects of genetic background, developmental status, and experience upon attack behaviors. In the left panel, the comparisons begun prior to puberty are shown. Note that significant differences between genetic lines do not emerge until following the onset of puberty (approximately day 42). The lines converge again at day 235 after the individuals in each line have had four test experiences. The other cohorts (middle and right panels of Figure 4.3) confirm that (a) the behavior is strongly influenced by genetic background following puberty, (b) there is an effect of experience at each of the assessment points, (c) attacks increase as a function of age/maturation in both genetic lines in the absence of experience, and (d) the effects of genetic differences may be eliminated, depending on the age of the individuals and the amount of experience that they have had.

One of the most important outcomes of this experiment is not shown in the figures because it would require still another time dimension. In the absence of repeated experience, the line differences remain robust at all ages in the initial 10 minutes of testing. But if the assessments are extended longer—to one hour, two hours, or two days—the line differences that were so strong in the initial phases of the assessment diminish in magnitude, even though the severity and levels of fighting do not. That is, the major effects of genetic bias are observed in the very early phases of assessment, then other factors relative to adaptation take over.

Such findings illustrate the inherent limitations of assigning static "proportions" of influence to the environment, to genes, and to their interaction. The "explained variance" is itself a relative figure that varies with the timing of the observations, with the developmental stage, and with the experiential context in which the observations were made.

The paradox is that genetic influences have been shown to be stable and enduring as well as plastic and time-bound. Which view of genetic influence is correct and which is wrong? The empirical findings indicate that the statements are not mutually exclusive and both may be correct. Resolving these seemingly contradictory propositions requires an experimental strategy

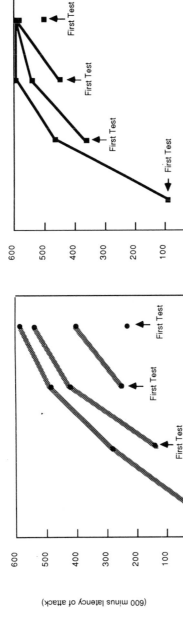

Figure 4.2 Speed of dyadic attack as a function of the selectively bred line animals from two different strains: NC-100 (low aggressive) in the left panel, and NC-900 (high aggressive) in the right panel. The day-of-age tested (day 28=prepubertal; day 45=early sexual maturity; day 72=young adults; day 210=late maturity) refers to a 10 minute dyadic test. Successive longitudinal studies were conducted with male twins obtained from the same litter (from Cairns, MacCombie & Hood, 1983; Cairns, Gariépy & Hood, 1990) but who were first tested at different ages

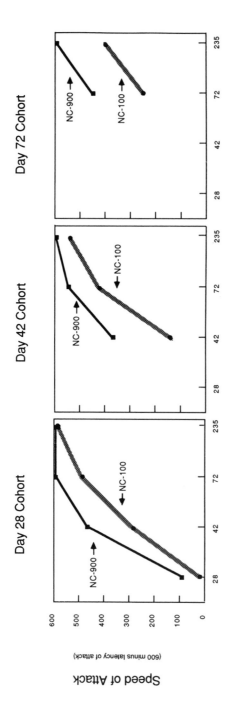

Figure 4.3 Speed of dyadic attack in two genetic lines in the 4th generation of selective breeding shown as a function of cohort (tested first at day 28, 45, or 72). The difference between the points at any one day reflects the effect that may be attributed to difference in genetic background

that extends beyond a boxscore of research outcomes. The scientific issue becomes one of understanding how genetic influences are fused with intra-organismic and environmental influences in order to permit the individual to behave in an effective, adaptive fashion. To address these issues, it is necessary to examine the dynamic processes of behavior organization and adaptation.

DEVELOPMENT–GENETIC RELATIONS: CORRELATED CONSTRAINTS AND TIMING

The study of behavioral genetics has been handicapped by the absence of studies of behavioral and biological pathways by which heritable influences may be exercised in development (Fuller & Thompson, 1978). Statistical models designed to establish the existence of genetic influences on behavior are not sufficient to track how genetic influences operate throughout development and mediate the organization of behavior. Proximal analyses of how genetic effects may be produced or inhibited are critical if the discipline is to go beyond mere demonstrations of genetic effects on behavior.

A proximal analysis begins with an analysis of the properties and developmental organization of the actions to be explained. This approach should be both "polythetic" (using multi-level measures) and developmental in order to take into account the behaviors as they occur by individuals in the context of their development and immediate physical and social surrounds (Jensen, 1967). The advantage of proximal analyses is that they lead directly to experimental manipulation of genes and experiences in addition to longitudinal and cross-generational tracking. Proximal analyses may also identify when, where, and how genetic factors most strongly influence behavioral organization, and when and where they do not.

However, to understand the role of genes in behavioral organization, one must first understand the organization of behavior in development. This principle holds as much for clarifying the role of genetic influence upon the aggressive behavior of 45-day-old mice as it does for understanding the role of genetic influence upon the intelligence test performance of 10-year-old children. To understand behavioral organization, one should first understand precisely what behavioral features are involved and how they are combined to promote the activity that is to be explained. It is not sufficient to summarize the effects by a simple score, whether IQ or attack latency.

Mayr (1988) observes that serious puzzles of genetic action remain unresolved by elementaristic approaches because of the persistent unity of the genotype, claiming that the fitness of individual genes tied up in complexes in the genotype "is determined far more by the fitness of the complex as a whole than by any functional qualities of individual genes" (Mayr, 1988, p. 424). It is equally important to observe that behaviors and the environments in which they occur also come in packages. Correlations between behaviors and environments appear in a wide range of observations, including the "homophily" of social groups, in which people tend to affiliate with others who share personality or social dispositions, and assortive mating, in which people tend to select similar others as mates (Buss & Barnes, 1986).

That behaviors are correlated with environments is precisely what is expected from an evolutionary perspective. In the longer course of development, spanning generations as well as individual ontogeny, there should be a mutual accommodation of behavioral propensities and the social and physical requirements for adaptation. The biological forces that operate to enhance adaptation should typically operate in the same direction as the environmental experiences so that nature–nurture competition should be the exception rather than the rule. Thus, it should not be surprising to find hot-tempered, impulsive children growing up with family members who themselves exhibit and reward these traits, or subcultures of aggressive adolescents in which aggressive behavior is viewed as an asset rather than a liability (see Scarr & McCartney, 1983).

To understand how associations between genes and environments emerge and become modified, one must go beyond the mere demonstration of correlations. Accordingly, research should (a) focus on the processes of behavioral organization over time, and (b) involve new strategies which permit experimental manipulation of the relevant processes. Studies of nonhuman development are useful in both tasks. On the first count, the study of behavioral organization requires a shift in the level of analysis from behavioral outcomes (e.g. "traits", "behavioral genotypes") to the study of behavioral processes. This is more easily proposed than accomplished. The problem has been that behavior–genetic studies of humans have been handicapped by the reification of such traits as "shyness", "aggression", and "intelligence". Once reified, such traits are viewed as structures that remain relatively constant over time and space, although their manifestations may vary as a function of age and context. Such a static view of behavior does not promote attention to the dynamics of adaptation and the processes by which action patterns emerge and become reorganized over ontogeny. By reformulating the scientific issues from the study of personality in humans to the behavioral adaptations in nonhumans, it may be possible to springboard research from the conceptual swampland in which it has been mired.

On the second, methodological count, behavior–genetic research in nonhuman species permits multiple strategies for the experimental unraveling of correlations between genes and environments. At the dawn of experimental psychology, Mills (1899) provided a blueprint for the new science which involved (i) the day-to-day study of behavioral development of a single animal over the first year of life, and (ii) the introduction of experimental modifications in order to understand the processes of behavioral development. In the late 1940s, modern behavior genetics was established as an experimental science when J. P. Scott, J. F. Fuller, and J. A. King began the intensive, developmentatl study of breeds of animals whose genetic differences could be precisely described. It became possible to assign individuals to rearing environments that are antithetical or supportive of biological propensities, or to place the same individuals in interactive conditions that are consistent with or inconsistent with their presumed genetic bias.

Correlated constraints

How might the correlations arise among behaviors and among behaviors and settings? Results from the above experimental studies indicate that these correlations arise from multiple sources: from within, from without, and from the properties of the behavioral organization itself. Consider, for example, the biological effects of puberty upon behavioral expression. Such constraints are not time-bound, nor do they have to appear early in ontogeny in order to be important and influential. Certain heritable effects on muturation rate do not appear until the transition from childhood to adulthood. Yet these effects may be of great importance for creating correlations among behavior patterns, including forms of deviance and early reproduction (Stattin & Magnusson, 1990). The effects of very early maturation in girls may be mediated through social affiliations with older males. In this case, sexual "deviance" occurs when the girls behave in accord with their maturational age rather than their chronological age.

Similarly, biological factors associated with configurations of gender differences in behavior may not appear in force until the onset of reproductive capacity and the associated sexual dimorphism (i.e. puberty in humans). It is also at the stage that social role differences in males and females become dominant in many cultures, along with expectations for interpersonal behaviors (including the expression of anger and interpersonal control). In this case, the biological constraints converge with social role expectations about "gender-appropriate" behavioral expression. Precisely when expectations for gender differences are enforced in ontogeny differs among societies (Beach, 1965).

Other correlated constraints are basically social and cultural in origin. This occurs, for example, when racial and social–economic class forces emerge from the background in childhood to the foreground in adolescence and adulthood. In this regard, it should not be surprising to expect to find that peer associations become increasingly sensitive in adolescence to racial and socio-economic class distinctions that earlier in development played a modest or negligible role in affiliations. Such emergent developmental constraints may be expected to arise as a direct outcome of age. Even in the absence of structural constraints of biology and culture, interpersonal correlations arise in dyads as a consequence of the organizational principles that underlie interactions. If the interaction is to be maintained, the responses of one individual necessarily create constraints on the actions of the other, and vice versa. But the similarities observed among dyads are not due only to reciprocal control processes. On the contrary, it seems likely that individuals select friends, and are selected to be friends, in terms of presumed similarities and likelihood of behavioral synchrony. In this regard, "assortative mating" would be a special case of selective affiliation (e.g. Kandel, 1978; Magnusson, 1988; Rodgers, Billy & Udry, 1984). At every stage, individuals are changed by their associations, and they carry to the next set of relationships the behavioral residue of the recent past. There is a dynamic exchange between enduring behaviors of the self and social relations with others, providing fresh meaning to Baldwin's (1897) assertion that personality is an "ever changing, never completed thing".

The broader point is that the correlations between environments, personal characteristics, and biological background reflect an ongoing alignment of developmental constraints. Risk factors in biology, behavior, and society tend to be correlated (Cairns & Cairns, 1991; Jessor & Jessor, 1977). In most accommodations, nature and nurture collaborate rather than compete. The disparate factors that serve to regulate behaviors tend to come in packages, not as independent entities. The task is to understand how configurations are formed across genetic–neurobiological–behavioral–social pathways. More broadly, social systems are usually formed in ways that are correlated with and support bio-behavioral dispositions. This principle holds in schools, informal social groups, families, and subcultures. Even powerful biological interventions (e.g. psychopharmacological, genetic) should not be viewed independently of the context in which they are employed, and the circumstances that might support or inhibit their influence. These constraints, and the correlations to which they give rise, are themselves adaptive and dynamic over ontogeny, relationships, and settings.

The relativity of time and adaptive mechanisms

Time is an essential and distinctive emphasis of the developmental perspective on genetic influence. Consider, for example, the relation between the time frames of ontogeny and transgenerational influences. Evolutionary study is addressed to the linkages across generations in the "development" of a species or class. Implicated at this level are those processes of developmental timing subsumed by the concept of heterochrony; namely, neoteny (extended immaturity of selected features in the descendants) and acceleration (facilitated maturity of selected features in the descendants).

Ontogeny, on the other hand, refers to mechanisms that operate in the life-span of the individual, from conception to death. In individual development, the distinctive mechanisms concern those of maturation and age-related changes in social role and expectations, as well as those of experiences that extend over a significant portion of the life-span of the person. Beyond maturational changes, this level of analysis involves most of the variables that have been implicated in "life-course" analyses, such as marriage, educational experience, military service, and economic depression (Elder, 1975). The nature–nurture conflict concerned the tension between microevolutionary–genetic mechanisms and those multiple processes of development.

But those are only two of the domains of time that have been implicated in developmental study. Modern behavioral research has been concerned with considerably shorter intervals, from the momentary micro-analyses to short-term studies, the episodic investigations, and brief longitudinal studies. Depending on the time interval involved, the same test–retest procedures may be labeled methodological analyses of reliability, longitudinal studies of stability, or life-course investigations of continuity. The nature–nurture dualism is but one of several possible interactions that exist between the mechanisms identified in the different time intervals. For example, Breland & Breland (1961) demonstrate how operant learning is typically overridden by species-typical maturational and sexual changes. They demonstrate how the effects of episodic and short-term learning are typically canceled out by maturational mechanisms. What works for adaptation in the short term may not be the most effective in the long term, in the light of inevitable changes in the nature of the internal and external context.

Such illustrations of long-term maturational changes overtaking short-term social learning adaptations should not be overdrawn, however. Existing evidence on mechanisms of development indicates that bidirectionality is more often the rule than the exception. Short-term learning mechanisms may, under specific conditions, minimize the effects of genetic difference and maturational changes as well as vice versa (Cairns, Gariépy & Hood, 1990).

John Fuller and his colleagues (e.g. Fuller & Sjursen, 1967; Scott & Fuller, 1965) have been at the forefront in examining the relations between time and genetic expression. In a provocative article, Fuller (1967) observed that the prime differences among breeds of dogs occurred during the initial stages of assessment. Once past the initial stage, the animals responded similarly to the demands of the assessment context. Accordingly, Fuller viewed the "emergence response" to be the phase where genetic biases in terms of emotional responses and temperamental differences were maximal.

Once beyond the introductory stage, other context-bound factors took over in behavioral regulation.

The "emergence reaction" presupposes a dynamic concept of behavioral organization. The genetic factors in the foreground in the initial stages of adaptation diminish in importance in behavioral organization during the very course of the observation. The distinctive genetic biases become melded with the characteristics of the context, and the weight of genetic contributions changes momentarily as the assessment continues. Lewis, Gariépy, and their colleagues have recently described the neurobiological and endocrinological substrata implicated by such a dynamic view (Lewis et al., in press).

The research indicates that selective breeding differences in aggressive behavior are mediated by differences in brain neurochemistry, specifically differences in dopaminergic activity and receptor concentrations (Lewis et al., in press). A primary effect of this difference in dopamine neurotransmitter is to increase the likelihood of freezing or social inhibition during the initial stages of an interchange. Such inhibition, in turn, diminishes the likelihood of attack initiation or counter-attacks in the first stages of interaction. However, preliminary data indicate that, like Fuller's "emergence response", the magnitude of the genetic bias rapidly diminishes. Other, situation-specific factors take over and become associated with other physiological mechanisms that are consistent with the individual's adaptation. In particular, endocrine functions become consistent with whether the individual is dominant or subordinate in the context. If the individual is winning, testosterone increases and corticosterone decreases. If the individual is losing, testosterone decreases and corticosterone increases. Apparently these endocrine factors are continuously updated in function in order to be correlated with the individual's social behavior patterns, and to provide support for future adaptation.

Taken overall, this research program provides an elegant demonstration of how genes, neurobiological states, physiological pathways, maturational changes, and experiences are dynamically interwoven over time in social behavior. The genetic bias observed in attack behavior was surprisingly time-bound, being expressed primarily in the initial stages of interaction. If and when environmental experiences failed to substantiate or reinforce the bias, a new set of biobehavioral processes were called into play. This sequential interplay between biological and behavioral mechanisms arose during the organization process itself. It would be neither efficacious nor efficient to have all alternatives for behavioral expression to be programmed in the genome, with the particular pathways triggered by contextual feedback. One lesson of developmental research is that, short of behavioral pathology, behavioral patterns cannot be frozen in form or function over time.

Such findings belie Henderson's (1990, p. 295) dismal conclusion that "it is these kinds of complexities [such as multiple determination and situational relativity] that have made the study of social behaviors so challenging and progress slower than in other areas of developmental behavior genetics". Significant social behaviors, because of their relevance for individual and species adaptation, are likely to provide the most parsimonious and elegant models of developmental–genetic influence. Viewed over time, the patterns of coherence and systematic features of social interactions emerge with clarity. They seem complex only because their dynamics do not permit simplistic assumptions about behavior stability and unidirectionality of influence. On this score, the study of the heritability of simple reflexive patterns, such as audiogenic seizures or conditioned reflexes, may have been a false economy. The developmental study of social behaviors promises to provide the field with models which show how genetic influences are woven into virtually all action patterns.

In order for individuals to adapt, a key feature is the sequential organization and mutual support of these components. And as the behavior system graduates from one level of organization and time to another, different processes can be implicated, even though the functions of the behavior remain the same. Hence the same outcome may be supported by different processes, depending upon the time and point in organization that the observations are made. This generalization is not limited to social adaptations: it has been identified in various behavioral domains, from the processes of short-term and long-term memory in children (Ornstein, 1978) to the mechanisms of echolocation in bats (Griffin, 1958) and hormonal supports for sexual arousal (Rosenblatt, 1965).

CONCLUDING COMMENTS

Biological, interactional, and genetic factors typically operate together in achieving behavioral adaptation. An understanding of the processes by which this collaboration occurs—or becomes challenged—has been handicapped by the commonsense view that behaviors can be reified and parsed into genetic or environmental "causes". The reification has been associated, in turn, with a search for the physiological pathways and brain structures that regulate specific behavioral attributes (e.g. maternal aggression, kin selection, empathy, cooperation). The *one gene→one behavior* conception is inconsistent with modern concepts of genes, neurobiology, and behavioral dynamics. The system perspective brings attention to the interactive processes by which behavioral outcomes arise rather than focus merely upon summary outcomes. It appears, for example, that a modest physiological bias can produce multiple behavioral outcomes. But the magnitude, pervasiveness, and permanence of the effect depends upon the timing of the influence and the context in which it occurs. In many intraspecific cases, genetic biases may be short-lived, giving way to contextual determinants during the organization of behavior. Such time-bound effects are nonetheless critical in behavioral adaptations.

A dynamic developmental perspective on how environmental–genetic influences are coalesced does not diminish the importance of biology in behavior. Nor does it obfuscate the research task. To the contrary, the perspective underscores the significance of the issue for biology as well as behavior. It also serves to redefine the research problem as being one amenable to experimental, embryological, and neurobiological research procedures. Do developmental considerations of gene and behavior fusion preclude a concept of causation? Yes, to the extent that "causation" presupposes a unidirectional, reductionistic view of behavior regulation. No, if "causation" is taken more broadly to mean the fabric of dynamic relationships by which behaviors are supported. In a developmental sequence, "causes" may become "outcomes" in a recursive, emergent fashion, depending upon the level of organization and developmental stage that is analyzed. Hence the arrow of causality may go around in circles rather than in a straight line.[5] Bidirectionality of influence does not, however, imply equality of influence. The scientific problem is to understand how the network of influences becomes fused to establish and regulate particular actions in particular settings.

Systems of internal regulation operate in conjunction with equally complex systems of behavior in achieving adaptation. Hence as much attention should be given to the study of behavior and its organization as to the study of genetic functions and molecular biology. Given the elegance and complexity of behavioral organization, the science can ill afford to continue to rely upon nouns of everyday speech to describe action patterns and environments. Nor can we afford to continue to employ commonsense concepts of genes and the biological substrata of behavior. In a developmental analysis, there are no separable "main effects" of environments and genes, and the concept of gene-by-environment interaction is too inclusive and vague to be of value in guiding empirical research.

Many contemporary investigators, including ourselves, argue that the behavioral–genetic research task should be enlarged in vision and in methodology. Priority should be given to understanding the development of meaningful behavior patterns in context. Specifically, the five steps of research strategy call for:

(1) Defining the behavior pattern that is to be explained in concrete operations;
(2) Tracking the natural development of this behavior pattern in explicitly defined conditions and contexts;
(3) Identifying the primary short-term events and long-term conditions that

contribute to changes in the pattern through experimental–longitudinal and cross-cultural analysis;

(4) Locating the possible pathways by which physiological and/or neurobiological effects may operate upon the behavior pattern;

(5) Examining through convergent behavior–genetic research designs the precise links between genetic influences, mediating pathways, and the concrete behaviors.

In sum, we suggest that the field has been grand in its aspirations yet modest in its methods. It risks becoming trapped by a limited vision of what is required to solve the enormous questions that it has chosen to address. A holistic approach to behavior development does not preclude precise genetic and ontogenetic analysis. On the contrary, it encourages such study albeit with a new set of requirements. No single method of study should be viewed as sacrosanct; ultimately, the solution must be compatible with both quantitative genetics and developmental genetic findings. If behavioral processes are to serve distinctive functions in biological adaptation, they must be responsive to changes in contexts, in relationships, and in maturational status. The interplay between neurobiology and behavior demands a fresh, dynamic view on the role of genes. John Paul Scott recently asked the question, "What do genes do?" His brief answer summarizes a main point of this chapter (Scott, 1990, p. vii):

> They organize nonliving material into living systems. Development, whose study began as the biological science of embryology, is the study of organizational processes. Therefore, the study of development is a fundamental method of analyzing gene action.

ACKNOWLEDGEMENTS

This research was supported in part by an NIMH grant to RBC. The three authors were colleagues in the Carolina Consortium on Human Development during the period that this chapter was prepared.

NOTES

1. This modest effect of genetic factors is confirmed by the biometric–genetic models that were fitted to these data (Lytton, 1980, pp. 225–241).
2. Intelligence is also relatively simple and economical to measure, and the tests that have evolved over the past century have robust psychometric properties.
3. Attention should be drawn to some of the admirable projects in progress on adoption and twins at the University of Colorado, and the collaborative adoption study conducted jointly at the University of Virginia, Pennsylvania State

University, and Georgetown University. When the work is currently at an early stage, each project promises to cover several steps of the above outline.
4. The distinction between evolutionary and proximal causation has been drawn from Wilson (1975). A more neutral designation of "ultimate" or "evolutionary" would have been "distal".
5. The authors thank Dr Angold for this succinct statement of the issues.

REFERENCES

Alexander, R. D. (1979). *Darwinism and Human Affairs*, University of Washington Press, Seattle.

Baldwin, J. M. (1897). *Social and Ethical Interpretations in Mental Development: A Study in Social Psychology*, Macmillan, New York.

Beach, F. A. (1965) (ed.) *Sex and Behavior*, John Wiley, New York.

Bell, R. Q. (1968). A re-interpretation of the direction of effects in studies of socialization. *Psychological Review*, **75**, 81–95.

Bell, R. Q. & Harper, L. V. (1977). *Child Effects on Adults*, Erlbaum, Hillsdale, NJ.

Bertalanffy, L. von (1962). *Modern Theories of Development: An Introduction to Theoretical Biology*, Harper & Brothers, New York. First published in 1932.

Breland, K. & Breland, M. (1961). The misbehavior of organisms. *American Psychologist*, **16**, 681–684.

Broadhurst, P. L. (1960). Experiments in psychogenetics: applications of biometrical genetics to inheritance of behavior. In H. J. Eysenck (ed.), *Experiments in Personality*, vol. 1. *Psychogenetics and Psychopharmacology*, Routledge & Kegan Paul, London. pp. 3–102.

Bronfenbrenner, U. (in press). The ecology of cognitive development: research models and fugitive findings. In R. H. Wozniak & K. Fischer (eds), *Specific Environments: Thinking in Context*, Erlbaum, Hillsdale, NJ.

Buss, D. M. & Barnes, M. (1986). Preferences in human mate selection. *Journal of Personality and Social Psychology*, **50**, 559–570.

Byrne, R. & Whiten, A. (eds) (1988). *Machiavellian Intelligence: Social Expertise and the Evolution of Intellect in Monkeys, Apes, and Humans*, Clarendon Press, New York.

Cairns, R. B. (1966a). Attachment behavior of mammals. *Psychological Review*, **72**, 409–426.

Cairns, R. B. (1966b). Development, maintenance, and extinction of social attachment behavior in sheep. *Journal of Comparative and Physiological Psychology*, **62**, 298–306.

Cairns, R. B. (1979). *Social Development: The Origins and Plasticity of Interchanges*, Freeman, San Francisco.

Cairns, R. B. (1990) Toward a developmental science. *Psychological Science*, **1**, 42–44.

Cairns, R. B. & Cairns, B. D. (1991). *Adolescents In Our Time: Lifelines and Risks*. (in preparation).

Cairns, R. B., Gariépy, J-L, & Hood, K. E. (1990). Development, microevolution, and social behavior. *Psychological Review*, **97**, 49–65.

Cairns, R. B., MacCombie, D. J. & Hood, K. E. (1983). A developmental–genetic analysis of aggressive behavior in mice: I. Behavioral outcomes. *Journal of Comparative Psychology*, **97**, 69–89.

Cairns, R. B. & Scholz, S. D. (1973). Fighting in mice: dyadic escalation and what is learned. *Journal of Comparative and Physiological Psychology*, **85**, 540–550.

Cairns, R. B. & Werboff, J. (1967). Behavior development in the dog: an interspecific analysis. *Science*, **158**, 1070–1072.

Cole, M. & Cole, S. (1989). *The Development of Children*, Scientific American, New York.

Corley, R. P. & Fulker, D. W. (1990). What can adoption studies tell us about cognitive development? In M. E. Hahn, J. K. Hewitt, N. D. Henderson & R. Benno (eds), *Developmental Behavior Genetics: Neural, Biometrical, and Evolutionary Approaches*, Oxford University Press, New York, pp. 236–265.

DeFries, J. C. & Hegmann, J. P. (1970). Genetic analysis of open-field behavior. In G. Lindzey & D. Thiessen (eds), *Contributions to Behavior–genetic Analysis: The Mouse as a Prototype*, Irvington Publishers, New York.

Dobzhansky, T. H. (1967). Of flies and men. *American Psychologist*, **22**, 41–48.

Eaves, L., Hewitt, J. K., Meyer, J. & Neale, M. (1990). Approaches to the quantitative genetic modeling of development and age-related changes. In M. E. Hahn, J. K. Hewitt, N. D. Henderson & R. Benno (eds), *Developmental Behavior Genetics: Neural, Biometrical, and Evolutionary Approaches*, Oxford University Press, New York, pp. 266–280.

Ebert, P. D. & Hyde, J. S. (1976). Selection for agonistic behavior in wild female *Mus musculus*. *Behavior Genetics*, **6**, 291–304.

Ebert, P. D. & Sawyer, R. G. (1980). Selection for agonistic behavior in wild female mice. *Behavior Genetics*, **10**, 349–360.

Elder, G. H., Jr (1975). Age differentiation and the life course. *Annual Review of Sociology*, **1**, 165–190.

Elder, G. H., Jr., Caspi, A. & Burton, L. M. (1988). Adolescent transitions in developmental perspective: historical and sociological insights. In M. Gunnar (ed.), *Minnesota Symposia on Child Psychology*, vol. 21. Erlbaum, Hillsdale, NJ, pp. 151–179.

Falconer, D. S. (1960). *Introduction to Quantitative Genetics*, Ronald Press, New York.

Fisher, R. A. (1930). *The Genetical Theory of Natural Selection*, Oxford University Press, London.

Fossey, D. (1983). *Gorillas in the Mist*, Houghton-Mifflin, Boston.

Fuller, J. L. (1967). Experiential deprivation and later behavior. *Science*, **158**, 1645–1652.

Fuller, J. L. & Sjursen, F. H. (1967). Audiogenic seizures in eleven mouse strains. *Journal of Heredity*, **58**, 135–140.

Fuller, J. L. & Thompson, W. R. (1960). *Behavior Genetics*, Wiley, New York.

Fuller, J. L. & Thompson, W. R. (1978). *Foundations of Behavior Genetics*, Mosby, St. Louis, Mo.

Gariépy, J-L., Hood, K. E. & Cairns, R. B. (1988). A developmental–genetic analysis of aggressive behavior in mice: III. Behavioral mediation by heightened reactivity or increased immobility? *Journal of Comparative Psychology*, **102** (4), 392–399.

Ginsburg, B. E. (1971). Developmental behavioral genetics. In N. B. Talbot, J. Kagan & L. Eisenberg (eds), *Behavioral Science in Pediatric Medicine*, Saunders, Philadelphia, pp. 228–242.

Ginsburg, B. E. & Allee, W. C. (1942). Some effects of conditioning on social dominance and subordination in inbred strains of mice. *Physiological Zoology*, **15**, 485–506.

Goldsmith, H. H. (1983). Genetic influences on personality from infancy to adulthood. *Child Development*, **54**, 331–355.

Goodall, J. (1986). *The Chimpanzees of Gombe: Patterns of Behavior*, Harvard University Press, Cambridge, Mass.

Gottlieb, G. (1983). The psychobiological approach to developmental issues. In P. H. Mussen, (ed.), *Handbook of Child Psychology*, 4th edn, vol. 2, John Wiley, New York, pp. 1–26.

Gottlieb, G. (1991). The experiential canalization of behavioral development: theory. *Developmental Psychology*, **27**, 3–34.

Griffin, D. R. (1958). *Listening in the Dark*, Yale University Press, New Haven, Conn.

Hahn, M. E., Hewitt, J. K., Henderson, N. D. & Benno, R. (eds) (1990). *Developmental Behavior Genetics: Neural, Biometrical, and Evolutionary Approaches*, Oxford University Press, Oxford.

Hall, C. S. (1951). The genetics of behavior. In S. S. Stevens (ed.), *Handbook of Experimental Psychology*, John Wiley, New York.

Hall, J. C., Kulkarni, S. J., Kyriacou, C. P., Yu, Q. & Rosbash, M. (1990). Genetic and molecular analysis of neural development and behavior in *Drosophila*. In M. E. Hahn, J. K. Hewitt, N. D. Henderson & R. Benno (eds), *Developmental Behavior Genetics: Neural, Biometrical and Evolutionary Approaches*, Oxford University Press, New York, pp. 100–112.

Henderson, N. D. (1990). Quantitative genetic analysis of neurobehavioral phenotypes. In M. E. Hahn, J. K. Hewitt, N. D. Henderson & R. Benno (eds), *Developmental Behavior Genetics: Neural, Biometrical, and Evolutionary Approaches*, Oxford University Press, New York, pp. 283–297.

Hewitt, J. K. (1990). Genetics as a framework for the study of behavioral development. In M. E. Hahn, J. K. Hewitt, N. D. Henderson & R. Benno (eds), *Developmental Behavior Genetics: Neural, Biometrical, and Evolutionary Approaches*, Oxford University Press, New York, pp. 298–303.

Jensen, D. D. (1967). Polythetic operationism and the phylogeny of learning. In W. C. Corning & S. C. Ratner (eds), *Chemistry of Learning: Invertebrate Research*, Plenum Press, New York.

Jessor, R. & Jessor, S. L. (1977). *Problem Behavior and Psychosocial Development: A Longitudinal Study of Youth*, Academic Press, New York.

Kandel, D. B. (1978). Homophily, selection, and socialization in adolescent friendships. *American Journal of Sociology*, **84**, 427–436.

Kuo, Z-Y. (1930). The genesis of the cat's responses to the rat. *Journal of Comparative Psychology*, **11**, 1–35.

Kuo, Z.-Y. (1967). *The Dynamics of Behavioral Development: An Epigenetic View*, Random House, New York.

Lagerspetz, K. M. J. (1964). Studies on the aggressive behavior of mice. *Annales Academiae Scientiarum Fennicae*, Sarja-ser. B. **131** (3), 1–131.

Lerner, I. M. (1954). *Genetic Homeostasis*, Oliver & Boyd, Edinburgh and London.

Lewis, M. H., Devaud, L. L., Gariépy, J-L., Southerland, S. B., Mailman, R. B. & Cairns, R. B. (in press). Dopamine and social behavior in mice bred for high and low levels of aggression. *Brain Research Bulletin*.

Lorenz, K. Z. (1965). *Evolution and the Modification of Behavior*, University of Chicago Press, Chicago.

Lytton, H. (1980). *Parent–child Interaction: The Socialization Process Observed in Twin and Singleton Families*, Plenum Press, New York.

Magnusson, D. (1988). *Individual Development from an Interactional Perspective: A Longitudinal Study*, Erlbaum, Hillsdale, NJ.

Mason, W. A. & Kinney, M. D. (1974). Redirection of filial attachments in rhesus monkeys: dogs as mother surrogates. *Science*, **183**, 1209–1211.

Matheny, A. P., Jr. (1990). Developmental behavior genetics: contributions from the Louisville Twin Study. In M. E. Hahn, J. K. Hewitt, N. D. Henderson & R. H. Benno (eds), Developmental Behavior Genetics: Neural, Biometrical, and Evolutionary Approaches, Oxford University Press, Oxford, UK, pp. 25–39.

Mayr, E. (1974). Behavior programmes and evolutionary strategies. *American Scientist*, **62**, 650–659.

Mayr, E. (1988). *Towards a New Philosophy of Biology: Observations of an Evolutionist*, Harvard University Press, Cambridge, Mass.

Michard, C. & Carlier, M. (1985). Les conduites d'agression intraspecifique chez la souris domestique: différences individuelles et analyses génétiques [Intraspecific aggressive behaviors in the domestic mouse: individual differences and genetic analyses]. *Biology of Behavior*, **10**, 123–146.

Mills, W. (1899). The nature of animal intelligence and the methods of investigating it. *Psychological Review*, **6**, 262–274.

Ornstein, P. A. (1978). (ed.) *Memory Development in Children*. Erlbaum, Hillsdale, NJ.

Oyama, S. (1985). *The Ontogeny of Information*, Cambridge University Press, New York.

Plomin, R. (1986). *Development, Genetics, and Psychology*, Erlbaum, Hillsdale, NJ.

Rodgers, J. L., Billy, J. O. G. & Udry, J. R. (1984). A model of friendship similarity in mildly deviant behaviors. *Journal of Applied Social Psychology*, **14**, 413–425.

Rosenblatt, J. S. (1965). Effects of experience of behavior in male cats. In F. A. Beach (ed.), *Sex and Behavior*, John Wiley, New York, pp. 416–439.

Rosenblum, L. A. & Kaufman, I. C. (1968). Variations in infant development and response to maternal loss in monkeys. *American Journal of Orthopsychiatry*, **38**, 418–426.

Rowe, D. C. (1987). Resolving the person–situation debate: invitation to an interdiscplinary dialogue. *American Psychologist*, **42**, 218–227.

Sackett, G. P. (1967). Some persistent effects of different rearing conditions on preadult social behavior in monkeys. *Journal of Comparative and Physiological Psychology*, **64**, 363–365.

Sameroff, A. J. (1983). Developmental systems: contexts and evolution. In P. H. Mussen (gen. ed.) & W. Kessen (vol. ed.), *Handbook of Child Psychology: History, Theory, and Methods*, 4th edn, vol. 1, John Wiley, New York, pp. 237–294.

Scarr, S. (1986). Cultural lenses on mothers and children. In L. Friedrich-Cofer (ed.), *Human Nature and Public Policy: Scientific Views of Women, Children, and Families*, Praeger, New York, pp. 202–238.

Scarr, S. & Kidd, K. K. (1983). Developmental behavior genetics. In P. H. Mussen (ed.), *Handbook of Child Psychology*, 4th edn, vol. 2, John Wiley, New York, pp. 345–434.

Scarr, S. & McCartney, K. (1983). How people make their own environments: a theory of genotype–environment effects. *Child Development*, **54**, 426–423.

Schneirla, T. C. (1966). Behavioral development and comparative psychology. *Quarterly Review of Biology*, **41**, 283–302.

Scott, J. P. (1977). Social genetics. *Behavior Genetics*, **7**, 327–346.

Scott, J. P. (1990). Foreword. In M. E. Hahn, J. K. Hewitt, N. D. Henderson & R. Benno (eds), *Developmental Behavior Genetics: Neural, Biometrical, and Evolutionary Approaches*, Oxford University Press, Oxford.

Scott, J. P. & Fuller, J. L. (1965). *Genetics and the Social Behavior of the Dog*, University of Chicago Press, Chicago.

Smuts, B. B. (1985). *Sex and Friendship in Baboons*, Aldine de Gruyter, New York.

Stattin, H. & Magnusson, D. (1990). *Pubertal Development in Girls*, Erlbaum, Hillsdale, NJ.

Symons, D. (1987). If we're all Darwinians, what's the fuss about? In C. Crawford, M. Smith, & D. Krebs (eds), *Sociobiology and Psychology: Ideas, Issues and Applications*, Hillsdale, NJ.

Tinbergen, N. (1974). Ethology and stress diseases. *Science*, **185**, 20–26.

Trivers, R. L. (1971). The evolution of reciprocal altruism. *Quarterly Review of Biology*, **46**, 35–57.

Trivers, R. L. (1985). *Social Evolution*, Benjamin/Cummings, Menlo Park, Calif.

Valsiner, J. (1987). *Culture and the Development of Children's Action*. John Wiley, Chichester.

Valzelli, L. & Bernasconi, S. (1979). Aggressiveness by isolation and brain serotonin turnover changes in different strains of mice. *Neuropsychobiology*, **5**, 129–135.

van Oortmerssen, G. A. & Bakker, Th. C. M. (1981). Artificial selelction for short and long attack latencies in wild *Mus musculus domesticus*. *Behavior Genetics*, **11**, 115–126.

Waddington, C. H. (1957). *The Strategy of the Genes*, George, Allen & Unwin, London.

Whitney, G. (1990). A contextual history of behavior genetics. In M. E. Hahn, J. K. Hewitt, N. D. Henderson & R. Benno (eds), *Developmental Behavior Genetics: Neural, Biometrical, and Evolutionary Approaches*, Oxford University Press, New York, pp. 7–24.

Whitney, G., McClearn, G. E. & DeFries, J. C. (1970). Heritability of alcohol preference in laboratory mice and rats. *Journal of Heredity*, **61**, 165–169.

Wilson, E. O. (1975). *Sociobiology: A New Synthesis*, Harvard University Press, Cambridge, Mass.

Wimer, C. (1990). Genetic studies of brain development. In M. E. Hahn, J. K. Hewitt, N. D. Henderson & R. Benno (eds), *Developmental Behavior Genetics: Neural, Biometrical, and Evolutionary Approaches*, Oxford University Press, New York, pp. 85–99.

Wrangham, R. W. (1979). On the evolution of ape social systems. *Social Science Information*, **18**, 334–368.

Wright, S. (1923). Mendelian analysis of the pure breeds of live stock. II. The duchess family of shorthorns as bred by Thomas Bates. *Journal of Heredity*, **14**, 339–348.

Chapter 5

Infant Precursors of Childhood Intellectual and Verbal Abilities

Marian D. Sigman and Peter Mundy

INTRODUCTION

The aim of this chapter is to explore our current knowledge regarding the infant precursors of childhood intellectual and verbal abilities. Although the investigation of individual differences is not the most active area of child study, significant effort has been devoted to identifying early markers and manifestations of subsequent cognitive abilities. The aims, methods, and results of these efforts will be discussed in this chapter with reference to normally developing children, children at risk because of early medical problems, and children whose development is clearly deviant.

Goals of identifying precursors

The purposes of identifying precursors of childhood cognitive skills are both theoretical and clinical. In terms of understanding the nature of development, the establishment of stability in a characteristic from infancy to childhood suggests that the characteristic is partly inherent in the infant, at least after the point when it was measured. The demonstration of stability in an individual characteristic may also help to define the characteristic more fully.

From a clinical viewpoint, establishing stability in cognitive functions enables the early identification of children who are likely to have cognitive limitations. This, in turn, may be useful for determining who should be treated and the nature of the treatment. In some pediatric settings, parents and clinicians are concerned about infants who have suffered early physical illness so that valid assessment techniques are needed. Even in groups of children whom we know will have cognitive limitations, such as children

Precursors and Causes in Development and Psychopathology.
Edited by D. F. Hay and A. Angold © 1993 John Wiley & Son Ltd

with Down's syndrome, identification of precursors is important. There are variations in intellectual and verbal competence among such children. If the processes important for more advanced development can be identified, then interventions may be designed to optimize cognitive skills. It may be important to analyze skills in terms of developmental constituents in order to understand how to intervene with extant cognitive disturbance.

Precursors and causes

The concept reflected in the term "precursor" is more narrow than the concept reflected in the term "cause". A precursor is an event that precedes and indicates the approach of another event or a substance from which another substance is formed. Thus, an ontogenetic relationship is presumed but the notion of causation is avoided. The extent to which the precursor is a prerequisite varies with the theory suggested. The evidence necessary to support the suggestion that some ability is a precursor is indirect, as it is for causal factors; no single correlational or experimental design can establish that any ability is a precursor of another ability, although extensive evidence from both designs can be compelling.

Types of studies

Two types of studies focused on identifying early manifestations or precursors have dominated the field of investigation. One type has focused on the sequential development of discrete sets of abilities in individual children. In these studies, precursors are defined as particular abilities that may be necessary, but not necessarily sufficient, for other abilities to develop. The logic here is that, although many variables may be involved, a particular ability (X) must be adequately developed before another different ability (Y) may emerge. A frequent assumption in this type of research is that the two sets of abilities tap a similar underlying process. If the precursor is clearly necessary, the skill is referred to as a prerequisite. An example of this line of research is the study carried out by Gopnik & Meltzoff (1987) showing that the infant's use of high-level categorization skills is often followed by the onset of the naming explosion.

The second type of study examines the infant's performance on a continuous behavior in comparison to the performance of other infants. The infant is ranked relative to other infants on a particular behavior shown by all infants, and evidence for stability is simply that the ranking on a later skill remains similar. In contrast to the prerequisite model described above, this model establishes the predictive validity and an inferred line of continuity between variables across age. Both models of continuity will be discussed in this chapter.

Influence of sample characteristics

When stability is identified by similar rankings across age, the characteristics of the sample used in any study can influence the findings in two ways. First, if the sample includes heterogeneous groups, individual stability may really be attributable to stable group differences. For example, longitudinal studies of full-term and preterm infants in which the preterm infants are tested at postnatal rather than conceptional ages may show stability in scores because the preterm infants remain ranked below the full-term infants at all ages due to their lesser maturity. The sample also influences the extent to which individual differences are identified by its homogeneity or heterogeneity. In a very homogeneous sample, individual rankings are likely to fluctuate more than when there is more spread so stability is more difficult to document. Moreover, the characteristics of the sample may influence the kind of stability identified. For example, stability in certain traits may be more genetically sustained in an economically prosperous sample where environmental variation is limited than in studies of poorer samples with wider environmental variations.

Defining the nature of continuity

Three types of continuity between infant and childhood behaviors seem possible (Bornstein & Sigman, 1986). The first, continuity of identical behaviors, is very rare because of the developmental transformations that occur in all cognitive processes during infancy and childhood. The second, continuity of developmental status, refers to an association between an infant behavior and childhood behavior due to rates of maturity. Since studies of individual differences rank the child relative to the group, two children could rank similarly as infants and children because one was developmentally more mature than the other at both points. This is quite likely in longitudinal studies of normal children whose development is quite regular across domains. Studies of children with more uneven development are useful for determining whether developmental status is the major form of continuity between behaviors. Continuity of underlying processes, the third type proposed, refers to stability which exists because the infant and childhood behavior both reflect a process which is continuous from infancy to childhood. In this case, the infant behavior is usually considered an early manifestation of the childhood behavior. However, the word "manifestation" is somewhat unsatisfactory because of the transformation in behavioral processes from infancy to childhood. The concept of precursor is more satisfactory in this regard because infant behaviors can be considered precursors of childhood skills despite differences in the actual behaviors measured.

Definitions of outcomes

The nature of our search for precursors is influenced by our understanding of the outcome variables. A great deal has been written about the limitations in our capacity to predict childhood and adult intelligence because of our incomplete knowledge of infant development. However, one of the central difficulties in designing infant measures stems from the lack of clarity in our understanding of childhood and adult intelligence. There is wide variation in what is considered intelligent behavior in adulthood (see Sternberg & Detterman, 1986 for 25 views on this issue). Our concepts of intelligence in adulthood willl necessarily guide the search for similar kinds of intelligence in childhood.

Environmental influences

One of the major issues in defining precursors is how to deal with environmental influences or the interaction of the child with other people. Environmental effects may account for stability or instability. Traits that appear stable in children may really reflect stability in the environment's treatment of the child. For example, the identification of a child as a slow learner may shape the expectations of the child's teachers so that identification becomes a self-fulfilling prophecy. As another example, if the infant's level of play and language is shaped by the quality of maternal activities, then a child may be advanced in play at one age and in language at another because of the stability in the quality of the mother's activities.

The current scientific convention seems to be that traits of the infant, rather than characteristics of the environment, are considered precursors to later development and environmental influences are treated separately. In the words of attribution theory, precursors are usually internal and stable. However, the current conventions allow a relationship between the infant and another person to be considered a precursor. For example, the nature of the attachment relationship between infant and caregiver is currently one of the major precursors examined in social and emotional development. Distinguishing environmental influences and infant traits is empirically useful for examining the ways in which different environments sustain or disrupt continuity. On the other hand, this separation is somewhat artificial in that the infant and environment are always in interaction and likely to be continuously transforming each other.

The considerations outlined in this introduction will be referred to more specifically throughout this chapter. In order to narrow the field, the chapter will focus on behaviors that develop in the first 18 months of life for which some stability has been demonstrated. Behavioral characteristics, rather than physical characteristics such as head size or health, will be discussed and these will generally be continuous qualities rather than discrete abilities since the focus is on prediction of intelligence which is itself a continuous variable. In general, outcome assessments will consist of intelligence tests although we will also discuss other measures, particularly verbal measures, where these are used. The discussion will be limited to infant traits although the part that the environment plays in fashioning and sustaining these traits will also be considered.

Overall approaches

Two approaches to summarizing the study of individual differences in cognitive development suggest themselves. First, we could attempt to apply an adult information-processing model to infant cognition and then discuss methods of assessing individual abilities in the component processes. This might be a useful strategy if the age range we were reviewing was narrower. However, across the first 18 months of life, developmental transformations are so marked that the kind of information-processing model used at one age would not fit for another. Furthermore, the study of individual differences in infancy has not evolved out of such an information-processing approach. Instead, the focus has been on emergent skills. The assumption has been that individual differences will be most meaningful in those abilities that are just developing and where the range of skills between infants is likely to be greatest. For this reason, the overall approach we will use in this chapter is to select areas of investigation that relate to the emerging abilities at three time periods.

DEVELOPMENTAL PHASES

In the early months of life, the principal task for the infant and caregiver is the regulation of states of arousal as the infant begins to integrate responses to stimulation in various modalities. Individual differences in state regulation and responsiveness to stimuli, especially visual stimuli, are the predominant characteristics studied in the first 6 months of life. In the second half-year, the infant has more organized responses to other people and objects. Individual differences in social communicative and exploratory behavior can be investigated in this period. After 12 months of age the infant begins to integrate social and cognitive understanding into symbolic systems which are manifested earliest in play behaviors. The infant's dawning representational system can be investigated by observing how the infant plays with objects and people, and variations among infants can be noted. This chapter will begin with three sections in which studies of individual differences in responsiveness to stimuli, social communicative skills, and exploratory behaviors and symbolic play in relation to later cognitive abilities are reviewed.

Early visual responsiveness and state regulation

Interest in individual differences in infants' responses to visual stimuli began with the first studies showing that infants responded differentially to stimuli. Robert Fantz, a pioneer in infant studies, recognized the importance of individual differences in infant responses at the same time as he was discovering the full extent of infant abilities. Some of the earliest studies of individual differences were carried out by Fantz and his students, Joseph Fagan and Simon Miranda, at Case Western Reserve (Fantz, Fagan & Miranda, 1975; Fantz & Nevis, 1967).

Two different approaches to measurement of individual differences in infant attention have been used. One technique is the investigation of the amount of attention the infant gives to an unchanging or repeated stimulus. Infants between birth and 7 months of age are seated in an infant seat and shown a single stimulus for a protracted period or over repeated trials and the infants' eyes are observed. The length of time that a reflection of the stimulus appears over the pupil of the eye is recorded. This is an easy observation to make and all studies report high inter-rater reliabilities. Most studies of infants older than 2 months of age use an infant-controlled habituation procedure. The infant is shown a stimulus until she or he looks away when the stimulus, usually presented as a slide or transparency, is turned off. At this point, a bright light is illuminated. After the infant fixates this attention getter, the light is replaced by the repeated stimulus. The process is continued until the length of fixation of the stimulus has declined to some absolute amount or to some percentage of the original fixation time. The measures derived from this procedure include the amount of habituation, the length of longest look, the length of first look, the time to a set criterion of habituation, and average duration time.

The second approach measures preference for novelty. The same stimulus is repeated on several familiarization trials and is then paired with a novel stimulus for several trials. The dependent measure is the percentage of looking time devoted to the novel stimulus. Infant attention patterns measured with these procedures have been found to be associated with later intelligence in about 12–15 studies (Bornstein & Sigman, 1986; Fagan & Singer, 1983; Rose & Wallace, 1985). These studies have been carried out with infants of different ages ranging from term to 7 months and from varying family backgrounds. Infants who fixate an unchanging stimulus more briefly, habituate more rapidly, or show greater preference for the novel rather than the familiar stimulus perform better on measures of intelligence later in life.

Visual habituation and novelty paradigms may also be used to examine the development of cognitive concepts in infants and nonverbal, clinical samples of young children. For example, we have used the visual attention paradigm to study category knowledge of form, color, and function in young autistic children as well as to assess the extent to which autistic children differentiated between facial expressions. Nonetheless, a limiting factor in the utility of these paradigms is that infants become increasingly restless with looking at slides by the end of the second half-year of life. At this point, assessment procedures need to focus on manipulative behaviors with objects as well as on the emerging social communicative abilities that are shown by 9 to 12-month-olds.

Social communicative development

The infant's social capacities are considerable by the second half of the first year. Up to about 5–6 months, the infant and others interact with face-to-face affective exchanges. While these kinds of social interactions continue in games involving physical contact and turn-taking, interactions become increasingly triadic involving the infant, caregiver, and objects (Adamson & Bakeman, 1982, 1985). In this phase of development, communication involves the coordination of the child's and caregiver's attention with respect to some object or event.

The intentionality of the child's communicative acts also becomes more apparent in this phase as the child begins to use conventional gestures (e.g. pointing, showing) and eye contact and direction of eye gaze to coordinate attention with others (Bates, 1979; Bruner & Sherwood, 1983; Rheingold, Hay & West, 1976). Alternating looks between interesting object events and a caregiver, often called "referential looking", is a common activity of 6- to 9-month-old infants. Pointing as a social gesture of reference emerges between 9 and 12 months (Hannan, 1987; Leung & Rheingold, 1981).

These behaviors seem to be used by infants for several different purposes. For example, social referencing behavior may be used to gain information from the caregiver in ambiguous situations (Campos, 1983; Hornik & Gunnar, 1988; Walden & Ogan, 1988). Requesting or protoimperative gestures are used to obtain assistance in obtaining or manipulating objects. A third class, joint attention or protodeclarative gestures are used to share an experience with another person (Bates, 1979; Bruner & Sherwood, 1983). Recent research suggest that these three classes of behavior may be distinguished vis-à-vis their affective involvement. Social referencing is associated with the display of quizzical or fearful expression, joint attention is associated with the display of positive affect, and requesting is associated with neutral affect (Hornik & Gunnar, 1988; Kasari et al, 1990).

Surprisingly few studies have been carried out to determine whether infants who develop these social–cognitive skills early are also more intelligent, verbally competent, or socially adept later in childhood. The level of speech used by 24-month-old-infants in the home was modestly predicted by the level of 13-month object communication in a study of 120 normal children (Olson, Bates & Bayles, 1984). The 13-month measure tapped both the extent to which the infant initiated joint attention by pointing and bringing objects to the mother and responded to requests by the mother. Elizabeth Bates and her colleagues have reported associations between a 13-month measure that combined joint attention and requesting gestures and later language development (Bates et al., 1979).

Exploratory behavior and representational play

In the second 6 months of life, infants become capable of more complicated actions with objects as well as people so that object exploration and play replaces visual attention to two-dimensional slides in studies of individual differences. Developmental changes in play have been described in numerous studies (Belsky & Most, 1981; Bretherton & Bates, 1984; Fein, 1981; Garvey, 1977; Lowe, 1975; McCune-Nicolich, 1981; Ungerer et al., 1981; Watson & Fisher, 1977).

At about 6 months, the infant begins to transfer objects from one hand to another, wave and bang objects, and examine objects closely. Later in this period the infant begins to combine objects by stacking them, lining them up, hitting one against another, and placing one within another. This simple manipulation is succeeded by functional or conventional use of objects in play. The most elementary form of functional play consists of combining objects in conventional ways such as putting a toy chair in front of a toy table or pouring from a teapot into a cup. By 13–14 months, normal infants direct conventional acts with objects to themselves, other people, and dolls. A hair brush is used to comb the child's hair, the mother's hair, and the doll's hair. Conventional acts are soon engaged in sequentially, as in the example above or when the acts remained focused on one person but follow from each other. An example is when a doll is fed with a bottle, her faced is wiped, and she is put in a toy crib. At about 20 months, the infant engages in truly symbolic play in that the infant pretends that one object is another, carries out an action with an imaginary object, or attributes animacy to a doll so that the doll carries out actions of her own.

Individual differences can be identified in two aspects of object play. First, observations can be used to determine the extent to which the infant sustains attention to objects, a capacity that increases with age (Jennings et al., 1979; Krakow, Kopp & Vaughn, 1981). Second, the level of symbolic representation can be assessed by measuring the extent to which play is dominated by more sophisticated forms of object use (Belsky & Most, 1981;

Bretherton & Bates, 1974; Tamis-LeMonda & Bornstein, 1989). Play competence, at least at 13 months of age, appears to reflect two different underlying mental capacities, exploratory competence and representational competence, that may have different origins, correlates, and consequences (Tamis-LeMonda & Bornstein, 1990).

Only a few studies have examined individual differences in exploratory behavior in normal children. We do not know how stable these differences are nor whether they predict later abilities. Leon Yarrow and his group conducted several studies of object exploration, mastery motivation, and persistence in relation to cognitive development. Infants who explored novel objects more at 6 months were cognitively more advanced in the second year than infants who explored novel objects less (Yarrow et al., 1983; Yarrow, Rubinstein & Pedersen, 1977). Holly Ruff and her collaborators have also investigated the relation between object exploration in the second half-year of life and later attentional patterns in both preterm and full-term children (Ruff et al., 1990).

There are also relatively few studies of the consequences of individual differences in representational play competence in normal infants. Most studies have not found a great deal of stability in the level of pretend play skills assessed over several weeks or months (Power, Chapieski & McGrath, 1985; Tamis-LeMonda & Bornstein, 1991). Bretherton & Bates (1984) also report only limited stability in play observation and minimal predictions from play to later language behavior in a sample of 27 infants followed from 13 to 28 months of age. In contrast, maternal reports of play behaviors at 13 months were predictive of language skills at 28 months. This may indicate that mothers are more accurate in their observations of their children's play skills and/or that mothers who report accurately also encourage symbolic development.

INVESTIGATIONS OF HETEROGENEOUS SAMPLES

Studies of preterm infants

Studies of infants whose development is placed at risk because of medical complications are useful for several reasons. First, clinical concern with these infants is very great so that longitudinal studies have been carried out to determine how they develop and to identify markers of later academic and adjustment difficulties (Friedman & Sigman, in press). Second, the range of variation in abilities at any age is generally greater with high-risk infants. While the majority of preterm infants show normal development throughout their lives, a greater percentage of preterm infants than full-term infants are mildly to severely retarded. The greater heterogeneity of the preterm group enhances the possibility of predictive relations between variables.

Infant attention

The infant attention paradigm has been used to predict later intelligence with normal full-term infants (Bornstein, 1985; Caron, Caron & Glass, 1983; Colombo et al., 1989; Fagan & McGrath, 1981; Lewis & Brooks-Gunn, 1981; Miller et al., 1980; Slater et al., 1985) and with preterm infants (Rose, 1980; Rose & Wallace, 1985; Sigman et al. 1986a). As a group, infants who are born preterm show longer fixation times and less preference for novelty after fixed amounts of familiarization (Sigman & Parmelee, 1974; Sigman et al., 1977). In one of the elegant studies carried out by her research group, Susan Rose (1983) has demonstrated that preterm infants will show preference for novel stimuli if they are provided with longer familiarization times. The use of the visual attention paradigm with very sick preterm infants, many of whom have developmental disorders in later life, has allowed both Fagan and Rose to identify mentally retarded children accurately in infancy.

Social communicative behaviors

The level of nonverbal communication skills as measured by the Early Social Communication Scales (Seibert, Hogan & Mundy, 1982) at 13 months was related to intelligence and language abilities at 2 and 3 years of age in a group of low birthweight infants varying in degree of medical complications (Ulvund & Smith, 1991). The relation between the early social communication measure and later abilities was significant even when the contribution of socio-economic status (SES) and score on the 13 month-Bayley Mental Scale was considered.

Exploration and play

A number of studies have shown that high-risk preterm infants explore novel objects less (Sigman, 1976), shift focus of attention between a number of objects less, and look at fewer objects than full-term infants, although the duration of attention to objects may be similar for the two groups (Landry et al., 1988). The extent to which the infant shifted gaze was associated with later development for the highest risk group in the study by Landry et al. As noted below, several studies suggest that this type of disturbance in attention regulation also appears in children with Down's syndrome (Krakow & Kopp, 1983; Landry & Chapieski, 1989; MacTurk et al., 1985). Thus, this type of attention deployment disturbance may be a general marker of cognitive delay. While preterm infants who experienced serious medical complications do show different exploration patterns than full-term infants, preterm infants who had fewer complications and are developing more normally show exploration patterns that are appropriate for their corrected age (Ungerer & Sigman, 1983; Landry, Chapieski & Schmidt, 1986; Ruff et al. 1990).

Representational play skills also develop normally in preterm infants when the latter group are compared to a sample of full-term infants of comparable conceptional age (Ungerer & Sigman, 1983). We have used observations of representational play skills as an assessment tool in a study of preterm infants. In this study, 13-month-old infants who showed more functional play, particularly play directed to other people, were more verbally able at 22 months (Ungerer & Sigman, 1984). One play measure, the amount of simple relational play at 22 months, was predictive of general intelligence at 5 years of age. The 22-month-old preterm and full-term infants who spent a significant proportion of play time in simply combining objects rather than in functional or symbolic play were less intelligent 5-year-olds (McDonald, Sigman & Ungerer, 1989). The play observation added to the prediction of intelligence at 5 years of age even when information from the Gesell Scale administered at 22 months was considered.

Observations of play have been conducted with infants whose development is at risk for reasons other than preterm birth. For example, 18–20-month-old children of drug-abusing mothers showed less representational play than a preterm control group (Rodning, Beckwith & Howard, 1989). The total amount of play, particularly symbolic play, was related to nutritional adequacy and verbal stimulation in a group of children in rural Kenya who were observed for two hours in their homes every other month from 18 to 30 months (Sigman et al., 1988, 1989). Infants who were well-fed and talked to more frequently showed more play over the year and more symbolic play at 30 months. Despite the sensitivity of play to environmental influences, play behaviors did not predict cognitive abilities at age 5 years in this sample (Sigman et al., 1991b).

Studies of mentally retarded and autistic children

As mentioned above, the study of children whose development is clearly delayed or more irregular may shed particular light on the identification of precursors. Normal children tend to have limited amounts of variability in their development in different domains, so one cannot see how one domain develops in the absence of development in another domain. Deviance in development, particularly when a particular ability or characteristic does not emerge at all or is markedly delayed, may illuminate the extent to which a particular ability is necessary and/or sufficient for the development of another ability.

Infant attention

Understanding the association between infant attention measures and intelligence may be facilitated through the study of infant attention in groups of young children with mental retardation (Butcher, 1977; McDonough, 1982). One set of studies has attempted to determine the extent to which handicapped infants are able to attend and process visual information. For example, Miranda & Fantz (1973), using a novelty preference paradigm, reported that children with Down's syndrome were quite capable of processing visual information, but they were also delayed in development of this capacity at 13, 24 and 36 weeks of age. However, delays in novelty response among infants with Down's syndrome and other handicapping conditions appear to be commensurate with their mental age (Lewis & Brooks-Gunn, 1984).

Social communicative behaviors

In our own work, we have investigated the social–communicative behaviors of three groups of developmentally delayed children, those with autism, Down's syndrome, and children with a variety of other pathologies. We have shown that autistic children have a specific deficit in their tendency to share joint attention with others, particularly in the service of sharing affect and experience with other people (Mundy et al., 1986; Kasari et al., 1990; Sigman et al., 1986b). Moreover, nonverbal communication skills, especially joint attention behaviors, are concurrently and predictively related to language abilities among autistic children (Mundy et al., 1987; Mundy, Sigman & Kasari, 1990). Thus, these findings are consistent with theory that suggests that the nonverbal capacity to share experiences with others may be a precursor for verbal communication skills (Bruner & Sherwood, 1983).

In contrast to normally developing children and other developmentally delayed children, young children with Down's syndrome are less likely to use nonverbal requesting gestures in order to obtain objects or assistance. Moreover, those children who do use such requesting gestures are more likely to have better expressive language skills concurrently and subsequently than children with Down's syndrome who do not use nonverbal requesting gestures (Mundy, et al., 1988; Smith & Tetzchner, 1986).

These data confirm that an association between the development of nonverbal and of verbal communication exists in atypical samples, but that different variables appear to be important precursors of development in different populations of children. Nonverbal requesting but not joint attention skill is an important correlate of language development among young children with Down's syndrome while the converse appears to be true for children with autism. However, part of this difference may be due to the nature of the outcome measures. Nonverbal requesting skills appear to be particularly important for the expressive language skills of children with Down's syndrome (who are specifically limited in expressive language abilities) whereas joint attention skills are related to both receptive and expressive language skills in autistic children. Different profiles of continuity may exist for different groups of children depending on the domains or functions that are delayed or deviant with the group.

Exploration and play

Studies of social and object exploration have identified what may be an abnormality in the attention deployment of children with Down's syndrome in that these children tend to display more face-to-face gaze and less looking to objects than normal controls (Berger & Cunningham, 1981; Gunn, Berry & Andrews, 1982). In contrast, in object play, young Down's syndrome children tend to display more looking to objects and less looking to people than do normal controls (MacTurk et al., 1985) or controls with mental retardation (Krakow & Kopp, 1983). These data suggest that children with Down's syndrome may have an overfocused attentional style (Hall, 1970) that may be the result of an inability to inhibit and shift attention (Loveland, 1987). These data and their current interpretation have an obvious alliance with the hypothesis discussed above that early established mechanisms for the regulation of attention contribute to individual differences in intellectual development.

As with social communicative behavior, autistic children show very different patterns of symbolic play than normal or mentally retarded children. Aside from their pecularities in attention deployment, mentally retarded children show play skills that are generally consonant with their developmental skills (Sigman & Ungerer, 1984). In contrast, autistic children show play skills which are quite immature for their developmental level (Ungerer & Sigman, 1981). We are presently studying the extent to which capacities for symbolic play are precursors for language and cognitive skills in both autistic and mentally retarded children.

DEFINING THE NATURE OF CONTINUITY

To the extent that prediction has been possible between these measures of attention, social communication, object exploration and play with later outcomes, the question immediately arises as to the nature of the continuity. Since social communication changes from the gestural form observed in infancy to the more largely verbal form used after 2 years of age, continuity is unlikely to be found in identical behaviors. This is also true for exploration and play with objects where, aside from the worlds of art and drama, representation becomes almost entirely internalized or verbal. While there may be some continuity of identical attention patterns, generally predictions have been more substantial between early attention behaviors with later measures of general or verbal intelligence than with later measures of visual discrimination or recognition memory (Bornstein & Sigman, 1986).

Continuity of developmental status cannot be ruled out so easily, particularly since the strongest stabilities have been identified with preterm and ill infants, some number of whom are developmentally delayed. One way to deal with this issue is to measure developmental status and determine whether the infant variable contributes to the outcome predictor when developmental status is covaried. An example given above is the demonstration by Ulvund & Smith (1991) that the social communication measure predicts later cognitive and language development even when an earlier Bayley score is taken into account. It would also be of interest to know whether predictive relations hold when only a normal sample is investigated. In the social communication study, it may only be the 13-month-olds who do not communicate gesturally and who later are diagnosed as mentally retarded who account for the significant correlations across ages. If the relation holds for normal children as well, one might argue that preverbal and verbal skills tap similar processes so that the child who is advanced in one might also be advanced in the other. If the relation does not hold when the data from the low-functioning children are excluded, it may indicate that some absolute level of preverbal communicative skills is critical for language development so that infants who do not develop these skills or do so only very much later are limited or delayed in their language acquisition. Variation above this level would then be nondiscriminating.

If one assumes that predictions over age are due to continuity in underlying processes, then the underlying processes have to be identified. As an example, the question has been asked why the length of time that an infant spends looking at a repeated pattern or a novel stimulus tells us anything about vocabulary skills at age 6.

Several underlying processes have been suggested as the basis for the continuity between infant attention and childhood intelligence. First, one of the early tasks of infancy is the modulation of state of arousal. The infant who is able to regulate his or her state well may be able to maintain attention so that processing occurs quickly (Lécuyer, 1988). This capacity to self-regulate may itself be continuous so that the child is able to focus on intellectual tasks and learn efficiently. The process may be self-perpetuating in that the self-regulated infant may learn more quickly so there is more to build on as the child develops.

A second possibility is that both infant attention and childhood intelligence assess the rate of information processing (Colombo & Mitchell, 1990). Many theories of adult intelligence include some factor which reflects the efficiency with which information is conveyed to short-term memory. The infant who fixates briefly, habituates rapidly, and consistently discriminates novel and familiar stimuli following a fixed familiarization time may be the child who takes in information most easily in the school years. The third hypothesis suggests that infants vary in terms of their comfort with and/or interest in novel stimuli (Berg & Sternberg, 1985). The infant who is more comfortable in dealing with novel stimuli may become the more exploratory child, at ease with novel intellectual problems. A variant of this explanation is that the infant who is interested in novelty may become the more curious child so that continuity is motivational in nature. This construct underlay much of the work of Leon Yarrow and his collaborators (Yarrow et al., 1972) when they measured exploration of novel objects in relation to later intelligence.

In our own work we have tried to examine these three hypotheses using divergent validation approaches (Sigman et al., in press). The sample of infants whose attention to unchanging stimuli was assessed at term and 4 months of age were retested at age 12 yeares. Among the measures administered were a test of sustained attention, a measure of speed of encoding information, and an assessment of reasoning using verbal analogies with novel information. The infant attention measure was associated with the speed of encoding information and not with sustained attention or novel verbal reasoning. These results suggest that infant attention is a precursor to later information processing. However, the results still do not completely solve the issue since the infant measure could assess state regulation or interest in novelty and yet be associated later with efficiency of information intake.

THE ROLE OF THE ENVIRONMENT

The environment may also influence the behavioral patterns of the infant and be responsible for the observed continuity. To put the issue more concretely, certain home environments may shape the infant to be more interested in novel visual stimuli or more adept at processing quickly, while other home environments are less facilitative in this way. For example, if parents are able to help the infant regulate states of arousal effectively, the infant may be freer to respond to visual stimuli. The continuity might then emerge from the infant or from the environment. Two studies have addressed the relation between parental behavior and infant attention. Bornstein (1985) found that infant attention and parental teaching were associated with each other in the first 6 months of life and with receptive language at age 12 months. However, the association of the infant's rate of habituation with receptive language was independent of the frequency of maternal teaching.

In our own study, both attention patterns and the frequency of vocalization by the caregiver in the neonatal period were associated independently with 12-year-intelligence (Sigman et al., 1991a). Thus, these two studies suggest that the continuity documented from infant attention to later intelligence is independent of environmental effects on the infant.

The issue of disambiguating the stability in the home environment from prediction is different for measures of social communication, exploration, and play behaviors than for measures of attention. Since there is still very little evidence as to whether the former abilities have consequences for later development in normal children, there has been little effort to disentangle these factors. In any case, the influence of the home environment on social communicative abilities has only rarely been investigated. Olson, Bates & Bayles (1984) have shown that the frequency with which mothers engaged in teaching of their 13-month-old-infants in the home was associated with concurrent infant object communication, a measure both of the extent to which the infant initiated joint attention and responded to requests. These findings need to be replicated with measures made in independent settings. In contrast, specific types of maternal activity have been shown to play a meaningful part in the early development of attention span (Belsky, Goode & Most, 1980; Landry, Chapieski & Schmidt, 1986; Yarrow et al., 1982) and play competence (Belsky, Goode & Most, 1980; Tamis-LeMonda & Bornstein, 1989, 1990, 1991; Vibbert & Bornstein, 1989). In these studies concurrent relations between maternal activities and play competence are more notable than predictive relations.

CONCLUSIONS

In summary, we have examined the extent to which the infant's abilities in responding to visual stimuli, communicating nonverbally, exploring objects, and playing symbolically are predictive of later intelligence and verbal skills. Clearly, the most progress has been made in terms of visual attention. Infant visual behaviors appear to vary with medical risk factors and developmental delay. Infants who are slower to process stimuli, possibly because of an overfocused attentional style, are less intelligent later in childhood. While infant attentional patterns may be related to maternal activities, stability appears to reside in the infant so that there is prediction from infant behavior to later intelligence even when the contribution of the home environment is considered.

We have made less progress in determining whether communicative and play skills are predictive of later abilities. For nonverbal communication, there appears to be a predictive relation to later verbal communicative skills for high-risk and delayed groups of children. Whether this relation exists across the whole continuum of normal development has not been examined.

There is some indication from studies of autistic children that an elementary capacity for shared attention may be a precursor, or even a prerequisite, for language acquisition. Play skills also seem to predict later abilities in high-risk and delayed samples but less clearly do so in normal samples.

Several issues continue to limit what can be concluded regarding infant precursors of childhood abilities. First, the identification of infant abilities that predict later development has only begun. We need to know whether prediction holds across all levels of abilities or whether the important issue is the infant's achievement of some critical level of skill. Second, disambiguation of continuity of developmental status from continuity of underlying process must be addressed. Third, there has been only minimal identification of the underlying processes accounting for the continuity of cognitive functions in the three domains described in this chapter. Until we can say more precisely what essential process is shared by the infant precursor and childhood ability, the link between the two will continue to be ephemeral.

ACKNOWLEDGEMENT

This work was supported by NINCDS GRANT, NS 25243, and NICHD grant, HD 17662.

REFERENCES

Adamson, L. & Bakeman, R. (1982). Affectivity and reference: concepts, methods, and techniques in the study of communication development of 6-to-18-month-old infants. In T. Field & A. Fogel (eds), *Emotion and Early Interaction*, Erlbaum, Hillsdale, N.J., pp. 213–236.

Adamson, L. & Bakeman, R. (1985). Affect and attention: infants observed with mothers and peers. *Child Development*, **56**, 582–593.

Bates, E. (1979). *The Emergence of Symbols: Cognition and Communication in Infancy*, Academic Press, New York.

Bates, E., Bretherton, I., Carlson, V., Carpen, K. & Marcia, R. (1979). Next steps: follow-up study and some pilot research. In E. Bates (ed.), *The Emergence of Symbols: Cognition and Communication in Infancy*, Academic Press, New York, pp. 271–314.

Belsky, J., Goode, M. K. & Most, R. K. (1980). Maternal stimulation and infant exploratory competence: Cross sectional, correlational, and experimental analyses. *Child Development*, **51**, 1168–1186.

Belsky, J. & Most, R. (1981). From exploration to play: a cross-sectional study of infant free-play behavior. *Developmental Psychology*, **17**, 630–639.

Berg, C. A. & Sternberg, R. J. (1985). Response to novelty: continuity vs. discontinuity in the developmental course of intelligence. In H. W. Reese (ed.), *Advances in Child Development and Behavior*, **19**, 1–47.

Berger, J. & Cunningham, C. C. (1981). The development of eye contact between mothers and normal versus Down's syndrome infants. *Developmental Psychology*, **17**, 678–689.

Bornstein, M. H. (1985). How infant and mother jointly contribute to developing cognitive competence in the child. *Proceedings of the National Academy of Science (U.S.A.)*, **82**, 7470–7473.

Bornstein, M. & Sigman, M. D. (1986). Continuity in mental development from infancy. *Child Development*, **57**, 251–274.

Bretherton, I. & Bates, E. (1984). The development of representation from 10 to 28 months; differential stability of language and symbolic play. In R. W. Emde & R. J. Harmon (eds), *Continuities and Discontinuities in Development*, Plenum Press, New York, pp. 229–261.

Bruner, J. & Sherwood, V. (1983). Thought, language, and interaction in infancy. In S. D. Call, E. Galenson & R. L. Tyson (eds), *Frontiers of Infant Psychiatry*, Basic Books, New York, pp. 38–52.

Butcher, M. (1977). Recognition memory for colors and faces in profoundly retarded children. *Intelligence*, **1**, 344–357.

Campos, J. J. (1983). The importance of affective communication in social referencing: a commentary on Feinman. *Merrill-Palmer Quarterly*, **29**, 83–87.

Caron, A. J., Caron, R. F. & Glass, P. (1983). Responsiveness to relational information as a measure of cognitive functioning in non-suspect infants. In T. Field & A. Sostek (eds), *Infants Born at Risk: Physiological, Perceptual, and Cognitive Processes*, Grune & Stratton, New York, pp. 181–209.

Colombo, J. & Mitchell, D. W. (1990). Individual differences in early visual attention: fixation time and information processing. In J. Colombo & J. Fagen (eds), *Individual Differences in Infancy*, Erlbaum, Hillsdale, NJ, pp. 193–229.

Colombo, J., Mitchell, D. W., Dodd, J., Coldren, J. T. & Horowitz, F. E. (1989). Longitudinal correlates of infant attention in the paired-comparison paradigm. *Intelligence*, **13**, 33–43.

Fagan, J. F. & McGrath, S. K. (1981). Infant recognition memory and later intelligence. *Intelligence*, **5**, 121–130.

Fagan, J. F. & Singer, L. T. (1983). Infant recognition memory as a measure of intelligence. In L. P. Lisitt (ed.), *Advances in Infancy Research*, vol. 12, Ablex, Norwood, NJ, pp. 31–78.

Fantz, R., Fagan, J. & Miranda, S. (1975). Early visual selectivity. In L. Cohen & P. Salapatek (eds), *Infant Perception: From Sensation to Cognition*, vol. 1, Academic Press, New York, pp. 249–345.

Fantz, R. L. & Nevis, S. (1967). The predictive value of changes in visual preferences in early infancy. In J. Hellmuth (ed.), *The Exceptional Infant*, vol. 1, Special Child Publications, Seattle, pp. 349–414.

Fein, G. (1981). Pretend play in childhood: an integrated review. *Child Development*, **52**, 1095–1118.

Friedman, S. & Sigman, M. D. (in press). *The Psychological Development of Low Birthweight Children*, Ablex, Norwood, NJ.

Garvey, C. (1977). *Play,* Harvard University Press, Cambridge, Mass.

Gopnik, A. & Meltzoff, A. (1987). The development of categorization in the second year and its relation to other cognitive and linguistic developments. *Child Development*, **58**, 1523–1531.

Gunn, P., Berry, P. & Andrews, R. J. (1982). Looking behavior of Down syndrome infants. *American Journal of Mental Deficiency*, **87**, 344–347.

Hall, B. (1970). Somatic deviations in newborn and older mongoloid children. *Acta Paediatrica Scandinavica*, **59**, 199.

Hannan, T. E. (1987). A cross-sequential assessment of the occurrences of pointing in 3- to 12-month-old human infants. *Infant Behavior and Development*, **10**, 11–22.

Hornik, R. & Gunnar, M. (1988). A descriptive analysis of infant social referencing. *Child Development*, **59**, 626–634.

Jennings, K. D., Harmon, R. J., Morgan, G. A., Gaiter, J. L. & Yarrow, L. J. (1979). Exploratory play as an index of mastery motivation: relationships to persistence, cognitive functioning, and environmental measures. *Developmental Psychology*, **15**, 386–394.

Kasari, C., Sigman, M., Mundy, P. & Yirmiya, N. (1990). Affective sharing in the context of joint attention interactions of normal, autistic and mentally retarded children. *Journal of Autism and Developmental Disabilities*, **20**, 87–100.

Krakow, J. B. & Kopp, C. B. (1983). The effects of developmental delay on sustained attention in young children. *Child Development*, **54**, 1143–1155.

Krakow, J. B., Kopp, C. B. & Vaughn, B. E. (1981). Sustained attention in young children. Paper presented at the Biennial Meeting of the Society for Research in Child Development, Boston, Mass.

Landry, S. H. & Chapieski, M. L. (1989). Joint attention and infant toy exploration: effects of Down syndrome and prematurity. *Child Development*, **60**, 103–119.

Landry, S., Chapieski, L., Fletcher, J. & Denson, S. (1988). Three year outcome for low birth weight infants: differential effects of early medical complications. *Journal of Pediatric Psychology*, **13**, 317–327.

Landry, S. H., Chapieski, M. L. & Schmidt, M. (1986). Effects of maternal attention directing strategies on preterms' response to toys. *Infant Behavior and Development*, **9**, 257–271.

Lécuyer, R. (1988). Please infant, can you tell me exactly what you are doing during a habituation experiment? *European Bulletin of Cognitive Psychology/Cahiers de Psychologie Cognitive*, **8**, 476–481.

Leung, E. & Rheingold, H. (1981). Development of pointing as a social gesture. *Developmental Psychology*, **17**, 215–220.

Lewis, M. & Brooks-Gunn, J. (1981). Visual attention at three months as a predictor of cognitive functioning at two years of age. *Intelligence*, **5**, 131–140.

Lewis, M. & Brooks-Gunn, J. (1984). Age and handicapped group differences in infants' visual attention. *Child Development*, **55**, 858–868.

Loveland, K. (1987). Behavior of young children with Down syndrome before the mirror: finding things reflected. *Child Development*, **58**, 928–936.

Lowe, M. (1975). Trends in the development of representational play in infants from one to three years: an observational study. *Journal of Child Psychology and Psychiatry*, **16**, 33–47.

McCune-Nicolich, L. (1981). Toward symbolic functioning: structure of early pretend games and potential parallels with language. *Child Development*, **52**, 785–797.

McDonald, M. A., Sigman, M. & Ungerer, J. A. (1989). Intelligence and behavior problems in five-year-olds in relations to representational abilities in the second year of life. *Journal of Developmental and Behavioral Pediatrics*, **10**, 86–91.

McDonough, S. (1982). Attention and memory in cerebral palsied infants. *Infant Behavior and Development*, **5**, 347–353.

MacTurk, R. H., Vietze, P. M., McCarthy,, M. E., McQuiston & Yarrow, L. J. (1985). The organization of exploratory behavior in Down syndrome and nondelayed infants. *Child Development*, **56**, 573–581.

Miller, D. J., Spiridigliozzi, G., Ryan, E. B., Callan, M. P. & McLaughlin, J. E. (1980). Habituation and cognitive performance: relationships between measures at four years of age and earlier assessments. *International Journal of Behavioral Development*, **3**, 131–146.

Miranda, S. B. & Fantz, R. L. (1973). Visual preferences of Down syndrome and normal infants. *Child Development*, **44**, 555–561.

Mundy, P., Sigman, M. & Kasari, C. (1990). A longitudinal study of joint attention and language development in autistic children. *Journal of Autism and Developmental Disorders*, **20**, 115–123.

Mundy, P., Sigman, M.,, Kasari, C. & Yirmiya, N. (1988). Nonverbal communication skills in Down syndrome children. *Child Development*, **59**, 235–249.

Mundy, P., Sigman, M., Ungerer, J. A., & Sherman, T. (1986). Defining the social deficits in autism: the contribution of non-verbal communication measures. *Journal of Child Psychology and Psychiatry*, **27**, 657–669.

Mundy, P., Sigman, M., Ungerer, J. A. & Sherman, T. (1987). Nonverbal communication and play correlates of language development in autistic children. *Journal of Autism and Developmental Disorders*, **17**, 349–364.

Olson, S. L., Bates, J. E. & Bayles, K. (1984). Mother–infant interaction and the development of individual differences in children's cognitive competence. *Developmental Psychology*, **20**, 166–179.

Power, T. G., Chapieski, M. L. & McGrath, M. P. (1985). Assessment of individual differences in infant exploration and play. *Developmental Psychology*, **21**, 974–981.

Rheingold, H. L., Hay, D. G. & West, M. J. (1976). Sharing in the second year of life. *Child Development*, **47**, 1148–1158.

Rodning, C., Beckwith, L. & Howard, J. (1989). Characteristics of attachment organization and play organization in prenatally drug-exposed toddlers. *Development and Psychopathology*, **1**, 277–289.

Rose, S. A. (1980). Enhancing visual recognition memory in preterm infants. *Developmental Psychology*, **16**, 85–92.

Rose, S. A. (1983). Differential rates of visual information processing in full-term and preterm infants. *Child Development*, **54**, 1189–1198.

Rose, S. A. & Wallace, I. F. (1985). Visual recognition memory: a predictor of later cognitive functioning in preterms. *Child Development*, **56**, 843–852.

Ruff, H. A., Lawson, K. R., Parrinello, R. & Weissberg, R. (1990). Long-term stability of individual differences in sustained attention in the early years. *Child Development*, **61**, 60–76.

Seibert, J., Hogan, A. J. & Mundy, P. (1982). Assessing interactional competencies: the early social communication scales. *Infant Mental Health Journal*, **3**, 244–258.

Sigman, M. (1976). Early development of preterm and full-term infants: exploratory behavior in eight-months-olds. *Child Development*, **47**, 606–612.

Sigman, M., Cohen, S. E., Beckwith, L., Asarnow, R. & Parmelee, A. H. (1991a). Continuity in cognitive abilities from infancy to 12 years of age. *Cognitive Development*, **6**, 47–59.

Sigman, M., Cohen, S. E., Beckwith, L., Asarnow, R. & Parmelee, A. H. (in press). The prediction of cognitive abilities at 12 years from neonatal assessments of preterm infants. In S. Friedman & M. Sigman (eds), *The Psychological Development of Low Birthweight Children*, Ablex, Norwood, NJ.

Sigman, M., Cohen, S. E., Beckwith, L. & Parmelee, A. H. (1986a). Infant attention in relation to intellectual abilities in childhood. *Developmental Psychology*, **22**, 788–792.

Sigman, M., Kopp, C. B., Littman, B. & Parmelee, A. H. (1977). Infant visual attentiveness in relation to birth condition. *Developmental Psychology*, **13**, 431–437.

Sigman, M., McDonald, M. A., Neumann, C. & Bwibo, N. (1991b). Prediction of cognitive competence in Kenyan children from toddler nutrition, family characteristics and abilities. *Journal of Child Psychology and Psychiatry and Allied Disciplines*, **32**, 307–320.

Sigman, M., Mundy, P., Sherman, T. & Ungerer, T. A. (1986b). Social interactions of autistic, mentally retarded and normal children with their caregivers. *Journal of Child Psychology and Psychiatry*, **27**, 647–656.

Sigman, M., Neumann, C., Baksh, M., Bwibo, N. & McDonald, M. A. (1989). Relations between nutrition and development of Kenyan toddlers. *Journal of Pediatrics*, **115**, 357–364.

Sigman, M., Neumann, C., Carter, E., Cattle, D. J., D'Souza, S. & Bwibo, N. (1988). Home interactions and the development of Embu toddlers in Kenya. *Child Development*, **59**, 1251–1261.

Sigman, M. & Parmelee, A. H. (1974). Visual preferences of four-month-old preterm and full-term infants. *Child Development*, **45**, 959–965.

Sigman, M. & Ungerer, J. A. (1984). Cognitive and language skills in autistic, mentally retarded, and normal children. *Developmental Psychology*, **20**, 231–244.

Slater, A., Cooper, R., Rose, D. & Perry, H. (1985). The relationship between infant attention and learning and linguistic and cognitive abilities at 18 months and at $4\frac{1}{2}$ years. Paper presented at the International Society for the Study of Behavioral Development, Tours, France.

Smith, L. & Tetzchner, S. (1986). Communicative, sensorimotor, and language skills of young children with Down syndrome. *American Journal of Mental Deficiency*, **91**, 57–66.

Sternberg, R. J. & Detterman, D. K. (1986). *What is Intelligence? Contemporary Viewpoints on its Nature and Definition*, Ablex, Norwood, NJ.

Tamis-LeMonda, C. S. & Bornstein, M. H. (1989). Habituation and maternal encouragement of attention in infancy as predictors of toddler language, play, and representational competence. *Child Development*, **60**, 738–751.

Tamis-LeMonda, C. S. & Bornstein, M. H. (1990). Language, play, and attention at one year. *Infant Behavior and Development*, **13**, 85–98.

Tamis-LeMonda, C. S. & Bornstein, M. H. (1991). Individual variation, stability and change in mother and toddler play, *Infant Behavior and Development*, **14**, 143–162.

Ulvund, S. E. & Smith, L. (1991). The predictive validity of nonverbal communicative skills in infants with perinatal hazards. Paper presented at the Biennial Meeting of the Society for Research in Child Development, Seattle, Wash.

Ungerer, J. A. & Sigman, M. (1981). Symbolic play and language comprehension in autistic children. *Journal of the American Academy of Child Psychiatry*, **20**, 318–338.

Ungerer, J. A. & Sigman, M. (1983). Developmental lags in preterm infants from 1 to 3 years of age. *Child Development*, **54**, 1217–1228.

Ungerer, J. A. & Sigman, M. (1984). The relation of play and sensorimotor behavior to language in the second year. *Child Development*, **55**, 1448–1455.

Ungerer, J. A., Zelazo, P. R., Kearsley, R. B. & O'Leary, K. (1981). Developmental changes in the representation of objects in symbolic play from 18 to 34 months of age. *Child Development*, **52**, 186–195.

Vibbert, M. & Bornstein, M. H. (1989). Specific associations between domains of mother–child interaction and toddler referential language and pretense play. *Infant Behavior and Development*, **12**, 163–184.

Walden, T. & Ogan, T. (1988). The development of social referencing. *Child Development*, **59**, 1230–1240.

Watson, M. & Fisher, K. (1977). A developmental sequence of agent use in late infancy. *Child Development*, **40**, 828–836.

Yarrow, L. J., McQuiston, S., MacTurk, R. H., McCarthy, M. E., Klein, R. P. &

Vietze, P. M. (1983). Assessment of mastery motivation during the first year of life: contemporaneous and cross-age relationships. *Developmental Psychology*, **19**, 159–171.

Yarrow, L. J., Morgan, G. A., Jennings, K. D., Harmon, R. J. & Gaiter, J. L. (1982). Infants' persistence at tasks: relationships to cognitive functioning and early experience. *Infant Behavior and Development*, **5**, 131–141.

Yarrow, L. J., Rubinstein, J. L. & Pedersen, F. A. (1977). *Infant and Environment: Early Cognitive and Motivational Development*, Hemisphere, Washington.

Yarrow, L. J., Rubinstein, J. L., Pederson, F. A. & Janowski, J. J. (1972). Dimensions of early stimulation and their differential effects on infant development. *Merrill-Palmer Quarterly*, **18**, 205–218.

Chapter 6

Causes and Precursors of Children's Theories of Mind

Douglas Frye

How do children come to understand that people have intentions and beliefs? The development of this understanding, which has been dubbed a "theory of mind" (Premack & Woodruff, 1978), has been the theme of intense research of late (Astington, Harris & Olson, 1988; Frye & Moore, 1990; Perner, 1991; Wellman, 1990). It is an important question because the greater part of everyday behavior is intentional and rooted in belief. We do things on purpose and choose how to do them based on what we believe about how the world (and other people) work. Even so, intention and belief must present a problem for the child. Because both are mental states, they cannot be observed directly—their presence must be inferred.

There is abundant evidence that the overwhelming majority of children do come to hold a theory of mind. The clearest experimental evidence for such a theory in childhood can be found in tasks of unfulfilled intention (Astington, 1990) and false belief (Wimmer & Perner, 1983). These tasks are convincing because they ask the child to infer someone's intention or belief even though the intention or belief is not in agreement with reality. For example, in one version of the false belief task, the child is told a story about a character who hides something in one location, and then is not present when the object is moved somewhere else. The child must say where the story character will look for the object when he or she returns. Three-year-olds in this task almost always say the character will look where the object actually is. Four-year-olds recognize that the character will have a false belief about the location of the object and will search there. The one exception to this pattern, which will be discussed later, is autistic children, who rarely ever succeed on these tasks.

The false belief task and the definition of theory of mind give the impression that a theory of mind must be a social phenomenon. After all, people are the ones who have intentions and beliefs. There is no doubt that

Precursors and Causes in Development and Psychopathology.
Edited by D. F. Hay and A. Angold © 1993 John Wiley & Son Ltd

a theory of mind is social. It has social precursors, is a social phenomenon, and has extensive consequences for the child's later social understanding and conduct. However, there are also indications that the effect is wider in scope. The appearance–reality distinction (Flavell, Flavell & Green, 1983) is a good example. When 3-year-olds are shown an ambiguous object—e.g. a sponge painted to look like a rock—they say it must be one thing or the other. Four-year-olds, on the other hand, are able to say that it *is* a sponge but *it looks* like a rock. In spite of the fact that drawing a distinction between appearance and reality would seem primarily to require the cognitive ability to represent objects in multiple ways, responses on the appearance–reality and the false belief tasks have been found to correlate (Gopnik & Astington, 1988; Moore, Pure & Furrow, 1990).

Zaitchik (1990) has provided firsthand verification of the broader scope of the change in the child's thinking at 4 years. She devised an analogue of the false belief task that only tests representation, not belief. In Zaitchik's task, children watched an instant photograph being taken of a salient toy in a specific place. The toy was then moved. The children were asked what location the photograph would show the toy to be in. The task produced the familiar 3- versus 4-year-old split. The younger children said the picture would show the toy in the new place. The older children realized that the picture would still show the toy in the old location. Zaitchik argues that the results demonstrate that 3-year-olds have trouble with more than just other minds. They have difficulty understanding representation, whether it is another person's (incorrect) representation of the world or a photograph's representation of the world at an earlier time.

These findings suggest that cognition has central importance for the development of a theory of mind. It is reasonable that cognition would be implicated in theory of mind except that no major cognitive change was previously identified at the 3- to 4-year-old point. The generally recognized cognitive changes in this period coincide with the end of infancy at 2 years and with the beginning of formal schooling at 5 or 6 years. The new research on theory of mind, then, may have also found evidence for a "new" cognitive change in early childhood. The discovery of a new cognitive change would be significant because it could explain theory of mind and point to the specific disability in autism. This chapter considers what the recent research on theory of mind indicates about the course of cognitive development in early childhood. To do so, it briefly reviews findings of some basic theory of mind effects, examines the research on theory of mind with autistic children, considers likely precursors to the theory of mind, and discusses what cognitive changes might be implicated in the development of theory of mind itself.

THREE THEORY OF MIND EFFECTS

For an aspect of development that has been under study until only recently, theory of mind has been found to encompass a diverse set of effects, perhaps as diverse as thought itself. Three types of effects have been chosen here to reflect that diversity. The effects can basically be classified by their application to other people, to children themselves, and to objects in the world. In the first category—the children's understanding of the beliefs and intentions of other people—the main findings discussed are drawn from the false belief task. Theory of mind has also been found to be relevant to children's understanding of their own beliefs and intentions. In this second category, illustrations are taken from research on children's identification of the sources of their own beliefs and their understanding of how those beliefs change. Finally, the application of this type of thought to objects is shown through studies on the appearance–reality distinction mentioned earlier.

False belief

Wimmer and Perner's group has been responsible for devising the two basic versions of the false belief task. The specific story told in the first version (Wimmer & Perner, 1983) has a character called Maxi returning home after a shopping trip with his mother. Maxi and his mother put some chocolate they have bought in one cupboard. When Maxi is out, his mother takes down the chocolate and returns it to a different cupboard. These events are acted out for the children in the study using small props. The question posed is where Maxi will look for the chocolate when he returns home hungry from playing. In other words, the children are asked where Maxi *believes* the chocolate is even though they know it has been moved to a new location. Three-year-olds, of course, are found to be unlikely to ascribe false belief, so they say Maxi will search where the chocolate actually is.

A number of control questions have been added to the task to determine if young children's difficulty with it is indeed due to false belief. In the Wimmer and Perner experiment, 3-year-olds were able to answer reality and memory questions that were given at the end. For the reality question, the children were able to say where the chocolate really was when Maxi came home. They were also able to say where Maxi had originally put the chocolate in response to a memory question. Perner, Leekam & Wimmer (1987) found children could successfully answer a second set of memory questions that asked if Maxi was present when the chocolate was moved and if he saw where it was put the second time. Thus, there is good evidence that children younger than 4 years of age do not understand that Maxi will have a false belief about the location of the chocolate in spite of their knowing where the chocolate is at the end of the story, where Maxi originally put it, and that Maxi does not see it being moved.

Wimmer and Perner's second version of their false belief task (Hogrefe, Wimmer & Perner, 1986) is even simpler than the first. A pair of children are shown an easily identifiable box; for example, a box of dominoes. After one child has been asked to leave the room, the contents of the box are changed. A glove is substituted for the dominoes. The child who has observed the switch is then asked a belief question about the child who is not in the room. What will your friend say is in the box when he or she comes back? Three-year-olds perform as badly on this version of the false belief task as on the original. Given the choice between dominoes and the glove, they state that the other child will say that there is a glove in the box.

The two versions of the false belief task can be seen as two parts of the same act. Notice that the children in the studies are being asked to understand another person's intentional action. In the hiding situations in these studies, the action is to gain access to a cupboard or box to retrieve an object. The other person's action can be broken down into a means and a goal. Either of the two can be made inappropriate after the change in the situation. So the two versions of the task could be labeled false belief (means) and false belief (goal). In first version of the task, Maxi has the wrong means for retrieving the chocolate because it has been moved to a new place. In the second version, the other child's goal—what they expect to find by opening the domino box—is wrong because the contents have been switched. The false belief tasks indicate that young children do not realize that another's beliefs about what means will work or what outcome will be produced can be out of step with the world. Instead of ascribing false belief, they tend to credit the other person with the correct means or goal.

Later research has extended Wimmer and Perner's results. Moses & Flavell (1990) engineered an even more convincing demonstration of the false belief (goal) version of the task. They showed children videotapes of real people acting out a script where the contents of a container were changed. Some of the tapes provided even more information than was given in the original task. In one condition, the actor went so far as to begin to look in the container. In another, the actor searched in the container, and then expressed great surprise that the contents were different. The experimenter furnished a running commentary on what the actor was looking for, where the actor was looking, and when the actor was surprised. The tapes were then shown a second time. At the point where the actor came back to look for the object, the usual belief question was posed. Giving the children information about the actor's action and surprise made some difference, but at least two-thirds of the 3-year-olds still said that the uninformed actor would expect the new object to be in the container.

There have been several investigations of ways the false belief effect can be reduced. Lewis & Osborne (1990) have found that variations in the belief question make a partial difference in 3-year-olds' performance. Flavell et al., (1990) have shown that 3-year-olds are somewhat more able to appreciate that someone else's "value beliefs" may be different—that they like a foul-smelling liquid—than their "fact beliefs"—that they mistakenly think that an empty milk carton is full. Finally, Wellman & Bartsch (1988) have discovered that the false belief effect can be lessened if the apparent conflict between the character's beliefs and reality is reduced. So, in the false belief (means) task where there are two hiding locations, if the story does not make it clear which location the desired object is in or if there is an identical object in each location, young children are more likely to understand that the character will search according to his or her own belief of where the object is. The results from these tasks do not negate those of the standard false belief tasks but they may give clues to how the child eventually comes to understand false belief.

Own beliefs

Just as the theory of mind refers to children's understanding of other people's intentions and beliefs, it also applies to their understanding of their own intentions and beliefs. Of course, children should not have to infer their own intentions and beliefs as they must other people's. It is possible, however, to ask whether they understand aspects of their own mental states in the same way adults do. For example, beliefs are formed on the basis of information. In the simplest case, the information is perceptual. Given children specific perceptual information—say, by allowing them to look at the contents of a box—makes it possible to ask them about their subsequent knowledge or belief. Once they have seen the contents, can they now say that they know what is in the box? Assume they were told what was in the box rather than seeing it. Are they able to identify the source of their knowledge? (The source is important because it ought to influence how strongly something should be believed.) And, finally, what if new information becomes available, do they recognize that beliefs change?

Wimmer, Hogrefe & Perner (1988) tested children's understanding of the relation between informational access and knowledge. They allowed the child to look at the contents of a box when a peer did not, or allowed the peer to look and not the child. Three-year-olds in this situation were able to report accurately whether they knew the contents of the box. On the other hand, the results seem to indicate that they could not make the same judgment of the other child. They were unable to report accurately when the other child knew what was in the box even though they saw when the other child had perceptual access to the contents of the box (see also Ruffman & Olson, 1989). Two studies (Pillow, 1989; Pratt & Bryant, 1990) have questioned this latter conclusion. Simplifying the test question in this type of study appears to show that in addition to being able to say what they know, 3-year-olds take into account perceptual access to judge what someone else knows.

Young children may be able to say what they know but they are not as aware of the sources of their knowledge. Wimmer, Hogrefe & Perner (1988) reported that before 4 years children are unable to explain how they know something. Gopnik & Graf (1988) investigated this issue directly by having children look in two boxes to see their contents, telling them the contents of another two, and having them infer the contents of two more from simple clues. Immediately after these experiences, 3-year-olds were found to be significantly worse than 4 and 5-year-olds in identifying the source of their beliefs about the contents of the boxes. When the youngest children were able to identify the source, their memory for it deteriorated just in the course of the experimental session. Memories of the 5-year-olds, on the other hand, seemed to be better for the sources of their beliefs regarding the contents of the boxes than it was for the actual contents themselves.

There is further evidence that young children do not remember that beliefs change. Gopnik & Astington (1988) adapted a variant of the false belief (goal) task (Hogrefe, Wimmer & Perner, 1986) to explore representational change. As in the usual false belief (goal) task, the children were shown a very familiar box—e.g. a box of candies. This time, however, the contents of the box had already been switched, so when they opened it expecting to find candies, they found a pencil instead. The change in procedure made it possible to ask about the children's own beliefs. After they knew the contents, they were asked about first seeing the box. Did they think there was a pencil or candy in it? Three-year-olds said that when they first saw the box they thought it contained a pencil. There response was even more remarkable in comparison to their performance on a control task. In the control task they were shown a house that had one toy in it, that toy was removed, and a new one put in. Three-year-olds could subsequently say which toy had been in the house when they first saw it. Thus, young children appear to realize when the contents of something change but they do not realize when the contents of their beliefs change (see also Moses & Flavell, 1990).

Appearance–reality distinction

Drawing a distinction between appearance and reality telescopes theory of mind effects even further. Like representational change, the phenomenon applies to individuals; unlike it, the issue is not the change in beliefs over time. To draw an appearance–reality distinction, the child must simultaneously realize that something can seem one way but in reality be another. There are a variety of different possible contrasts that call on this broad distinction (see further Woolley & Wellman, 1990). The one that has been found to produce results comparable to the other theory of mind effects is illusion versus reality or the child's reaction to genuinely deceptive objects.

Young children can be shown a sponge that has been painted to look exactly like a rock. After they have examined the object, they are asked what it really is and what it seems to be. Or, they can view a glass of milk that has been placed behind a green plastic filter. They are asked what color the object is and what color it appears to be. Flavell, Flavell & Green (1983) have labeled these tasks, respectively, *identity* and *property* appearance–reality discrimination. Children younger than 4 years tend to fail these tasks by giving consistent answers to both parts of the test question. They will make intellectual realism mistakes by stating that the sponge really is a sponge and also looks like one. Or, they will make phenomenism mistakes by claiming that the milk looks green and really is green. In fact, it has been found that young children tend to make realism errors with the identity version of the task and phenomenism errors with the property version (Flavell, Flavell & Green, 1983; Taylor & Flavell, 1984). In either case, it is clear that they are failing to appreciate that something can appear one way and really be another.

The authenticity of the appearance–reality results have been probed more deeply than any other theory of mind task. Flavell, Green & Flavell (1986) established that 3-year-olds fail appearance–reality tasks even though they can solve a memory pretest that showed them a glass of milk being covered by a colored filter and asked them what color the milk would be when the filter was removed. This same series of studies also attempted to make the tasks easier through changes in the displays and in the language used to pose the test questions. For example, familiar objects like sunglasses were used as the color filter and it was emphasized that the appearance and reality were "different" questions. None of these changes convincingly removed the effect. The effect has also proven highly resistant to short-term training (Flavell, Green & Flavell, 1986; Taylor & Hort, 1990). Showing the child what color something is, then hiding it behind different colored filters, describing all the time what color it is and what color it appears to be, does not improve 3-year-olds' success on appearance–reality tasks. Even having young children pay attention to what color something is beneath a filter as a part of a meaningful game does not allow them to grasp the appearance–reality distinction.

Appearance–reality effects are not limited to visual perception; however, the type of task does seem to affect when children can provide a solution. Flavell, Green, & Flavell (1989) tested children's understanding of appearance versus reality when they were presented with tactile problems. For example, children were asked to touch an ice cube while wearing a heavy glove. They had to say that the ice cube did not feel cold but that it really was cold. Three-year-olds drew the appearance–reality distinction for the tactile tasks before they could do so for visual ones. In contrast, Harris et al., (1986) discovered that discriminating between real and apparent emotion is a later development. They told children stories in which the main character had cause to feel one way but wanted to disguise that feeling. So, in one of their stories, the character had a stomach ache but tried to act as if she were feeling well so she could visit a friend. It was not until 4 years that children began to be able to say what the character's real and apparent emotions were.

In spite of some variation in the onset of the appearance–reality distinction for different types of judgments, the relationship of these tasks to others is stable. Flavell (Flavell, Green & Flavell, 1986, 1989) discovered a relationship between appearance–reality and perspective-taking tasks based on his distinction between levels 1 and 2 of perspective taking (Flavell et al., 1981). In Level 1 perspective taking, the child can determine whether someone is experiencing something or not; for example, whether they can see it or are touching it. Level 2 perspective taking requires the child to be able to specify the contents of the other's experience, what they are seeing or feeling. For both the visual and tactile modalities, Flavell has shown that drawing the appearance–reality distinction and solving level 2 perspective-taking problems are correlated. Furthermore, two studies (Gopnik & Astington, 1988; Moore, Pure & Furrow, 1990) have now shown that children's performance on appearance–reality, representational change and false belief tasks all correlate with age controlled.

Summary

The preceding overview does not touch on all theory of mind effects or even exhaust the ones that have been extensively studied. Substantial literatures have accrued on theory of mind's role in referential communication and deception. The overview does illustrate the range of theory of mind effects and points to the features they have in common. Each requires that the child maintain conflicting representations (Wimmer & Perner, 1983). In the false belief tasks, the child must represent where the target object is or what it is, and at the same time maintain the understanding that the character in the situation will have a different idea of its location or identity. Representational change requires children to remember that they thought something was one way before and think it is another way now. In appearance versus reality, they must be able to think about what something seems like and what it actually is. Even the level 2 perspective-taking tasks ask children to specify what they are currently perceiving compared to someone else's perceptions. The similar developmental pattern and the correlations among the tasks back the conclusion that they should be grouped together.

PSYCHOPATHOLOGY

One of the more remarkable discoveries about a theory of mind is that it may be linked to a distinct childhood psychopathology. Baron-Cohen, Leslie & Frith (1985) have initiated the collection of a variety of evidence indicating that a specific developmental delay in theory of mind is involved in childhood autism. Of course, if borne out, this possibility represents a major advance in the understanding and potential treatment of autism. At the same time, it makes what is otherwise known about autism relevant in a new way to normal development, especially in regards to theory of mind.

The evidence for theory of mind being a stumbling block in autism is impressive. The large majority of autistic children fail both the means (Baron-Cohen, Leslie & Frith, 1985; but see also Prior, Dahlstrom & Squires, 1990) and goal (Perner, et al., 1989) versions of the false belief task. They do so whether the task is carried out with story characters or live actors (Leslie & Frith, 1988), and fail even though they pass the standard memory control questions. Perhaps more important, the accumulated results strongly support the difficulty being specific. Autistic children do not solve the false belief tasks in spite of having verbal mental ages several years beyond the 4-year mark. Children from various comparison groups—Down's syndrome, specific language impairment, normal preschool—with similar or lower mental ages are successful on the tasks. The pattern of results is persuasive that autistic children's difficulty with theory of mind is not primarily a function of mental retardation or language limitations.

Baron-Cohen, Leslie & Frith (1985, 1986) and Baron-Cohen (1988) interpret their results as showing that the major impairment in autism is specific and cognitive. They argue that autistic children suffer a severe developmental delay in being able to form metarepresentations. Leslie (1987, 1988) has defined metarepresentation, and explicated its necessary role in theory of mind and symbolic pretend play. Metarepresentation, very roughly, is being able to adopt a propositional attitude toward a primary representation of the world or, in other words, form embedded representations on the order of "I believe X" or "I pretend X". Of course, if autistic children have difficulty with metarepresentation, then their developmental disorder should include deficits in theory of mind and pretend play, as it seems to. Baron-Cohen, Leslie and Frith have systematically gathered evidence indicating that metarepresentation is crucial to the three defining features of autism: impairments in social understanding (Baron-Cohen, Leslie & Frith, 1986), communication (Baron-Cohen, 1989a), and imagination (Baron-Cohen, 1987).

The metarepresentational explanation has been challenged for giving an overly cognitive and not sufficiently affective account of autism (Hobson, 1990; Mundy & Sigman, 1989). The issue at present is being contested, as it should be, through research and debate on how well metarepresentation and the competing affective explanations account for the facts of autism (see the above, and Simon-Cohen, 1988; Leslie & Frith, 1990). The other side of the question has not been given as much attention. Research on theory of mind in autism began before the recent convergence of findings on theory of mind effects. If a cognitive deficit is responsible for the autistic child's difficulty with theory of mind, indeed if a cognitive change underlies theory of mind itself, then autistic children should exhibit consistent delays across the theory of mind tasks. It has been found in a related area of development that autistic children are competent at level 1 perspective taking (Hobson, 1984; Baron-Cohen, 1989b) but not level 2 (Dawson & Fernald, 1987). They have also been found to fail the appearance–reality task (Baron-Cohen, 1989a). Autistic children's difficulty with this task adds particular support to the cognitive account because it is not obvious why affective understanding should lead to a change in the perception of objects.

The other major criticisms of Baron-Cohen, Leslie and Frith's theory of autism can be subsumed under the claim that it is not sufficiently developmental (Mundy & Sigman, 1989). This shortcoming can probably be traced to the researchers' initial concentration on the false belief task. Baron-Cohen (1989c) has begun to recast the theory in developmental terms, especially for the later periods. He has made the argument that theory of mind in autism is the result of a specific developmental delay by showing that the small percentage of autistic children who succeed on the false belief task nonetheless are stymied by the later steps in theory-of-mind development. The one exception to this general picture is the recent finding that autistic children, unlike the typical three-year-old, perform well on the Zaitchik photo task (Leekam & Perner, 1991; Leslie & Thaiss, 1992) described earlier. This finding suggests that either the Zaitchik task is an ambiguous measure of metarepresentation or that the metarepresentational deficit in autism is partially different from the one overcome in normal development (cf. Baron-Cohen, 1992).

DEVELOPMENT OF THEORY OF MIND

How children typically acquire a theory of mind stands to be one of the more interesting research topics in this field in the years to come. It is perplexing how it might be possible for the child to acquire such a theory. Having a theory of mind, of course, requires that children recognize the mental states of others and of themselves. Yet, other people's mental states cannot be directly observed and our own mental states can only be directly experienced. This problem gives credence to the choice of "theory of mind" as a label for these developments because the problem children are being asked to solve is that of discerning that other people have minds and that they themselves have them.

It may be possible to begin considering this question by breaking it down into two others. The first asks *why* a theory of mind develops. In other words, what are the causes of the development of a theory of mind? This question may be slightly premature, but several suggestions have been advanced for possible causes of theory of mind. The other question, which seems slightly more tractable, is to ask *what* develops in theory of mind. What do children acquire when they acquire a theory of mind? An answer to this question would specify the contents and precursors of the child's theory of mind. Such an answer would help explain how it is possible for the child to acquire a theory of mind because it would indicate just what it is children have to acquire. Do they truly have to intuit the unobservable mental states of others or are there other clues they can follow into the mental world?

CAUSES

Two broad classes of causes have thus far been proposed for the development of theory of mind. One suggested cause is the enormous social benefits a theory of mind affords the child (Moore & Frye, 1990). Being cognizant of the intentions and beliefs of others allows the child to understand what others are doing, to influence their actions, and to conduct social exchanges with them. If children carry any impetus for making sense of the behavior of others, then they will confront problems that they will need a theory of mind to solve. An example already at hand is the false belief (means) task. Children will not be able to make sense of Maxi's searching in the wrong place until they understand that Maxi's behaviour is not a fluke, but follows from Maxi's belief about the toy's location. On a more natural level, children will not be able to make sense of lying or deception in general until they realize that the other person is intentionally making a statement that is at variance with the truth. The social utility approach would argue that children are impelled to construct a theory of mind precisely because their naive predictions for the behaviour of others fail.

Bretherton (1990) has identified another cause. She argues that theory of mind emerges first from communication and later from language. Several pieces of evidence support her suggestion. Children use words ("I thirsty", "You sad, mommy") at the end of the second year that are normally interpreted as making reference to inner states (Bretherton, McNew & Beeghly-Smith, 1981). Dunn (1990) has discovered that young children of families who talk more about feelings, behaviour, and intentions are more likely to participate in conversations about inner psychological states. Hay (Hay, Stimson & Castle, 1990) has preliminary evidence that mothers who make reference to their own thoughts and understanding in the context of an interaction with their 2-year-old child have children who are more likely to state their desires (what they "want"). Individual differences in early talk about the social world within the family are associated with earlier success on theory of mind tasks (Dunn et al., 1991). These findings give a positive indication that communication and language may alert very young children that there are inner states people talk about. The use of particular words in context may help children isolate specific inner states so that they can learn how those states affect what people do (e.g. Maxi searched there because he *thought* that was where the toy was).

PRECURSORS

The contents of children's first theories of mind are not obvious. We do not know what terms they think in when they try to solve theory of mind problems. The line of thought pursued in this chapter is that the means and goals of human action are the primitives in children's early theories of mind. A means-and-goals explanation for the contents of early reasoning about mental life has the advantage that it has natural application to several of the core theory of mind tasks. Means and goals also retain a close connection to action, or what people do, so they furnish a more plausible account of how children are able to become aware of the importance of mental states.

The false belief tasks lend themselves to an interpretation in means–goals terms. In fact, means and goals are necessary for understanding these stories, much less solving them. In the Maxi or false belief (means) task, children must first understand that Maxi has the goal of finding the chocolate, and will search as a means of satisfying that goal. Solving the task requires that the child realize that the means Maxi has will no longer be effective with the change in the chocolate's location. Similarly, to understand the story in the false belief (goal) task, where a glove is substituted for the usual contents of a dominoes box, the child at a minimum must accept that one opens a container in order to get at its contents; in other words, as a means to a goal. The solution of the task then depends on the child understanding that a naive person's goal in opening the box will be formed by the box's markings rather than by its undisclosed contents.

Long before children begin to solve theory of mind tasks, means and goals may provide the pathway needed to other's mental states. Children need to recognize the means and goals in other people's actions. Means and goals make it possible to look beyond the other's current behavior (Premack & Woodruff, 1978). For example, if we see someone jumping up and down on a platform with an arm outstretched towards a suspended object, we can either interpret the behavior simply as someone jumping or as someone jumping to try to reach the object. Adults automatically place an intentional interpretation on the behavior. When children begin to make the same type of interpretation, they are realizing that the jumping is really a means to the goal of reaching the object. But ascribing a goal to the person goes beyond the behaviour given. It is crediting the other person with something else besides their physical movements. In other words, it is the first step towards understanding that there is a mental component to people's actions.

Because the means–goals explanation assumes that the child begins to infer mental characteristics by examining the behavior of other people, the child is granted a starting point that depends on observation. The child is not being asked to intuit another's mental state pure and simple, or do so without the aid of evidence. The means–goals explanation has the further advantage that it fits with what must be the important features of the child's life. Children are inherently tied to other people. It has to be of great benefit when they become able to understand, predict, and influence what other people are doing, especially their caregivers. Therefore, it would make sense to speculate that the child's first understanding of the mental comes from ordinary experiences with other people.

Adopting a means–goals explanation does not solve the problem of how the child acquires a theory of mind; however, it does make it possible to search for developmental precursors. If means and goals form the contents of children's first theories of mind, then it becomes important to determine exactly how they isolate means and goals in the behavior of others. It is possible to answer this problem in a variety of ways. An approach worth exploring is that children must have means and goals in their own actions in order to recognize them in others. Thus, when the child is able to search intentionally for something, they should gain the chance of interpreting someone else's search as being directed towards a goal as well. More generally, when children can employ a particular means to a goal, it then becomes possible for them to interpret that behavior when shown by someone else as evidence that the other is using it as a means to a goal. According to the means–goals explanation, then, the precursors of a theory of mind are that the child must be able to act intentionally and come to discover means and goals in the actions of others.

Infant intention

There is evidence that the ability to act intentionally develops over the course of infancy (Frye, 1990; but see also Lewis, 1990, for an opposing view). An act is intentional if it is done in relation to some future state of affairs and if what is being done is directed to bringing about that future state of affairs (Anscombe, 1957). This definition has several critical advantages. It does not state that an act must be successful to be intentional. As long as what is being done is directed to bringing about another specific outcome, it is not crucial whether or not the outcome is achieved. We can try to do something intentionally and fail. The definition excludes coincidences and fortuitous successes from being intentional. Having something desirable come about that had nothing to do with our current actions may be beneficial to us but it does not mean we brought about the change intentionally. Reflexes and conditioning are also excluded. The act must be directed towards achieving a specific, known outcome. It cannot simply be elicited by some environmental event or be emitted because it produces some generally positive result.

The two parts of the definition can essentially be identified as goals and means. When both are present, an act is intentional. It is possible to search for goals and means in infant behaviour. Frye (1990) presented 8-, 16-, and 24-month-old infants with a variety of gimmicked versions of the support task, where babies must pull a cloth to bring a toy resting on it into reach. A *changed consequence* manipulation was imposed to test for goals. After the baby pulled the toy into reach three times, when the cloth was pulled the fourth time, the gimmicked apparatus made the toy move away from the child. If the infants were surprised by this event, it showed that they had some expectation for the specific outcome of pulling the cloth. Expectation of an outcome is not sufficient for intention. What the baby is doing must be directed towards bringing about the outcome. To test for means, a *mismatch of means and goal* manipulation was instituted. Here the apparatus was gimmicked so that pulling a cloth 12 inches off to the side of the toy nonetheless brought the toy into reach. If the infants were surprised by this outcome, it showed that they knew specifically which of their actions should bring about the outcome, simply getting the toy was not enough.

The study found clear evidence for means and goals in the actions of the 16- and 24-month-olds. They were surprised by both manipulations. The 8-month-olds were only surprised by the changed-consequence manipulation, so the results did not strongly indicate that their behaviour was intentional. The intention-testing manipulations obviously need to be tried in other contexts. It is always possible that if they were presented as a part of other tasks, then 8-month-olds or even younger babies would show signs of acting intentionally. Related results in the experiment did signal that the 16- and 24-month-olds differed in their facility for acting intentionally. As a whole, these initial findings confirm there are changes in the development of intention in infancy, and that the presence of means and goals in the infant's actions is well established in the second year of life.

Recognition of means and goals

There may be evidence for means and goals in the infant's actions in the second year, but is the infant able to detect the means and goals in the actions of others? Children show numerous signs of being aware of others' means and goals before the end of infancy. Initially their understanding may be tied to action, yet it extends to almost every social situation where the infant coordinates actions with another. To pick one example from many (see Frye, 1981, 1989, 1990), after the first year, babies are able to indicate to another person by pointing that they want an out of reach object. They are also able to give an object to another if the other makes the same sort of indication (Bates, 1979). The first of these exchanges represents the infant employing the other person as a means to a goal. The second, however, reveals that the infant recognizes the goal of the other's action. If infants at this age only saw the other's behavior, and did not see what the other was intending or trying to do, then presumably they would be no more likely to hand the object over in this situation as in any other. The understanding that is granted by this new accomplishment opens the social world to the child. The baby now has a chance of knowing what other people are doing, and consequently can understand, help, and hinder others.

Gaining the ability to recognize means and goals in the actions of others probably occurs in just the sorts of simple interactions between infant and caregiver described above. Actions are likely to play an important mediating role. When babies discover that they can point and then be handed a toy, they have the information necessary to recognize that someone else's pointing can be directed towards something as well. Because both gestures can be seen, the infant is able to connect the two. Of course, the infant will need to formulate a new reply to the request. To satisfy the other's goal they must actually pass the toy over. It is possible that infants also learn this part of the exchange by analogy with the instances when they point and are handed toys by other people. Alternatively, they may simply devise the means that satisfies the situation. Piaget's (1952) observations show that infants in the second year become increasingly able to experiment with different means and discover new ones when the occasion requires. In any case, by the end of infancy, babies are sufficiently accomplished that they are able to coordinate their means with another child's in order to pursue shared goals as can be illustrated by the simple 2-year-olds' game of taking turns placing blocks to build a tower (Mueller & Vandell, 1979).

The beginnings of means–goals reasoning

Very soon after the end of infancy, children show definite signs that they are able to reason explicitly about the means and goals of others. Three-year-olds demonstrate that they are aware of other's means and goals not just by adjusting their own actions in relation to others, but by being able to state what the means and goals of others are as disclosed by their actions. Their reasoning about means and goals at this point is still limited. If given a means, they can designate a goal; given a goal, they can provide a means; and given both, they can specify what the actor's satisfaction is likely to be with the outcome of the act. Even within these limits, the early means–goals accomplishments make it possible for the child to begin to decipher what others' actions are all about.

Experiments of Wellman and his co-workers have effectively explored the means–goals reasoning of young preschool children. All of the experiments present very simple stories to children that then serve as the basis for questions about the actions of characters in the story. The simplest stories in Bartsch & Wellman (1989) were of the form, "Here's Jane. Jane is looking for her kitten under the piano." The children were then asked, "Why do you think Jane is doing that?" The majority of the 3-year-olds made reference to psychological states in answering the question. They often said that Jane "wants her cat" or "thinks the cat is under the piano". Although Bartsch and Wellman do not adopt exactly the same terminology, their results are straightforward evidence that 3-year-olds pursue means–goals reasoning. When Jane's action is described, the 3-year-olds construe it as a means, and are on their own able to supply the goal the means is most likely directed towards.

Studies by Wellman & Woolley (1990) and Wellman & Bartsch (1988) illustrate that young children are able to conduct means–goals reasoning in the opposite direction—from goal to means—as well. One of Wellman and Woolley's stories embodies the most economical version of this task. Preschoolers were told a story about a person who wanted some bananas. The story also revealed that there were bananas in two specific locations. All the child had to do was to consider the character's goal and the state of the described world in order to identify the means for the character to fulfill the goal. Children who had just turned 3 years old were able to succeed on this task. In two related tasks in Wellman and Bartsch, the child was not told where the bananas had been hidden. Here it was found that children half a year older were also able to specify correctly which of the two locations the character would search in on the basis of where the *character* thought the bananas were. The children were successful on another version when they were first asked where they thought the bananas were hidden and then the story was told with the character thinking that the bananas were in the other location. So, at $3\frac{1}{2}$ years, children can designate another's means to a stated goal even when the means does not agree with the one the child would have initially formulated.

The preceding examples establish that children can identify simple goals from another's apparent means, as well as provide plausible means for another's stated goals, all before 4 years of age. Several studies (Hadwin & Perner, 1991; Wellman & Woolley, 1990; Yuill, 1984) have further shown that, if both the means and goal of the other are furnished, preschoolers can judge in advance what the other's emotional reaction will be to the different outcomes the action may have. Wellman and Woolley told children stories about a character who wanted a specific object, searched in one of two locations for it, and either found nothing, the object, or another attractive object. Children who were approaching 3 years of age were able to say that character would be happy only when the object was found and would be sad in the two other situations. They were also able to say that the character would stop searching in the "found" condition and continue to search in the other two.

THE CHANGE IN THEORY OF MIND AT 4 YEARS

Four years has been acclaimed as the turning point in the development of the child's theory of mind. It is not until this time that children can understand false belief in others, recognize changes in their own beliefs, and reconcile the difference between the appearance and reality of particular objects in the world. Different explanations have been proposed for the change at 4 years. Perner (1990) and Flavell (1988) have argued that the change is a real one. Their theories stipulate that the child does not have an understanding of belief before 4 years. At 4 years they acquire one. Wellman (Wellman & Woolley, 1990) has adopted more of a gradualist's position. He contends that in spite of their poor performance on the false belief task there is evidence that children have an understanding of belief as early as 3 years. He has refined this point by suggesting that there might be an earlier period at 2 years when children only understand others' desires (what they want) and not their beliefs.

If it is true that means–goals reasoning serves as the precursor to theory of mind, then it should provide an indication of the cognitive change that underlies the new development at 4 years. According to the means–goals explanation, it is a mistake to partition the child's understanding at 3 years into beliefs. The recent research shows that more than anything else children are beginning to pursue means–goals reasoning in the period after infancy.

They try to make sense of others' behavior by searching for the means and goals in what others are doing. It follows, then, that their understanding of others' actions is likely to be cast in these very same terms of means and goals.

The means–goals account provides a different look at 3-year-olds' performance on theory of mind tasks testing belief. It argues that children fail the false belief tasks precisely because they are trying to make sense of (i.e. make sensible) the behavior of the character in the story. In the false belief (means) task, for instance, the children know Maxi's goal of retrieving the chocolate, they also know the location of the chocolate, so they ascribe the suitable means that Maxi will search where the chocolate is. Children employ this same type of means–goals reasoning to make sense of what they observe others do in real life. However, if they apply it to the false belief task, then Maxi's action will only be explicable if he searches where the chocolate really is.

Other results support the position that children's means–goals reasoning is restricted at 3 years. In the Wellman stories (Wellman & Bartsch, 1988) where identical goal objects are placed in both locations, 3-year-olds provide the means of searching in one location or the other, and if they told the character has some preference (where Maxi "thinks" it is), they will give a means that fits the situation and the preference, saying that Maxi will search where he thinks the object is. In this case the children are not following a strategy of reality assessment, they are trying to select a means from the available information. When no information about the location of the object is given but the character's preference is stated (Bartsch & Wellman, 1989), then the only reasonable means for fulfilling the goal is to have the character search where he thinks the object is. This answer does not ascribe false belief but, again, just solves the means–goals problem posed. Finally, it is known that young children tend to overgeneralize means–goals reasoning in other ways. For example, they tend to apply it to reflexes when older children do not (Shultz, Wells & Sarda, 1980).

It has been proposed that 3-year-olds can reason forwards from means to goals and backwards from goals to means. To solve false belief tasks, children need to be able to represent both means and goals, and recognize that the representations are independent of what actually exists in the world. It is interesting in this regard to note the similarities between the tasks that were used to test for intention in the infant's actions and the false belief tasks that test for the child's understanding of intention in others. Basically the false belief tasks have children predict the outcome of someone else being exposed to the intention tasks. The false belief (goal) task, for instance, has the child reason about someone else experiencing a changed consequence manipulation. The child must say what another person will expect to find inside a characteristic container even though the child knows that the contents of the container have been changed. (Hadwin & Perner (1991) have made the logic of the two tasks even more similar by also asking if the child can predict that the other person will be surprised by the unexpected change in the outcome of opening the container.) The parallels between the tasks illustrate that the understanding demanded by the false belief task is extensive. The child must not only determine the means and goals of the other, but also judge how those means and goals will interact with the current state of the world. As we have seen, children do not appear to be able to cope with all of these different considerations until they are about 4 years old.

What is it that prevents children younger than 4 years from solving the false belief tasks? They do seem to be able to recognize and reason individually about means and goals, so it is possible that their difficulty comes in following a level of reasoning that will allow them to draw conclusions from the two. In the false belief tasks, the children must use both the story character's goal and means to infer what the character will do. This same level of inference is not required in the Wellman means–goals reasoning tasks. They only ask for the means that produces a particular goal or the goal that commonly goes with a given means. This analysis hints that the cognitive capability 3-year-olds lack, but 4-year-olds have, may be the ability to form inferences that cover means, goals and situations. If this hypothesis is true, then the form of these inferences might be related to the cognitive change underlying all of the theory of mind effects.

There is independent evidence that there is a change in children's powers of inference between 3 and 4 years. The evidence comes from a domain that presumably has little to do with mental states. Das Gupta & Bryant (1989) investigated causal inference by testing children's understanding of causal sequences. They presented preschoolers with pictures of an apple and then a cut apple. Three-year-olds were very good at choosing the instrument from several alternatives (knife from water, knife, writing implement) that could have caused the change in the apple. They were not as good when the task was made slightly more complicated. When 3-year-olds were given pictures of a broken cup and then a wet broken cup, they tended to choose a hammer as the instrument, rather than water. Four-year-olds had no difficulty with either version of the task. Das Gupta and Bryant interpreted the results as showing 3-year-olds are able to identify a cause for a given result. However, when they have to make an inference based on both the initial and final state in a sequence or, in other words, consider what changed from the broken cup to the wet broken cup and choose an instrument for that, their performance was much worse.

In their paper, Das Gupta and Bryant noted that young children's inability to make genuine causal inferences may underlie their difficulty with appearance versus reality. Generalizing Das Gupta and Bryant's suggestion from causal inference to inference itself provides a possible explanation for all of the 3–4-year theory of mind effects. For example, in the false belief (means) task, 3-year-olds can work from the real location of the object to supply a means by which the character can find the object. In contrast, 4-year-olds can consider the character's means and goal in order to infer where the character will really search. In the representational change task, 4-year-olds seem to be able to conclude that they thought the contents of the container was one thing before, they think it is something else now, so their thoughts must have changed. In appearance versus reality, as Das Gupta and Bryant argue, when 4-year-olds see an object one way and then see it another way under a colored filter, they can infer that the filter is responsible for the color change, and that the object does not actually change color.

SUMMARY AND CONCLUSIONS

In the present examination of theory of mind development, it has been suggested that means and goals are the precursors to children's early theories of mind. They offer a possible solution to the problem of how the child is able to assign others' mental states. With the infant's own development of intention, the child becomes able to identify similar means and goals in the actions of others. During the period immediately after infancy, 3-year-olds can not only show recognition of others' intentions through action, but they can begin to reason about means and goals explicitly. They are able to state the means that lead to known goals and goals that commonly follow from known means. A cognitive change in the child's ability to reason inferentially has been proposed as the explanation for the change in theory of mind at 4 years. Such a change would be sufficiently basic to account for the related developmental effects seen in reasoning about false belief, representational change, and appearance versus reality.

Obviously, a broad array of studies will be necessary to begin to test this theory. One preliminary criterion it must meet is to fit what is known about autism. The theory of mind interpretation of autism has been criticized for not throwing light on the course of development prior to false belief (Leslie & Happe, 1989). It is possible that autistic children's characteristic development in this early period can be explained by a delay in the means–goals reasoning outlined previously, especially since the deficits that have been discovered are in intentional pointing (Mundy & Sigman, 1989) and judging characters' reactions to outcomes of intentional acts (Harris, 1989). If the inference hypothesis is correct, it must also apply to autism. It necessitates that autistic children should have an impaired capacity for inference. Baron-Cohen, Leslie & Frith (1986) have assessed autistic children's causal reasoning on mechanical, behavioral, and mental state events. The autistic children's performance was poor only for the mental state sequences, although it is noted that on average there may have been relatively more events in these sequences (Baron-Cohen, Leslie & Frith, 1986, p. 123). A strong test of the inference hypothesis would be to give autistic children Das Gupta & Bryant's (1989) causal reasoning task because it does not refer to mental events. Should autistic children do poorly on this task, inference would be much strengthened as an explanation for the cognitive change involved in theory of mind.

REFERENCES

Anscombe, G. E. M. (1957). *Intention*, Blackwell, London.
Astington, J. (1990). Intention in the child's theory of mind. In D. Frye & C. Moore (eds), *Children's Theories of Mind: Mental States and Social Understanding*, Erlbaum, Hillsdale, NJ, pp. 157–172.
Astington, J. W., Harris, P. L. & Olson, D. R. (1988). *Developing Theories of Mind*, Cambridge University Press, New York.
Baron-Cohen, S. (1987). Autism and symbolic play. *British Journal of Developmental Psychology*, **5**, 139–148.
Baron-Cohen, S. (1988). Social and pragmatic deficits in autism: cognitive or affective? *Journal of Autism and Developmental Disorders*, **18**, 379–402.
Baron-Cohen, S. (1989a). Are autistic children "Behaviorists"? an examination of their mental–physical and appearance–reality distinctions. *Journal of Autism and Developmental Disorders*, **19**, 579–600.
Baron-Cohen, S. (1989b). Perceptual role taking and protodeclarative pointing in autism. *British Journal of Developmental Psychology*, **7**, 113–127.
Baron-Cohen, S. (1989c). The autistic child's theory of mind: A case of specific developmental delay. *Journal of Child Psychology and Psychiatry*, **30**, 285–297.
Baron-Cohen, S. (1992). On modularity and development in autism: a reply to Burack. *Journal of Child Psychology and Psychiatry*, **33**, 623–629.
Baron-Cohen, S., Leslie, A. M. & Frith, U. (1985). Does the autistic child have a "theory of mind"? *Cognition*, **21**, 37–46.
Baron-Cohen, S., Leslie, A. M. & Frith, U. (1986). Mechanical, behavioural and intentional understanding of picture stories in autistic children. *British Journal of Developmental Psychology*, **4**, 113–125.
Bartsch, K. & Wellman, H. (1989). Young children's attribution of action to beliefs and desires. *Child Development*, **60**, 946–964.
Bates, E. (1979). *The Emergence of Symbols: Cognition and Communication in Infancy*, Academic Press, New York.
Bretherton, I. (1990). Intentional communication and the development of an understanding of mind. In D. Frye & C. Moore (eds), *Children's Theories of Mind: Mental States and Social Understanding*, Erlbaum, Hillsdale, NJ, pp. 15–38.
Bretherton, I., McNew, S. & Beeghly-Smith, M. (1981). Early person knowledge as expressed in gestural and verbal communication: When do infants acquire a "theory of mind"? In M. E. Lamb & L. R. Sherrod (eds), *Infant Social Cognition*, Erlbaum, Hillsdale, NJ, pp. 333–373.
Das Gupta, P. & Bryant, P. (1989). Young children's causal inferences. *Child Development*, **60**, 1138–1146.
Dawson, G. & Fernald, M. (1987). Perspective-taking ability and its relationship to

the social behavior of autistic children. *Journal of Autism and Developmental Disorders*, **17**, 487–498.

Dunn, J. (1990). Young children's understanding of other people: evidence from observations within the family. In D. Frye & C. Moore (eds), *Children's Theories of Mind: Mental States and Social Understanding*, Erlbaum, Hillsdale, NJ, pp. 15–38.

Dunn, J., Brown, J., Slomkowski, C., Tesla, C. & Youngblade, L. (1991). Young children's understanding of other people's feelings and beliefs: individual differences and their antecedents. *Child Development*, **62**, 1352–1366.

Flavell, J. H. (1988). The development of children's knowledge about the mind: From cognitive connections to mental representations. In J. W. Astington, P. L. Harris & D. R. Olson (eds), *Developing Theories of Mind*, Cambridge University Press, New York, pp. 244–267.

Flavell, J., Everett, B., Croft, K. & Flavell, E. (1981). Young children's knowledge about visual perception: further evidence for the level 1–level 2 distinction. *Developmental Psychology*, **17**, 99–103.

Flavell, J. H., Flavell, E. R. & Green, F. L. (1983). Development of the appearance–reality distinction. *Cognitive Psychology*, **15**, 95–120.

Flavell, J., Flavell, E., Green, F. & Moses, L. (1990). Young children's understanding of fact beliefs versus value beliefs. *Child Development*, **61**, 915–928.

Flavell, J. H., Green, F. L. & Flavell, E. R. (1986). Development of knowledge about the appearance–reality distinction. *Monographs of the Society for Research in Child Development*, **51** (1), Serial No. 212.

Flavell, J., Green, F. & Flavell, E. (1989). Young children's ability to differentiate appearance–reality and level 2 perspectives in the tactile modality. *Child Development*, **60**, 201–213.

Frye, D. (1981). Developmental changes in strategies of social interaction. In M. Lamb & L. Sherrod (eds), *Infant Social Cognition*, Erlbaum, Hillsdale, NJ, pp. 315–331.

Frye, D. (1989). Social and cognitive development in infancy. *European Journal of Psychology of Education*, **4**, 129–140.

Frye, D. (1990). The development of intention in infancy. In D. Frye & C. Moore (eds), *Children's Theories of Mind: Mental States and Social Understanding*, Erlbaum, Hillsdale, NJ, pp. 15–38.

Frye, D. & Moore, C. (1990). *Children's Theories of Mind: Mental States and Social Understanding*, Erlbaum, Hillsdale, NJ.

Gopnik, A., & Astington, J. W. (1988). Children's understanding of representational change and its relation to the understanding of false belief and the appearance–reality distinction. *Child Development*, **59**, 26–37.

Gopnik, A. & Graf, P. (1988). Knowing how you know: young children's ability to identify and remember the sources of their beliefs. *Child Development*, **59**, 1366–1371.

Hadwin, J. & Perner, J. (1991). Pleased and surprised: children's cognitive theory of emotion. *British Journal of Developmental Psychology*, **9**, 215–234.

Harris, P. (1989). The autistic child's impaired conception of mental states. *Development and Psychopathology*, **1**, 191–195.

Harris, P., Donnelly, K., Guz, G. & Pitt-Watson, R. (1986). Children's understanding of the distinction between real and apparent emotion. *Child Development*, **57**, 895–909.

Hay, D., Stimson, C. & Castle, J. (1990). A meeting of minds in infancy: imitation and desire. In D. Frye & C. Moore (eds), *Children's Theories of Mind: Mental States and Social Understanding*, Erlbaum, Hillsdale, NJ, pp. 15–38.

Hobson, R. P. (1984). Early childhood autism and the question of egocentrism. *Journal of Autism and Developmental Disorders*, **14**, 85–104.

Hobson, R. P. (1990). On acquiring knowledge about people and the capacity to pretend: response to Leslie (1987). *Psychological Review*, **97**, 114–121.

Hogrefe, G.-J., Wimmer, H. & Perner, J. (1986). Ignorance versus false belief: a developmental lag in attribution of epistemic states. *Child Development*, **57**, 567–582.

Leekam, S. & Perner, J. (1991). Does the autistic child have a metarepresentational deficit? *Cognition*, **40**, 203–218.

Leslie, A. M. (1987). Pretense and representation: the origins of "theory of mind". *Psychological Review*, **94**, 412–426.

Leslie, A. M. (1988). Some implications of pretense for mechanisms underlying the child's theory of mind. In J. Astington, P. Harris & D. Olson eds, *Developing Theories of Mind*, Cambridge University Press, Cambridge, UK, pp. 19–46.

Leslie, A. M. & Frith, U. (1988). Autistic children's understanding of seeing, knowing and believing. *British Journal of Developmental Psychology*, **6**, 315–324.

Leslie, A. M. & Frith, U. (1990). Prospects for a cognitive neuropsychology of autism: Hobson's choice. *Psychological Review*, **97**, 122–131.

Leslie, A. M. & Happe, F. (1989). Autism and ostensive communication: the relevance of meta representation. *Development and Psychopathology*, **1**, 205–212.

Lewis, C. & Osborne, A. (1990). Three-year-olds' problems with false belief: conceptual deficit or linguistic artifact? *Child Development*, **61**, 1514–1519.

Leslie, A. M. & Thaiss, L. (1992). Domain specificity in conceptual development: neuropsychological evidence from autism. *Cognition*, **43**, 225–251.

Lewis, M. (1990). The development of intentionality and the role of consciousness. *Psychological Inquiry*, **1**, 231–247.

Moore, C. & Frye, D. (1990). The acquisition and utility of theories of mind. In D. Frye & C. Moore (eds), *Children's Theories of Mind: Mental States and Social Understanding*, Erlbaum, Hillsdale, NJ, pp. 15–38.

Moore, C., Pure, K. & Furrow, D. (1990). Children's understanding of the modal expression of speaker's certainty and uncertainty and its relation of the development of a representational theory of mind. *Child Development*, **61**, 722–730.

Moses, L. & Flavell, J. (1990). Inferring false beliefs from actions and reactions. *Child Development*, **61**, 929–945.

Mueller, E. & Vandell, D. (1979). Infant–infant interaction: an empirical and conceptual review. In J. Osofsky (ed.), *Handbook of Infant Development*, John Wiley, New York, pp. 591–622.

Mundy, P. & Sigman, M. (1989). The theoretical implications of joint-attention deficits in autism. *Development and Psychopathy*, **1**, 173–183.

Perner, J. (1990). On representing that: the asymmetry between belief and desire in children's theory of mind. In D. Frye & C. Moore (eds), *Children's Theories of Mind: Mental States and Social Understanding*, Erlbaum, Hillsdale, NJ, pp. 15–38.

Perner, J. (1991). Understanding the Representational Theory of Mind, MIT Press, Cambridge, Mass.

Perner, J., Frith, U., Leslie, A. M. & Leekam, S. (1989). Exploration of the autistic child's theory of mind: knowledge, belief, and communication. *Child Development*, **60**, 689–700.

Perner, J., Leekam, S. & Wimmer, H. (1987). Three-year-olds' difficulty with false belief: the case for a conceptual deficit. *British Journal of Developmental Psychology*, **5**, 125–137.

Piaget, J. (1952). *The Origins of Intelligence in Children*, International Universities Press, New York.

Pillow, B. (1989). Early understanding of perception as a source of knowledge. *Journal of Experimental Child Psychology*, **47**, 116–129.

Pratt, C. & Bryant, P. (1990). Young children understand that looking leads to knowing (so long as they are looking into a single barrel). *Child Development*, **61**, 973–982.

Premack, D. & Woodruff, G. (1978). Does the chimpanzee have a theory of mind? *The Behavioral and Brain Sciences*, **1**, 515–526.

Prior, M., Dahlstrom, B. & Squires, T. (1990). Autistic children's knowledge of thinking and feeling states in other people. *Journal of Child Psychology and Psychiatry*, **31**, 587–601.

Ruffman, T. & Olson, D. R. (1989). Children's ascriptions of knowledge to others. *Developmental Psychology*, **25**, 601–606.

Shultz, T., Wells, D. & Sarda, M. (1980). Development of the ability to distinguish intended actions from mistakes, reflexes and passive movements. *British Journal of Social and Clinical Psychology*, **19**, 301–310.

Taylor, M. & Flavell, J. (1984). Seeing and believing: children's understanding of the distinction between appearance and reality. *Child Development*, **55**, 1710–1720.

Taylor, M. & Hort, B. (1990). Can children be trained in making the distinction between appearance and reality? *Cognitive Development*, **5**, 89–99.

Wellman, H. M. (1990). *The Child's Theory of Mind*, Bradford Books/MIT Press, Cambridge, Mass.

Wellman, H. & Bartsch, K. (1988). Young children's reasoning about beliefs. *Cognition*, **30**, 239–277.

Wellman, H. & Woolley, J. (1990). From simple desires to ordinary beliefs: the early development of everyday psychology. *Cognition*, **35**, 245–275,

Wimmer, H., Hogrefe, G.-J. & Perner, J. (1988). Children's understanding of informational access as a source of knowledge. *Child Development*, **59**, 386–396.

Wimmer, H. & Perner, J. (1983). Beliefs about beliefs: representation and constraining function of wrong beliefs in young children's understanding of deception. *Cognition*, **13**, 103–108.

Woolley, J. & Wellman, H. (1990). Young children's understanding of realities, nonrealities, and appearances. *Child Development*, **61**, 946–961.

Yuill, N. (1984). Young children's coordination of motive and outcome in judgments of satisfaction and morality. *British Journal of Developmental Psychology*, **2**, 73–81.

Zaitchik, D. (1990). When representations conflict with reality: the preschooler's problem with false beliefs and "false" photographs. *Cognition*, **35**, 41–68.

Chapter 7

Inhibitory Influences in Development: The Case of Prosocial Behavior

Marlene Caplan

An underlying assumption in much of the literature on prosocial behavior is that acts of sharing, comforting, helping, and cooperating increase with age. Emerging cognitive capabilities, motoric advances, internalization of moral norms, and the affective experiences of both empathy and guilt are expected to bring about greater displays of valued social behaviors. And indeed several studies do, in fact, report increased prosocial tendencies over the course of childhood (see Bar-Tal, 1982 and Underwood & Moore, 1982 for reviews). However, there are also numerous studies whose findings do not reveal age-related linear trends in prosocial behavior, but rather complex developmental pathways not easily explained by measurement error, demand characteristics, or setting effects (Eisenberg-Berg, Hand & Hake, 1981; Gottman & Parkhurst, 1980; Midlarsky & Hannah, 1985; Severy & Davis, 1971; Staub, 1970; Yarrow & Waxler, 1976).

What, then, are we to make of the equivocal findings regarding the development and maintenance of prosocial behavior? Studies demonstrating that young children outperform their older counterparts are often dismissed on the basis of irrationality (Kagan & Madsen, 1971) or misunderstanding (Green & Schneider, 1974) on the part of younger children. As Radke-Yarrow, Zahn-Waxler & Chapman (1983; p. 487) point out, there is "considerable investment in believing that children become more civilized" in their social interactions with others as they get older. Consequently, the search for causal connections in prosocial behavior has focused on enhancements, factors that promote the development and maintenance of such behavior. Identifying precursors and causal connections becomes especially difficult when a target behavior undergoes apparent oscillation and in some instances decline, depending on other constraining and regulating causal influences in the system.

Social development, however, may not simply be a matter of learning

Precursors and Causes in Development and Psychopathology.
Edited by D. F. Hay and A. Angold © 1993 John Wiley & Son Ltd

how to interact positively with others and controlling negative impulses, as socialization processes may indicate. This chapter is designed to explore an alternative assumption, namely that prosocial behavior should not by necessity increase as children grow older. Certain causal influences may be operative that constrain, rather than enhance, prosocial inclinations. Rather than ask research questions pertaining only to variables that promote prosocial responding, as most studies do, we might also benefit from systematic inquiry into variables that inhibit such behavior. In the real world, a variety of constraints may dampen children's tendencies to engage in prosocial acts. It will be argued that such constraints emanate from a constellation of internal, contextual, and social-system influences, and may, in fact, be serving important adaptive functions in children's development.

It should be noted at the outset, however, that different types of developmental pathways undoubtedly exist for different children, resulting in various degrees of affective sensitivity, cognitive processing, and behavioral responsiveness to others. These trajectories would appear to be a function of numerous inputs of socialization, experience, and disposition. An emphasis on age-related changes alone does not permit conclusions to be drawn about these different developmental courses. However, an exploration of variables that facilitate as well as constrain prosocial tendencies will shape our understanding of the general principles that guide prosocial reasoning and functioning, thereby increasing the predictability of behavior.

This chapter will be concerned with voluntary, presumably intentional, behaviors that are commonly viewed to benefit another person, such as sharing, comforting, helping, and cooperating (Eisenberg & Mussen, 1989; Staub, 1979). The task of establishing guiding principles to explain the development of prosocial behavior, however, is complicated by the observation that various modes of prosocial action represent somewhat separate behavioral responses, elicited by distinct behavioral cues, and regulated by different mechanisms (Radke-Yarrow, Zahn-Waxler & Chapman, 1983). As such, the developmental course of each may follow different patterns. Bearing this in mind, the present chapter examines selected causal influences as they impact on specific types of prosocial responding.

EARLY DISPLAYS OF PROSOCIAL BEHAVIOR

As a backdrop, the origins of prosocial action will be examined. There is evidence to suggest that the capacity for prosocial behavior originates very early in development. Sharing, for example, represents a characteristic feature of social interaction in the first 2 years of life. In a series of playroom studies conducted by Rheingold, Hay & West (1976), seven samples of 15- and 18-month-old children were observed in a laboratory playroom. All of the children engaged in sharing (as indexed by showing or giving an object) at least once with their mother, father, or an unfamiliar adult, and most did so several times. Sharing occurred across a variety of experimental conditions, with familiar as well as unfamiliar toys, when caretakers were and were not responsive to their actions, and on occasions when the recipient of the sharing requested or did not request the toy. Several other studies have reported similar sharing behaviors among young peers, both unfamiliar and familiar, in the course of observations (Eckerman, Whatley & Kutz, 1975; Hay, Caplan, Castle, & Stimson, 1991).

In addition to the prosocial act of sharing, very young children appear to be responsive to the distress of their companions. An early sensitivity to the distress of others is documented by the newborn's tendency to cry in tandem with other newborns (Simner, 1971) and the 6-month-old's tendency to watch and eventually become distressed when a peer cries (Hay, Nash & Pedersen, 1981). Instrumental attempts to comfort distressed companions are seen as early as the second year in the home (Dunn & Kendrick, 1985), and between peers in the laboratory (Iannotti, 1985) and play groups (Murphy, 1937). In a longitudinal study of children between the ages of 15 and 30 months (Zahn-Waxler, Radke-Yarrow & King, 1979), mothers' reports indicated that children responded by physically or verbally trying to comfort the distressed person, providing objects such as food or bandages, offering physical assistance, or locating other persons who could help. Such active attempts to intervene occurred on about one-third of the observed occasions, and were engaged in by virtually all of the children. Over the first 3 years of life, affective reactions were developmentally replaced by more focused efforts to intervene on behalf of persons in distress. Other observational studies substantiate these findings (Hoffman, 1975; Murphy, 1937).

Helping behavior also appears to have its roots in early childhood. In a laboratory environment simulating that of a typical home, Rheingold (1982) observed 18-, 24-, and 30-month-olds' participation in the everyday tasks of adults. The setting contained a range of ordinary, uncompleted household tasks, including a table to set, a bed to make, books and cards to pick up from the floor, scraps to sweep up, and laundry to fold. All of the children engaged in some form of helping, ranging from simply holding the dustpan to distributing dishes so as to set the table for a meal. Parents were assisted, on the average, by their 18-month-olds on 63%, by their 24-month-olds on 78%, and by their 30-month-olds on 89% of the tasks they performed. With age, children were more competent in carrying out the helping acts, but even the youngest group engaged in the some form of helping, however rudimentary.

Cooperative behavior also represents a characteristic feature in young children's social interaction. Dunn & Munn (1986) observed children at the ages of 18 and 24 months in the presence of their older siblings at home.

The majority of children (88%) engaged in cooperative behavior, defined as performing a complementary action directed toward the same goal as their older brother or sister. Similar findings are revealed in observations of peer interaction. Children engage in complementary and reciprocal social behaviors with agemates, involving the ability to exchange turns and roles in action toward a mutual goal. These behaviors become more sustained and more complex in form over the first few years of life (Holmberg, 1980; Eckerman, Whatley & Kutz, 1975; Howes, 1987).

Collectively, these findings suggest a remarkably early appearance of prosocial capabilities. In reviewing the literature on such early displays, Hay & Rheingold (1983) trace a systematic progression in the course of early prosocial development. In the first 6 months of life, infants demonstrate a general social and emotional responsiveness to the world, smiling when others smile and fussing or crying when others cry. Such responsiveness provides a pivotal base for all prosocial behaviors. During the second half of the first year, capabilities increase such that children participate more actively in social interactions, which include the sharing of toys and cooperative games. During the second year, children refine these skills, and their prosocial displays become increasingly coordinated. They display knowledge of caregiving skills and can assist adults with routine household tasks. Hay & Rheingold (1983) speculate that emerging motoric, cognitive, and linguistic capabilities contribute to these advances. With greater motoric capabilities and manual dexterity, young children can perform more complex helping and comforting acts. As children learn to use diverse means to accomplish certain ends, they become better equipped to comfort, cooperate with, and assist others. And with increased understanding of language, they are better able to interpret the needs and wants of their companions.

To the extent that these prosocial displays constitute precursors to later sharing, helping, and cooperation, they provide important information about the early propensities for prosocial action. Certainly, these early displays show surface similarity to later prosocial action, and would appear to serve corresponding functions in so far as they sustain positive social interaction. On the other hand, Staub (1978) has argued that such displays in infancy and toddlerhood may represent expressions by children of their desire to have someone share their own perspective, and not of their desire to benefit another. While the intentions underlying these prosocial displays cannot be assessed directly, it is apparent that very young children are sensitive to emotional signals in their environment and can engage in coordinated social behaviors that promote positive interaction with others, and sometimes benefit them, as in the case of responding to distress and helping.

As such social behaviors are displayed, they would appear to be enhanced by observational learning, verbal instruction, and encouragement by caregivers offered in the course of everyday activities. Children tend to comfort others in the same distinctive ways that they themselves receive comfort from a parent (Zahn-Waxler, Radke-Yarrow & King, 1979). An adult's request for an object, in conjunction with give-and-take play, tends to facilitate sharing (Hay & Murray, 1982). And in the course of interaction, caregivers respond positively to many of their infants' attempts at and actual prosocial behaviors (West & Rheingold, 1978). The enthusiasm displayed when engaging in such acts, as indexed by smiles and promptness, also suggests that such early prosocial behaviors, at least in very young children, may be intrinsically rewarding as well.

FACILITATORS OF PROSOCIAL BEHAVIOR

What happens to these early inclinations toward prosocial behavior? How are the positive tendencies observed in the first few years of life altered, strengthened, or tempered over the course of childhood? Advances in cognitive abilities would appear to propel prosocial tendencies to both a higher frequency and elevated level of complexity. With greater cognitive sophistication, children should be better equipped to perceive accurately the need states of others, make appropriate attributions about the cause of others' behavior, and reason in a morally based manner (Bar-Tal, 1982; Flavell et al., 1968). In addition, developmental changes in affective factors such as empathy, sympathy, and guilt would appear to be instrumental in promoting motivations for and actual prosocial behavior. Hoffman (1975), for example, has suggested that empathic capabilities are present in early life, but with decreasing egocentrism, they become more generalized to encompass a wider range of individuals.

Such expanding cognitive skills and affective sensitivities, while increasing over the course of development, however, do not appear to be sufficient to induce prosocial responding. The data substantiating the link between cognitive and affective abilities and prosocial behavior, even at the same point in time, are equivocal; and age-related changes in these abilities do not correlate highly with age-related changes in prosocial behavior (see review by Shantz, 1983). The capacity to better understand the need states of others and empathize with their plight does not appear to be sufficient to elicit active attempts to help, comfort, share, or cooperate.

Obviously, socialization influences also play a critical role in determining the prosocial behaviors of children. Numerous experimental studies have been conducted, documenting the enhancing effects of nurturance, modeling, attributional statements, reinforcement, assignment of responsibility, moral exhortations, and direct instruction on children's motivations for and actual displays of prosocial action (see reviews by Grusec, 1982; Rushton, 1982; Staub, 1979). These studies illustrate the powerful influence of social learning procedures on sharing, helping, and comforting behavior, at least in the laboratory. But to what extent do these processes operate in the real world and influence children's tendencies to behave prosocially in everyday life? The fact that sharing and helping can be increased by modeling and reinforcement is by no means sufficient to explain developmental trends, or individual variations for that matter, in children's prosocial behavior.

The contrived laboratory setting, in which most of these studies are based, is undoubtedly very different from other settings encountered by the child. In a typical modeling experiment, for example, a child observes the model's performance once, and the model is routinely a stranger to the child. In the real world, the child's models are likely to be parents or teachers or others with whom there is an established relationship, and such modeled behaviors may not be very consistent across situations and time. In addition, the recipients are often comprised of a hypothetical, abstract group of children, such as the poor, and are devoid of direct interaction with the person in need. Children's comprehension of these abstract groups and the impersonal nature of these behaviors complicates interpretation (Radke-Yarrow, Zahn-Waxler & Chapman, 1983). Parke (1976) has argued that social learning theorists need to demonstrate empirically how principles of modeling and reinforcement apply to naturalistic socialization practices. Thus, it is critical to look to naturalistic data to ascertain the particular aspects of socialization, as well as children's understanding of the social world, that serve to enhance or inhibit prosocial responding.

CONSTRAINTS ON PROSOCIAL BEHAVIOR

Several investigators have offered anecdotal information to explain children's reasons for failing to behave in a prosocial manner toward others. For example, in a study of kindergarten-age children, Staub (1971) cited fear of potential disapproval from an adult and respect for privacy rights as possible explanations for the lack of intervention on behalf of a distressed person in another room. Similarly, in a study of 3- to 7-year-olds' reactions to an adult's simulated distress, Yarrow & Waxler (1976) referred to fear of adult disapproval, respect for privacy, lack of perceived competence in handling the situation, and norms that people should "be brave as possible" as explanations for nonintervention. As evidence, these investigators reported that some children first approached the crying adult, then hurried back to their seats pretending to do something else when the experimenter returned. Other children informed the experimenter about the crying in a whisper or pointed silently. Furthermore, the decrease with age in willingness to intervene in this latter study suggests that perhaps children become more sensitive to some of these concerns as they get older.

To address this issue more systematically, Midlarsky & Hannah (1985) queried first-, fourth-, seventh-, and tenth-grade children about reasons for not intervening on behalf of a distressed peer. Younger children most often justified their behavior with explanations of lacking competence ("I'm too young to help" or "I wouldn't know how to help") whereas older children more commonly referred to sensitivity to the distressed peer's privacy and potential embarrassment. Although the interviews took place within a debriefing period for the entire group (versus individually which might have yielded more valid responding), such data provide valuable information about internalized constraints that may guide behavior. Clearly, children's lack of responding to a peer in distress does not imply a lack of sensitivity to the other's plight.

In our own work, we investigated younger children's understanding about the general rules of social conduct guiding their responses to peers' distress (Caplan & Hay, 1989). The spontaneous reactions of preschoolers to the distress of their peers were recorded in the classroom. Interviews were also conducted, with the aid of a videotaped segment depicting a classmate's distress as a stimulus material. Observational findings revealed that the children often paid attention to distressed peers, and most were capable of active intervention. Virtually all of the children intervened to alleviate a peer's distress on at least one occasion. Overall, however, a low rate of prosocial responding was observed. The interviews disclosed that the children held systematic beliefs about how to aid a distressed companion, suggesting a number of general acts of nurturance and comfort (e.g. "help him", "make him feel better", "make him happy") as well as specific forms of aid (e.g. "bring a tissue", "put a band-aid on it", "hold him", "wash it off"). However, the considerable knowledge these children possessed was only infrequently put into practice. These preschool-age children did not believe that they were supposed to help when competent adult caregivers were present. Most (92%) concluded that the teacher was supposed to tend to the upset peer, while the remaining 8% of children reported that the mother is supposed to help. None of the children believed that they themselves were supposed to aid the distressed peer.

These findings indicate that children's attention to peer distress is not automatic and that, even when they do pay attention, they are not automatically likely to try to intervene. Bystander intervention in adults is influenced by a variety of situational, motivational, and experiential factors; such factors apparently influence young bystanders as well. A general social responsibility norm does not seem to be what these children are learning. Rather, they seemed to be conforming to a more adult-like norm, namely, that not all distress is worth paying attention to or acting upon, and that designated individuals are charged with the responsibility of helping persons in distress.

One model that may be useful for conceptualizing an individual's lack of prosocial behavior in a given circumstance is provided by Peterson (1982).

She posits the existence of an internal rule that governs prosocial behavior, comprised of several rule qualifiers. The salience of any particular qualifier is influenced by a child's developmental level, personality characteristics, and situational factors. An elaborated rule for helping is as follows (Peterson, 1982, p. 202):

> I should help or give to *deserving* individuals who are in *X level of need*, and are *dependent* on me for help when I can *ascertain* and *perform* the necessary behavior and when the *cost* or *risk* to me does not exceed *Y amount* of my currently *available resources*.

This information-processing rule takes into account a number of variables that may influence the display of prosocial behavior at any given time point. Cognitive factors are important in determining who is deserving, the needs of the recipient, the level of responsibility on the part of the child, whether or not the child believes he can perform the act competently, and the relative cost to the child. Individual differences in temperament, mood state, and previous experience would also affect the way in which a particular qualifier is processed.

There is abundant experimental research evidence to indicate that each of the specified qualifiers in Peterson's model exerts some influence on prosocial behavior. Children alter their sharing and helping behavior as a function of need and deservingness perceptions (Miller & Smith, 1977). Responsibility assignment enhances children's prosocial tendencies (Maruyama, Fraser & Miller, 1982). Knowledge about the appropriate response to a situational cue, usually through modeling, tends to increase prosocial action (Staub & Sherk, 1970). Perceived cost affects prosocial responding, as evidenced by children's sharing of more nonpreferred than preferred candy with others (Zinser & Lydiatt, 1976). Finally, perceptions of one's own resources, or lack thereof, tends to be commonly cited as a reason for not responding to a peer in need (Midlarsky & Hannah, 1985).

Peterson's model of prosocial responding assumes that with increasing age, social experience, and cognitive sophistication, the information-processing rule undergoes transformation by the progressive addition of rule qualifiers. It is theorized that children's initial prosocial behavior is nondiscriminating, and later becomes quite clearly defined and unique by the inclusion of these rule qualifiers. Children's internal beliefs concerning when, where, and to whom help should be offered becomes more complex with development. As such, prosocial displays may not increase linearly, but ebb and flow according to the addition of qualifiers and the salience of them during the course of development. According to the model, the development of progressively more elaborated rules, as well as increases in competency, responsibility, and resources can lead to age-related increases in prosocial behavior. On the other hand, the addition of qualifiers might lead to *decreased* generosity or comforting behavior, because an undeserving person might be perceived as less in need of assistance, or perceptions of one's own capabilities in aiding a victim become more realistic.

Age-related trends in the acquisition and salience of these qualifiers have not been adequately researched. There is some evidence to indicate that children become more attuned to issues of deservingness and need as they get older. In a study by Staub (1970), for example, older children provided less aid than younger children when the person in distress had become injured as a result of continuing a prohibited play activity. Other studies, however, indicate that the tendency to make discriminations among potential recipients of aid decreases with age (Ladd, Lange & Stremmel, 1983; Eisenberg, 1983). It is difficult to determine, however, to what extent demand characteristics are operative in these studies. In the Ladd, Lange & Stremmel (1983) study, for example, helping was defined as compliance to an adult's request (rather than spontaneous helping behavior directed toward a peer). Such compliant prosocial acts reflect functionally different patterns of behavior than spontaneous prosocial acts (Eisenberg, Cameron & Tryon, 1984).

Moreover, the supporting evidence for the role of these and other qualifiers in children's prosocial behavior has been derived primarily from experimental evidence. To what extent do any of these qualifers guide children's prosocial behavior in everyday life? What kinds of prosocial activities do children engage in when left to their own resources? It is in the natural settings that sensitivity or insensitivity to the other's behavior and affect, as well as one's own thoughts and feelings, may combine in complex ways to elicit, maintain, or inhibit helping, comforting, sharing, and cooperating. Furthermore, if these rule qualifiers do guide behavior, when in development do children incorporate them in their cognitive repertoire? And by what mechanisms do they learn such qualifiers?

I turn now to three areas of inquiry that may prove useful in understanding the lack of prosocial responding under certain conditions, as well as the equivocal findings with regard to age-related linear increases. It is argued that the early displays of prosocial actions may become more focused and differentiated with increasing cognitive skills, affective sensitivities, and socialization experiences. The three areas selected are but a few examples of developmental influences that may be operating to temper prosocial displays. It would be beyond the scope of this paper to review all the possible contributing factors; the goal is to stimulate further inquiry into the processes potentially underlying the inhibition of prosocial responding. In this way, the normative developmental pathways for prosocial behavior may be better understood.

Balancing prosocial inclinations with self-interest

One potentially fruitful direction for understanding children's lack of prosocial responding under specified conditions pertains to the developing balance between prosocial inclinations and self-interest. On the one hand, children tend to seek out positive social interaction with others, as evidenced by offering, showing, and sharing objects (Rheingold, Hay & West, 1976). On the other hand, Dunn (1988) has suggested that, even in the first few years of life, children become increasingly concerned with their own self-interest, often pursuing their desires and needs in subtle, sophisticated ways. How do these potentially conflicting inclinations affect children's tendency to share, help, and cooperate with others, and when do such constraints begin to emerge in development?

The work of several investigators suggests that early in life, children show prosocial behavior in a generalized fashion. For example, at 6 months, they willingly share objects contacted by a peer without resorting to protest (Hay, Nash & Pedersen, 1981); at 15 months, children share with unfamiliar and familiar companions spontaneously as well as in response to requests (Rheingold, Hay & West, 1976). There is some evidence to indicate that the prosocial act of sharing declines in frequency, however, after the second year. For example, children between 29 and 36 months of age did not share with a peer who had no toys unless they were requested by their mothers to do so (Levitt et al., 1985). Observations in the preschool reveal a decline in sharing behavior between the ages of 30 and 48 months (Eisenberg-Berg, Hand & Hake, 1981). And in a longitudinal study, toddlers' games involving the giving of objects appeared to peak at 20 months of age and decline in frequency, relative to other types of games, thereafter (Eckerman, Davis & Didow, 1989).

One explanation for these findings is that, with increasing verbal skills, children replace sharing with other means of achieving and sustaining social interaction (Eckerman, Davis & Didow, 1989; Howes, 1987). An alternative explanation, however, is that with increasing age and knowledge about the social world, children come to learn that there are certain costs for sharing. For example, preschoolers are more likely to share nonpreferred as opposed to preferred food with others (Zinser & Lydiatt, 1970). Interviews also reveal that they would rather share with a friend than an unfamiliar child, and that they would be less likely to share a consumable item than a toy that they could reasonably expect to get back (Liu & Hay, 1986). Sharing may become more restricted to particular environmental conditions (when costs are low) and to specific peers based on relationship factors such as friendship. An increasing preoccupation with self-interest coupled with an equally powerful motivation to interact harmoniously with others may result in more strategic and context-specific acts of sharing.

In a study of 12- and 24-month-old children, my colleagues and I charted spontaneous sharing and sharing in response to peers' expressions of interest in toys (Hay et al., 1991). Children were observed in small groups of three under two conditions: once when toys were plentiful and once when toys were scarce. Spontaneous sharing was defined as explicitly giving an object to a peer. Expressions of interest in a peer's toy consisted of pointing to or reaching for, talking about, or asking for a toy; taking a toy that a peer had just put down or that was part of an array the peer was playing with; or touching or tugging on a toy that the peer was holding. Sharing in response to these expressions of interest was defined as releasing the toy into the peer's hands without sign of protest or objection.

In this study, spontaneous sharing of toys with peers occurred just as often in the 1-year-olds as the 2-year-olds sampled. However, the 2-year-olds were less likely to share in response to peers' expressions of interest in their possessions. This tendency was affected to some degree by the availability of toys. When toys were abundant and particular items were available in duplicate, the 2-year-olds shared as frequently as the 1-year-olds. One-year-olds, by contrast, appeared to be relatively unaffected by the nature and extent of resources present when responding to a peer's expression of interest in their possessions.

Other investigators have noted that 2-year-olds, as opposed to 1-year-olds, are more capable of sustaining coordinated, complementary interaction with peers (Eckerman, Davis & Didow, 1989; Howes, 1987). However, when one considers the content of the interaction, it is not completely evident that 2-year-olds are more prosocial than children a year younger. Rather, as Dunn (1988) has noted about family interaction, very young children become capable of pursuing their own interests in more discriminating ways. As development proceeds, sharing may become less of a conventional way to interact with others and more of a logical, informed decision.

Further support for this speculation comes from the conflicts that actually ensued over the possession of objects in our study, instances in which a child objected to a peer's expression of interest in a possessed toy (Caplan et al., 1991). Under such circumstances, prosocial means of resolving conflicts over toys (e.g. sharing the desired object with the antagonist) were more likely among 2-year-old than 1-year-old children, especially when resources were in short supply. Thus, the presence of scarce resources had a prosocial effect on the 2-year-old children, resulting in more explicit sharing of resources to resolve disputes. Sensitivity to environmental conditions, while not apparent in the frequency of conflict, was evidenced in the way 2-year-olds negotiated their way out of conflict. Thus, both forces of self-interest and prosocial tendencies appear to be at work as children decide when and when not to share with their peers.

Rules regarding possession rights also appear to guide children's sharing of resources. Even among 18-month-olds, children who enjoyed first possession are more likely to retain that possession when a peer seeks access to a toy, suggesting some shared understanding of a "prior possession rule" (Bakeman & Brownlee, 1982). There is also evidence to suggest that children's comprehension or adherence to such a rule becomes more pronounced with age. Bakeman & Brownlee (1982) found that possession episodes tended to occur less frequently among preschoolers than toddlers, and preschoolers were less likely to resist a taker who had prior possession than were toddlers. These findings indicate children's increasing attention to and comprehension of the role the partner is playing in the current interaction. According to these investigators, children acquire such a social rule to regulate interaction because of its adaptiveness in managing group conflict. They suggest that such rule acquisition is a "heavily canalized characteristic requiring only moderate encouragement from the environment"; social rules emerge spontaneously in the context of peer play, as a natural consequence of a fundamental human propensity to manage social interaction in an equitable manner.

Another rule that appears to be operating among young children pertains to reciprocity and equity rights. In their study of 2-year-olds, Levitt et al. (1985) found that sharing was related to whether or not children had been shared with by the peer. The number of toys shared, furthermore, was most likely to be equivalent or greater than the amount shared with that child. It is clear from these examples that prosocial behavior represents not a simplistic response to a stimulus cue, but a multifaceted response guided by numerous pushes and pulls as children confront a world of conflicting needs and desires and restricted number of resources. At least with regard to sharing, rules for when to act prosocially appear to emerge early in life and undergo systematic developmental change.

When charting the sharing behaviors of older children, the research method tends to shift from naturalistic observations of sharing to laboratory studies of generosity. A typical paradigm consists of children playing a bowling game, winning prizes, and having the opportunity to share their earnings with another person (usually a hypothetical needy peer). It should be noted that these lab analog conditions come closer to observational situations in which the child possesses an abundant supply of the resources. In such cases, sharing behavior generally increases with age (see review by Rushton, 1982). The cost of abdicating the resource, however, is certainly quite different under conditions of ample and scarce resource availability. While it is difficult to compare naturalistic observation of sharing behavior at younger ages to these lab analog studies of generosity at older ages, consideration of the similarities and differences in the situational tasks may help to provide more interpretable information regarding developmental pathways for prosocial behavior over the course of childhood.

PARTNER SPECIFICITY IN PROSOCIAL BEHAVIOR

The ongoing nature of the relationship between two or more individuals would also appear to be important to the prediction of prosocial behavior. Very early in life, infants smile and vocalize to any person who approaches, familiar or unfamiliar (Hay & Rheingold, 1983). However, as their power to distinguish among individuals increases, children tend to interact in different ways with familiar and unfamiliar peers. Mueller & Brenner (1977) observed the social interchange patterns between groups of 2-year-olds over a six-month period. One play group was already well acquainted at the outset of the study while the other play group was not. Relative to less-acquainted agemates, acquainted toddlers more frequently engaged in sustained social interactions and used coordinated social behaviors in their interactions.

In observations of older children, Strayer, Wareing & Rushton (1979) found that preschoolers discriminate in the selection of recipients for prosocial behavior, directing more prosocial overtures to some children than others. On the average, children directed prosocial behavior to an average of 5.4 classmates. However, when only those targets who received at least two prosocial acts during the 30 hours of observation were included (demonstrating some consistency in prosocial behavior), the average dropped to 3.4. Sociograms, based on the frequency of dyadic approaches observed, confirmed that the majority of children were found to direct most of their prosocial overtures to a specific group member. In addition, individual rates of initiated and received prosocial activity were intercorrelated.

One explanation for the increased rates of prosocial behavior with well-acquainted peers may be that children typically interact with them more often than less well-acquainted peers, thereby providing more opportunity for observers to witness the behavior in that context. However, experimental findings substantiate the tendency for young children to engage in more prosocial acts with their friends, controlling for interaction frequency. In a study of preschoolers' food sharing, Birch & Billman (1986) paired children with a friend and an acquaintance. Food was unequally distributed, with the target children receiving more of both a preferred and nonpreferred food, and the potential recipient receiving a small amount of each. Although boys did not share differentially with the two partners, girls shared more with friends than with acquaintances.

Such social specificity may be in place very early in development. Howes & Farver (1987) observed 1- and 2-year-olds' spontaneous prosocial responses to their peers' distress, as indexed by crying. Friendships between children were gathered independently through teacher assessments. Children were three times as likely to respond to the distress of a friend than to a nonfriend. The social specificity of responding held true even after controlling for base rates of interaction between friends and other classmates. According to the investigators, these differential responses in toddler-age children indicate that young children may perceive and interpret the emotional displays of a partner and accommodate their behavior according to the affective relationship between themselves and the other person.

The social specificity of prosocial behaviors noted in these studies corresponds to sociobiological theories of altruism (see Trivers, 1971), emphasizing how relationships between individuals affect the likelihood of altruistic behavior. Such altruism can include helping in time of danger, sharing food, helping the less able, sharing tools, and sharing knowledge. Trivers (1971) has outlined several conditions that contribute to greater chances of selection for reciprocal altruism: extended period of contact, low dispersal rate in geography, and interdependence. Youniss (1986) suggests that friendship constitutes a relationship that best fits these parameters, and thus provides an arena in which prosocial behaviors may be most often displayed.

There are several important implications of these differential displays of prosocial behavior toward selected individuals for tracking the development course of prosocial behavior. First, as others have pointed out (Strayer, Wareing & Rushton, 1979), social specificity calls into question the validity of experimental procedures claiming to measure children's prosocial proclivities by offering the opportunity to help, rescue, or give to a complete stranger. While demand characteristics inherent in experimental settings may produce overestimates of prosocial response tendencies, they may also result in underestimates of children's capacity for prosocial behavior. Second, assessing children's prosocial behavior under one set of conditions may lead to very different conclusions than when assessed under another set of conditions. Reviews of the literature tend to amass the various interpersonal contexts together, with the assumption that an underlying prosocial trait is being measured by each. An alternative view may be that various interpersonal contexts place constraints on prosocial behavior. It is interesting to note that several studies, often cited as evidence for increasing prosocial behavior with age, measure acts of sharing within the context of friendship (Ugurel-Semin, 1952; Wright, 1942). Children's prosocial overtures may show more consistency within rather than outside the friendship context. Third, the lack of consistency in prosocial behavior may be due, in part, to comparisons in different interpersonal settings. Sensitivity to these issues may be critical to understanding how prosocial tendencies actually translate into prosocial action in the real world.

One of the reasons why children may display more prosocial behavior toward friends is that friends typically are not reticent about requesting such behavior from one another. In Birch & Billman's (1986) study of food sharing among preschoolers, spontaneous (as opposed to requested) sharing occurred only rarely, even among friends. Friends, however, were more likely to request the food under inequitable conditions, to which their partners acquiesced. Thus, one explanation for increased sharing, and perhaps helping behavior, observed among friends may be that friend partners request the sharing of valued resources to which the other partner complies. In older children, sharing also is more common among friends than acquaintances, although other context-specific variables, such as the particular goal of the behavior, impact on the display of this behavior (Berndt, 1986).

Theories of moral development offered by Kohlberg, Piaget, and Youniss would suggest the prosocial skills acquired and demonstrated within friendship should be applied to interactions with all people as they mature. However, there is insufficient evidence to support such a hypothesis, at least in actual observations (Berndt, 1986). While such a progression appears to take place in children's reasoning abut moral dilemmas (Eisenberg & Mussen, 1989), there is no supporting research to verify that such a progression transpires in actual behavior. Friendship does not seem to be only a context in which various prosocial sensitivities and behaviors are learned and refined, but also a relationship that may be viewed as deserving of reciprocity and self-sacrifice in a way that other relationships are not.

Strayer, Wareing & Rushton (1979) argue that such discriminative processes are linked to the development of affectional systems that underlie family attachments, and have biological value. The reciprocity in young children's prosocial behavior may provide important information for the developing child that allows the formation of discriminative, but realistic, expectations concerning the probability that peers will reciprocate resources. Such learning, occurring early in development, may be necessary for the formation and stabilization of prototypic social relationships that provide natural constraints for the majority of adult altruistic behaviors. Such norms of reciprocity supply society with a cohesion necessary for stable relationships and community life (Gouldner, 1960).

In addition to friendship *per se*, there is also evidence to suggest that children are learning whom to respond to and whom not to respond to in everyday situations. Murphy (1937) reported striking individuality in the recipients of sympathetic behavior from peers. Across many months of observation, some children never received prosocial overtures when they experienced distress. Older children, unpopular children, and children without a friend were found to receive a disproportionately smaller amount of prosocial reactions from the peer group. In our study of preschoolers mentioned previously (Caplan & Hay, 1989), we examined the relationship between the frequency of distress on a child's part and the tendency of peers to react to that child. Children who became distressed most frequently received the least attention and the fewest prosocial overtures from peer bystanders. One explanation for this finding is that certain children may be acquiring a reputation of being "cry-babies", and as a result are deemed less deserving of attention than children who rarely become distressed. Similar results were obtained in a study by Zahn-Waxler, Friedman & Cummings (1983), who noted that successive presentations of infant cries resulted in a significant decrease in empathic responding.

Taken together, these findings suggest the importance of considering partner specificity in models of prosocial responding. Of particular relevance are friendship relationships and children's reputation in the peer group, which appear to entail sets of expectations that affect the likelihood of prosocial responding.

SOCIALIZATION PRACTICES AND THE DEVELOPMENT OF INTERNAL RULES

What role do socialization practices play in children's tendency to engage in prosocial acts? To what extent do socializers teach children how, when, and with whom to display prosocial behavior? In reviewing the proposed mechanisms underlying prosocial behavior, Radke-Yarrow, Zahn-Waxler & Chapman (1983, p. 494) have noted that research has often proceeded with little consideration of social, situational, and experiential contexts: "The adults and peers available to a child at various ages, the interpersonal responsibilities assigned or assumed, and the home, school, or societal settings imposed all provide predictably different developmental pressures and opportunities for prosocial behavior."

One of the premises underlying social learning theory is that people will abstract standards of appropriate conduct from the environmental contingencies to which they are exposed, taking on society's values as their own. If socialization proceeds according to plan, children will have witnessed many altruistic models, been reinforced for behaving altruistically at least intermittently, been reasoned with by nurturing adults, and received social attributions consonant with prosocial behavior. As a result, prosocial behavior should increase with age. However, in many cases, children fail to come to the aid of a person in distress or share something of a value with another person. And such behaviors do not, for the most part, become more frequent with age.

In interpreting the finding that many children do not come to the aid of someone in distress, presumably because of fear of potential punishment for leaving the room, Staub (1979, p. 90) laments: "The decline in initiative in response to another's need is presumably an unintended consequence of socialization." But can it really be characterized as such? As cognitive and metacognitive abilities become more sophisticated, children may be learning society's expectations for their behavior and the conditions under which prosocial action is required. To clarify the processes of socialization, it is essential to take a look at the practices, considered fundamental to the facilitation of prosocial behavior, that occur *outside* of the laboratory. Although sparse, some data are available to provide a preliminary picture of general socializing practices with respect to prosocial behavior in children.

In one study, mothers were trained to conduct on-the-spot recording of their 1- and 2-year-olds' reactions and their own reactions to others' distress (Zahn-Waxler, Radke-Yarrow & King, 1979). Instances in which a child merely observed the distress were recorded as well as those instances in which the child actually precipitated the distress of another. When their children witnessed the distress, mothers were most likely not to respond at all (56%). In 36% of cases, mothers reassured and supported their own children with words such as "Don't worry", or "It's okay.". In 21% of cases, mothers ministered to the distressed child themselves, thereby modeling prosocial behavior. Explanations, sometimes accompanied by statements of empathy, occurred in 12% of cases. Suggestions of a positive prosocial action to be taken by their own children occurred even less frequently (1%).

In situations whereby children precipitated the distress of another person, mothers were most likely to provide explanations (40%), often accompanied by affective statements with a moral or prohibitive message (e.g. "You made Doug cry, it's not nice to bite"). In 31% of occasions in which children precipitated another's distress, there was no caregiver reaction. Verbal prohibitions without an explanation occurred in 15% of incidents. Suggestions of a positive prosocial action to be taken by children were relatively infrequent (13%). Other maternal reactions included punishment (9%), reassurance to her own child (8%), and prosocial responding to the victim (5%). Correlational findings indicated that mothers who focused their children's attention on another's distress and modeled prosocial responding tended to have children who themselves behaved prosocially toward their own children.

These data suggest that mothers of very young children (1- and 2-year-olds) do not always use opportunities of distress to foster prosocial responses in their children. They seem to be more concerned with preventing transgressions, as indexed by the greater response tendencies on the part of parents when their child caused the distress of another. While modeling effective caregiving in many instances, mothers also convey to their children that the situation will be taken care of, as evidenced by their common use of reassurances to their own child. Only rarely do they suggest positive prosocial actions that the children themselves could take, unless their children were the ones who precipitated the distress. Given that responsibility assignment and participation in prosocial actions lead to more prosocial responding to others (Bathurst, 1933; Staub & Fotta, 1978), the intentional or unintentional ways in which parents' expectations for prosocial responding are conveyed are important to consider.

Using a similar recording method, Grusec & Dix (1986) gathered maternal reports concerning naturally occurring reactions to their 4- and 7-year-olds' prosocial overtures. Unlike the Zahn-Waxler, Radke-Yarrow & King (1979) study in which reactions to distress were recorded, mothers were asked to chart reactions to a variety of their children's prosocial displays (e.g. helping, sharing, giving, defending, comforting, concern). In only half of the incidents observed did mothers acknowledge, provide social approval, or praise the child for the act. Attributions of helpfulness, which have been found to be extremely effective in experimental studies for inducing prosocial responding, were rarely employed (less than 4% of occasions). Unlike Zahn-Waxler, Radke-Yarrow & King's (1979) study of younger children's response to distress, there was no association between level of children's prosocial behavior and reported usage of any maternal socialization practice.

Mothers' reactions to their children's *failure* to behave prosocially (by not showing concern for someone who is injured, not helping someone, and failing to share) as well as antisocial acts (disobedience, lying, stealing, physical aggression) were also charted by Grusec & Dix (1982). From their description, although not explicitly mentioned, failure to behave prosocially often occurred when children precipitated the distress of another. The most common responses to children's failure to behave prosocially were moral exhortation ("It's not your house", "You could put somebody's eye out") (31%), direct instruction or forcing the child to behave (25%), scolding ("That was selfish") (16%), and empathy training (directing the child's attention to the feelings of others) (5%). There were no responses on 11% of occasions and punishment was never employed. In responding to antisocial behavior, mothers more commonly forced children to behave more appropriately and resorted to punishment.

Given the scant data, it is difficult to provide any definitive conclusions about parental socialization practices around prosocial behavior provided in the real world. However, some preliminary conclusions can be drawn. First, mothers report sometimes using the socialization techniques that have proven effective in the laboratory, but not as frequently as might be expected. Second, more hands-on training tends to be provided in instances whereby their child has caused the distress of another or otherwise behaved in an antisocial fashion; less feedback is given in situations of observed distress or spontaneous prosocial behavior. Third, there may be differential relationships between caregivers' socialization practices and children's prosocial behavior depending on the age of the child and type of prosocial behavior. Maternal socialization practices were associated with comforting behaviors in response to distress incidents, but maternal socialization practices were unrelated to children's spontaneous displays of sharing, helping, and cooperating. Finally, one might also speculate that the socialization of prosocial behaviors takes on less significance with development. As children broaden their social world, other issues (e.g. the deterrence of transgressions and other antisocial behavior) may assume a more prominent role in socialization.

Valuable information concerning caregivers' reactions to children's prosocial displays also comes from actual observations in the preschool (Eisenberg et al., 1981). Unlike maternal records which may be subject to bias, observations of preschool teachers' responses provide objective data on the feedback actually given by caregivers. The naturally occurring prosocial behaviors (sharing, alleviating distress, helping) of 3- to 5-year-old children were charted, as well as teacher and peer reactions to these behaviors. The positive reactions of interest consisted of smiles, approval, gratitude, reciprocity, initiating or sustaining social interaction with the child. Surprisingly, on most occasions, teachers did not respond positively when a child behaved in a prosocial manner. Observations revealed that teachers never responded positively to any of the boys' prosocial behaviors and reacted positively to only 11% and 5% of the girls' spontaneous and requested prosocial overtures respectively.

Similar findings were obtained in our own observational study (Caplan & Hay, 1989). Preschoolers' reactions to the distress of their classmates, as well as teacher reactions to the event, were charted. Teachers did little to .encourage children's own prosocial responses to peer distress; there was no evidence of positive feedback from teachers when children expressed concern for a distressed peer. Adults explicitly asked children to perform sympathetically on only four occasions, and each of these instances occurred in the course of pretend play (instructing children to pretend to comfort a doll or toy animal). Reinforcement of pretend play, however, would not be expected to enhance actual prosocial responding. In a study of preschoolers, Yarrow, Scott & Waxler (1973) found that symbolic modeling of helping behavior (tending to the needs of pretend people and animals) did not facilitate actual prosocial responding.

Related to this result is the finding that children without day care experience are more likely to help and comfort another person than children with previous day care experience (Schenk & Grusec, 1987), despite no differences between groups in knowledge of appropriate helping behavior or the use of reasoning involving concern for the distressed person. A greater number of siblings is also associated with lowered level of helping among preschool-age children (Staub, 1971). Diffusion of responsibility may, in part, account for the lowered rates of responding in these studies. Given that caregivers do little actually to encourage prosocial responding to peers' distress out of the confines of pretend play, such findings should probably not be so surprising.

What are the implications of these naturally occurring socialization practices for our understanding of the development and maintenance of prosocial behavior? As Zahn-Waxler, Radke-Yarrow & King (1979) point out, the actions taken by caregivers in the face of distress may influence how children learn to discriminate the ingredients of a situation and also the best procedures for how to behave toward distressed others. If children are not being encouraged to engage in prosocial acts, what are they learning from the information, discipline practices, and models around them? One study bearing on this issue was conducted by Smetana (1981), who interviewed preschoolers about their attitudes to a variety of misdemeanors. Children believed that behaviors such as hitting, throwing water at another child, and shoving were wrong regardless of whether or not the school had a proscribed rule against them. On the other hand, refusing to share a toy, a failure to be prosocial, was not considered wrong if a school did not have a specific rule requiring it. Thus, in general, children seem to be abiding by the parameters set by socialization agents, who appear to place more emphasis on the deterrence of antisocial behavior than the fostering of prosocial acts. Smetena's (1981) study emphasizes the necessity of understanding the child both as knower of, and participant in, the social world.

Other data bearing on the issue of caregiver socialization practices around prosocial behavior come from a study by Petersen & Reaven (1984). Parents of 4-, 7-, and 12-year-olds completed a questionnaire regarding their attitudes toward their children's prosocial behavior under a variety of conditions (age and cost to their child, age and familiarity of the recipient). Interestingly, parents tended to advocate sharing on the part of their children most often when the cost was low. For example, parents were more likely to espouse their children's sharing of cookies when they had an ample supply than to espouse their children's sharing an only sweater on a cold day. Furthermore, parents were more likely to advocate their children's helping of familiar people rather than strangers, and younger as opposed to older children. Follow-up interviews indicated that parents had thoughtful, convincing rationales to support the constraints imposed on children's prosocial behavior. In the case of not helping strangers, parents indicated that strangers would be more likely physically to harm or take advantage of the child, hurt the child's feelings by refusing help, and would be less likely to reciprocate the act.

Taken together, these findings suggest that although most socializing agents probably advocate general norms of social responsibility, they may also inhibit prosocial responding in subtle ways. Modeling effective caregiving, without providing opportunities for the child to take part, may result in a definite message about who should come to the aid of a distressed peer. Lack of feedback about a child's spontaneous sharing or helping, even on an intermittent schedule, may foster less positive attitudes about engaging in such behaviors. And parental beliefs about the potential negative costs of helping and sharing may bring about greater reticence on the part of a child to engage in these acts with everyone. As a whole, developmental researchers have not studied the nature of subtle restrictions placed by parents on children's prosocial behavior.

As we think about the child actively constructing his world from the cues around him, we need to consider the variety of explicit and subtle messages about who does what, when, and how. Many societal norms dictate that as children grow older, they should show more consideration for others. At the same time, socialization experiences may be at work that dampen what could be considered as natural early impulses to show concern for others. From the work of Zahn-Waxler, Yarrow and their colleagues, it appears that caregivers play a considerable role in the development of concern for the feelings of others, in terms of providing nurturance and models for effective action in the face of distress. Subtle messages also need to be considered.

Grusec & Dix (1986) suggest that perhaps caregivers are not socializing their children in the best possible way, given the experimental findings indicating the succcess of modeling, social praise, and attributional statements in facilitating prosocial behavior. However, if we take a step back and consider the implications of inculcating in children the necessity of sharing, helping, comforting, and cooperating with every human being, regardless of relationship, need, and cost, would that really be adaptive? Notwithstanding the expense of time and energy, how reasonable would it be to expect children to engage in such acts indiscriminately? Should preschoolers really be the ones to come to the aid of a classmate in distress? Should children share toys and other resources with all children who are in their presence or who ask for them? Should children assist others with every task when they witness someone having difficulty? Should children engage in cooperative, reciprocal activities whenever the opportunity presents itself?

Perhaps socializers could go further in providing opportunities for children to practice engagement in prosocial behaviors, rather than taking care of things so efficiently themselves (Rheingold, 1982). At the same time, it may be important to consider the possibility that such socializing practices are not arbitrary, but functionally adaptive. Caregivers may be socializing their children in effective ways, teaching them when, where, how, and who should respond, as well as who should be responded to, based on numerous factors of relationship, need, and available resources. Burton (1976) has suggested that parents teach social information to their children in ways that will help children classify moral situations. It may be that the rule qualifiers inherent in Peterson's (1982) model, indicating when and when not prosocial responding is necessary, may not be arbitrary, but learned systematically from the training received.

Socialization of prosocial behavior operates at many different levels, occurring by direct interaction, environmental settings created, as well as the inculcation of societal and cultural norms on modes of thinking, norms of behavior, and conditions of life (Radke-Yarrow, Zahn-Waxler & Chapman, 1983). Such practices may serve both to enhance and dampen prosocial inclinations, depending on the particular circumstances.

IMPLICATIONS FOR NORMAL DEVELOPMENT AND PSYCHOPATHOLOGY

As the preceding discussion suggests, the search for predictable developmental pathways over the course of childhood is complicated by the lack of consistency found across situations even at the same point in time (Radke-Yarrow, Zahn-Waxler & Chapman, 1983), by various qualifiers that appear to be operative in any given setting (Peterson, 1982), and by a number of internal, contextual, and system-level variables that have yet to be fully taken into account in any model of prosocial functioning. As a result, our knowledge about what constitutes "normal" prosocial responding is limited, rendering it difficult to delineate and track adaptive and maladaptive patterns.

An additional complicating factor is that, unlike aggression (which, for the most part, is deemed socially unacceptable), the failure to engage in prosocial overtures is not construed as unacceptable from the perspective of either children or adults. The work of Grusec & Dix (1986) as well as Smetena (1981) suggests that acts of sharing, helping, and comforting represent a choice rather than a moral edict. The failure to be prosocial, furthermore, cannot be equated with antisocial behavior, although some interconnections between the two behaviors are apparent (see Cummings et al., 1986).

Notwithstanding these difficulties, there would probably be consensus among professionals that the absence of prosocial responding, under circumstances when it should be most likely to occur, represents a form of psychopathology. Zahn-Waxler (1986) points out that the failure to establish significant social bonds, to feel empathy and guilt, and to be able to refrain from hurting others are often cited as descriptors in different diagnostic categories. Importantly, one of the findings to emerge from Zahn-Waxler and her colleagues' longitudinal study of children's responses to distress was an "unemotional passive reaction" category that remained highly stable from the second year of life to age 7 (Cummings et al., 1986). Toddlers who displayed a lack of responsiveness to the distress of others, across a variety of incidents charted by their mothers, were highly likely to continue this pattern into the early school years.

On the other hand, extreme sensitivity and attention to the needs of others may not be adaptive either. Anna Freud (1936) describes a state of "altruistic surrender" in which the individual's needs are subordinated to the interests of others as a means of managing intrapsychic conflict. This subordination results ultimately in symptoms of psychopathology. Children's heightened preoccupation with others' distress, in addition, might reflect an excessive amount of empathy as in the case of children reared with a depressed parent (Zahn-Waxler et al., 1984). Such a preoccupation, to the detriment of one's own self-interest, may be indicative of maladjustment as well.

Between these two extremes, there would appear to be a wide range of prosocial functioning that would fall within a typical "normal" continuum. As this chapter has attempted to elucidate, the tendency to engage in prosocial acts is mediated by a variety of internal rules, interpersonal contexts, and system-level constraints over the course of development. The way in which children conceptualize, reason about, and reflect on their social worlds represents a critical determinant of prosocial responding. With development, cognitive capabilities bring about changes in sensitivities to and reasoning about social events (Shantz, 1983). However, such competencies may not, by necessity, result in increased prosocial behavior. Sensitivity to the other's behavior and affect, as well as one's own thoughts and feelings, may combine in complex ways to elicit, maintain, or inhibit prosocial action.

Longitudinal study of individual differences will provide essential information about the developmental course of prosocial behavior. It is important to note that, despite findings from many studies indicating that most toddlers and preschoolers engage in prosocial behaviors, there are indeed some children who fail to do so. Murphy's (1937) detailed analysis of 2- to 4-year-olds revealed that 18 of the 70 children observed failed to emit a sympathetic response in the course of observations. The manner of response also appears to be individualistic. In a study of young children, Radke-Yarrow & Zahn-Waxler (1984) found that some children imitated others' emotional expressions in a reflexive manner (crying when another child was distressed). For other children, affective arousal was not apparent; rather these children responded by continued gazing at the distressed peer while ceasing their own activity, as if deciding what was going on and what could be done to alleviate the distress. The authors speculate that cognitive and affective components may have differential prominence for different children and that such differences in thresholds may lay the foundation for later developmental differences in prosocial behavior. Such speculations require further study.

At the same time, as Cairns (1986) notes, not all of the variance is "in the child", and we need to look to the child's history of socialization, social networks, and physical environments for modifying influences. Data concerning children who show little or no prosocial responding in later childhood would be particularly informative. Did these children never show much prosocial behavior even at early ages? Or are those the children whose initial impulses were more completely inhibited? Clearly, longitudinal observations are necessary to clarify the relative contribution of disposition, affective arousal, information processing, and socializing influences on prosocial displays.

The ability to recognize an appropriate opportunity to cooperate, help, share, and comfort may also provide a useful marker for charting adaptive and maladaptive patterns. Socially competent children tend to be more cognizant of social conventions concerning where and when different responses are appropriate (Asher & Hymel, 1981). Ladd & Oden (1979) demonstrated that children of high sociometric status, relative to low-status children, were more knowledgeable about the appropriate response to situations requiring prosocial behavior. Rubin & Schneider (1973) have speculated that changes in prosocial behavior may not be due to differences in norms of social behavior, but simply to differential awareness of the environmental cues delineating when and where action is appropriate. Strayer, Wareing & Rushton, (1979), furthermore, have suggested that the ability to recognize the circumstances in which prosocial behavior is appropriate may account for many differences in children's behavior across situations.

This line of reasoning may help to explain the mixed findings concerning age-related changes in prosocial behavior and the lack of correspondence between social–cognitive skills and prosocial behavior. In the real world, individuals may seek out a model to help them define the situation and the appropriate response. In the case of responding to distress, children may learn from their adult models that not all distress is worth paying attention to, and more importantly, that certain individuals (such as competent adult caregivers) may be more capable of handling the situation. The role of social experience in children's ability to recognize when, where, and how to behave prosocially, and how to carry out such behavioral actions in a competent manner, may provide a fruitful direction to pursue in the understanding of the development of prosocial behavior.

In the case of aggression, consistency across situations predicts chronic aggressive patterns (Loeber, 1982). If the same principle were applied to prosocial behavior, one could speculate that children who consistently fail to show prosocial behaviors, even with familiar persons, even when self-interest would not be undermined, may be particularly at risk for maladjustment. I have conducted a study that provides some support for this speculation. Children's prosocial response tendencies were assessed in response to two hypothetical situations, potentially provocative of conflict. In the first situation, the partner in the scenario was a friend and in the other situation, the partner was an acquaintance (who was not disliked). As would be expected, the children arrived at more prosocial means of resolving the conflict with their friends than their acquaintances. The prosocial response tendencies in the two situations were then correlated with teacher ratings of students' competence in multiple domains. Importantly, the tendency to respond in a prosocial manner with a friend, by cooperating or compromising, was associated with higher competence ratings by teachers; the tendency to respond in a prosocial way with an acquaintance was unrelated to teacher judgments of competence.

One of the implications of this finding is that the manner in which children behave with individuals they consider important in their lives may be more predictive of maladjustment than how they behave with others more generally. Perhaps it may not be adaptive to behave prosocially with everyone, but if a child does not share, help, comfort, or cooperate with selected individuals, then that child may be at risk for psychopathology.

Given the difficulties inherent in demonstrating, at the very least, cross-situation consistency, it is not surprising that so few studies are available on the stability of prosocial behavior in childhood, and no follow-up studies trace the development of prosocial behavior into adolescence or adulthood. The few studies that are available suggest some stability of individual differences in prosocial behavior over time, at least in childhood, and when global indices are used (see Eisenberg & Mussen, 1989). This differs quite markedly from other aspects of behavior, such as aggression (Loeber, 1982; Olweus, 1979), where numerous follow-up and follow-back studies can be drawn upon. In part, this lack of longitudinal inquiry would appear to stem from the difficulty in getting a handle on the normative development of prosocial responding across the life span, to which atypical patterns could be compared.

CONCLUSION

Actions taken on behalf of others are essential to the survival of the individual as well as the group, and presumably undergo considerable transformation throughout the life span. Tracing the developmental course and causal influences on prosocial behavior, however, has proven difficult, owing to changes in its quality and form, in the types of events eliciting its display, and in the principles underlying motivations to engage in such acts. The picture is further complicated by the apparent oscillation in prosocial responding over time, an observation that has yet to be fully acknowledged with respect to its implications for social development.

From the preceding discussion, it is clear that prosocial behavior does not develop in a simple, unidirectional trend. In the first few years of life, chidlren's affective arousal and capacity for social interaction appear to create an early propensity to engage in prosocial acts. While there are many factors both within and outside the child that enhance these early prosocial propensities, there may also be certain causal influences that constrain such inclinations. It is critical to identify the conditions and experiences that shape the generality and selectivity of children's prosocial behavior under certain circumstances and over time. Social development may not be simply a matter of learning to interact positively with others, as socialization processes may indicate. An understanding of the developmental course of prosocial behavior needs to take into account enhancements as well as constraints with respect to affective arousal and regulation, cognitive and motivational components, and the circumstances in which prosocial action occurs.

Consideration of the ways in which prosocial behavior may become more focused and differentiated over the course of development may help to provide a framework for charting developmental pathways. Throughout development, children are learning about how to balance concerns for others with concerns for themselves, about appropriate contexts for prosocial behavior, and about mutual obligations and expectations in relationships. Socialization influences operate at multiple levels, influencing children by direct interactions, providing opportunities for prosocial action, as well as the inculcation of societal norms on modes of thinking and behaving. Such learning may result in increases or declines in prosocial behavior over the course of development, and longitudinal study will be necessary to trace and clarify the guiding principles underlying development, individual differences in pathways, as well as the role of disposition, affective arousal, cognitive processing, and socialization factors in the development of prosocial behavior. The failure to engage in a prosocial act under certain circumstances, however, should not automatically be construed as a deficit, but perhaps as an adaptive response, often sanctioned by nurturing, responsible caregivers, to the way in which the world operates.

REFERENCES

Asher, S. R. & Hymel, S. (1981). Children's social competence in peer relations. Sociometric and behavioral assessment. In J. D. Wine & M. D. Smye (eds), *Social Competence*, Guilford Press, New York, pp. 122–157.

Bakeman, R. & Brownlee, J. (1982). Social rules governing object conflicts in toddlers and preschoolers. In K. Rubin & H. Ross (eds), *Peer Relationships and Social Skills in Childhood*, Springer-Verlag, New York, pp. 99–111.

Bar-Tal, D. (1982). Sequential development of helping behavior: a cognitive-learning approach. *Developmental Review*, 2, 101–124.

Bathurst, J. E. (1933). A study of sympathy and resistance (negativism) among children. *Psychological Bulletin*, **30**, 625–626.

Berndt, T. J. (ed.) (1986). Sharing between friends. In *Process and Outcome in Peer Relationships*, Academic Press, New York, pp. 105–127.

Birch, L. L. & Billman, J. (1986). Preschool children's food sharing with friends and acquaintances. *Child Development*, **57**, 387–395.

Burton, R. V. (1976). Honesty and dishonesty. In T. Lickona (ed.), *Moral Development and Behavior: Theory, Research, and Social Issues*, Holt, Rinehart, & Winston, New York.

Cairns, R. B. (1986). A contemporary perspective on social development. In P. S. Strain, M. J. Guralnick & H. M. Walker (eds), *Children's Social Behavior: Development, Assessment, and Modification*, Academic Press, New York, pp. 331–372.

Caplan, M., Bennetto, L. & Weissberg, R. P. (in press). The role of interpersonal context in the assessment of social problem-solving skills. *Journal of Applied Developmental Psychology*.

Caplan, M. & Hay, D. F. (1989). Preschoolers' responses to peers' distress and beliefs about bystander intervention. *Journal of Child Psychology and Psychiatry*, **30**, 231–242.

Caplan, M., Vespo, J. E., Pedersen, J. & Hay, D. F. (1991). Conflict over resources in small groups of one- and two-year-olds *Child Development*, **62**, 1513–1524.

Cummings, E. M., Hollenbeck, B., Iannotti, R., Radke-Yarrow, M. & Zahn-Waxler, C. (1986). Early organization of altruism and aggression: developmental patterns and individual differences. In C. Zahn-Waxler, E. M. Cummings & R. Iannotti (eds), *Altruism and Aggression*, Cambridge University Press, Cambridge, pp. 165–188.

Dunn, J. (1988). *The Beginnings of Social Understanding*, Harvard University Press, Cambridge, Mass.

Dunn, J. & Kendrick, D. (1985). *Siblings: Love, Envy, and Understanding*, Harvard University Press, Cambridge, Mass.

Dunn, J. & Munn, P. (1986). Siblings and the development of prosocial behavior. *International Journal of Behavioral Development*, **9**, 265–284.

Eckerman, D. O., Davis, C. C. & Didow, S. M. (1989). Toddlers' emerging ways of achieving social coordinations with a peer. *Child Development*, **60**, 440–453.

Eckerman, C. O., Whatley, J. L. & Kutz, S. L. (1975). Growth of social play with peers during the second year of life. *Developmental Psychology*, **11**, 42–49.

Eisenberg, N. (1983). Children's differentiations among potential recipients of aid. *Child Development*, **3**, 594–602.

Eisenberg, N., Cameron, E. & Tryon, K. (1984). Prosocial behavior in the preschool years: methodological and conceptual issues. In E. Staub, D. Bar-Tal, J. Karylowski & J. Reykowski (eds), *Development and Maintenance of Prosocial Behavior*, Plenum Press, New York, pp. 101–115.

Eisenberg, N., Cameron, E., Tryon, K. & Dodez, R. (1981). Socialization of prosocial behavior in the preschool classroom. *Developmental Psychology*, **17**, 723–729.

Eisenberg, N. & Mussen, P. H. (1989). *The Roots of Prosocial Behavior in Children*, Cambridge University Press, Cambridge.

Eisenberg-Berg, N., Hand, M. & Hake, R. (1981). The relationship of preschool children's habitual use of space to prosocial, antisocial, and social behaviors. *Journal of Genetic Psychology*, **138**, 111–121.

Flavell, J. H., Botkin, P., Fry, C., Wright, J. & Jarvis, P. (1968). *The Development of Role-taking and Communication Skills in Children*, John Wiley, New York.

Freud, A. (1936). *The Ego and the Mechanisms of Defense,* International Universities Press, New York, rev. ed. 1966.

Gottman, J. M. & Parkhurst, J. T. (1980). A developmental theory of friendship and acquaintanceship processes. In A. Collins (ed.), *Minnesota Symposia on Child Psychology*, vol. 13, Erlbaum, Hillsdale, NJ.

Gouldner, A. J. (1960). The norm of reciprocity: a preliminary statement. *American Sociological Review*, **25**, 161–178.

Green, F. P. & Schneider, F. W. (1974). Age differences in the behavior of boys on three measures of altruism. *Child Development*, **45**, 248–251.

Grusec, J. E. (1982). The socialization of altruism. In N. Eisenberg (ed.), *The Development of Prosocial Behavior*, Academic Press, New York, pp. 65–90.

Grusec, J. E. & Dix, T. (1982). The socialization of prosocial behavior: theory and reality. In C. Zahn-Waxler, E. M. Cummings & R. Iannotti (eds), *Altruism and Aggression*, Cambridge University Press, Cambridge, pp. 218–237.

Hay, D. F., Caplan, M., Castle, J. & Stimson, C. A. (1991). Does sharing become increasingly "rational" in the second year of life?, *Developmental Psychology*, **27**, 987–993.

Hay, D. F. & Murray, P. (1982). Giving and requesting: social facilitation of infants' offers to adults. *Infant Behavior and Development*, **5**, 301–310.

Hay, D. F., Nash, A. & Pedersen, J. (1981). Responses of six-month-olds to the distress of their peers. *Child Development*, **52**, 1071–1075.

Hay, D. F. & Rheingold, H. L. (1983). The early appearance of some valued social behaviors. In D. Bridgeman (ed.), *The Nature of Prosocial Development: Interdisciplinary Theories and Strategies*, Academic Press, New York, pp. 73–94.

Hoffman, M. L. (1975). Developmental synthesis of affect and cognition and its implications for altruistic motivation. *Developmental Psychology*, **11**, 607–622.

Holmberg, M. C. (1980). The development of social interchange patterns from 12 to 42 months. *Child Development*, **51**, 448–456.

Howes, C. (1987). Social competence with peers in young children: developmental sequences. *Developmental Review*, **7**, 252–282.

Howes, C. & Farver, J. (1987). Toddlers' responses to the distress of their peers. *Journal of Applied Developmental Psychology*, **8**, 441–452.

Iannotti, R. J. (1985). Naturalistic and structured assessments of prosocial behavior in preschool children: the influence of empathy and perspective taking. *Developmental Psychology*, **21**, 46–55.

Kagan, S. & Madsen, M. C. (1971). Cooperation and competition of Mexican, Mexican–American, and Anglo-American children of two ages under four instructional sets. *Developmental Psychology*, **5**, 32–39.

Ladd, G. W., Lange, G. & Stremmel, A. (1983). Personal and situational influences on children's helping behavior: factors that mediate compliant helping. *Child Development*, **54**, 488–501.

Ladd, G. W. & Oden, S. (1979). The relationship between peer acceptance and children's ideas about helpfulness. *Child Development*, **50**, 402–408.

Levitt, M. J., Weber, R. A., Clark, M. C. & McDonnell, P. (1985). Reciprocity of exchange in toddler sharing behavior. *Developmental Psychology*, **21**, 122–123.

Loeber, R. (1982). The stability of antisocial and delinquent child behavior: a review. *Child Development*, **53**, 1431–1446.

Liu, Y. C. & Hay, D. F. (1986). Young children's knowledge of the cost of sharing. Paper presented at the American Psychological Association, Washington, DC.

Maruyama, G., Fraser, S. C. & Miller, N. (1982). Personal responsibility and altruism in children. *Journal of Personality and Social Psychology*, **42**, 659–664.

Midlarsky, E. & Hannah, M. E. (1985). Competence, reticence, and helping by children and adolescents. *Developmental Psychology*, **21**, 534–541.

Miller, D. T. & Smith, J. (1977). The effect of own deservingness and deservingness of others on children's helping behavior. *Child Development*, **48**, 617–620.

Mueller, E. & Brenner, J. (1977). The origins of social skills and interaction among playgroup toddlers. *Child Development*, **48**, 854–861.

Murphy, L. (1937). *Social Behavior and Child Personality*, Columbia University Press, New York.

Olweus, D. (1979). Stability and aggressive reaction patterns in males: a review. *Psychology Bulletin*, **86**, 852–875.

Parke, R. D. (1976). Social cues, social control, and ecological validity. *Merrill-Palmer Quarterly*, **22**, 111–123.

Peterson, L. (1982). Altruism and the development of internal control: an integrative model. *Merrill-Palmer Quarterly*, **28**, 197–222.

Peterson, L. & Reaven, N. (1984). Limitations imposed by parents on children's altruism. *Merrill-Palmer Quarterly*, **30**, 269–286.

Radke-Yarrow, M. & Zahn-Waxler, C. (1984). Roots, motives, and patterns in children's prosocial behavior. In E. Staub, D. Bar-Tal, J. Karylowski & J. Reykowski (eds), *The Development and Maintenance of Prosocial Behavior: International Perspectives on Positive Morality*, Plenum Press, New York, pp. 81–99.

Radke-Yarrow, M., Zahn-Waxler, C. & Chapman, M. (1983). Prosocial dispositions and behavior. In P. Mussen (ed.), *Manual of Child Psychology*, vol. 4. E. M. Hetherington (ed.), *Socialization, Personality, and Social Development*, John Wiley, New York, pp. 469–545.

Rheingold, H. L. (1982). Little children's participation in the world of adults, a nascent prosocial behavior. *Child Development*, **53**, 114–125.

Rheingold, H. L., Hay, D. F. & West, M. (1976). Sharing in the second year of life. *Child Development*, **47**, 1148–1158.

Rushton, J. P. (1982). Social learning theory and the development of prosocial behavior. In N. Eisenberg (ed.), *The Development of Prosocial Behavior*, Academic Press, New York, pp. 77–105.

Schenk, V. M. & Grusec, J. E. (1987). A comparison of prosocial behavior of children with and without day care experience. *Merrill-Palmer Quarterly*, **33**, 231–240.

Severy, L. J. & Davis, K. E. (1971). Helping behavior among normal and retarded children. *Child Development*, **42**, 1017–1031.

Shantz, C. V. (1983). Social cognition. In P. H. Mussen (ed.), *Handbook of Child Psychology: Cognitive Development*, vol. 3, John Wiley, New York, pp. 495–555.

Simner, M. L. (1971). Newborn's response to the cry of another infant. *Developmental Psychology*, **5**, 136–150.

Smetena, J. G. (1981). Preschool children's conception of moral and social rules. *Child Development*, **52**, 1333–1336.

Staub, E. (1970). A child in distress: the influence of age and number of witnesses on children's attempts to help. *Journal of Personality and Social Psychology*, **14**, 130–140.

Staub, E. (1971). A child in distress: the influence of nurturance and modeling children's attempts to help. *Developmental Psychology*, **5**, 124–132.

Staub, E. (1978). *Positive Social Behavior and Morality*, vol. 1, *Social and Personal Influences*. Academic Press, New York.

Staub, E. (1979). *Positive Social Behavior and Morality: Socialization and Development*, vol. 2, Academic Press, New York.

Staub, E. & Fotta, M. (1978). *Participation in Prosocial Behavior and Positive Induction as a Means of Children Learning to be Helpful*. Unpublished Manuscript, University of Massachusetts, Amherst, Mass.

Staub, E. & Sherk, L. (1970). Need for approval, children's sharing behavior, and reciprocity in sharing. *Child Development*, **41**, 243–252.

Strayer, F. F., Wareing, S. L. & Rushton, J. P. (1979). Social constraints on naturally occurring altruism. *Ethology and Sociobiology*, **1**, 1–11.

Trivers, R. L. (1971). The evolution of reciprocal altruism. *Quarterly Review of Biology*, **46**, 35–57.

Ugurel-Semin, R. (1952). Moral behavior and moral judgment of children. *Journal of Abnormal and Social Psychology*, **47**, 463–474.

Underwood, B. & Moore, B. S. (1982). The generality of altruism in children. In N. Eisenberg (ed.), *The Development of Prosocial Behavior*, Academic Press, New York, pp. 25–52.

West, M. J. & Rheingold, H. L. (1978). Infant stimulation of maternal instruction. *Infant Behavior and Development*, **1**, 205–215.

Wright, D. (1942). Altruism in children and the perceived conduct of others. *Journal of Abnormal and Social Psychology*, **37**, 218–233.

Yarrow, M. R., Scott, P. M. & Waxler, C. Z. (1973). Learning concern for others. *Developmental Psychology*, **8**, 240–260.

Yarrow, M. R. & Waxler, C. Z. (1976). Dimensions and correlates of prosocial behavior in young children. *Child Development*, **47**, 118–125.

Youniss, J. (1986). Development in reciprocity through friendship. In. C. Zahn-Waxler, E. M. Cummings & R. Iannotti (eds), *Altruism and Aggression*, Cambridge University Press, Cambridge, pp. 88–106.

Zahn-Waxler, C. (1986). Conclusions: lessons from the past and a look to the future. In C. Zahn-Waxler, E. M. Cummings & R. Iannotti (eds), *Altruism and Aggression*, Cambridge University Press, Cambridge, pp. 303–324.

Zahn-Waxler, C., Cummings, E. M., McKnew, D. & Radke-Yarrow, M. (1984). Altruism, aggression, and social interactions in young children with a manic-depressive parent. *Child Development*, **55**, 112–122.

Zahn-Waxler, C., Friedman, S. & Cummings, E. M. (1983). Children's emotions and behaviors in response to infant cries. *Child Development*, **54**, 1522–1528.

Zahn-Waxler, C., Radke-Yarrow, M. & King, R. A. (1979). Child-rearing and children's prosocial initiations toward victims of distress. *Child Development*, **50**, 319–330.

Zinser, O. & Lydiatt, E. W. (1976). Mode of recipient definition, affluence of the recipient, and sharing behavior in preschool children. *Journal of Genetic Psychology*, **129**, 261–266.

Chapter 8

Relationships in Infancy as Precursors and Causes of Later Relationships and Psychopathology

Alison Nash and Dale F. Hay

OBJECTIVES

Countless stories, myths, and proverbs point to events in infancy as the determining forces in life. In the common wisdom, children are fathers to men; as twigs are bent, so grow the trees. Within this general tradition, particular power is accorded to the relationship between an infant and its mother. Belief in the impact of the relationship between mother and child is summed up in Freud's (1938, p. 188) often quoted words, describing that relationship as "unique, without parallel . . . the prototype of all future love relations". By linking manifestations of neurosis in adulthood to early deficiencies or distortions in that first, prototypical relationship, Freud's writings characterized experiences with one's mother as a primary cause of, as well as precursor to, later relationships and psychopathology.

Freud's thesis was translated into empirically testable claims by John Bowlby (1958, 1969, 1982) and Mary Ainsworth (Ainsworth & Wittig, 1969). Bowlby's and Ainsworth's writings led to the first decade of attachment research, which empirically investigated the Freudian hypothesis by searching for correlations between the quality of the infant's relationship with the mother and various measures of subsequent functioning (for a review, see Waters, Hay & Richters, 1986). Success in identifying such associations has led to the pre-eminent position attachment theory holds in contemporary developmental theory.

In formulating his theory, Bowlby (1958, p. 350) was at pains to note that he was not restricting his argument to the case of the biological mother: "Although in this paper I shall usually refer to mothers and not mother-figures, it is to be understood that in every case I am concerned with the person who mothers the child and to whom he becomes attached rather

Precursors and Causes in Development and Psychopathology.
Edited by D. F. Hay and A. Angold © 1993 John Wiley & Son Ltd

than to the natural mother." However, the bulk of the empirical research on correlates of early attachment relationships has happened to focus on infants' relationships with their biological mothers, and misinterpretations of Bowlby's position continue to influence clinical practice. For example, in the UK, special psychiatric hospital units exist to support severely depressed or otherwise psychiatrically ill women in caring for their infants. The women are encouraged to breast-feed if possible, even if they are being prescribed psychotropic medication. Thus this treatment policy asserts the fundamental importance of close contact with the biological mother in the first months of life, even if that consigns the infant to institutional rearing by multiple caregivers and passive exposure to potentially toxic levels of drugs.

Such policies have been adopted on the grounds that they are in keeping with Bowlby's theory of human development (R. Kumar, personal communication). However, as we have seen, Bowlby had in fact broadened his analysis to "mothering figures", and, in particular, made no special claims about the importance of breast-feeding. Thus Bowlby himself might have argued that it would be better for a baby to be cared for consistently by a nurturant father or grandmother than to reside on a hospital ward with an ill mother. (This is not of course to deny the possible therapeutic advantages the presence of the baby creates for depressed mothers.) Moreover, the bulk of scientific evidence does not confirm the importance of care by the biological mother (for a review, see Rutter, 1991). Rather, contemporary scientists see infants as part of a social network (Rheingold & Eckerman, 1975; Lewis, 1982), in which emotional attachments to several people may be formed. Investigators have found that the quality of infants' relationships with fathers (Lamb, 1977), professional caregivers (Fox, 1977; Howes et al, 1988; Sagi et al., 1985), grandmothers (Myers, Jarvis & Creasey, 1987) and siblings (Teti & Ablard, 1989) may be assessed in the same way as attachments to mothers.

What these investigators have largely done, however, is describe various sorts of early relationships and acknowledge their probable contribution to infants' subsequent development. They have not provided any theoretical basis on which to examine whether all or any of these relationships serve as precursors of later ones, and whether they have similar or distinct causal functions. There is no encompassing theoretical alternative to Freud's strong claim about the primacy of the relationship with the mother. Despite the acknowledgement of the infant's multiple relationships, reviews of the effects of early attachment on later development and psychopathology concentrate almost exclusively on mother–infant attachment (see e.g. Belsky & Nezworski, 1988). We have no conceptual framework in which to understand how different sorts of early relationships exert their effects on children's later lives. This in turn provides no clear guidelines for social policy and clinical practice, beyond the misinterpretations of Bowlby's notions discussed above.

In this chapter, we are trying to provide the needed theoretical framework by considering how multiple relationships in infancy might serve as precursors and causes of later development and psychopathology. By doing so, with respect to the general concerns of the book, we hope to illustrate some of the conceptual and methodological issues that arise when attempting to identify precursors and causes in any developmental trajectory. Of particular note is the fact that all four types of causation described by Aristotle (see Hay & Angold, Chapter 1 this volume; Hopkins & Butterworth, 1990) have been applied to the study of social relationships: material causes (the Freudian assertion that anatomy is destiny), efficient causes (deprivation of normal rearing experiences), final causes (evolutionary adaptation) and formal causes (the structure and operation of mental representations within the developing organism). In addition, causal reasoning has been invoked at three different levels of analysis: the episode of interaction, the ontogeny of the individual, and the phylogeny of the species (see Hay, 1980). It is especially important to examine whether evidence secured about one sort of causal hypothesis at one level of analysis is applied to issues that arise about other sorts of causation at other levels of analysis.

With respect to the particular case of social relationships, we are trying to provide the building blocks for a theory of human relationships that extends the insights of ethological attachment theory. In doing so, we chose to start in one of the same places that Bowlby did—with birds. In setting forth his initial theoretical statements, Bowlby (1958, 1969) synthesized three different perspectives: psychoanalytic theories of object relations, contemporary cognitive theory, and ethological studies of the evolutionary principles guiding social adaptations. Theorists in the 1980s continued to explore the first two avenues (e.g. Bretherton, 1985; Stern, 1985), but have rather neglected the third. In contrast, we shall turn for new ideas, as Bowlby did, to current evolutionary, ethological and biological theories and studies of social behaviour, in both birds and humans.

Interestingly, the recent interest in the formation of multiple early relationships in humans is paralleled by a similar trend in studies of imprinting in birds. In both the fields, investigators now view the social context of infancy as important, and are beginning to examine the formation of multiple early attachments or imprinting objects, and the combined influences of these on later development. Most importantly, human attachment theorists are talking about the importance of internal representations and "working models" as causal forces in development, but investigators who study birds are coming up with research designs showing that such models actually exist and exert causal force.

Bowlby himself was at pains to note that human infants' attachments to their mothers were not identical to young birds' relations with their imprinting objects. None the less, he was aware that some general biological principles can be applied to the formation and disruption of social attachments across many species. We agree with this assumption. Obviously, if one were to attempt a comprehensive review of comparative studies of social relationships, there would be considerable relevant evidence from studies of many different species, in particular the non-human primates. That is not, however, our objective here. We have returned for an update on the imprinting literature because we wish to generate a few testable hypotheses, based on current thinking about the simplest case of the precursor hypothesis. Different methodologies are required to test the hypothesis in different species. We believe that the possibility of experimentation on birds' rearing environments elucidates important causal principles that may apply in other species, even though they cannot be so easily studied. By reviewing recent imprinting studies in which the importance of multiple relationships is assumed, and contrasting findings there with those stemming from correlational studies and "experiments in nature" applied to human development, we shall be able to consider different rules of evidence for identifying precursors and causes in development.

In reviewing the current work on birds' relationships, we have arrived at five specific propositions which are set forth in the argument that follows:

(1)   In many social species, multiple relationships are formed in the earliest days and months of life, and these all contribute to the young organism's subsequent development;

(2)   An infant's earliest relationships are not necessarily more powerful than those that occur at a somewhat later time;

(3)   Therefore organisms' "internal representations" of conspecifics and potential mates are drawn from multiple sources;

(4)   The nature of an adult's contemporary relationships mediate and constrain the influence of earlier ones;

(5)   Interpretation of the links between early experiences and adult adjustment requires an understanding of the natural social ecology of a group or species.

We shall now examine some evidence for each of these propositions. First we demonstrate how these principles emerge from current experimental studies of avian imprinting and then we show how the same principles may be used to explain the findings from correlational studies of children's social relationships.

MULTIPLE RELATIONSHIPS AND EVOLUTION

Primary attachment or multiple relationships?

The concepts of precursor and cause are very tightly woven in theories of social relationships. In Freud's (1938) statement about the importance of the mother–infant relationship, claims about its primacy are closely linked to the hypothesis about its causal status. It is described as unique, without parallel, different from all other relationships and therefore of peculiar importance in setting the stage for later development. Additionally, it is characterized as a prototype of adult love relationships, which implies that it bears both formal resemblance and functional continuity with the later occurring relationships. This in turn implies that one must scrutinize the nature and formation of the mother–child relationship, in terms of its determinants and functions in the period of infancy itself, before examining its further development and causal force. This approach has indeed been taken by John Bowlby and his colleagues; however, somewhat different levels of analysis have been applied to the origins of attachment relationships, as opposed to their long-term consequences. In particular, Bowlby (1969, 1982) focused at length on phylogenetic factors influencing the initial development of attachments. He was especially concerned to demonstrate the biological functions of attachment behaviour (final causation, in Aristotelian terms).

Bowlby anchored his belief in the fundamental importance of the infant–mother relationship to the prevailing biological theory of behaviour of that time—ethological–evolutionary theory. When thus anchored to ethology the infant–mother relationship began to be studied empirically. Thus Bowlby, by examining the phylogeny of social attachments, opened up the way for developmental psychologists to examine their ontogeny. According to Bowlby, infants have an innate predisposition to maintain proximity with familiar caregivers (ofen though not necessarily the mother). They are able to maintain this proximity at first through signals, such as crying and smiling, which bring and/or keep an adult near by, and later through locomotion as well as signals. Although the behaviours used to effect proximity may change as the infant gets older, their goal remains the same.

Infants are assumed to get a feeling of security through proximity. This latter notion was probably introduced into the theory largely through the efforts of Bowlby's colleague, Mary Ainsworth. Ainsworth began her career under the supervision of Canadian personality theorist, William Blatz, who argued that security was a central construct in adult development and adjustment (Blatz, 1966). Ainsworth's contribution to the theory linked Bowlby's psychoanalytic and ethological perspective to the North American psychometric tradition of studying individual differences in personality.

Furthermore, by attempting to measure a particular dimension of the infant's internal world, Ainsworth reiterated the concerns of the psychoanalytic object relations theorists whose work followed from Freud's initial formulations. In Ainsworth's theory, the child's feeling of security took on its own explanatory role; the child's representation of attachment experiences became the causal link between early stimulation or deprivation and later outcomes. Thus, again in Aristotelian terms, formal causation (the structure of representations) was invoked, in addition to efficient and final causal forces (adverse early experiences and biological function, respectively).

Bowlby's phylogenetic discussion referred to a particular dimension of relationships, and not to interpersonal relationships in general. Furthermore, this dimension of relationships, i.e. attachment and the quest for security, was said to emerge primarily with one person, the infant's primary caregiver. Bowlby proposed that infants were monotropic: they could form attachments to several people, but would form a primary attachment with their mothers. His theory grew out of work with infants who had no central mothering figures in their lives. Through their absence, the importance of such central figures was revealed to him. He developed his theory in terms of supporting the notion that, for healthy functioning and later adjustment, an infant needs a central person in his or her life. His evolutionary argument thus focused on the need for central relationships rather the need for mothers in particular.

Nash (1988) recently examined Bowlby's evolutionary theory of attachments in the light of more recent advances in evolutionary theory, where accounts of the origins of social behaviour have moved from an emphasis on species survival (the "group selection" hypothesis) to a focus on individual survival (i.e. an argument that social phenomena emerge from the forces of natural selection being applied to individual organisms). Although Bowlby, in 1982, acknowledged these revisions in evolutionary thinking, by referring to individual survival, rather than species survival as he had done in his earlier statements, he did not include the newer view of the evolution of social behaviour. The individual selection view focuses on the costs and benefits of specific behaviours to each individual involved in various kinds of social relationships (e.g. Chase, 1980; Emlen & Oring, 1977; Hamilton, 1964; Orians, 1969; Maynard-Smith, 1974; Trivers, 1971, 1972, 1974). If "attachments" have evolved through natural selection, both the costs and benefits (in terms of fitness) of "attachment behaviours" to the infant, and the costs and benefits of the reciprocal care-providing behaviours to the caregivers need to be elucidated. When this form of evolutionary analysis is applied to attachment phenomena, there is no reason to assume a biological predisposition for attachments to primary caregivers, in particular. Rather, it appears to be simpler to assume that a biological preparedness may exist for relationships in general (for a fuller discussion, see Nash, 1988).

The issue becomes important because of Bowlby's recognition that biological parenthood was not necessary for attachments to form; attachments are formed between infants and their caregivers, whether related or not (Bowlby, 1982, p. 29). This feature of the theory stems at least partially from Bowlby's psychoanalytic heritage. Ainsworth (1969) has traced how developments in ego psychology and in object relations theories stem from two statements about the early mother–child relationship in Freud's writings. According to Ainsworth, in his earlier writings, Freud speculated that the bond between mother and child derived secondarily from the child's need to be nurtured—the earliest attachment then forming to the mother's breast. In later statements, the emotional relationship between mother and child was seen to be primary, and not an epiphenomenon of the child's need for sustenance. Ainsworth noted that social learning theories of dependency derived from the earlier statement, but Bowlby's ethological attachment theory derived from the latter one. Clearly, with the conceptual separation of the child from the breast, there would be decreased emphasis on the mother as a biologically related figure.

Nevertheless, this development in psychoanalytic thinking poses difficult problems for the evolutionary side of Bowlby's argument. Concepts like inclusive fitness, kin selection, and, in particular, reciprocal altruism need to be invoked to explain attachments between infants and non-related caregivers. Both kin selection and reciprocal altruism require that a sustained relationship exist between the individuals involved. It then becomes simpler to assume a biological preparedness for behaviours involved in relationship formation in general, not attachment formation in particular. The many studies of infants' early capacities to relate to others (inspired in part by Bowlby's legitimizing the study of early infant relationships) support this view (for fuller discussions see Hay, 1985; Lamb & Nash, 1989; Nash, 1988).

What, then, are the developmental implications of this shift in emphasis regarding the evolutionary basis of infants' relationships with others? If attachment between mother and infant is in fact not primary, in terms of having been specially selected for in the course of evolution, does it still serve as a precursor of, and prototype for, all future love relationships? Does it still hold unique causal force, in terms of the child's subsequent relations and adjustment? In more general terms, does evidence against a particular proposal regarding final causation undermine attachment's status as a formal cause of subsequent development? Or, alternatively, does the evolutionarily based capacity for multiple relationships begin a network of precursors and causes with respect to the variety of subsequent relationships an individual embarks upon?

Although, at the phylogenetic level of analysis, theories of behavioural biology have placed renewed emphasis on the individual rather than the group as the unit of selection, several theorists have reaffirmed the importance of social influences with respect to cultural evolution and individual development. At the ontogenetic level of analysis, there has been much recent emphasis on the greater social context in which individual development occurs (e.g. Hinde, 1983). For example, T. C. Schneirla's (see Aronson et al., 1972) notion of the fusion of genetic and environmental influences, as opposed to their interaction (a term which implies that they might somehow be sorted out) is being used to revise evolutionary analyses of behavioural development: " . . . natural selection has operated on the entire developmental manifold (the developing organism and its typical early social context) and not merely on genetic, organic, or organismic aspects of that system" (Lickliter & Gottlieb, 1988, p. 320). Gottlieb (1991) argues that a major causal force in development is what he calls environmental canalization, the flowering of species-appropriate behaviour under species-appropriate environmental conditions. Thus, discussions of final causation themselves are beginning to encompass environmental as well as genetic determinants.

In other words, the process of reproduction entails the inheritance of both the genes and the developmentally relevant aspects of a species' environment, including the social environment. West & King (1988) have coined the term "ontogenetic niche" to signify the ecological and social legacies that accompany genes, emphasizing the importance of the inherited environment. They remind us that organisms inherit not only their parents' genes, but their parents, siblings, peers, and others as well. This emphasis on the greater social context has been formalized as a higher order, "systems" approach to evolution (Oyama, 1985), which is a major theme in contemporary discussions of developmental causality (see Hay and Angold, Chapter 1, this volume). Thus, recent developments in biological theory set the stage for a re-examination of the imprinting process.

The imprinting hypothesis: filial relationships constrain possibilities for sociosexual ones

Filial and sexual imprinting

As Bowlby (1982, p. 223) himself pointed out, the "way in which attachment behaviour develops in the human infant and becomes focused on a discriminated figure is sufficiently like the way in which it develops in other mammals, and in birds, for it to be included, legitimately, under the heading of imprinting . . . ". Bowlby also noted, in his revised statement in 1982, that the imprinting process is now understood to be more flexible than when it was first proposed. It is no longer believed to be "irreversible"; under some circumstances imprinting can be reversed. But since Bowlby's treatise, recent studies have led to alternative ways of understanding the notion of "reversibility".

Viewing imprinting to a second figure as a "reversal" of the imprinting to the first figure still implies that the imprinting process is monotropic, i.e. the young bird can be imprinted to only one individual at any given time. But perhaps the young bird who acquires a second imprinting figure has not reversed an earlier preference but has simply become imprinted to two individuals.

In many species of birds, the figure to which a young bird imprints forms the basis of later recognition of suitable mating partners (Lorenz, 1935/1970). For example, Lorenz found that geese who had been imprinted to a human (Lorenz himself) would follow him rather than an adult female of their own species or another human. When mature, the male birds would court human beings in preference to members of their own species. Thus the first relationship appeared to form a prototype, for the young, of what future mates should look like. Although Bowlby (1982) believed that filial imprinting worked in a similar way in humans and birds, he specified that their sexual systems were quite distinct. We agree that studies of factors influencing sexual preferences in birds may not reveal much about the development of sexual preferences in humans. Nevertheless, we think that the sexual imprinting model is helpful in illuminating the conceptual issues involved in looking for links between early mother–child relationships and mature social and sexual relations.

Empirical studies of sexual imprinting: the importance of multiple relationships

Like Darwin, many more recent investigators have attempted to test general principles by examining one genus of birds, finches. Immelmann (1972) attempted to support the notion of "sensitive" periods in his work with zebra finches. He concluded that sexual imprinting was complete by about the twentieth day after hatching in normally raised zebra finches, and suggested that transfer of the attachment to another species (Bengalese finches are typically used as the alternative preference) should occur before day 20, if a previously established mate preference is to be altered. However, Ten Cate, Los & Schilperoord (1984) found that one-third of their sample of zebra finches transferred to Bengalese finches later than 20 days after hatching (30–60 days) reimprinted on Bengalese finches.

Why might Immelmann's birds have preferred females only of the first species to which they were exposed, during the so-called "sensitive period", whereas Ten Cate's males courted females of both the first and second species to which they were exposed? As Clayton (1987) has pointed out, the disparity in these results can be explained by differences in the procedures used in each laboratory. Three critical differences were noted. Firstly, Immelmann tested later preferences using normally raised Bengalese finch females as sexual objects. Ten Cate's group used cross-fostered Bengalese females, i.e. Bengalese finch females who themselves had been raised by zebra finch parents. This becomes important when we consider that females' responses to a courting male, as well as his image of his mother, may influence his choice of a mate. A female of one species may not be sufficiently responsive to a male of a different species. But a female raised by the second species may well be responsive. Secondly, Immelmann transferred whole clutches of zebra finches to a pair of Bengalese finches, whereas Ten Cate and his colleagues placed individual male zebra finches with a group of Bengalese finches. And, finally, Ten Cate's birds were exposed to the second species for a longer period of time than were Immelmann's.

These procedural differences may reflect different underlying assumptions about the influences of relationships other than the first relationship on later mate choice. First, Ten Cate assumed that the behavior of the females themselves may influence male mate choice. Second, Ten Cate gave his male zebra finches the opportunity to relate to many Bengalese finches, whereas Immelmann placed his with only two others, and for a shorter time period. Extended interaction with these Bengalese finches may have contributed to subsequent preferences for them.

Finally, Ten Cate considered that relationships with siblings may influence later mating behaviour. Ten Cate's birds were placed alone, without siblings, with the foster species, whereas Immelmann's birds continued to relate to their siblings (members of their own species) when they were placed as a group with the second species. Indeed, Kruijt, Ten Cate & Meeuwissen (1983) found that siblings do in fact influence later mate preferences. Zebra finches raised with conspecific siblings and Bengalese finch parents would later court either Bengalese finches or zebra finches or both. These authors concluded (p. 238) that, "in addition to parental influences, experience with siblings has an influence on the development of the sexual preferences of males".

Kruijt and his colleagues also found that sibling influence increases with the presence of more than one or two siblings. With many siblings, the offspring may interact more with one another than with the parent. It is interesting to note that in large human families, common in many cultures (see Rogoff, 1990), an infant may interact more with brothers and sisters than with his or her mother.

Sibling influences have been found for a variety of bird species besides finches, including mallard ducks (Lickliter & Gottlieb, 1985, 1988, see below; Klint, 1978), snow geese (Cooke, 1978), and Japanese quail (Bateson, 1982). Even greater sibling influences have been found for these latter species than for zebra finches. For example, Lickliter & Gottlieb (1985) compared filial imprinting in mallard ducklings raised in different social situations. All of the ducklings were given the opportunity to follow a female mallard model when they were one day old. Preferences for this female were again tested several days later, after the ducklings had been placed in different rearing conditions. No preference was found for the familiar mallard model when the ducklings were reared in isolation but allowed to see another duckling, or when they were reared in a group of ducklings but denied the opportunity for direct social interaction. In contrast, those ducklings who were able to engage in unrestricted, reciprocal interaction with siblings did show preferences for natural maternal models in choice tests. In a later experiment (Lickliter & Gottlieb, 1988), these investigators found that mallard ducklings' interaction with "foster siblings", other young ducks from other species, does not support preference for their own species. This indicates that the later preference for mallards in particular is influenced by earlier interaction with mallard siblings only.

   Lickliter & Gottlieb (1985, p. 379) concluded that, in forming attachments, "non-obvious, normally occurring experiential precursors may be more widespread than currently recognized . . .". In this case, in order to prefer a particular figure, social interaction with other members of that species was important. Lickliter and Gottlieb stress the importance of the role of the social context in understanding development. For ducklings and many other birds, the typical early environment includes both siblings and mother, and all of these companions appear to influence development.

   It is interesting to note that ducks, geese, and quail are all precocial, and thus the young are far more capable of interacting with one another from the first day of life on than are zebra finch young, who are altricial. Perhaps sibling influences are greater when siblings are more motorically and perceptually capable of direct interaction. This illustrates a general principle that holds for humans as well, namely that the impact of a given social experience may be partially determined by the receptivity of the growing organism, in terms of the stage of development of its perceptual and motor capacities.

Early experiences and somewhat later ones: primacy or joint influence?

Two different models of the impact of early relationships on later ones underlie the studies of Immelmann (1972) and Ten Cate, Los & Schilperoord (1984) described above. Immelmann assumed that, if early relationships do influence later ones, the primary source of influence is the parent–infant relationship. In examining only parental influences, he did not provide for opportunities to test for other influences. Ten Cate, on the other hand, allowed for the influences of other relationships and found them. In fact, in a subsequent experiment, Ten Cate (1986) attempted to examine whether adult social experiences affect mate preferences. Young zebra finch males were exposed first to their own species, and then later to Bengalese finches. Many of these males, as adults, courted females of both species. Ten Cate then either isolated these "dithering" males, as he called them, or placed them with members of their own species. After this manipulation, the preferences of the males given experience with conspecifics became more zebra finch oriented than for the males in isolation. Thus adult relationships influenced mate preference. However, the influence of earlier relationships still persisted, as most males still "dithered".

Ten Cate (1986) next examined whether dithering indicates a double preference, or a lack of preference. He found that dithering males, given experience with both normally coloured zebra finches and Bengalese finches, preferred females of both of these species over white zebra finches and over a related species, silverbills. Ten Cate concluded that dithering indicated parallel imprinting to both zebra and Bengalese finches.

Two hypotheses about the effects of multiple early relationships have been suggested. Immelmann & Suomi (1981) have suggested that later relationships interfere with or mask the effects of earlier ones (a process referred to previously as a temporary "reversal" of earlier established preferences). They placed cross-fostered zebra finches with conspecifics for a period ranging from 3 to 60 days, and found that, the longer their exposure to conspecifics, the greater their preferences for females of their own species. They concluded from this that exposure to the second species (in this case their own) temporarily interfered with a stable preference for the first species. In other words they were again assuming that the first relationship forms the prototype for future mate preferences. In contrast to this view, Ten Cate, Los & Schilperoord (1984) argued that secondary influences are stable, resulting from partial imprinting on the second stimulus as well.

Clayton (1987) attempted to distinguish between these two hypotheses. To do this, he exposed zebra finches to a third stimulus, and examined whether or not the third period of exposure overruled the effect of secondary exposure, a prediction based on the "interference" hypothesis. He found that zebra finch young placed first with Bengalese finches, then with zebra finches, then again with Bengalese finches later courted both finches (as did young placed first with zebra finches, then Bengalese, and then zebra finches). Both sets of relationships appeared to have stable effects on later mating choices. When exposed to the third stimulus, which had been the same as the first, the birds did not all revert back to a preference for the first stimulus, as would be predicted by the interference hypothesis.

Thus these experimental studies of sexual imprinting have indicated that the first relationship may not be the overriding influence on later relationships it was previously believed to be. Several relationships, both early and contemporary ones, may have an impact on adult courtship.

Models of the influence of multiple early relationships on later ones: the issue of internal representation

Differential attention to various individuals can thus explain why young birds' later behaviour may be influenced by various companions, not just the first individual they see or hear. But can we explain how these various influences combine to affect later behaviour? How do the influences of siblings, for example, combine with parental influences?

The simple hypothesis that the first relationship an organism has constrains all later ones is appealing because there are relatively straightforward ways of envisioning how it might work. But if there are several early influences, how are these combined? Do we simply add up the effects of each individual? Or might a relationship with one individual override other influences?

Theories of imprinting are quite advanced compared to theories of human attachment in that empirical studies have elucidated the processes whereby multiple relationships might influence later development. Interestingly, the link between early relationships and later behaviour has recently been described using very similar concepts to the notion of "internal working models" used by attachment theorists (e.g. Bretherton, 1985). Both Ten Cate (1987) and Bateson (1981) attempt to understand later behaviour in terms of internal representations of earlier relationships. They each attempt to explain precisely how more than one relationship might become incorporated in a young bird's internal representation of whom to court in adulthood.

Bateson, in his work with Japanese quail (1982), envisioned internal representations of each individual to whom young birds are exposed. He proposed that a kind of double imprinting might occur, resulting in two separate standards which are stored in the bird's recognition system. Thus he posited an additive model, in which the effects of various individuals are added together, so that the separate influences of each are retained.

Ten Cate's model, in contrast, can be viewed as synergistic rather than additive. Rather than assuming that imprinting information from two different individuals is stored separately, he suggested that it may become combined during the imprinting process. This would result in one standard only, combining characteristics of both species. Ten Cate calls this the "mixed standard" model, in contrast with Bateson's "separate standards". He devised a clever study to test between these two models. He focused on zebra finches who had become imprinted on both zebra and Bengalese finches, and who as adults had become "ditherers" with a 50–50 preference in zebra finch versus Bengalese finch choice tests. Ten Cate reasoned that if preferences were stored as suggested by the "separate standard model", that these ditherers who find finches of both species equally attractive would be less attracted to a hybrid formed from both these species. They might court hybrids, finding them somewhat attractive due to generalization from each of the separate standards, but would prefer pure zebra finches and pure Bengalese finches to hybrids. The "mixed standard" model, however, predicts a preference for hybrids, i.e. for individuals who combined characteristics from both species. This is, in fact, just what Ten Cate found; the "dithering" birds sang more often to hybrids than to pure representatives of either species.

Ten Cate used this model to explain the Japanese quail's preference to mate with cousins rather than siblings (see Bateson, 1982). Siblings resemble one another, and as they are a young quail's constant early companions, one internal representation is formed consisting of the composite appearance of all the siblings. This composite may then resemble a more distantly related individual, like a cousin, more than any one particular sibling. Such an internal representational process would, of course, promote exogamy while retaining some degree of assortative mating. It is interesting to note that, in a recent study of human courtship preferences, faces rated as the most attractive were those that were composites of a large number of real faces (Langlois & Roggman, 1990).

The mediating or constraining role of relationships in adulthood

In making predictions about the effects of early social experiences on mating choices, one must consider the influence of current relationships, at the time that mating choices are being made. The behaviour of the female being courted may affect the male's behaviour, as indicated by Ten Cate Los & Schilperoord's (1984) study described above, and males may be more responsive to females who are themselves responsive. Female influences on male courting behaviour have been found in a number of bird species. For example, West & King (1985) found that female brown-headed cowbirds were able to influence the development of male songs; the song of juvenile males housed only with females (who themselves do not sing), and who never heard males sing, was influenced by the particular subspecies of females with whom they were housed. Although in nature juvenile males will typically hear other males sing, and be influenced by these songs, West and King showed that the male's courting behaviour was affected by the responses of females as well. In addition, Ten Cate's experiments described above (1986; Ten Cate, Los, & Schilperoord, 1984) indicate that adult peer relations also influence mate choice.

The importance of the natural social ecology

The history of studies of avian imprinting draws attention to the importance of combining experimental strategies with naturalistic observation of particular species in their natural settings. Consider, for example, the case of the zebra finch. Zebra finches live in colonies. Many nests are found together and members of a colony are quite sociable with one another. Their sociability entails, for example, frequent visits to one another's nests. These neighbourly visits have been observed both in the wild (Immelmann, 1965) and in semi-natural aviary studies (A. Nash, unpublished observations). In the latter studies, in focused observations of several nests, the average number of visits by others in a two-hour period was 25. Often the same individuals repeatedly visited particular nests. This means that young zebra finches are often repeatedly exposed to individuals in addition to their parents. They hear males other than their fathers sing, and, once fledged, interact with many individuals other than their parents.

Even while still in their nests, young zebra finches may interact with individuals other than their parents and siblings. In one intensively observed nest, the female was persistently courted by a male who was not the father of the young. The father attempted somewhat to keep this male away, but the interloper eventually managed to replace the father at the nest. The father left with one of the young, and continued to feed that fledgling. The "stepfather" fed the other young at the nest until they fledged, and continued to feed them in various places in the aviary after they fledged. Thus, in a semi-natural situation, these young were exposed to two imprinting figures. Such goings on may or may not occur in the wild, but their occurrence revealed the potential of the young to imprint to two "father figures".

It is important to note that such flexibility might be quite adaptive, given the ecological conditions under which the species resides. Zebra finches normally live in semi-desert regions in Australia, where rainy periods are unpredictable. The birds come quickly into breeding condition when water is available, and must quickly go about the business of pairing and raising young while the water lasts. They continue to breed as long as there is water. All of the breeding must be done during these brief, sporadic periods of water availability (Immelmann, 1965; Serventy, 1971, 1977). Life in colonies helps adults quickly come to breeding condition physiologically, through the processes of social facilitation and synchrony. It permits many opportunities for relationships to be formed and mates secured. Thus social flexibility and multiplicity of relationships may be very helpful for zebra finches in expediting the securing of mates and raising of their young. In general, the particular models tested and experimental manipulations made in laboratory studies of the imprinting process must take into account the social ecology of the species in question.

Summary

The foregoing review of some recent studies of imprinting in birds indicates that links between early experiences and adult mating choices are flexible and multifaceted. Multiple influences are present quite early in life, and sibling relationships may be particularly important. Different relationships experienced in sequence each appear to have long-term effects, and so the concept of "reversals" of imprinting appears overly simplistic. Indeed, birds' "internal representations" of conspecifics with whom it is appropriate to mate appear to be amalgams of various earlier schemas. In addition, the behaviour of prospective mates in adulthood may mediate or constrain the effects of early socializing experiences. And, finally, the particular patterns of early and later social relations that arise may be best understood with respect to the overall ecological constraints on the species in question.

We now turn to the case of human children. To what extent do our five theoretical propositions derived from the imprinting studies of the 1980s elucidate the literature on the critical importance of early social relationships for human beings?

STUDIES OF HUMAN RELATIONSHIPS: SINGLE PRECURSORS OR CAUSAL NETWORKS?

Some remarks must be made at the outset regarding the comparison of the human studies with the literature on imprinting. First of all, the hypothesis being tested is not exactly the same. The imprinting hypothesis states baldly that young birds of a given species need experience with a particular mothering figure if they are to figure out what species they belong to and, therefore, mate appropriately with a member of that species. In contrast, with the possible exception of severe autism, species recognition abilities in human children are not generally in question, and the precursor hypothesis becomes a more qualitative one: positive experiences with a mothering figure in infancy facilitate psychological adjustment in adulthood, which presumably includes successful mating and rearing of young. Thus the task is to find a suitably non-deviant, compatible, responsible mate, not just another obvious human being.

Secondly, the literatures on imprinting in birds and socio-emotional development in humans are not easily compared. Experimental manipulations of human rearing environments are unethical and impracticable. With respect to prospective longitudinal analyses, there are only a few long-term longitudinal studies where one can actually look at the links between early experiences and mating choices. These did not use Ainsworth's "strange situation", the currently well-regarded methodology for measuring the quality of infant–mother relationships. The children assessed with the "strange situation" are yet to be studied in adulthood.

Thus, what is necessary here, is to examine each of the propositions set forth about imprinting with respect to somewhat incomplete, inadequate data on human children. Rather than examining mate choice *per se*, in most cases we shall be focusing on the capacity for social relationships in later childhood and on other measures of psychological adjustment and its opposite, forms of psychopathology.

Infants' multiple relationships and their long-term influences

Much correlational evidence has accumulated regarding links between the quality of early mother–infant relationships and later outcomes for the child (for a review see Waters, Hay & Richter, 1986). What evidence is there for similar links, at least at the level of correlation, between other types of relationships early in life and later adjustment?

Fathers

An initial question regarding the impact of early father–infant relationships concerns the actual level of paternal involvement in caregiving. Studies (reviewed by Yogman, 1990) have indicated that infants whose fathers participate highly in caretaking are more sociable than infants with less involved fathers. Furthermore, intervention studies (reviewed by Yogman, 1990) indicated that teaching new fathers about infant development and care led to more paternal caregiving. Of particular concern to developmental psychologists, however, has been the quality of the infant's relationship with the father, whatever degree of caregiving responsibilities the father takes on. After a plethora of studies on infants' attachments to their mothers, some investigators began examining the infant–father relationship, and found that infants form attachments to fathers in much the same way as they do with mothers (see Lamb, 1981). Additionally, as predicted by attachment theory, the quality of the attachment relationships with mothers and fathers were independent. Infants who have insecure relationships with their mothers can still have secure relationships with their fathers (Lamb, 1977; Main & Weston, 1981). However, most studies investigating early relationships as precursors of later adjustment looked only for correlations between the quality of the infant–mother attachment and other indices of psychological functioning (reviewed by Lamb et al., 1985). There are only very few studies that search for such long-term influences of father–infant attachments.

One such group of studies examined the impact of attachment quality to both fathers and mothers on toddlers' sociability with strangers. Sociability with others is hypothesized to be an important link between early relationships and later functioning. Inability to relate well to others puts children at risk for psychological problems. Main & Weston (1981) examined influences of both infant–mother and infant–father attachments on infants' readiness to form new relationships. They found the relationships to fathers as well as to mothers influenced infants' responses to the social overtures of an unfamiliar person. Infants who had insecure attachments with mothers but secure attachments with fathers were friendlier than infants without any secure attachments. Similarly, attachments to fathers were found to influence sociability with strangers in traditional and non-traditional Swedish families (Lamb et al., 1982) and in Israeli kibbutz-reared children (Sagi, Lamb & Gardner, 1986).

Another hypothesized mediator between early relationships and later functioning is the child's sense of self, which is thought to emerge within the context of relationships (Mahler, Pine & Bergman, 1975; Emde, 1983; Bretherton, 1985). Although there have been several studies which examined the relationship between infant–mother attachment and the developing sense of self (e.g. Schneider-Rosen & Cicchetti, 1984; Lewis, Brooks-Gunn & Jaskir, 1985), there has been only one that we know of which also examined paternal influences. Pipp, Easterbrooks & Harmon (1992) examined the effects of attachment quality to each parent, mother and father, on infants' knowledge of self and others. They found that fathers were influential, in that infants with secure relationships with both parents passed more tests of self- and other-knowledge than did infants who were insecurely attached to one or both parents. Similarly, Easterbrooks & Goldberg (1990) found that kindergarteners who, as toddlers, had had secure attachments to both of their parents, had better ego control than children who had had at least one insecure attachment. Children with only one secure attachment appeared to overcontrol their impulses and emotions more than children with two secure attachments.

Alternative caregivers

Oppenheim, Sagi & Lamb (1988) conducted the first empirical investigation of influences of non-parental attachments on development. In their sample, as predicted by attachment theory, the quality of attachment to a kibbutz metapelet was independent of infant–parent attachments (Sagi et al., 1985). The type of early relationships infants had with their metaplot was found to be a better predictor of various aspects of socio-emotional development than were infant–parent attachments. Children who as infants had secure attachments with metaplot were later more empathic, dominant, independent, achievement-oriented, ego-undercontrolled (seen as better adjusted than being too overcontrolled), and purposive as kindergarteners than children previously classified as insecure with metaplot.

It should be noted that Oppenheim and his colleagues did not interpret this to mean that parents were not that influential in the kibbutz setting.

They suggest that relationships with each attachment figure may serve as precursors to different facets of later development. Attachments with metaplot may relate to later functioning in group settings, such as kindergarten, as the metaplot directly socialize children every day in this out-of-home context. D. Oppenheim (personal communication) has suggested that measures of emotional functioning may have been better predicted by early infant–parent relationships.

Non-parental caregivers have been found to be influential in other societies as well. Howes et al. (1988) examined the quality of infant–mother and infant–caregiver attachments in US day care centres, and their effects on later peer interaction. Security of attachment to caregiver was a better predictor of later peer relations than was the security of the infant–mother attachment. Both infant–mother attachment and infant–caregiver attachment was related to current infant–caregiver relationships: children categorized as insecure with their mothers engaged in less high-level play with caregivers than children categorized as insecure with caregivers. Additionally, children categorized as insecure with both mother and caregiver had the lowest level of play with adults and spent the least time engaged with peers.

Howes similarly found caregiver influences in another study in which she used indices other than attachment to examine early relationships (Howes, 1990). In this study she examined the influences of early entry into centre-based care on later adjustment to kindergarten. She found that teachers' socialization practices, as assessed in toddlerhood, were better predictors of later kindgergarten adjustment than were parental socialization practices. (These were assessed for the "primary" parent only, again in toddlerhood.) A key measure of teachers' socialization practice was the teachers' involvement and persistence in children's compliance, which was found to be greater in high-quality centres than low-quality ones. Howes, like Oppenheim, Sagi & Lamb (1988) above, explained the continuity between teacher socialization practices and later adjustment as based on the setting similarity between centre care and school, as opposed to home and school. Children in both school and centre-based care must adjust their behaviour to function in a group. Thus parental socialization practices might affect other aspects of later functioning, which were not tapped in this study.

Siblings

Although in many parts of the world infants spend a good part of their day cared for by older siblings (Dunn, 1988; Rogoff, 1990; Zukow, 1989), there are only very few studies of sibling influences. There are as yet no studies that we know of that investigate the correlations between infant–sibling attachments and later functioning, and only very few studies that use the "strange situation" attachment paradigm to investigate infant–sibling relationships (Teti & Ablard, 1989). Thus the influences of siblings on later functioning is somewhat difficult to assess, as there is no standard paradigm in which to do so. However, investigators of sibling relationships believe that such influences exist. For example, Howe & Ross (1990) found preschoolers to be influenced by their infant siblings in that friendly interaction with siblings increased children's perspective-taking abilities. They concluded that "although the sibling system is not independent of the quality and frequency of exchanges children have with their mothers, it appears to have a structure and impact of its own" (Howe & Ross, 1990, p. 165). Dunn (1988) very richly documents the enhanced arena for the development of social understanding provided by siblings, and infants' considerable practical understanding of the feelings and intentions of other family members, siblings and parents alike. In addition, siblings provide a variety of experiences not often provided by parents.

How are the influences of different early relationships combined?

Our second proposition states that *the earliest occurring relationships are not necessarily more influential than later developing ones*. The findings presented above suggest that people other than mothers may influence children's later functioning; as in the imprinting literature, multiple relationships occurring early in life appear to have long-term consequences. Here we ask about the human evidence for the second proposition derived from the imprinting studies: how are somewhat later experiences integrated with the earliest ones?

Because there has not been much theory-building in the area of multiple influences on children's lives, most studies that examine them are not guided by an explicit underlying model. The quality of attachments to mother, and perhaps father or professional caregiver are assessed, and correlations with aspects of later functioning are examined, but a good deal of further exploration of the theoretical underpinnings of this work is urgently needed.

Models of multiple influences

There have been periodic attempts to describe the complexity of very young children's social relationships and attachments to various individuals (e.g. Schaffer & Emerson, 1964; Rheingold & Eckerman 1975; Lewis, 1982). Recently, both Tavecchio & van IJzendoorn (1987) and Thompson (1990) have urged a reconceptualization of the construct of attachment to include members of the infants' social network. Van IJzendoorn and Tavecchio analysed attachment theory as a scientific theory and concluded that certain aspects of it might block its further development. One of these was its emphasis on mothers, or on primary caregivers. They proposed (Tavecchio & Van IJzendoorn, 1987, pp. 24–25)

> to replace the monotropy-thesis with the "extension" hypothesis: the optimal caregiving arrangement would consist of a network of stable and secure attachment relationships between the child and both its parents and other persons such as professional caregivers, members of the family, or friends. In research, attachment should be considered in light of a network of relationships the child builds up in the first years of life.

Similarly, Thompson (1990, p. 50) suggests that

> broadly based ecological interventions with families may prove as salutary as an exclusive focus on the mother and her quality of care. In this sense, infants are provided with redundant opportunities for positive growth in the early years as early attachments become constructed—and reconstructed—in relation to a changing and broadening social ecology.

Easterbrooks & Goldberg (1990) have suggested ways to combine the influences of both attachment figures: the predictive validity of each indpendent relationship can be examined, as well as joint parental influences and compensatory relationships. In other words, we can ask whether or not the type of attachment with fathers, as well as mothers, predicts later functioning. Or, we can ask whether a child who has secure attachments to both mother and father does better than a child who has only one secure attachment (this tests the effect of joint influences). Finally, we can ask whether a secure relationship with one parent compensates for an insecure relationship with the other. This model implies that infants with insecure attachments to mothers may not be at risk for later problems when they have a secure relationship with someone else.

Much of the empirical literature on the impact of multiple relationships on human development focuses on this latter issue of compensation. Investigators have asked, firstly, in extreme cases can later relationships compensate for the ill effects of maternal deprivation in the earliest years? And secondly, in less extreme cases, can a satisfactory attachment relationship with one figure compensate for the adverse effects of an insecure relationship with another?

Rehabilitation of children deprived of mothering: attachment formation in later childhood

An initial question about the primacy of early relationships that is often posed is whether, in human development, there is a critical period for the formation of attachment relationships. In other words, if infants are deprived of adequate mothering, can they ever form loving relationships with a parental figure? The evidence suggests that, in the absence of gross biological insult, they can.

Such evidence was provided in a review of several case studies of children reared under conditions of extreme physical and social deprivation (Skuse, 1984) and, quite compellingly, in the classic observations of young concentration camp victims made by Anna Freud & Sophie Dann (1951). In the latter case, a group of very young children formed strong, supportive attachments to each other and were later able to form attachments to nurses and adoptive parents. Similar findings were provided by a longitudinal study of British children reared in institutions in which numerous changes of caregivers took place over the first few years of life (Tizard & Hodges, 1978; Hodges & Tizard, 1989). When adopted later in childhood, these children established secure attachment relationships with their adoptive parents. In general, for these institution-reared children, the parent–child relationships in middle childhood were more satisfactory if the child had been adopted into new homes than if he or she were returned to the original biological parents. Thus it appears that attachment relationships can be formed with different figures in the years that follow infancy.

It is important to note, however, that there may be a statute of limitations on the number of attachments any child may be expected to form. Girls who lived for most of their childhoods in group homes (i.e. were not adopted into families at some point in childhood), particularly if they had been admitted into institutional care in the first two years of life, had an increased risk of psychiatric illness and problems in rearing their own children in later life (Quinton, Rutter & Liddle, 1984). Girls in that sample may have had over 50 different caregivers in the course of their childhoods. Parallel findings were found for boys reared in the same institution, although, in males, poor outcomes in adulthood were primarily related to personality disorder, which in turn was predicted by a history of criminality or psychiatric illness in the biological parents, even when the influence of institutional rearing was statistically controlled (Rutter, Quinton & Hill, 1990). The long-term follow-ups of institutionally reared children suggest that, although they may have been capable of forming secure relationships with other caregivers, the institutional environment may not have afforded them the opportunities to do so.

It is also important to note that the formation of close attachments later in childhood may compensate for some effects of deprivation in infancy, but not others. For example, in the study of institutionally reared children who were later adopted (Hodges & Tizard, 1989), both those children who were adopted and those who were restored to their biological families showed distinctive patterns of relating to peers and teachers that might put them at risk in the school situation. Such persisting effects of the early institutional rearing could not be discerned in the domains of cognitive development or family relationships.

Compensation for insecure relationships to parents

Within the population of home-reared children, who have more or less secure relationships with their parents, compensatory influences have also been identified. Goossens & Van IJzendoorn (1990) suggested that a secure attachment with a professional caregiver may compensate for a completely insecure network of attachments within the family. They assessed the quality of infants' attachments to both mothers and professional caregivers, and found that half of the infants with no secure relationships at home had a secure relationship with a caregiver (10% of all the infants in the study). Follow-up studies are needed to see if the secure relationships provided by caregivers lessen the influences of insecure attachments at home. We would also like to note that Goossens and Van IJzendoorn's study is the only one of which we are aware in which antecedents of attachments to professional caregivers were examined. They found that coming from a "solidly middle-class" background or having younger caregivers increased the likelihood of having secure attachments to caregivers. In addition, the complexity of the compensatory model is highlighted by the finding that infants who spent more time with caregivers were more likely to have secure attachments with them than children who spent less time. Goossens and van IJzendoorn conclude that their findings, taken together with Belsky's view that increased time away from mother puts infants at risk of insecure attachments with her, indicate that spending more time with mother puts infants at risk of insecure attachments with caregivers, and vice versa. Thus the implications of the compensatory model are intricate.

Compensatory influences are implied by some findings in studies designed for other purposes. For example, Werner & Smith's (1982) study of resilient children, that is, children who were at risk of later problems for a variety of reasons, but in fact developed no behaviour problems, indicated that many of these resilient children were very sociable and able to form strong relationships with people outside the immediate family. Vandell (1988) examined the influences of full-time non-maternal care during infancy on children's functioning when they were in third grade. She found that infants who had received full-time maternal care and whose parents later divorced were rated as functioning more poorly in third grade than children in full-time non-maternal care (whether or not there was later divorce in these families). Thus an exclusive infant–mother relationship was not necessarily what was best for children.

Similarly, Easterbrooks & Goldberg (1990) found that mothers' employment (with infants consequently placed in alternative care arrangements) was beneficial for some infants. They examined the effects of changes in child care environment (the most common being mothers' return to outside employment) on the stability of infant–mother attachments. They found such changes had a positive effect on children who had been insecurely attached to their mothers, with the least adaptive behaviour found when the caregiving environment for insecurely attached children did not change. Once again, an exclusive infant–mother relationship was not necessarily best. A recent study by Hock & DeMeis (1990) indicated that mothers who wanted outside employment, but stayed home because they felt it was best for their infants, were at risk of depression (which in turn is a risk factor for infants). Thus it is not necessarily always optimal for infants to receive full-time care from their mothers. Although poor infant–mother relations may be viewed as precursors of later problems, at the same time good relationships with others may be viewed as being protective against later problems.

Are children's internal representations additive or multiplicative?

Our third proposition states that *developing organisms construct internal representations of their companions and potential mates from multiple sources.* Just as imprinting theorists have attempted to explain apparent reversals of imprinting and the coexistence of multiple relationships in terms of birds' mental representations of their companions, so much theorizing about human attachments has focused on the mediating role of "internal working models" of attachment objects (Bowlby, 1969; Bretherton, 1985). It is in this context that alternatives to the compensation hypothesis are proposed. One alternative view to the compensatory effects of secure relationships is the view that insecure attachments, even one, place infants at risk.

Easterbrooks & Goldberg (1990) found that infants securely attached to both parents were rated as having more adaptive patterns of ego-control than infants with an insecure attachment to one parent. Similarly, Pipp, Easterbrooks & Harmon (1992) concluded that an insecure attachment to even one parent is a risk factor in the development of knowledge of self and parent, rather than a secure attachment with father providing a buffering role against an insecure attachment with mothers.

Yet another way of combining several influences can be envisioned. Working models of several relationships can be retained and continuously reconstructed with the continuing transactions that are basic to relationships. But rather than averaging across the various models, as is assumed in an additive model, aspects of later relationships may be linked to particular aspects of earlier ones. For example, Oppenheim, Sagi & Lamb's (1988) suggested that relationships that focused on getting along in a group, such as the infant–metapelet relationship for kibbutz children, might influence later functioning in groups.

Similarly, Howes (1990) found that teacher socialization style during infancy better predicted children's functioning with teachers in kindergarten than did parents' earlier socialization style. In both of these studies, early infant–group caregiver relations predicted later children's later adjustment to group settings. Further studies designed explicitly to test this model require that the particular aspects of later functioning of interest are conceptually linked to relevant aspects of particular early relationships.

Impact of early versus contemporary relationships on adult adjustment

The fourth proposition derived from the imprinting literature states that *the impact of early relationships on adult life may be mediated by contemporary relationships in adulthood*. Support for this proposition is provided by the longitudinal studies of psychiatric illness and mating choices in institutionally reared women and men (Quinton, Rutter & Liddle, 1984; Rutter, Quinton & Hill, 1990). These studies indicate that a harmonious marital relationship in early adulthood appears to protect institutionally reared individuals from psychiatric illness and problems in rearing their own children. The extent to which this protective factor was available to an individual, however, appeared to depend upon the individual's gender. The women reared in institutions were almost twice as likely as their male counterparts to marry "deviant" men—i.e. men with a history of criminality or psychiatric disorder. When compared with home-reared women from similar disadvantaged communities, the institution-reared women were two and a half times more likely to marry "deviant" men. The women were also much more likely to become parents themselves as teenagers, both in comparison to the home-reared women and the institutionally reared men. Thus the lot of many of the institutionally reared women was either to become immersed in an unsatisfactory partnership or to take on the responsibilities of a single parent.

In contrast, only 27% of the men married "deviant" women, a proportion that was not significantly different from that characterizing men from similar communities who had not been reared in institutions. This perhaps simply reflects the base rates of criminality and psychiatric disorder in men and women in the population; women are more likely than men to be presented with "deviant" future mates. None the less, this fact then implies that compensatory marital relationships in adulthood are less available to one half of the population than the other. Quinton and his colleagues were at pains to demonstrate that the choice of a satisfactory mate seemed a better planned activity for women than for men. They interpreted a sequence of events in a woman's life in terms of her individual ability to "plan" her life, in terms of making plans for successful completion of schooling, entry into the workforce, avoidance of early pregnancy, and decision to marry a man whom she had known for at least six months and who was not psychiatrically ill or holding a criminal record. Such women who made plans tended to have fewer psychiatric symptoms and fewer child-rearing problems in adulthood, in contrast to their peers who planned ahead less. Successful school experiences seemed to be particularly important in compensating for the adverse effects of institutional rearing in this regard.

This interpretation of course places the responsibility for life choices squarely on the woman herself, and does not take into account either intellectual differences that might have made schooling more or less successful, or the existence of other, potentially compensatory relationships with teachers, grandparents, peers, and so on that might have made the adolescent years easier for some women than others. By focusing primarily on the marital relationship as the primary compensatory influence, much useful information is lost. However, it is worth noting that the men in the sample apparently did not have to plan. Their successful choice of a non-deviant spouse was unrelated to their tendency to plan in the realms of school and work, and even to their own tendency to show "deviant" behaviour. The assumption must be that their prospective spouses, like the other women, were the ones doing the planning.

Thus, in general, the longitudinal studies of institutionally reared children point to the importance of compensatory relationships in adulthood, but do not go far enough in exploring earlier relationships that might have set a sequence of life choices into motion. Again, the absence of theoretical models of the impact of multiple relationships constrains the possibilities investigated.

One possible model that might clarify some of the links between early relationships and choice of mate, which in turn may provide a compensatory influence with respect to subsequent relations with one's own children, derives quite directly from the imprinting literature—the hypothesis that individuals exposed to multiple figures may form a composite representation of a suitable mate. With this hypothesis in mind, it is important to contrast the representations likely to be formed by girls and boys reared in children's homes. Adult caregivers in children's homes are almost entirely female—thus boys may be forming their internal representations of human females from as many as 50 exemplars, whereas girls may hardly ever see adult males at all. Surely, it is rare for "father figures" to be provided. In such circumstances, extrapolation of a principle from the imprinting literature would suggest that it is "sibling" influences that might become of particular importance. To the extent that institutional rearing enhances behavioural problems in boys (Rutter, Quinton & Hill, 1990), the male peers of institutionally reared girls provide somewhat "deviant" models. Such models may be quite influential in shaping the girls' expectations of male behaviour, which in turn may influence their subsequent choices of mate.

The social ecology of human child rearing

Our final proposition states that *interpretation of the links between early experiences and adult adjustment requires an understanding of the natural social ecology of the group or species*. Humans, like other social animals, are surrounded by a network of individuals. Human infants interact, form relationships, and learn from all these individuals. Several developmental theorists have attempted to conceptualize social development in terms of the network of relationships in which infants are involved (Dunn, 1988; Hinde, 1983; Lewis, 1982; Rogoff, 1990; Tavecchio & van IJzendoorn, 1987). This approach has revealed much greater social understanding by infants and toddlers than had previously been realized (see Dunn, 1988). The rich and varied interaction provided by people other than mothers contribute to this increased social understanding.

In many places, siblings, older children, grandparents, or other adults in the village share in infant care. In some places, mothers take care of infants' physical needs, but other children and/or adults take care of their social needs. For example, Rogoff et al. (in preparation) found that, when asked to demonstrate how a toy worked to their infants, women from a rural Indian village demonstrated the toy to older siblings, so that they in turn could teach the infants. These mothers saw such tasks as the siblings' responsibility. When asked to play with their infants, these mothers laughed; they did not view this as their role.

Similarly, Watson-Gegeo & Gegeo (1989, p. 66) describe the sibling caregiving among the Kwara'ae, a Melanesian people of the south-west Pacific. Once infants are eating solid foods (at about 5 or 6 months), they spend many hours a week with sibling caregivers. These older children not only physically care for their charges, but "carry on a running stream of talk with infants, speaking to them and for them, stimulating them to respond, and interpreting their vocalizations". Bryant (1989, p. 162) examined sibling caregiving in the USA and concluded that siblings are unique contributors to the social–emotional functioning and development of younger siblings: "Both aspects of supportive sibling caretaking, nurturance and challenge, as well as more conflictual style characterized by punishment, predicts children's socio-emotional functioning." Rogoff describes cultures in which mothers hold infants so that they face the same direction as their mothers are facing, rather than facing the mothers themselves (as in the typically studied face-to-face interaction situation). Mothers who direct their infants to face others are revealing their belief in the importance of learning to function in a social setting; by observing the relations of others, infants can begin to understand how they themselves can fit in. Rogoff, like Dunn (1988), proposes that group interaction, rather than dyadic interaction, may be the prototype for social engagement.

It becomes helpful to re-examine the information about institutionally reared individuals in this context. Children reared in institutions are brought up in groups of fluctuating membership, with no constant parental figures, but also no constant community of siblings, peers, and interested elders. Such fluctuation in group membership stands in contrast to other forms of group rearing in stable communities with stable and accessible parental figures, for example, the Israeli kibbutz. Given the ecological constraints, what would be adaptive responding? It might be argued that the distinctive ways in which children who spent their early years in institutions now relate to peers—i.e. showing "overly friendly" behaviour, and having more than one "best friend" (Hodges & Tizard, 1989)—might represent highly adaptive behaviour in one set of circumstances that does not transplant easily to another context. It is also of course possible that children who are forming close attachments to family members for the first times in their lives, in later childhood and early adolescence, are less likely to seek intimacy in the peer group. Not having resided with their parents all their lives, the late-adopted adolescents may be less frustrated with parental values and supervision, and may be less likely to turn to peer relationships for compensation. All these possibilities underscore the fact that is is premature to call a certain mode of relating to others "pathological" without reference to the social ecology of the species in general and the population of interest in particular.

CONCLUSIONS

Is the mother–child relationship unique, without parallel? Is it the prototype of all future love relationships? Is it thus both precursor and ultimate cause of later adjustment and psychopathology? We can answer those questions with an unequivocal "no". Parallel theoretical developments in research on avian imprinting and human relationships indicate that there are multiple pathways, in both nests and human dwellings, to healthy development. There does not appear to be one way that is optimal or one particular, biologically constrained relationship that is absolutely crucial. It does seem important that young organisms' interpersonal experiences not be completely fleeting or chaotic—but compensatory attachment relationships may be formed after infancy.

In evaluating the impact of any early relationship on later adjustment, it becomes important to examine adaptation to a particular set of circumstances and the extent to which new adaptations are required in new social contexts. Both the imprinting theorists and theorists of human attachments see the need to study individuals' representations of their social lives, as well as overt behaviour, in tracing such adaptations and readaptations throughout the life span.

The lessons learned in the studies of imprinting and human relationships are relevant for other attempts to identify a single precursor of a later outcome. One must examine the proposed precursor not simply in terms of its morphological resemblance to a later outcome, and not simply in terms of the stability of individual differences on some dimension of precursor and outcome, but within a causal network of contemporary and subsequent influences. This effort is aided in situations, such as the imprinting literature, where experimentation is possible. It is, however, necessary to attempt to specify a network of causation in non-experimental studies as well.

Furthermore, in doing so, it is important to consider the impact of formal as well as efficient and final causation (see Hopkins & Butterworth, 1990; Hay and Angold, Chapter 1 this volume). To the extent that mental representations, once formed, have a life span of their own, and shape subsequent experiences accordingly, individuals' views of themselves and their prospective companions acquire their own causal status. Thus it may not be an early relationship itself, but its subsequent interpretation and representation that has causal force in later life (see e.g. Waters et al., 1986; Main, Caplan & Cassidy, 1985). The impact of an early condition or event may indeed be discerned for years, but the same sort of condition or event may be represented by different individuals in different ways. In humans, tracing the evolution of a sense of self and personal myth, starting with, but not restricting oneself to, bare facts about early deprivation and insecurities, may be a more profitable exercise than the attempt to identify particular precursors with later problems. At least, this more complicated, more cognitive, and more culturally informed approach to developmental causality seems to be what is required to understand birds' social lives. We cannot believe that human development and pathogenesis are less complex.

REFERENCES

Ainsworth, M. D. S. (1969). Object relations, dependency, and attachment: theoretical review of the infant–mother relationship. *Child Development*, **40**, 969–1025.

Ainsworth, M. D. S. & Wittig, B. A. (1969). Attachment and exploratory behaviour of 1-year-olds in a strange situation. In B. M. Foss (ed.), *Determinants of Infant Behaviour*, vol. 4, Methuen, London, pp. 111–136.

Aronson, L. R., Tobach, E., Rosenblatt, J. S. & Lehrman, D. S. (1972). *Selected Writings of T. C. Schneirla*, Freeman, San Francisco.

Bateson, P. (1981). Ontogeny of behavior. *British Medical Bulletin*, **37**, 159–164.

Bateson, P. (1982). Preferences for cousins in Japanese quail. *Nature*, **295**, 236–237.

Belsky, J. & Nezworski, T. (1988). *Clinical Implications of Attachment*, Erlbaum, Hillsdale, NJ.

Blatz, W. E. (1966). *Human Security: Some Reflections*, Toronto University Press, Toronto.

Bowlby, J. (1958). The nature of the child's tie to his mother. *International Journal of Psychoanalysis*, **39**, 350–373.

Bowlby, J. (1969). *Attachment*, Basic Books, New York.

Bowlby, J. (1982). *Attachment and Loss*. vol. 1, *Attachment*, 2nd edn, Basic Books, New York.

Bretherton, I. (1985). Attachment theory: retrospect and prospect. In I. Bretherton & E. Waters (eds), *Growing Points of Attachment Theory and Research. Monographs of the Society for Research in Child Development*, **50**(1,2), Serial No. 209, 3–35.

Bryant, B. K. (1989). The child's perspective of sibling caretaking and its relevance to understanding social–emotional functioning and development. In P. G. Zukow (ed.), *Sibling Interaction Across Cultures. Theoretical and Methodological Issues*, Springer-Verlag, New York, pp. 143–164.

Chase, I. D. (1980). Cooperative and noncooperative behavior in animals. *The American Naturalist*, **115**, 827–857.

Clayton, N. (1987). Mate choice in male zebra finches: some effects of cross-fostering. *Animal Behavior*, **35**, 596–597.

Cooke, F. (1978). Early learning and its effect on population structure. Studies of a wild population of snow goose. *Zeitschrift für Tierpsychologie*, **46**, 344–358.

Dunn, J. (1988). *The Beginnings of Social Understanding*, Harvard University Press, Cambridge, Mass.

Easterbrooks, M. A. & Goldberg, W. A. (1990). Security of toddler–parent attachments: relation to children's socio-personality functioning during kindergarten. In M. Greenberg, D. Cicchetti & M. Cummings (eds), *Attachment in the Preschool Years: Theory, Research, and Intervention*, University of Chicago Press, Chicago, pp. 221–244.

Emde, R. N. (1983). The pre-representational self and its affective core. *Psychoanalytic Study of the Child*, **38**, 440–452.

Emlen, S. T. & Oring, L. W. (1977). Ecology, sexual selection, and the evolution of mating systems. *Science*, **197**, 215–223.

Fox, N. (1977). Attachment of kibbutz infants to mother and metapelet. *Child Development*, **48**, 1228–1239.

Freud, A. & Dann, S. (1951). An experiment in group upbringing. *Psychoanalytic Study of the Child*, **6**, 127–168.

Freud, S. (1938). *An Outline of Psychoanalysis*, Hogarth, London.

Goossens, F. A. & van IJzendoorn, M. H. (1990). Quality of infants' attachments to professional caregivers: relation to infant–parent attachment and day-care characteristics. *Child Development*, **61**, 832–837.

Gotlieb, G. (1991). Experiential canalization of behavioral development: theory. *Development Psychology*, **29**, 4–13.

Hamilton, W. D. (1964). The genetical evolution of social behavior. I., II. *Journal of Theoretical Biology*, **7**, 1–16, 17–52.

Hay, D. F. (1985). Learning to form relationships in infancy: parallel attainments with parents and peers. *Developmental Review*, **5**, 122–161.

Hinde, R. (1983). *Primate Social Relationships: An Integrated Approach*, Blackwell Scientific Publications, Cambridge.

Hock, E. & DeMeis, D. K. (1990). Depression in mothers of infants: the role of maternal employment. *Developmental Psychology*, **26**, 285–291.

Hodges, J. & Tizard, B. (1989). Social and family relationships of ex-institutional adolescents. *Journal of Child Psychology and Psychiatry*, **30**, 77–97.

Hopkins, B. & Butterworth, G. (1990). Concepts of causality in explanations of development. In G. Butterworth & P. Bryant (eds), *Causes of Development*, Harvester Wheatsheaf, Hemel Hempstead.

Howe, N. & Ross, H. S. (1990). Socialization, perspective-taking, and the sibling relationship. *Developmental Psychology*, **26**, 160–165.

Howes, C. (1990). Can the age of entry into child care and the quality of child care predict adjustment in kindergarten? *Developmental Psychology*, **26**, 292–303.

Howes, C., Rodning, C., Galluzzo, D. C. & Myers, L. (1988). Attachment and child care: relationships with mother and caregiver. *Early Childhood Research Quarterly*, **3**, 403–416.

Immelmann, K. (1965). *Australian Finches in Bush and Aviary*, Angus & Robertson, Sydney.

Immelmann, K. (1972). Sexual and other long-term aspects of imprinting in birds and other species. *Advances in the Study of Behavior*, **4**, 147–174.

Immelmann, K. & Suomi, S. J. (1981). Sensitive phases in development. In K. Immelmann, G. W. Barlow, L. Petrinovitch & M. Main (eds), *Behavioral Development*, Cambridge University Press, Cambridge,

Klint, T. (1978). Significance of mother and sibling experience for mating preferences in the mallard. *Zeitschrift für Tierpsychologie*, **47**, 50–60.

Kruijt, J. P., Cate, C. J. Ten & Meeuwissen, G. B. (1983). The influence of siblings on the development of sexual preferences of male zebra finches. *Developmental Psychobiology*, **16**, 233–239.

Lamb, M. E. (1977). The development of mother–infant and father–infant attachments in the second year of life. *Developmental Psychology*, **13**, 237–244.

Lamb, M. E. (ed.) (1981). *The Role of the Father in Child Development*, revised edn, Wiley, New York.

Lamb, M. E., Hwang, C.-P., Frodi, A. M. & Frodi, M. (1982). Security of mother- and father–infant attachment and its relation to sociability with strangers in traditional and nontraditional Swedish families. *Infant Behavior and Development*, **5**, 355–367.

Lamb, M. E. & Nash, A. (1989). Infant–mother attachment, sociability, and peer competence. In T. J. Berndt & G. W. Ladd (eds), *Peer Relationships in Child Development*, John Wiley, New York, pp. 217–245.

Lamb, M. E., Thompson, R. A., Gardner, W. & Charnov, E. L. (1985). *Infant–mother attachment: the Origins and Developmental Significance of Individual Differences in Strange Situation Behavior*, Erlbaum, Hillsdale, NJ.

Langlois, J. H. & Roggman, L. A. (1990). Attractive faces are only average. *Psychological Science*, **1**, 115–121.

Lee, P. C. (1983). Ecological influences on relationships and social structures. In R. A. Hinde (ed.), *Primate Social Relationships: An Integrated Approach*, Blackwell, Oxford, pp. 225–229.

Lee, P. C. (1984). Ecological constraints on the social development of vervet monkeys. *Behaviour*, **91**(4), 245–262.

Lewis, M. (1982). The social network systems model: toward a theory of social development. In T. Field (ed.), *Review of Human Development*, vol. 1, John Wiley, New York, pp. 180–209.

Lewis, M., Brooks-Gunn, G. & Jaskir, J. (1985). Individual differences in infant self-recognition as a function of the mother–infant attachment relationship. *Developmental Psychology*, **21**, 1181–1187.

Lickliter, R. & Gottlieb, G. (1985). Social interactions with siblings is necessary for visual imprinting of species-specific maternal preferences in ducklings (*Anas platyrhynchos*). *Journal of Comparative Psychology*, **99**, 371–379.

Lickliter, R. & Gottlieb, G. (1988). Social specificity: interaction with own species in necessary to foster species-specific maternal preferences in ducklings. *Developmental Psychobiology*, **21**, 311–321.

Lorenz, K. (1935/1970). Companions as factors in the bird's environment. In K. Lorenz (ed.), *Studies on Animal and Human Behavior*, vol. 1, Harvard University Press, Cambridge, Mass, pp. 101–258.

Mahler, M. S., Pine, F. & Bergman, A. (1975). *The Psychological Birth of the Human Infant*. Basic Books, New York.

Main, M., Kaplan, A. & Cassidy, J. (1985). Security in infancy, childhood, and adulthood: a move to the level of representation. In I. Bretherton & E. Waters (eds), *Growing Points in Attachment Theory and Research. Monographs of the Society for Research in Child Development*, **50**(1–2), Serial No. 209, 66–104.

Main, M. & Weston, D. R. (1981). The quality of the toddler's relationship to mother and to father: related to conflict behavior and the readiness to establish new relationships. *Child Development*, **52**, 932–940.

Maynard-Smith, J. (1974). The theory of games and the evolution of animal conflicts. *Journal of Theoretical Biology*, **47**, 209–221.

Myers, R. J., Jarvis, P. A. & Creasey, G. L. (1987). Infants' behavior with their mothers and grandmothers. *Infant Behavior and Development*, **10**, 245–259.

Nash, A. (1988). Ontogeny, phylogeny, and relationships. In S. Duck (ed.), *Handbook of Personal Relationships*, John Wiley, Chichester, pp. 121–141.

Oppenheim, D., Sagi, A. & Lamb, M. E. (1988). Infant–adult attachments on the kibbutz and their relation to socioemotional development 4 years later. *Developmental Psychology*, **24**, 427–433.

Orians, G. H. (1969). On the evolution of mating systems in birds and mammals. *American Naturalist*, **103**, 589–603.

Oyama, S. (1985). *The Ontogeny of Information: Developmental Systems and Evolution*, Cambridge University Press, Cambridge.

Pipp, S., Easterbrooks, M. A. & Harmon, R. J. (1992). The relation between attachment and knowledge of self and mother in one- to three-year-old infants. *Child Development*, **63**, 738–750.

Quinton, D., Rutter, M. & Liddle, C. (1984). Institutional rearing, parenting difficulties and marital support. *Psychological Medicine*, **14**, 107–124.

Rheingold, H. L. & Eckerman, C. O. (1975). Some proposals for unifying the study of social development. In M. Lewis & L. A. Rosenblum (eds), *Friendship and Beer Relations*, John Wiley, New York, pp. 293–298.

Rogoff, B. (1990). *Apprenticeship in Thinking*, Oxford University Press, New York.

Rogoff, B., Mistry, J., Goncu, A. & Mosier, C. (1991). Cultural variation in the role relations of toddlers and their families. In M. Bornstein (ed.), *Cultural Approaches to Parenting*, Erlbaum, Hillsdale, NJ, pp. 173–183.

Rutter, M. (1991). A fresh look at "maternal deprivation". In P. Bateson (ed.), *The Development and Integration of Behaviour*. Cambridge University Press, Cambridge, pp. 331–374.

Rutter, M., Quinton, D. & Hill, J. (1990). Adult outcome of institution-reared children. In L. Robins & M. Rutter (eds), *Straight and Devious Pathways from Childhood to Adulthood*, Cambridge University Press, New York, pp. 135–157.

Sagi, A., Lamb, M. E. & Gardner, W. (1986). Relations between strange situation behavior and stranger sociability among infants on Israeli kibbutzim. *Infant Behavior and Development*, **9**, 271–282.

Sagi, A., Lamb, M. E., Lewkowicz, K. S., Shoham, R., Dvir, R. & Estes, D. (1985). Security of infant–mother, –father, and –metapelet attachments among kibbutz-reared Israeli children. In I. Bretherton & E. Waters (eds), *Growing*

Points in Attachment Theory and Research. Monographs of the Society for Research in Child Development, **50**(1–2), Serial No. 209, 257–275.

Schaffer, H. S. & Emerson, P. E. (1964). The development of social attachments in infancy. *Monographs of the Society for Research in Child Development*, **29**(3), Serial No. 94, 77pp.

Schneider-Rosen, K. & Cicchetti, D. (1984). The relationship between affect and cognition in maltreated infants: quality of attachment and the development of visual self-recognition. *Child Development*, **55**, 648–658.

Skuse, D. (1984). Extreme deprivation in early childhood. I. Diverse outcomes for three siblings from an extraordinary family. *Journal of Child Psychology and Psychiatry*, **25**, 523–541.

Serventy, D. L. (1971). Biology of desert birds. In D. S. Farner & J. R. Kings (eds), *Avian Biology*, vol. 1, Academic Press, New York, pp. 287–339.

Serventy, D. L. (1977). The timing of breeding by the zebra finch *Taeniopygia castantotis* at Mileura, Western Australia. *Ibis*, **119**, 369–372.

Stern, D. N. (1985). *The Interpersonal World of the Infant*. Basic Books, New York.

Tavecchio, L. W. C. & van IJzendoorn, M. H. (1987). *Attachment in Social Networks*, Elsevier, Amsterdam.

Ten Cate, C. (1986). Sexual preferences in zebra finch (*Taeniopygia guttata*) males raised by two species, *Lonchura striata* and *Taeniopygia guttata*: I. A case of double imprinting. *Journal of Comparative Psychology*, **100**, 248–252.

Ten Cate, C. (1987). Sexual preferences in zebra finch males raised by two species: II. The internal representation resulting from double imprinting. *Animal Behavior*, **35**, 321–330.

Ten Cate, C., Los, L. & Schilperoord, L. (1984). The influence of differences in social experiences on the development of species recognition in zebra finch males. *Animal Behavior*, **32**, 852–860.

Teti, D. M. & Ablard, K. E. (1989). Security of attachment and infant–sibling relationships: a laboratory study. *Child Development*, **60**, 1519–1528.

Thompson, R. A. (1990). Construction and reconstruction of early attachments: taking perspective on attachment theory and research. In D. Keating & H. Rosen (eds), *Constructivist Perspectives on Atypical Development and Developmental Psychopathology*, Erlbaum, Hillsdale, NJ, pp. 41–67.

Tizard, B. & Hodges, J. (1978). The effect of early institutional rearing on the development of eight-year-old children. *Journal of Child Psychology and Psychiatry*, **19**, 99–118.

Trivers, R. L. (1971). The evolution of reciprocal altruism. *Quarterly Review of Biology*, **46**, 35–57.

Trivers, R. L. (1972). Parental investment and sexual selection. In B. Campbell (ed.), *Sexual Selection and the Descent of Man*, Aldine, Chicago, pp. 136–179.

Trivers, R. L. (1974). Parent–offspring conflict. *American Zoologist*, **14**, 249–269.

Vandell, D. L. (1988). Early non-maternal care and later development. Paper presented at the International Conference on Infant Studies, Washington, DC, April.

Waters, E., Hay, D. F. & Richters, J. E. (1986). Infant–parent attachment and the origins of prosocial and antisocial behavior. In D. Olwens, J. Block & M. Radke-Yarrow (eds), *Development of Antisocial and Prosocial Behavior*, Academic Press, London, pp. 97–125.

Watson-Gegeo, K. A. & Gegeo, D. W. (1989). The role of sibling interaction in child socialization. In P. G. Zukow (ed.), *Sibling Interaction Across Cultures: Theoretical and Methodological Issues*, Springer-Verlag, New York, pp. 54–76.

Werner, E. E. & Smith, R. S. (1982). *Vulnerable but Invincible: A Longitudinal Study of Resilent Children and Youth*. McGraw-Hill, New York.

West, M. J. & King, A. P. (1985). Social guidance of vocal learning by female cowbirds: validating its functional significance. *Zeitschrift für Tierpsychologie*, **70**, 225–235.

West, M. J. & King, A. P. (1988). Settling nature and nurture into an ontogenic niche. *Developmental Psychobiology*, **21**, 543–552.

Yogman, Y. W. (1990). Male parental behaviors in humans and nonhuman primates. In N. A. Krasnegor & R. S. Bridges (eds), *Mammalian Parenting*, Oxford University Press, New York.

Zukow, P. G. (1989). *Sibling Interaction Across Cultures: Theoretical and Methodological Issues*, Springer-Verlag, New York.

Chapter 9

Precursors, Causes and the Development of Criminal Offending

Marc Le Blanc and Rolf Loeber

INTRODUCTION

The purpose of this chapter is to identify some precursors and potential causes of adult criminal offending. With respect to the overall concerns of this book, we propose that, by adopting an explicitly developmental perspective, one can better elucidate the causal processes underlying the activation and aggravation of, and sometimes desistance from, a criminal career. This requires taking a long-term view of the predictors of criminal offending, and examining their timing and duration of influence. It may also require analysis of the developmental course of criminality in terms of a sequence of precursor conditions and a constant redefinition of the network of causal influences.

Despite the longstanding existence of a few developmental approaches to criminology, such as psychodynamic theory (Feldman, 1969; Empey, 1978), labeling theory (Lemert, 1951) or developmental stage models (Sullivan, Grant & Grant, 1957; Jennings, Kilkenny & Kohlberg, 1983), for many years the study of the causes of offending has been dominated by several assumptions stemming from the cross-sectional approach and the analysis of between-individual differences. This has led to a near standstill in the identification of those correlates or risk factors of offending that are also most likely to be causes. It has hindered the development of new, empirically based theories and the development of another generation of much-needed innovative intervention and prevention strategies for reducing delinquency.

The first of these assumptions is that causes are invariant with the age of the offender, and that similar causes or constellations of causes operate for earlier onset of offending compared with later beginning (e.g. Hirschi & Gottfredson, 1983, 1987). This assumption flies in the face of evidence that when youngsters grow older they are exposed to considerable shifts in the

Precursors and Causes in Development and Psychopathology.
Edited by D. F. Hay and A. Angold © 1993 John Wiley & Son Ltd

presence of known risk and causal factors, such as parental influences, peer influences, and academic failure (Loeber, 1990; LaGrange & White, 1985; Loeber & Le Blanc, 1990). The assumption also implies that the ranking of the explanatory power of causal variables is the same whether offending is studied cross-sectionally or longitudinally; in other words, causal factors and their interrelationships operate at equal strength at any given point along the developmental time line.

The second in this set of assumptions is that a number of important causal factors often occur only in close temporal proximity to the delinquent acts. For example, increases in peer pressure to break rules may shortly thereafter be followed by youngsters' engaging in law-breaking. This assumption excludes the possibility that potential causal factors occur much earlier than the time of the actual delinquent event; further it excludes the possibility that causality evolves, in part, from a sequence of events often stretching over many years.

A third assumption is that it is sufficient to measure causal factors independent of the length of time that they have been operating. For example, peer influences are often measured within a particular recall period; but it can be safely assumed that persisting peer influences over a long period of time have a larger impact on the initiation and maintenance of offending than short-lived influences. In the area of parental influences on child behavior over time, Kagan & Moss (1962) have called attention to the importance of sleeper effects, i.e. effects which are initially weak but become stronger the longer the child is exposed to the particular parenting practices. Thus, the duration of causal factors, and their waxing and waning, could be thought to be pivotal parameters in explaining offending.

In our view, theorists in criminology generally have not explored all of the developmental implications or exploited all of the potential causal strengths of their theories. Only recently are some theoretical models with a developmental component now receiving more attention. Attention to developmental factors, however, immediately raises the issue of what methods best test particular theories and hypotheses within theories. For example, Ferdinand (1987) proposed that cultural deviance theory should be tested with longitudinal data and that control theory should be verified with cross-sectional data, because the first explains initiation into offending while the second explains its maintenance. Tests of models using these two categories of theories (Agnew, 1984; Liska & Reed, 1985) have demonstrated delayed effects and reciprocal or more proximal effects for cultural deviance variables. However, the recent fashion for integrative models (Elliott, Huizinga & Ageton, 1985; Elliott, Huizinga & Menard, 1989) and theories (Messner, Krohn & Liska, 1989) has done little to enhance our knowledge of the ordering of causal factors, aside from confirming that delinquency is the most powerful predictor of future delinquency. This integrative movement has not been developmental because these models and theories failed to emphasize processes over time or temporal ordering and changes in causal factors with age. Some new empirical models, however, are clearly developmental because they propose a specific time ordering of causal factors (Farrington, 1986; Ouimet, 1986; Le Blanc & Ouimet, 1986). Still, the ordering of factors often merely refers to the fact that certain classes of factors operate at specific age periods, while other factors are active at other ages rather than identifying distinct developmental processes.

In this chapter, we outline an approach to the study of offending that we call "developmental criminology". It consists of the examination of within-individual changes in offending over time with the help of the longitudinal design, in which comparisons are made between individuals' offending at one time and then at subsequent times. It also refers to systematic changes that are successive over time and to the specific forms of these changes. The nonrandomness of such changes in an individual's behavior during the life cycle is reflected in the orthogenetic principle, which states that development exists when a system changes from being organized in a very general, undifferentiated way to having differentiated parts that are organized into an integrated hierarchy (Werner, 1957; Kaplan, 1983). A further review on this approach can be found in Loeber & Le Blanc (1990).

A major concern of developmental criminology is with causal factors that explain individual differences among offenders in the age at onset, variety, seriousness, and duration of their offending. At the same time, developmental criminology is interested in the relationship between variations in offending and important transitions in the life cycle. Examples of transitions are the shift in youngsters' relationships from parents to peers, the transition from school to work, and from peers of the same sex to peers of the opposite sex.

Another goal of developmental criminology is to increase the options for differentiating between risk factors or correlates and causal factors. To achieve this goal, developmental criminology uses longitudinal studies with repeated measurements as a principal tool. In order to ascertain the potential status of causal factors, it is necessary to consider a variety of questions, such as: Which factors are correlated with offending? Which of these correlates also predate and predict later delinquency, and do so independently from third factors? Which discrete life events encourage a change in offending? Which variables (which may vary in frequency or duration) covary with within-individual changes over time in offending? Which sequences of antecedent factors best explain increments in offending?

These are merely quasi-experimental procedures and constitute a necessary preliminary screening of potential causal factors. When possible, a final and superior test of the causal status of risk factors is the experimental manipulation of the antecedent factors (Hirschi & Selvin, 1967; Loeber & Stouthamer-Loeber, 1986).

The main aim of this chapter is to illustrate how a developmental perspective can be used optimally to distinguish between correlates and causes of delinquency, and to point out strategies for establishing causality. It is posed that a developmental model of offending cannot only test causal assumptions more effectively than most concurrent criminological models, but also is more likely to increase knowledge about within-individual changes in offending over time. Such knowledge is relevant for addressing several critical questions:

(1) Which causal factors are responsible for some but not other youngsters progressing to serious delinquent outcomes?

(2) Why is it that, even within a group of individuals who reach the same serious outcomes over time, some do so within a shorter time-span and at an earlier age than others?

(3) Why is it that, even within a group of individuals after progressing to some degree in conduct problems and delinquency, some reach a plateau and desist from progressing to more serious levels?

(4) Which factors cause some individuals, after progressing to a serious pattern of delinquency, to desist from these behaviors later?

We shall, therefore, first describe how the study of various sorts of causal influences are tied to particular methodologies, and summarize some findings derived from each sort of research method for each class of influence.

Both in summarizing the descriptive literature and highlighting particular causal factors, we take account of the fact that causal factors may operate in different ways in relationship to various dimensions of offending. The three basic dimensions we consider are *activation*, *aggravation*, and *desistance*. Relying on the theoretical and empirical work of Le Blanc & Frechette (1989), we propose to define these processes in the following way.

Activation refers to the way the development of criminal activities, once begun, is stimulated and the way the continuity, frequency, and diversity of offending take place. We make a distinction among three subprocesses of activation, namely acceleration (increased frequency of offending over time), stabilization (increased continuity over time), and diversification (the propensity for individuals to become involved in more diverse criminal activities). The second process, aggravation, refers to the existence of a developmental sequence of diverse forms of delinquent activities which escalate or increase in seriousness over time. Individuals can progress or regress within this developmental sequence. The third process, desistance, concerns a slowing down in the frequency of offending (deceleration), a reduction in its variety (specialization), and a reduction in its seriousness (de-escalation). Evidence for the processes of activation, aggravation, and desistance are more fully reviewed in Loeber & Le Blanc (1990).

Insofar as developmental analyses almost always refer to age, it is important to establish whether age qualifies as a causal variable. Since developmental analyses often refer to age, it is important to establish whether age will be used here as a causal or explanatory variable. Whether or not changes in offending occur as a function of age is a matter of dispute in criminology (Hirschi & Gottfredson, 1983; Farrington, 1986a). However, psychologists are well aware that developmental trends cannot be inferred from comparisons of age groups, that age differences may reflect historical conditions and that development involves a complex mixture of continuities and discontinuities (see Rutter's review of these questions, 1989). We agree with Wohlwill (1970, p. 50) that it is imperative to search for "variables which actually determine or mediate the variation of behavior with age", rather than considering age a causal or explanatory variable. We sustain that point of view because age as an index of development can adopt various meanings, as discussed by Rutter (1989): mental age, biological maturation, duration of experiences, types of experiences, and social age of stages.

Developmental criminology of course focuses on various causal influences, in addition to age. We shall now consider some ways in which causal variables are specified and investigated in the study of offending, before examining the ways in which different types of causal hypotheses are investigated in different types of research designs.

METHODOLOGICAL CONSIDERATIONS

The choice of research strategy in the search for causes of offending depends partly on the nature of the independent variables that are examined, and partly on the importance of determining individuals' increased vulnerability to particular influences in certain life phases.Thus it is important to consider both the types of causes being hypothesized and the timing of their influence.

Different types of causal variables

Three categories of variables can be distinguished: *unchanging variables*, *discrete variables*, and *variable states*. In developmental criminology, unchanging variables are sometimes referred to as *structural variables* (such as race or sex, but also including parental criminality or schooling). The task is to examine which of the unchanging factors are long-acting, stable causal influences that may predict both activation and aggravation of offending and other manifestations of antisocial behaviour. This implies that, even though an unchanging variable may be seen as a long-term structural influence, its actual impact may not emerge instantly. Rather, the influence of a structural variable may emerge only gradually and then stabilize.

In developmental criminology, discrete variables and variable states are sometimes both referred to as *change variables*. Discrete variables index changes in a state (e.g. from being in school to being in the work force, from being single to being married), or the occurrence of a life event such as moving to another city. Usually the impact of discrete variables on the course of offending can be gauged by a subsequent change in the activation or aggravation of or desistance in offending. A discrete variable, however, is obviously limited in its variability; its impact on offending is often immediate and cannot affect more than one process at the time. Consequently, it can have an impact on either activation, aggravation, or desistance.

Lastly, variable states concern continuous variables that may vary over time in terms of their degree (e.g. attachment to parent, attitude to police, psychotism, father's alcohol consumption). In contrast to discrete variables, a change in a variable state can be related to positive and negative changes in offending, thus explaining activation, aggravation, and desistance. Discrete variables and variable states often occur in proximity to a change in offending.

Each type of variable has different options for causal analysis. Unchanging variables must be statistically controlled for or partialled out in analyses (Hirsch & Selvin, 1967). This is especially necessary for within-individual analyses, where the invariant nature of these variables cannot be linked readily to changes in offending over time. In this instance, invariant factors should be examined in between-group analyses, where groups of offenders are distinguished on the basis of some developmental characteristics, such as early versus late onset. However, as we shall see, certain methods cannot be used with unchanging variables, and so the options are limited for establishing their causal status.

As for discrete variables, when the point of transition falls outside the period in which offending takes place, these variables merely become background factors, similar to race or sex. Similar restrictions on causal analysis apply. However, when the transition from one state to another takes place closer to the offense history, such variables can be more directly incorporated into developmental models. Event history analyses are a potential tool for this purpose (Allison, 1985). It should be kept in mind, however, that the effect of discrete variables that occurred in the past may rest on other consequences that flow from the events. For instance, death of a father may be followed by poverty in the family and reduced supervision of the children.

The options for causal analyses increase even further when variable states are examined. Central to the quest for causality are such variables that either change naturally over time or can be made to vary by means of a systematic experimental manipulation. However, in any developmental study, stable factors with long-term effects are important, even though their causal status is more difficult to assess. It seems plausible that stable causal factors are of importance for the explanation of the continuity of antisocial behaviour over time. Within a longitudinal sample, one must examine whether a stable causal factor correlates with different manifestations of antisocial behaviour over time (such as the associations between conduct problems and offending), correlates with offending at different age periods, correlates positively with activation and aggravation but negatively with desistance. One must also determine whether the level of offending by those with the stable factor is significantly different from offending by those without the factor.

The timing of causes

Studies of offending seldom refer to the possibility that the timing of causal influences may be important, and that individuals may be more vulnerable to specific influences in certain life phases but not others. Criminologists often fail to acknowledge that causes of deviant behaviour do not operate equally strongly along the time line, but interact with children's susceptibility or vulnerability. Developmental psychology refers to this life-phase vulnerability as "sensitive periods" in development, in which susceptibility to causal influences is enhanced, compared with other periods (Bateson & Hinde, 1987). Thus causes would have a more powerful effect during a sensitive period than at other times in the child's life. For instance, it is especially likely that the preschool period is when children's attachment to adults is established. This is evident from studies comparing youngsters who experienced disruptions in the continuity of child care (adoption, exposure to many different caretakers, and marital breakdown) with those who did not experience such disruptions (Werner & Smith, 1977; Wadsworth, 1979; Cadoret & Cain, 1980; Behar & Stewart, 1984; MacDonald, 1985; Kolvin et al., 1988). Another example of the sensitive period concept concerns the development of the central nervous system in children, which from gestation to about age 6 is particularly vulnerable to neurotoxins, such as lead. Research findings show that exposure to even very small amounts may produce nonclinical degrees of handicaps in intelligence and impulsivity, eventually resulting in poor academic performance and behaviour problems (e.g. Needleman & Bellinger, 1981; Yule et al., 1981; Bellinger et al., 1984). As we shall see, some research strategies for identifying causal influence are sensitive to the timing of experiences, but most are not.

Strategies of causal analysis

We shall now consider the various ways in which criminologists have sought to determine the causes of offending. A logical step for developmental criminology is not only to introduce developmental concepts into the theoretical domain, but also to incorporate them into empirical studies in order to distinguish better between correlates and causes of offending. To do so, longitudinal studies and, eventually, experiments are required. In nonexperimental, cross-sectional studies, it is impossible to distinguish correlates from causes because the variables are measured at the same time, and temporal priority cannot be established. In that sense, longitudinal studies have obvious advantages (see Farrington, 1989b). Furthermore, longitudinal data obtained through a quasi-experimental before-and-after design offer the highest internal validity after the randomized experiment (Cook & Campbell, 1979).

Not everyone, however, is convinced of the need for longitudinal studies. Gottfredson & Hirschi (1987) claimed that findings on correlates of crime based on longitudinal surveys merely confirm those from cross-sectional surveys, rather than shedding light on new correlates. We find this argument impossible to refute: Farrington, Ohlin & Wilson (1986) and Blumstein et al.'s (1986) reviews of findings from longitudinal studies do not present any information on risk factors that was not already known from concurrent studies. We can note that even if there are an enormous number of cross-sectional studies that control for third factors (only the three criteria of causality proposed by Hirschi & Selvin, 1967) through part correlation, multiple regression and causal modeling techniques, these results have nothing to say about the temporal order of independent and dependent variables. However, despite the theoretical advantage of the longitudinal design, it is true that empirical criminology has not been advanced much by follow-up studies. This is because researchers did not make full use of the potentials of longitudinal designs (see Labouvie, 1986; Le Blanc, 1989). With some exceptions, they did not distinguish between correlates and causes or, at least, establish the temporal order of events.

What is necessary is to identify more clearly between factors that are causal as well. In this section we review seven different methods that can be applied to the problem, and summarize some findings derived from each method, first with respect to the activation of criminal offending and then with respect to aggravation and desistance. The methods are:

(1) Analysis of concomitant change;
(2) Long-term prediction from early experiences and behaviours;
(3) Cross-lagged analysis;
(4) Sequential covariation;
(5) The analysis of life events;

(6)   The stepping-stones approach;
(7)   Experimental manipulation.

These methods, as applied to the development of criminal offending, all take a longitudinal perspective in that they make measurements of problem behaviours and various correlates at more than one point in time. However, they differ in the length of time over which they are searching for associations and the extent to which they make specific causal hypotheses. Concomitant change analysis aids in the search for potential causes by describing parallel developments over relatively short periods of time in the evolution of offending and various correlates. Long-term prediction from childhood indicators seeks precursors and potential causes of later offending in the early years of childhood. Cross-lagged panel analysis attempts to extend such findings by establishing the temporal priority of hypothesized explanatory variables and outcomes. The method of sequential covariation analyzes the impact of the timing and duration of possible explanatory variables. The analysis of life events makes a specific prediction about the sequelae of particular normative or nonnormative events in the life span. The stepping-stones approach elaborates upon the strategy of long-term prediction by proposing a particular sequence of experiences and precursor conditions leading up to offending. And, finally, experimentation uses random assignment to test specific causal hypotheses.

It should be noted that the seven methods are differentially appropriate for the examination of different types of causal variables (i.e. unchanging variables, discrete variables and variable states). Thus the usefulness of each type of research design for generating and testing hypotheses about each type of variable is summarized in Table 9.1.

CORRELATES AND POTENTIAL CAUSES OF OFFENDING

Parallel developments over time: concomitant change analyses

Some potential causal variables may occur in such close proximity to offending that, for all practical purposes, it is impossible to measure which comes first. Moreover, there may be reciprocal influences between apparent causes and offending itself (Thornberry, 1987). The analysis of concomitant change is aimed at addressing this situation and allows an examination of the parallel evolution of problem behaviours and personal and social explanatory factors. This research strategy makes possible the generation of hypotheses about particular causal influences. For example, Le Blanc et al. (1980) studied a representative sample of adolescents and a sample of convicted youth over two waves of testing and noted four classes of changes on measures of behaviour, personality, bond to society, and internal and

Table 9.1 The relationship between type of independent variable and strategies to establish causality in developmental studies

| Independent variable | Causal strategies | | | | | | |
| | Correlational approach | | | Predictive approach | | | Experimental |
	Concomitant change	Cross lagged	Sequential covariation	Prediction	Life event analysis	Stepping stone	Manipulation
Invariant (e.g. sex, race)	N/A	N/A	N/A	YES*	N/A	YES*	N/A
Discrete event (e.g. death of parent)	YES*	YES*	N/A	YES*	YES*	YES*	N/A
Variable state (e.g. marital conflict, peer influence)	YES*	YES*	YES*	YES*	N/A	YES*	YES*

*Control is desirable for third variables.
N/A=not applicable.

external social constraints: the four types of changes were increases, decreases, stability at a low level and stability at a high level. Parallel and contrasting developments could then be examined for the four classes of variables in the two samples.

The analysis of concomitant change may support the four classes of variables in the covariation between offending and various explanatory variables, but usually fails to shed light on the temporal order between independent and dependent variables. However, the categorization of variables with respect to classes of change (increases, decreases, stability at various levels) permits the identification of different factors associated with different dimensions of offending, i.e. onset, continuation, desistance, or aggravation.

Activation

With respect to the onset of problem behaviours, Jessor & Jessor (1977) analysed concomitant change in a descriptive manner, in a four-wave panel study of high school and college youth. They concluded that there were consonant developments in the areas of personality, perceived context, and deviant behaviour. In the personality domain, those who developed problem behaviour showed a decline in value on achievement, and an increase in tolerance for deviance and religiosity, and an increase in value on independence and social criticism. In the social environment, there was a decline in parental control and an increase in friends' support and friends' approval for problem behaviours. Finally, there was increased problem drinking, drug use, sexual experience, and general deviance, and a decline in conventional behaviours, such as church attendance.

Aggravation

In the Le Blanc et al. (1980) study of representative adolescents and delinquents, aggravation of offending was associated with low-level stability of attachment and communication with parents, high-level stability or increase in attachment to delinquent peers, a reduction of parental supervision, being inactive, and a worsening of the scores on various personality scales. In contrast, maintaining the same high degree of offending across the two waves of testing had somewhat different correlates, including a poor respect for persons in positions of authority, a low involvement in family chores, a weak adherence to social norms, a late recourse by parents to harsh penalties, and weak scores on various personality scales. In studies of concomitant variation, it is not completely easy to distinguish aggravation from early and late activation for different individuals in the sample.

Desistance

For conventional adolescents in the Le Blanc et al. (1980) study, the following factors were associated with a reduction in offending: a stable, high level or increase in the level of attachment to parents; stable high levels or increases in parental supervision; an improvement in attachment to an intimate person; a firmer commitment to school; and a more realistic view of persons in positions of authority. Among the convicted youth, the regulatory effects seemed to come more from outside than inside the natural milieu. Delinquency diminished under the influence of meaningful adults and with an involvement in work. These positive experiences occurred in parallel with improved psychological functioning, which was associated with a reduction in self-reported delinquency.

Long-term prediction from childhood experiences and indicators

Unlike those just described, some longitudinal studies span much longer intervals. In such studies explicit links are explored between childhood behaviours and experiences and various dimensions of later offending. Remarkably, at least one study was able to predict future delinquency to some degree on the basis of data collected when youngsters were 2 years old (Werner & Smith, 1977). In such long-term studies, because temporal priority is known and the hypothesized causal variables were measured years earlier than the outcome variables, investigators are more likely to ascribe causal status to the independent variables. The usual cautions against inferring causality from correlational data must still be given, but the longitudinal studies do take us one step further than the documentation of parallel covariation.

Nonetheless, adoption of a long-term perspective does not necessarily mean adoption of an explicitly developmental approach. A commonly held assumption of earlier criminological investigations was that causes and correlates of offending are similar in different segments of the delinquency career. Therefore, researchers have rarely highlighted differential predictors of onset, aggravation, or desistance from offending. This is inconsistent with known developmental shifts in the social influences that youngsters experience in the first two decades of their lives, for example the transition from parents to peers as predominant socializing influences. Therefore we summarize the findings from the long-term prediction studies with respect to activation, aggravation, and desistance in turn.

Activation

Investigators have examined various dimensions of a child's early environment and various aspects of the child's own early functioning in an effort to predict the age of onset of offending. With respect to environmental influences, disruptions in the family have been of particular concern. For example, Kolvin et al. (1988) followed up a birth cohort of 847 boys and girls to age 33. Data for the males showed that nearly a third (29.9%) of those who had been exposed to marital instability during the preschool years were first convicted before age 15, compared to 13.8% who were first convicted after the age of 15. Likewise, 28.4% of those boys who experienced parental illness during the preschool years were first convicted before age 15, compared with 6.9% of those who were first convicted at age 15 or older[1].

Other studies have also examined aspects of the family environment. Recent analyses of the Cambridge Study in Delinquent Development have demonstrated that, in two-parent families, lack of involvement of a father with his son in leisure activities was particularly associated with early conviction, i.e. between ages 10 and 13 (Farrington & Hawkins, 1991). It is not clear, however, whether the causal influence derives from other aspects of the parents and their social milieu that are associated with marital breakdown and lack of parental involvement. For example, Mannheim & Wilkins (1955), in their study of Borstal boys, found that broken homes were not associated with the early onset of crime, but that parental delinquency was. This finding was not, however, replicated by Farrington & Hawkins (1991), who found that parental criminality predicted late onset of offending. With respect to more global environmental conditions, Wikström (1987) reported on Project Metropolitan in Stockholm and found that the activation of offending varied with parents' social class: the median age of onset for youngsters with lower-class parents was 16, compared with 17 for those with working-class or lower-middle-class parents, and 18 for upper-middle-class families.

Other studies have looked within the individual child for predictors of later offending. A number of studies have indicated that hyperactivity and impulsivity in childhood are associated with an aggravation of conduct problems and later delinquency. For example, Offord et al. (1979) found that hyperactivity in delinquents was associated with an earlier onset of antisocial behaviours. Hyperactive delinquents were on the average 10.8 years old when they were first reported to show four different antisocial symptoms; the average age for displaying the same symptoms was 12.5 years for nonhyperactive delinquents.

Hyperactivity and impulsivity are often associated with aggression and other conduct problems. This raises the issue of whether the early appearing behaviours are causal influences that activate offending some years later, or simply earlier precursors or early manifestations of the same phenomenon. However, studies of youngsters who score high on aggression and hyperactivity early in life show that they are particularly vulnerable to delinquency

(Loney, Kramer & Milich, 1982; Magnusson, 1988; Loeber, 1988), compared with those who score high on hyperactivity only or on aggression only.

It would follow that, since hyperactivity, impulsivity, and attentional problems predict an early onset of offending, late-onset delinquents would be much less likely to have been hyperactive in childhood. In a reanalysis of the data from the Cambridge Study in Delinquent Development (Farrington, Loeber & van Kammen, 1990), inner-city boys from London were divided into four groups on the basis of parents', teachers', and peers' reports of their behaviour at ages 8–10: those scoring high on hyperactivity and impulsivity only, those scoring high on conduct problems only, those scoring high on both sets of problems, and those failing to score high with respect to either. Attention deficit with hyperactivity and impulsivity was a better predictor of early conviction (before age 14) than were conduct problems. Relatively few (8%) of the hyperactivity-only subjects were first convicted in early adulthood, as opposed to 25% of those with conduct problems and 32% of those with both sorts of problems[2].

Other investigators have attempted to predict the age of onset of target problem behaviours by examining the earlier occurrence of other sorts of problems. For example, school discipline problems, stealing, vandalism, and truancy earlier in childhood predict early as opposed to late onset of drug use (Robins & Przybeck, 1985). Lack of obedience in childhood also correlates more highly with early versus late activation of drug use (Smith & Fogg, 1978, 1979).

In summary, the available evidence indicates that family circumstances, hyperactivity, and the occurrence of particular problem behaviours in childhood predict the early as opposed to late onset of criminal offending. Few studies, however, have examined systematically which factors uniquely predict the subprocesses of activation, namely, acceleration, stabilization, and diversification of the components of offending.

Aggravation

Very few studies have examined predictors of escalation in offending, and most that have search for causal influences within the individual. For example, Wadsworth (1979), observing a birth cohort studied until age 21, scaled juvenile delinquent acts according to the seriousness of offenses. Boys' physical maturity at age 15 was predictive of the seriousness of offending, but only in the case of boys from a low socioeconomic class. Various measures of childhood personality appear to predict an aggravation of drug use in adolescence (Brook et al., 1989).

Activation has itself been examined as a predictor of aggravation. Tontodonato (1988) and Tolan & Lorion (1988) concurred in showing that early onset was by far the best predictor of more frequent and serious delinquency. Structural variables and family experiences then entered the equation. Tolan & Lorion (1988) showed that, second only to age of onset, family systemic/interactional characteristics were most helpful for predicting subsequent frequency, while individual and school factors, family demographics, and social status had virtually no explanatory power.

Desistance

Most known predictors of desistance appear to be the reverse of risk factors predicting offending (Loeber & Stouthamer-Loeber, 1987). This is particularly evident with respect to family characteristics. Thus, since marital conflict is a strong predictor of offending, the lower the degree of marital conflict, the lower the likelihood of the offspring offending. Fathers' involvement in their sons' leisure activities at the age of 11 was associated with desistance from crime between the ages of 21 and 32.

There is an obvious need to identify "unique" predictors of desistance, which are not simply the opposite of predictors of activation or aggravation. One line of evidence suggests that a different set of problems within the individual militate against continued offending: emotional problems, anxiety, or neurotic problems all predict the absence or reduced likelihood of later offending (see evidence summarized by Loeber & Stouthamer-Loeber, 1987).

In summary, the causal status of risk factors in the long-term prediction studies still remains to be established. Rarely have these studied systematically controlled for a wide range of third variables. Although much emphasis has been placed on finding different predictors of activation and aggravation, many factors appear to affect both, and may reflect long-acting, structural influences. A possible avenue of exploration might be to study resilient individuals, as did Werner & Smith (1982), or subjects from particularly vulnerable backgrounds, as did Farrington et al. (1988). Identification of the protective factors operating on these individuals could help to rule out some hypothesized causal influences relating to activation, aggravation, or desistance.

Which comes first: cross-lagged panel analysis

Both the short-term studies of parallel developments and the long-term studies of prediction from childhood variables establish possible causal links for further investigation. Cross-lagged analyses represent a concerted attempt to establish the direction of causal influence in correlational studies. Some longitudinal studies have made full use of the two or more waves of testing by analyzing all of the independent and dependent variables in a cross-lagged model (Liska & Reed, 1985; Ouimet, 1986). The logic of the cross-lagged design is to determine whether the association between the putative cause at time 1 and the dependent variable at time 2 is greater than the association between a measure of the dependent variable at time 1 and the putative cause at time 2. These "cross-lagged" associations are contrasted with the overall level of stability over time for the putative causal influence and the outcome variable.

Studies using this approach have the advantage of informing us about the temporal ordering of events. However, these designs have several disadvantages for causal analysis (see Rogosa, 1980). They do not distinguish between behaviours that have emerged from those that persisted over time, and they often offer only a very limited time perspective on the causes of offending over two points in time. Although such analyses could be carried out over long periods of time, in criminological studies the interval between testing points is usually only one or two years. In other cases, however, cross-lagged designs are used with much greater inter-wave intervals (see e.g. Eron et al., 1972).

Studies of offending that have used cross-lagged analyses have been able to examine the differential impact of contemporary versus lagged influences. Liska & Reed (1985) clearly showed that the reciprocal effects at each time of measurement were stronger than the lagged effects. Attachment to parents was associated with delinquency which in turn determined attachment to school. Attachment to school had a reciprocal effect on attachment to parents. Ouimet (1986), with a larger set of explanatory variables, established that attachment to parents at time 1 had a stronger effect on subsequent delinquency than attachment to parents at time 2. Other variables, such as attachment to delinquent peers and external controls, only had an immediate effect on delinquency. Commitment to education and deviant activities at either time had similar effects on subsequent offending.

When self-reported delinquency is introduced as the independent variable at time 1, it is very common that the most important predictor of later delinquency is prior delinquency. When it comes to the content of the causal variables, Agnew (1985) and Elliott, Huizinga & Ageton (1985) agreed that social control variables were not very efficient in explaining subsequent self-reported delinquency. Elliott, Huizinga & Ageton (1985) showed that bonding to delinquent friends was the most important factor as compared with conventional bonding, social disorganization, and strain variables (see also Elliott, Huizinga & Menard, 1989). In such tests, both concurrent and prospective factors were included so that the causal status of delinquent friends remains to be elucidated (Loeber, 1990).

Duration and timing of causal influence: analysis of sequential covariation

The aforementioned designs make measurements at prespecified time points in development; they do not necessarily examine the onset and change over time in the hypothesized causal factors. In contrast, in an analysis of sequential covariation, a particular independent variable is specified and several things about it are measured, in particular its frequency, its duration of influence, and its timing of onset. We shall concentrate on the second and third of these, because we have not been able to unearth studies in criminology documenting sequential covariation between independent and dependent variables (see Loeber & Stouthamer-Loeber, 1986, for a review of studies showing sequential covariation in the frequency of children's conduct problems and parental behaviour).

The basic rationale for examining the effects of the duration of an independent variable is borrowed from epidemiological studies of dose–response relationships: the longer the exposure to a noxious influence, the more likely its effects on offending. These effects may include both activation and aggravation. For example, in an important study by Cohen & Brook (1987), children were followed up over a period of eight years. The duration of familial handicaps was associated with the later onset but greater aggravation of juvenile conduct problems. More particularly, worsening forms of child rearing were associated with increased prevalence of conduct disorder.

Analyses of sequential covariation can also be used when the timing of onset of offending is precisely known, but where the frequency and pattern of offending may subsequently evolve differently, depending on changes in other variables. Thus what the researcher is looking for is the behavioural, social, and psychological consequences of various points of onset of a particular problem behaviour. In other words, the timing of the activation of offending is itself examined as a possible cause of later persistence, aggravation, and desistance. For example, Jessor & Jessor (1977) have studied the impact of the time when an adolescent starts to drink alcohol, use marijuana, or become sexually active. They reported that there were different rates of change, depending on the time of onset. A later onset led to more rapid changes, implying both that an adolescent with a late onset of a problem behaviour would assume the characteristics of those who started earlier, and that the changes were pervasive across a variety of problem behaviours. In other words, it was more a change in general status than in specific behaviours. Starting to drink, use marijuana, or become sexually active all involved the same type of changes in other aspects of personality (a lowering of value placed on achievement, an increase in value placed on independence, increased tolerance of deviance, and a decrease in negative functions).

Le Blanc et al., (1991) have similarly looked at the consequences of the age of onset of offending. They compared 10-year-old boys who had started offending at earlier (ages 4, 5, and 6 years) as opposed to later (6, 7, and 8 years) points in development, in terms of their subsequent offending. An earlier as opposed to later onset had the following consequences at age 10: a higher frequency of offending and commission of more serious acts; a lower level of attachment to persons; lower commitment to institutions; lower involvement in conventional activities and beliefs in conventional norms; a higher level of external constraints and formal social reactions; and a personality profile at the age of 10 that resembled that of adolescent delinquents.

Analysis of life events

The method just discussed, the examination of what happens after offending begins, focuses on the timing of a discrete event and its later consequences. One can look at the sequelae of particular experiences that impinge on the individual, as well as the timing of the individual's own actions. Thus the last-mentioned example of sequential covariation analysis is paralleled by the study of the impact of life events.

The life-events approach is concerned with the impact of specific salient and discrete events on subsequent offending. Such events include leaving school, entering the labor force, going into the armed forces, and getting married. Over the last two decades, several longitudinal studies have addressed the influences of life events on within-individual changes in offending and substance use. These studies must be distinguished from those that simply correlate levels of certain sorts of experiences with certain sorts of offending (correlating employment and crime, for instance) or those that compare groups with and without the experience (e.g. comparing the delinquency of married and unmarried individuals).

Activation or aggravation

Some life events appear to activate or aggravate a criminal career. For example, unemployment in late adolescence increases delinquency (Farrington, Ohlin & Wilson, 1986). Young men become more delinquent after they begin to cohabit (Rand, 1987). Criminal conviction itself may be seen as a life event that aggravates subsequent offending: getting caught for the first time increases subsequent offending (Farrington, 1977), but a reconviction does not have such an amplification effect (Farrington, Osborn & West, 1978). Some life events may have delayed effects on offending: dropping out of school in adolescence increases the likelihood of criminality between the ages of 21 and 24 (Thornberry, Moore & Christenson, 1985), though it decreases offending if it is followed by an entry into the job market (Elliot & Voss, 1974; Pronovost & Le Blanc, 1980).

Desistance

Various sorts of life events are associated with desistance. Young men commit fewer criminal acts and become less deviant after marriage (West, 1982; Rand, 1987), espcially if they do not marry someone who is deviant herself (Bachman, O-Malley & Johnston, 1978; West, 1982). However, parenthood has a negligible impact on subsequent offending (Rand, 1987). Young men who move out of the city are less criminal in their new environments (West, 1982). Entry into the armed forces has no impact on the criminality of white men, but decreases the subsequent criminal activity of members of other racial groups, especially if they receive job training in the armed forces (Rand, 1987). Entry into the armed forces appears to increase some sorts of problem behaviours while decreasing others: it is followed by an increase in the use of tolerated substances but a decrease in restricted substances (Newcomb & Bentler, 1987).

The conclusions of the life-event studies are somewhat limited in that there is a scarcity of replications with different subject populations, and the impact of third variables has seldom been controlled. Furthermore, Hogan (1978) suggests that not only the presence or absence of life events, but their order may be critical for determining outcomes. Nonetheless, life-events analyses constitute an important approach to the study of the causes of offending because a change in the hypothesized causal variable can be timed very precisely and, in the case of normative events, its impact can be gauged from a comparison between prior and subsequent offending. Obviously this form of analysis requires the study of change variables; the study of ongoing influences, such as broader psychosocial factors, is more difficult.

The stepping-stones approach

The aforementioned methods of sequential covariation and life-events analysis take an explicitly developmental approach, insofar as they examine the impact of the timing and duration of particular conditions and events. The stepping-stones approach extends these by focusing not just on the timing of discrete events and outcomes, but on a more complex developmental sequence. The time frame that is adopted is that of the long-term prediction studies.

All of the preceding modes of analysis have assumed a relatively straightforward relationship between particular independent and dependent variables. A developmental approach to criminology, however, assumes that there are a multitude of such one-to-one causal relationships, that formerly dependent variables may become independent variables over time, that causality is best represented by a developmental network of causal factors or by a series of stepping stones representing the factors, and that such networks can extend over long time periods.

Given that the base rate of chronic offenders and substance abusers in representative populations is low, Robins, Davis & Wish (1977) suggested that a way out of the dilemma of studying low-base-rate events is to decompose these events into a series of stages or stepping stones and to calculate the transition rates from one stage to another. The stepping-stone model thus allows the identification of factors that are uniquely associated with particular developmental processes of offending and allows specification of the sequence and duration of potential causal factors along the developmental time line.

In the stepping-stones approach, identification of the time ordering of factors is fundamental. Factors from different age periods are used and their predictive ability on a distal outcome is assessed. A sophisticated stepping-stone model was developed by Farrington (1986b), using a range of factors measured during childhood, adolescence, and young adulthood to predict official criminality up to age 24. The results are twofold.

First, he demonstrated a stepwise continuity in antisocial behaviour: troublesomeness and daring behaviour at ages 8–10 predicted convictions at 10–13; the latter predicted convictions at age 14–16, which predicted convictions at 17–20, which, in turn, predicted convictions at 21–24. Convictions at ages 10–13 also predicted self-reported delinquency at age 14. The latter, and convictions at age 14–16, predicted antisocial tendency at age 18. All these predictions held when a number of other factors were taken into account.

Second, Farrington (1986b) identified four factors during late childhood (economic deprivation, family criminality, parental mishandling, and school failure) that were significantly associated with troublesomeness or daring behaviour at age 8–10. All of these factors independently predicted conviction in the juvenile years. Convictions in the young adult years (ages 18–20) were best predicted by two former predictors, family criminality measured at age 10 and economic deprivation measured at age 14, as well as two new predictors, truancy at 12–14, and delinquent friends at age 14. Economic deprivation at age 14 continued to predict adult offending, together with two new predictors at age 18, unstable job record and anti-establishment attitude.

Thus, some predictors, family criminality and economic deprivation, exerted nearly constant influence on antisocial behaviour throughout the age range under investigation, whereas others, parental mishandling and school failure, were particularly relevant for the early part of the career.

Truancy and delinquent friends were important predictors of offending in young adulthood, whereas unstable job record and anti-establishment attitude determined offending in adulthood. What is more significant is the fact that these predictors of delinquency and crime are also virtually the same for frequency offending (Farrington, 1987), adolescent aggression, and adult violence (Farrington, 1989a), suggesting that all these measures index a general antisocial tendency.

The stepping-stones approach to the study of causes of offending offers a wider perspective on the entire developmental sequence than do the other methods discussed so far. There were, however, some limitations in the Farrington (1986a) study. The number and type of variables used were rather small at each phase in the sequence, and most of them were structural variables. Psychosocial variables were relatively underrepresented.

Nevertheless, the effectiveness of the stepping-stone approach can be increased by means of the following modifications. First, prediction of onset of offending is needed within a given period, rather than lumping together in a given age period those whose delinquency is ongoing and those who have just started breaking the law. Second, measurement of the cumulative impact of risk factors occurring in prior phases is required, either in terms of their frequency or in terms of individuals' length of exposure to them. This allows the examination of a possible dose–response relation between the risk factors and offending, such as those explored in the shorter term by the method of sequential covariation. Third, it is necessary to examine sleeper effects (Kagan & Moss, 1962), where the effect of an independent variable tends to emerge over time rather than being present instantaneously or at equal strength along the developmental time line. Finally, examination of both short-term and long-term causal factors should be undertaken.

Experimental manipulation

In comparison with all the preceding techniques, experimental manipulation is the most powerful strategy for distinguishing between correlates and causes of crime. Its crucial feature is the random assignment of a sufficiently large number of subjects to experimental and control conditions. This should randomize potential causal factors other than those manipulated in the course of the intervention. Thus, the power of manipulation in randomized experiments rests on establishing control over other sources of influence, and then demonstrating that the introduction of a variable or variables is followed by a change of outcome in the experimental but not the control group.

Obviously certain categories of variables do not easily lend themselves to manipulation. However, when it is ethically permissible for variables to change, experimentation constitutes a powerful tool for discriminating between unexplained correlates and causes.

According to Schwartz, Flamant & Lelouch (1980), experimental manipulations can serve two basic purposes. Firstly, in a *pragmatic clinical trial*, they can show that a particular intervention or preventive strategy works. Secondly, in an *exploratory trial*, experimentation can demonstrate that causal control can be established in a small segment of the causal network.

Pragmatic clinical trials have as their direct goal the amelioration of existing problem behaviours or their prevention (i.e. it should encourage desistance or prevent activation). Ideally, subjects should be representative of the population at risk. Usually, the large number of variables manipulated in the course of an intervention or prevention study give only a hint of the causal status of each. In this way, such broad-stroke pragmatic trials are similar to correlational studies of concomitant variation, in that they serve to generate, not test, precise causal hypotheses.

An exploratory trial may serve to compensate for the imprecise nature of pragmatic interventions or prevention studies. The focus is on the proximal link between a potential cause and an intermediate (rather than an ultimate) outcome. For instance, the intervention may concentrate on showing that certain forms of teacher training improve classroom attendance (the reverse of truancy which predicts delinquent activities). Unlike pragmatic clinical trials, exploratory trials require relatively homogeneous groups of subjects. In this example the subjects should be those at risk for truancy, rather than all children in the classroom.

Lack of space does not allow us to review the findings of exploratory trials, although it seems clear they would provide the building blocks for pragmatic interventions (see several reviews of pragmatic interventions, e.g. Farrington, 1982; Loeber, 1984; Kazdin, 1985). Among the most successful early interventions, the Perry Preschool Project is the one best known among criminologists (Berreuta-Clement et al., 1984). It provided concentrated Head Start training to disadvantaged preschoolers and demonstrated a lower rate of delinquency in adulthood for the experimental group, as compared to the control group. Although a number of intervention studies focus on the preschool period (see also Kolvin et al., 1988), there are multiple entry points for intervention at several intermediate steps (see Loeber, 1990, for examples). For example, when delinquent youngsters were assigned either to an all delinquent peer group or to a prosocial peer group, the latter had a significantly better treatment outcome (Feldman, Caplinger & Wodarski, 1984).

It should be noted that experimental designs have an obvious superiority over the other methods in testing specific causal hypotheses. However, they do not always take an explicitly developmental perspective, and it is in this regard that the other methods have their strengths. Furthermore, some important sorts of causal variables are impossible to examine in experimental studies. In general, unchanging background factors do not yield to study by means of concomitant change, cross-lagged analyses, sequential covariation, or experimentation (see Table 9.1).

CONCLUSIONS

Causality

We attempted to demonstrate three points. First, few criminological theories have made optimal use of the developmental perspective to establish causality. Second, too few empirical studies have tried to sequence causal factors in relation to individual offending; those studies that did attempt to accomplish this task were hampered by methodological difficulties. Third, the nature of independent variables influences the options for making causal influences, with those variables that can vary over time being most optimal. We have drawn a distinction between causal factors that are long-acting and stable and those that occur proximally and are changeable. Not all causal influences appear equally potent at all life phases, and much remains to be learned about sensitive periods in which causal potency is enhanced.

Overall, the study of the correlates of individual offending is very well advanced, perhaps reaching a ceiling in cross-sectional studies. But the study of the causes of individual offending is only just beginning. We have outlined some ways to optimize causal inferences from longitudinal studies. We would warn readers, though, to guard against simplifying causal effects by conceiving them unidirectionally, that is, so that only independent factors have a causal impact on dependent variables. It is important to remember that independent and dependent factors may have reciprocal effects. Much work remains to be done before it will be possible to distinguish among the many putative causes of crime.

Developmental and explanatory theories of offending

Along with a renewed interest in theoretical criminology has come a few statements supporting a developmental explanation of offending. This orientation is of such importance that it must be emphasized and pursued with vigor. We can no longer be satisfied with a myopic view of the causes of individual offending, rooted in a specific moment in time, with the causes invariant with developmental stages. Rather, there is a need to adopt a systems view, in which numerous factors operate and interact along the developmental time line. The level of youngsters' commitment to education during adolescence, for example, cannot be viewed as a *sui generis* reality; it has emerged progressively through the influence of numerous structural and psychosocial influences in a context of specific antecedent factors (Hawkins et al., 1986). We think that more complete theories will emerge in criminology, not only through the integrative theoretical movement, but through consideration of the developmental perspective.

Future longitudinal studies

In North America a new generation of longitudinal studies is building momentum. Although still in their infancy, they have a potential for advancing our knowledge of individuals' offending, and are likely to exploit the advantages offered by the longitudinal design for distinguishing correlates from causes of crime. In the area of causation, these studies are enabling us to formulate and answer fundamental questions such as:

(1)   What is the time ordering of putative causal factors?
(2)   Do certain factors operate primarily and specifically during the perinatal period or infancy, and others during childhood, adolescence, or young adulthood, respectively?
(3)   Is it possible to distinguish stage-specific causal factors from the factors that may be stable, and long-lasting, influencing activation and aggravation throughout the delinquency career?
(4)   Are some factors primarily associated with the activation and aggravation of offending, while other factors are mainly associated with desistance?

Prevention and intervention

Researchers who have worked for decades with juvenile repeat offenders are convinced that some degree of desistance can be brought about through intensive efforts by adults in controlled environments, such as group homes supervised by trained surrogate parents or by specially trained foster parents (Hawkins et al., 1985; Wolf, Braukmann & Ramp, 1987). Once released into their old environment, however, relapse in offending and other problem behaviours is very common. Wolf, Braukmann & Ramp (1987) even speak of the chronic nature of the "social disability" displayed by these youngsters, a disability which requires long-term commitment and care.

It is not surprising that calls for preventive intervention have been sounded more frequently in recent years. As has been pointed out by Lorion (1982), knowledge of the etiology of offending is essential for the development of preventive programs, since the modification of etiological factors is the backbone of prevention. Advocates of early intervention have proposed that there are at least two viable strategies: (1) postponing the onset of the age-inappropriate behaviour, as in the case of early alcohol use or teenage pregnancy (e.g. Jessor, 1982); and (2) eliminating early problem behaviours (labeled "stepping stones" or "gateway behaviours"), in order to arrest the activation of subsequent antisocial behaviours (O'Donnell & Clayton, 1982; Voeltz & Evans, 1982).

The postponement strategy assumes that there is a period of vulnerability to activation and that once youngsters pass that period, activation is either less likely to occur or will take place more benignly and in accordance with age norms (as in the case of alcohol use). The second assumption of the postponement strategy is that postponement leads to a higher likelihood of youngsters' completion of age-normative milestones, such as the finishing of secondary school. In contrast, the stepping-stone/gateway approach assumes that the prevention of learning of one behaviour impedes the acquisition of behaviours that typically occur later in the developmental sequence. Thus, "intervention to prevent expression of the behavior at one age would have directly transmitted benefits at later ages" (Hewitt et al., 1988, p. 36).

The rationales for postponement or early intervention can be challenged. What if successive onsets are determined by a common underlying cause that is stable over time and has long-term rather than short-term effects? For example, Robins & Wish (1977, p. 466) studied black youngsters' developmental sequences in antisocial behavior, and examined whether one act was "either a necessary or a sufficient cause of the second". A necessary cause was inferred "if the second act almost never occurs unless preceded by the first . . . ; [while] a sufficient cause [can be inferred] if the first act is almost invariable followed by the second". The authors found only 3 sequences out of 78 comparisons that fulfilled these criteria, which hardly produced evidence that one behavior was "causing" another. Instead, it is more plausible that a common underlying tendency toward antisocial behavior could explain the findings, although the authors did not address this. If so, as Hewitt et al. (1988, p. 36) point out, "intervening to prevent the expression of behavior . . . at one age would not confer subsequent benefits *in the absence of continued intervention*".

Given our imperfect state of knowledge of stable and variable causes of crime, conclusions about optimal types of intervention are inherently premature. However, we see promise in the approaches offered by developmental criminology for addressing these issues and ultimately lending support to particular types of preventive or rehabilitative intervention, within both the mental health arena and the criminal justice system.

NOTES

1. The following variables did not distinguish between early and late conviction, but significantly distinguished between convicted and nonconvicted boys irrespective

of age: poor physical/domestic care of children/home, social dependency, overcrowding, and poor mothering.
2. Although hyperactivity, impulsivity, and attention problems are associated with early onset of delinquent acts, it should be stressed that a proportion of high hyperactivity–impulsivity–attention deficit (HIA) youngsters without appreciable conduct problems later became delinquent also. Although little is known about the developmental course of delinquent acts for this group, we assume that these youngsters adopted a delinquent way of life in adolescence, or perhaps eluded detection by the police.

ACKNOWLEDGEMENTS

An extended version of this chapter was first published under the title "Toward a developmental criminology" in M. Tonry & N. Morris (eds), *Crime and Justice, an Annual Review*, vol. 12, the University of Chicago Press, 1990, and is republished here in a revised and improved format with important revisions with permission from the University of Chicago Press. The authors are greatly indebted to the following individuals who provided inspiration for this chapter: Adrian Angold, Carol Baicker-McKee, E. Jane Costello, Marcel Fréchette, Magda Stouthamer-Loeber, and members of the Working Group on Onset of Delinquency and Crime, Program on Human Development and Criminal Behavior, sponsored by the MacArthur Foundation and the Nationl Institute of Justice. The authors also are grateful for the editorial comments by Michael Tonry and Richard Wills. Special thanks are due to Celia Nourse Eatman and Rebecca Cunningham for their excellent editing of earlier drafts, and to Debbie Tokar for her assistance in the preparation of the manuscript. The chapter was written with financial assistance under Grant No. 86-JN-CX-0009 from the Office of Juvenile Justice and Delinquency Prevention, Grant MH42528 of the National Institute of Mental Health, a grant from the Ministry of the Solicitor-General of Canada, and the Canadian Research Council for the Humanities and Social Sciences. Points of view or opinions in this document are those of the authors and do not necessarily represent the official position or policies of the US Department of Justice.

REFERENCES

Agnew, R. (1984). Appearance and delinquency. *Criminology*, **22**, 421–440.
Agnew, R. (1985). Social control theory and delinquency: a longitudinal test. *Criminology*, **23**, 47–61.
Allison, P. D. (1985). *Event History Analysis: Regression for Longitudinal Event Data*, Sage, Beverly Hills, Calif.
Bachman, J. G., Green, S. & Wirtanen, I. D. (1971). *Youth in Transition: Dropping Out, Problems or Symptom*, Institute for Social Research, Ann Arbor, Mich.
Bachman, J. G., O'Malley, P. M. & Johnston, J. (1978). *Youth in Transition: Adolescence to Adulthood. Change and Stability in the Lives of Young Men*, Institute for Social Research, Ann Arbor, Mich.
Bateson, P. & Hinde, R. A. (1987). Developmental changes in sensitivity to experience. In M. H. Bornstein (ed.), *Sensitive Periods in Development: Interdisciplinary Perspectives*, Erlbaum, Hillsdale, NJ, pp. 19–34.
Behar, D. & Stewart, M. A. (1984). Aggressive conduct disorder: the influence of social class, sex and age on the clinical picture. *Journal of Child Psychology and Psychiatry*, **25**, 119–124.

Bellinger, D. B., Needleman, H. L., Bromfield, R. & Mintz, M. (1984). A follow up study of the academic attainment and classroom behavior of children with elevated dentine lead levels. *Biological and Heavy Metal Research*, **6**, 207–223.

Berrueta-Clement, J. R., Schweinhart, L. J., Barnett, W. S., Epstein, A. S. & Weikart, D. P. (1984). *Changed Lives: The Effects of the Perry Preschool Program on Youths Through Age 19*, High Scope Press, Ypsilanti, Mich.

Blumstein, A., Cohen J., Roth, J. A. & Visher, C. V. (1986). *Criminal Careers and Career Criminals*, National Academy of Sciences, Washington, DC.

Brook, J. S., Whiteman, M., Scovell, G. A. & Cohen, P. (1989). Changes in drug involvement: a longitudinal study of childhood and adolescent determinants. *Psychological Reports*, **65**, 707–726.

Cadoret, R. J. & Cain, C. (1980). Sex differences in predictors of antisocial behavior in adoptees. *Archives of General Psychiatry*, **37**, 1171–1175.

Catalano, R. F. & Hawkins, J. D. (1986). The social development model: a theory of antisocial behavior. Paper presented at the Safeco Lecture on Crime and Delinquency, School of Social Work, University of Washington, Seattle, Wash.

Cohen, P. & Brook, J. (1987). Family factors related to the persistence of psychopathology in childhood and adolescence. *Psychiatry*, **50**, 332–345.

Cohen, P., Brook, J. & Kandel, D. (1991). Predictors of adolescent drug use. In R. M. Lerner, A. C. Petersen & J. Brooks-Gunn (eds), *The Encyclopedia of Adolescence*, vol. 2, Garland, New York, pp. 268–271.

Cook, T. D. & Campbell, D. T. (1979). *Quasi-experimentation*, Rand McNally, Chicago, Ill.

Elliott, D. S., Huizinga, D. & Ageton, S. S. (1985). *Explaining Delinquency and Drug Use*, Sage, Beverly Hills, Calif.

Elliott, D. S., Huizinga, D. & Menard, S. (1989). *Multiple problem youth: delinquency, substance use and mental health problems*. New York, Springer-Verlag.

Elliott, D. S. & Voss, H. L. (1974). *Delinquency and Dropout*, D. C. Heath, Lexington, Mass.

Empey, L. T. (1978). *American Delinquency: Its Meaning and Construction*, Dorsey Press, Homewood, Ill.

Eron, L. D., Huesmann, L. R., Lefkowitz, M. M. & Walder, L. O. (1972). Does television violence cause aggression? *American Psychologist*, **27**, 253–263.

Farrington, D. P. (1977). The effects of public labeling. *British Journal of Criminology*, **17**, 112–125.

Farrington, D. P. (1982). Randomized experiments on crime and justice. In N. Morris & M. Tonry (eds), *Crime and Justice*, vol. 4, University of Chicago Press, Chicago, Ill, pp. 257–308.

Farrington, D. P. (1986a). Age and crime. In M. Tonry & N. Morris (eds), *Crime and Justice*, vol. 7, University of Chicago Press, Chicago, Ill.

Farrington, D. P. (1986b). Stepping stones to adult criminal careers. In D. Olweus, J. Block & M. R. Yarrow (eds), *Development of Antisocial and Prosocial Behavior*, Academic Press, New York, NY.

Farrington, D. P. (1987). Early precursors of frequent offending. In J. Q. Wilson & G. C. Loury (eds), *From Children to Citizens*, Springer-Verlag, New York, NY.

Farrington, D. P. (1989a). Early predictors of adolescent aggression and adult violence. *Violence and Victims*, **4**, 79–100.

Farrington, D. P. (1989b). Studying changes within individuals: The causes of offending. In M. Rutter (ed.), *The Power of Longitudinal Data*, Cambridge University Press, Cambridge, UK, pp. 158–183.

Farrington, D. P., Ohlin, L. E. & Wilson, J. Q. (1986). *Understanding and Controlling Crime: Toward a Research Strategy*, Springer-Verlag, New York.

Farrington, D. P., Gallagher, L., Morley, L., St. Ledger, R. J. & West, D. J. (1988). Are there any successful men from criminogenic backgrounds? *Psychiatry*, **51**, 1114–1130.

Farrington, D. P. & Hawkins, J. D. (1991). Prediction of participation, early onset, and later persistence in officially recorded offending: the relevance of social development model constructs. *Criminal Behavior and Mental Health*, **1**, 1–34.

Farrington, D. P., Loeber, R. & van Kammen, W. B. (1990). Longterm criminal outcomes of hyperactivity–impulsivity–attention deficit and conduct problems in childhood. In L. Robins & M. Rutter (eds), *Straight and Devious Pathways to Adulthood*, Cambridge University Press, Cambridge, UK, pp. 62–81.

Farrington, D. P., Osborn, S. G. & West, D. J. (1978). The persistence of labeling effects. *British Journal of Criminology*, 18, 277–284.

Feldman, D. (1969). Psychoanalysis and crime. In D. R. Cressey & D. A. Ward (eds), *Delinquency, Crime and Social Process*, Harper and Row, New York, NY, pp. 433–442.

Feldman, R. A., Caplinger, T. E. & Wodarski, J. S. (1984). *The St. Louis Conundrum*, Prentice-Hall, Englewood Cliffs, NJ.

Ferdinand, T. N. (1987). The methods of delinquency theory. *Criminology*, **25**, 841–863.

Gottfredson, D. & Hirschi, T. (1987). The methodological adequacy of longitudinal research on crime. *Criminology*, **25**, 581–614.

Hawkins, J. D., Lishner, D. M., Catalano, R. F. & Howard, M. O. (1986). Childhood predictors of adolescent substance abuse: toward an empirically grounded theory. *Journal of Children in Contemporary Society*, **8**, 11–40.

Hawkins, R. P., Meadowcroft, P., Trout, B. A. & Luster, W. C. (1985). Foster family-based treatment. *Journal of Clinical and Child Psychology*, **14**, 220–228.

Hewitt, J. K., Eaves, L. J., Neale, M. C. & Meyer, J. M. (1988). Resolving causes of developmental continuity or tracking: I. Longitudinal twin studies during growth. *Behavior Genetics*, **18**, 133–151.

Hirschi, T. & Gottfredson, M. (1983). Age and the explanation of crime. *American Journal of Sociology*, **89**, 552–584.

Hirschi, T. & Gottfredson, M. (1987). Causes of white-collar crime. *Criminology*, **25**, 949–974.

Hirschi, T. & Selvin, H. C. (1967). *Delinquency Research: An Appraisal of Analytic Methods*, The Free Press, New York, NY.

Hogan, D. P. (1978). The variable order of events in the life course. *American Sociological Review*, **43**, 573–586.

Jennings, W. S., Kilkenny, R. & Kohlberg, L. (1983). Moral-development theory and practice for youthful and adult offenders. In W. S. Laufer & J. M. Day (eds), *Personality Theory, Moral Development, and Criminal Behavior*, Lexington Books, Lexington, Mass., pp. 281–356.

Jessor, R. (1982). Critical issues in research on adolescent health promotion. In A. C. Peterson & C. Perry (eds), *Promoting Adolescent Health*, Academic Press, New York, NY. pp. 447–465.

Jessor, R. & Jessor, S. L. (1977). *Problem Behavior and Psychosocial Development*, Academic Press, New York, NY.

Kagan, J. & Moss, H. A. (1962). *Birth to Maturity*, John Wiley, New York, NY.

Kaplan, H. B. (1983). *Patterns of Juvenile Delinquency*, Sage, Beverly Hills, Calif.

Kaplan, H. B. & Robbins, C. (1983). Testing a general theory of deviant behavior in longitudinal perspective. In K. Van Dusen & S. A. Mednick (eds), *Prospective Studies in Delinquent and Criminal Behavior*, Kluwer-Nijhoff, Boston, Mass, pp. 117–146.

Kazdin, A. E. (1985). *Treatment of Antisocial Behavior in Children and Adolescents*, Dorsey Press, Homewood, Ill.

Kolvin, T., Miller, F. J. W., Fletting, M. & Kolvin, P. A. (1988). Social and parenting factors affecting criminal-offense rates: findings from the Newcastle thousand family study. *British Journal of Psychiatry*, **152**, 80–90.

Labouvie, E. W. (1986). Methodological issues in the prediction of psychopathology: a life-span perspective. In L. Erlenmeyer-Kimling & N. E. Miller (eds), *Life-span Research on the Prediction of Psychopathology*, Erlbaum, Hillsdale, NJ, pp. 128–146.

LaGrange, R. L. & Raskin White, H. (1985). Age differences in delinquency: a test of theory. *Criminology*, **23**, 19–46.

Le Blanc, M. (1989). Designing a self-reported instrument for the study of the development of offending from childhood to adulthood: issues and problems. In M. W. Klein (ed.), *Cross-national Research in Self-reported Crime and Delinquency*, Kluwer-Nijhoff, Boston, Mass, pp. 371–398.

Le Blanc, M., Charland, R., Côté, G. & Provonost, L. (1980). *Développement psycho-social et évolution de la délinquance au cours de l'adolescence: Recherche, structure, et dynamique du comportement délinquent*, vol. 3, of final report, Groupe de Recherche sur Inadaptation Juvenile, University of Montreal, Montreal, Canada.

Le Blanc, M. & Fréchette, M. (1989). *Male Criminal Activity from Childhood through Youth: Multilevel and Developmental Perspectives*, Springer-Verlag, New York, NY.

Le Blanc, M, McDuff, P., Charlebois, C., Gagnon, C., Larrivée, S. & Tremblay, R. E. (1991). Social and psychological consequences, at 10 years old, of an earlier onset of self-reported delinquency, *Psychiatry*, **54**, 133–147.

Le Blanc, M. & Ouimet, M. (1986). Validation d'une théorie intégrative de la régulation de la conduite délinquante. In R. E. Tremblay, M. Le Blanc & A. E. Schwartzman (eds), *La Conduite délinquante des adolescents à Montréal (1974–1985)*, Université de Montréal, Montréal, Canada.

Liska, A. & Reed, M. (1985). Ties to conventional institutions and delinquency: estimating reciprocal effects. *American Sociological Review*, **50**, 547–560.

Loeber, R. (1984). Experimental studies to reduce antisocial and delinquent child behavior: implications for future programs and optimal times for intervention. Paper presented at the ADAMHA/OJJDP Conference on Juvenile Offenders with Serious Drug, Alcohol and Mental Health Problems, Bethesda, Md.

Loeber, R. (1988). Behavioral precursors and accelerators of delinquency. In W. Buikhuisen & S. A. Mednick (eds), *Explaining Crime*, Brill, London, pp. 51–67.

Loeber, R. (1990). Development and risk factors of juvenile antisocial behavior and delinquency. *Clinical Psychology Review*, **10**, 1–41.

Loeber, R., Brinthaupt, V. & Green, S. M. (1990). Attention deficits, impulsivity and hyperactivity with or without conduct problems: relationships to delinquency and unique contextual factors. In R. J. MacMahon & R. D. Peters (eds), *Behavior Disorders of Adolescence: Research, Intervention and Policy in Clinical and School Settings*. Plenum Press, New York, NY.

Loeber, R. & Le Blanc, M. (1990). Toward a developmental criminology. In M. Tonry & N. Morris (eds), *Crime and Justice: An Annual Review*, vol. 12, University of Chicago, Press, Chicago, Ill, pp. 375–473.

Loeber, R. & Stouthamer-Loeber, M. (1986). Family factors as correlates and predictors of juvenile conduct problems and delinquency. In N. Morris & M. Tonry (eds), *Crime and Justice: An Annual Review of Research*, vol. 7, University of Chicago Press, Chicago, Ill, pp. 29–150.

Loeber, R. & Stouthamer-Loeber, M. (1987). Prediction. In H. C. Quay (ed.) *Handbook of Juvenile Delinquency*, John Wiley, New York, NY, pp. 325–382.

Loney, J., Kramer, J. & Milich, R. S. (1982). The hyperactive child grows up: predictors of symptoms, delinquency, and achievement at follow-up. In K. D. Gadow & J. Loney (eds), *Psycho Social Aspects of Drug Treatment for Hyperactivity*, Westview Press, Boulder, Colo, pp. 381–415.

Lorion, R. P. (1982). Methodological criteria for prevention research. Paper presented at the Prevention Research Seminar to the Center for Studies of Prevention, National Institute of Mental Health, Rockville, Md.

MacDonald, K. (1985). Early experience, relative plasticity, and social development. *Developmental Review*, **5**, 99–121.

Magnusson, D. (1988). *Individual Development from an Interactional Perspective: A Longitudinal Study*, Erlbaum, Hillsdale, NJ.

Mannheim, H. & Wilkins, L. T. (1955). *Prediction Methods in Relation to Borstal Training*, HMSO, London.

Messner, S. F., Krohn, M. D. & Liska, A. E. (1989). *Theoretical Integration in the Study of Deviance and Crime: Problems and Prospects*, State University of New York Press, Albany, NY.

Needleman, H. L. & Bellinger, D. C. (1981). The epidemiology of low-level lead exposure in childhood. *Journal of the American Academy of Child Psychiatry*, **20**, 496–512.

Newcomb, M. D. & Bentler, P. M. (1987). Changes in drug use from high school to young adulthood: effects of living arrangement and current life pursuit. *Journal of Applied Developmental Psychology*, **8**, 221–246.

O'Donnell, J. A. & Clayton, R. R. (1982). The stepping-stone hypothesis—marijuana, heroin, and causality. *Chemical Dependencies: Behavioral and Biomedical Issues*, **4**, 229–241.

Offord, D. R., Sullivan, K., Allen, N. & Abrams, N. (1979). Delinquency and hyperactivity. *Journal of Nervous and Mental Disorders*, **167**, 734–741.

Ouimet, M. (1986). *Analyse causale d'un modèle extensif de régulation psychologique et sociale de la conduite délinquante des adolescents*, Mémoire de maîtrise inédit, Ecole de criminologie, Université de Montfeal.

Pronovost, L. & Le Blanc, M. (1980). Transition statutaire et délinquance. *Revue Canadienne de Criminologie*, **22**, 288–297.

Rand, A. (1987). Transitional life events and desistance from delinquency and crime. In M. E. Wolfgang, T. P. Thornberry & R. M. Figlio (eds) *From Boy to Man, from Delinquency to Crime*, University of Chicago Press, Chicago, Ill, pp. 134–162.

Robins, L. N., Davis, D. H. & Wish, E. (1977). Detecting predictors of rare events, demographic, family, and personal deviance as predictors of stages in the progression toward narcotic addiction. In J. S. Straus & H. M. Babigan (eds), *The Origins and Course of Psychopathology*, Plenum Press, New York, NY, pp. 379–406.

Robins, L. N. & Przybeck, T. R. (1985). Age of onset of drug use as a factor in drug and other disorders. *National Institute of Drug Abuse Research Monograph Series*, **56**, 178–192.

Robins, L. & Wish, E. (1977). Childhood deviance as a developmental process: a study of 223 urban black men from birth to 18. *Social Forces*, **56**, 448–473.

Rogosa, D. (1980). A critique of cross lagged correlation. *Psychology Bulletin*, **88**, 245–258.

Rutter, M. (1989). Age as an ambiguous variable in developmental research. *International Journal of Behavioral Development*, **12**, 1–34.

Schwartz, D., Flamant, R. & Lelouch, J. (1980). *Clinical Trials*, Academic Press, London.

Smith, G. M. & Fogg, C. P. (1978). Psychological predictors of early use, late use, and non-use of marijuana among teenage students. In D. B. Kandel (ed.), *Longitudinal Research on Drug Use*, John Wiley, New York, NY, pp. 101–112.

Smith, G. M. & Fogg, C. P. (1979). Psychological antecedents of teen-age drug use. In R. G. Simmons (ed.), *Research in Community and Mental Health: An Annual Compilation of Research*, vol. 1, JAI Press, Greenwich, Conn, pp. 87–102.

Sullivan, C. E., Grant, M. Q. & Grant, J. D. (1957). The development of interpersonal maturity: applications to delinquency. *Psychiatry*, **20**, 272–283.

Thornberry, T. (1987). Toward an interactional theory of delinquency. *Criminology*, **4**, 863–892.

Thornberry, T., Moore, M. & Christenson, R. L. (1985). The effect of dropping out of high school on subsequent criminal behavior. *Criminology*, **23**, 3–18.

Tolan, P. H. & Lorion, R. P. (1988). Multivariate approaches to the identification of delinquency proneness in adolescent males. *American Journal of Community Psychology*, 16, 547–561.

Tontodonato, P. (1988). Explaining rate changes in delinquent arrest transitions using event history analysis. *Criminology*, **26**, 439–459.

Voeltz, L. M. & Evans, I. M. (1982). The assessment of behavioral inter-relationships in child behavior therapy. *Behavioral Assessment*, **4**, 131–165.

Wadsworth, M. (1979). *Roots of Delinquency: Infancy, Adolescence and Crime*, Martin Robertson, Oxford.

Werner, H. (1957). The concept of development from a comparative and organismic point of view. In D. B. Harris (ed.), *The Concept of Development*, University of Minnesota Press, Minneapolis, Minn, pp. 125–148.

Werner, E. E. & Smith, R. S. (1977). *Kauais Children Come of Age*. University of Hawaii Press, Honolulu, Hawaii.

Werner, E. E. & Smith, R. S. (1982). *Vulnerable, But Invincible: A Longitudinal Study of Resilient Children and Youth*, McGraw-Hill, New York, NY.

West, D. J. (1982). *Delinquency: Its Roots, Careers, and Prospects*, Heinemann, London.

Wikström, P. O. (1987). *Patterns of Crime in a Birth Cohort: Age, Sex and Class Differences*, Project Metropolitan; a longitudinal study of a Stockholm cohort no. 24. Department of Sociology, University of Stockholm, Stockholm.

Wohlwill, J. F. (1970). The age variable in psychological research. *Psychology Review*, **77**, 49–64.

Wolf, M. M., Braukmann, C. J. & Ramp, K. A. (1987). Serious delinquent behavior may be part of a significantly handicapping condition: cures and supportive environments. *Journal of Applied Behavior Analysis*, **20**, 347–359.

Yule, W., Lansdown, T., Millar, I. & Urbanowicz, M. (1981). The relationship between blood lead concentrations, intelligence, and attainment in a school population: a pilot study. *Developmental Medicine and Child Neurology*, **23**, 567–576.

Chapter 10

Why Do We Not Know the Cause of Depression in Children?

Adrian Angold

Kraepelin (1921) reported that 4% of his manic-depressive cases first manifested their disorder before the age of 10, and since then hundreds of studies have attempted to delineate the causes of depression. The volume of research effort directed at this issue continues to increase, though to date no clear answers have emerged. This interest in causes springs both from a simple desire to know how and why these problems arise and the hope that, if the etiology and pathogenesis of depression were known, they would lead to the development of better treatment, or even the prevention of depression in the first place. In fact, treatment research and causal research often go hand in hand, since the discovery of efficacious treatments (such as antidepressant medications or cognitive therapy) often stimulate theories of the cause of a disorder. Thus we have suggestions that depression results from abnormalities in brain amine metabolism and/or negative biases in thinking, while the association between disordered family functioning and depression in children has begun to stimulate research on family therapy as a treatment for the disorder. In spite of this substantial effort, we still have no clear picture of why some individuals become depressed. On the other hand this investigative effort has provided some rather vivid demonstrations of a number of thorny issues in causal research, and the purpose of this chapter is to examine several causal hypotheses about depression in an attempt to understand why all this work has failed to offer a satisfactory answer to the question "What causes depression?" The aim here is not to provide a detailed review of all the literature relevant to the etiology of depression, but first to examine the concept of depression itself, and then to consider several lines of causal reasoning in order to get an idea of why we have failed so miserably in the task of determining why children and adolescents become depressed. We shall find that there are problems on both sides of the causal equation: in defining depression itself, in measuring

Precursors and Causes in Development and Psychopathology.
Edited by D. F. Hay and A. Angold © 1993 John Wiley & Son Ltd

it, in defining and measuring risk factors (or potential causes), in identifying patterns of relationship between risk factors and depression, and in identifying the causal status of those risk factors. On a more positive note, the exploration of this daunting list of difficulties suggests a number of research strategies that offer hope of clearing a path through the causal jungle.

At this stage it is useful to distinguish between three rather different questions that can easily become confused. The first is "Is depression in childhood, defined according to criteria originally developed for adults, the same thing as depression in adulthood?" This question involves determining whether the phenomenological presentation, associations with risk factors, and treatment responses of similarly defined depressive syndromes are the same across the span of development. The second question is "Are there phenomenological states in children that differ from adult depressions, but which share their patterns of risk factors and treatment responses?" In other words, are there early child-specific presentations of depression? The distinction between these first two questions is clear enough in principle, but it should be remembered that the degree of difference or similarity required to decide whether a condition is an age-specific manifestation of the later disorder is a matter of opinion.

The third question is "Are there childhood precursors of adult depression?" That is, are there childhood states that represent rungs on the ladder to full-blown depression? Consider for instance, the fact that miserable children often meet DSM-IIIR criteria for both major depression and dysthymia, and dysthymic children are at very high risk of having episodes of major depression, while children with major depression are at high risk of manifesting later dysthymia (Kovacs et al., 1984a, b). Should we, therefore, call dysthymia a precursor of depression, call depression a precursor of dysthymia, extend the boundaries of depression to include dysthymia, or recognize two forms of dysthymia—one associated with major depression and a pure dysthymic syndrome (as suggested by the emergence of the term "double depression")? It seems that in order for dysthymia to be seen as a precursor of depression, we need, at least, to show that some factor is associated with the transition from dysthymia to depression. In the absence of such a demonstration, it seems most parsimonious to regard the two conditions as being part of the same disorder, especially since the measurement error associated with these diagnoses is high. However, this is a judgment call, not a matter of demonstrating a "fact". Distinguishing between precursors and final outcomes is almost always a matter of parsing the phenomena in the most coherent fashion, rather than discovering an incontrovertible state of the universe. In other words, the status of a putative precursor is a matter of theory, as well as empirical demonstration. Note also that the precursor is a state of the organism that involves an increased likelihood of the manifestation of the final outcome. What if its appearance is associated with a 100% chance of that outcome occurring? Then it seems most sensible to regard it, not as a precursor, but as an early form of the disease—in this case the disease itself is a developmental process (cf. Anna Freud's, 1966, distinction between the development of the individual and the development of the disease).

In order to determine the answers to the three questions posed above, and to answer the more general question of how depression arises, we must first be able to identify depression when it occurs. The next section presents some reflections on our ability to perform that task.

PROBLEMS WITH THE DEFINITION AND MEASUREMENT OF DEPRESSION

The ability to identify the thing being caused is logical prerequisite of any demonstration of causality. This is not to say that research must always start from an outcome and look backwards for its cause. There is nothing wrong with starting with some action and then looking for its later effects (that is the basic logic of experimental design); however, those effects must be both definable and measurable. Relevant outcomes in psychiatry are rarely easy to measure in a satisfactory manner, and depression is an example of an outcome that has proved difficult both to describe and to measure, and it serves as an exemplar of some standard problems in psychopathologic research. In particular, we are faced with the fact that the word "depression" has multiple meanings, while our predetermined definitions may place troublesome restrictions on the range of causal analyses, both at the level of the outcome phenomena (i.e. depression) and that of putative causal variables.

The word "depression" has multiple meanings

To begin with, "depression" is a word with multiple lay and academic meanings (Angold, 1988b, discusses nine different meanings), with the result that different studies of depression may not be talking about the same thing at all. Thus, it is not uncommon to come across a research report with the word "depression" in its title in which a group of unselected schoolchildren is administered a "depression scale" and some characteristics of the highest-scoring quartile are compared with those of the rest. Such an approach seems to represent the use of "depression" as a description of the low end of the ordinary fluctuations of normal mood. On the other hand, the epidemiological literature suggests that the six-month prevalence of depressive disorders in the general population is more like 2% than 25%. We cannot suppose that it is necessarily the case that the causes of an extreme position on the distribution of misery are the same as those of a much less extreme position. The importance of this point is illustrated by considering the distribution of IQ, where the correlates of a very low score (say, less than 50) are very different from those of a score between 75 and 100. The use of clearly prespecified diagnostic criteria represents an attempt to standardize concentration on a particular part of the distribution with certain extreme phenomenological characteristics. However, as we shall see, there are some problems with the way that this group has been defined. Nevertheless, from this point on, we will use the term "depression" to refer to depressive *disorders*, by which we mean depressive syndromes (constellations of symptoms that are regularly found to occur together) that may be regarded as being deviant from normality, as defined in either the DSM-III (American Psychiatric Association, 1980), DSM-IIIR (American Psychiatric Association, 1987) or ICD-9 (World Health Organization, 1978) nosologies.

Defining deviance: problems with restricting the range of the causal analysis

This apparently simple specification of a disorder involves two criteria that prove to be problematic in the case of depression: (i) the notion of deviation from normality, and (ii) the appropriateness for children of the definition provided in those formal nosologies.

(i) *Deviation from normality: problems with narrowing the range of the dependent and independent variables*

Let us begin with the issue of deviance from normality, since it arises at two points—the first being in the identification of symptoms, while the second involves the deviance of the whole syndromes from normality. A "symptom" refers to the deviation of molecular behavioral or psychological states from normality. Thus symptoms constitute the building blocks of disorder. This deviation may be either (a) quantitative or (b) qualitative.

Quantitative deviation from normality. In the quantitative sense a symptom represents more or less of a particular phenomenon than is accepted as being normal. Thus the ebullient child who suddenly becomes sad for several hours a day may be said to be manifesting the symptom of depressed mood. But what if we discover that her mother died three days before? Most of us would say that this unhappiness was to be expected—but is it, therefore, "normal"? That all depends on what we mean by normal. If we went to the child's school and tested hundreds of her peers with a depression scale, we would probably find that her scores were at the extreme end of the distribution. Thus her sadness is abnormal in statistical comparison with her peer group. It is also abnormal in that it represents a deviation from her normal mode of functioning. However, most of us would say that hers was a normal reaction under the circumstances. In other words, it is just what we would have expected, and the child is showing the signs of a bereavement reaction, not a depressive disorder. This response is reasonable, even though she might also have lost her appetite, be sleeping poorly, be feeling unreasonable guilt about her mother's death, failing to concentrate in school, and unable to enjoy anything at all—meeting, in fact, all the criteria for a major depressive episode in DSM-IIIR (American Psychiatric Association, 1987), except for the fact that the DSM-IIIR rubric (p. 222) explicitly excludes responses to bereavement from that diagnosis. Thus we have a situation where symptoms are present, these symptoms conform to a recognized syndrome, but that syndrome is defined as being normal on account of its apparent cause.

Where then should we draw the line between normal and abnormal depressive syndromes? What if the mother only went to jail for 30 days or less? Then the presence of such a syndrome would take us into the arena of life events as a cause or precipitant of depression (Coddington, 1972a, b). On the other hand, if the child merely became sad and tearful 10 days after her mother's incarceration, and was found to be sleeping poorly, and having trouble concentrating at school, the diagnosis would be one of adjustment disorder with depressed mood (according to the DSM-IIIR), and the child would fall outside the ambit of most depression research. If this state persisted for more than a year, then the diagnosis would change to dysthymia. In the hiatus between the six-month limit for the duration of an adjustment disorder and the one-year lower limit for dysthymia, it is not clear that any diagnosis would apply. The point here is that we have restrictions in the range of both our predictor and outcome variables. Bereavement, though by all accounts it represents a major event in an individual's life, is excluded from consideration in research on major depressive disorders because bereaved individuals are excluded from the diagnosis of a major depression, while misery of relatively short duration that follows a life event is excluded precisely because if follows such an event. Thus the presence of the diagnosis of adjustment disorder with depressed mood in the DSM-IIIR nosology represents an explicit recognition that life events are involved in the genesis of depressive syndromes, but the fact that most studies of depression these days concentrate on major depression (plus or minus dysthymia), which both have more stringent criteria for their diagnosis, means that the study of the impact of life events tends to be limited to the severe end of the range depressive responses.

Concentration on the question "Do life events cause major depression?" limits the field of investigation in an arbitrary fashion, based on the definition of major depression. Perhaps a better question would be "What is the association between life's events and depressive symptomatology?" Under the heading of the latter question, lie the further questions "Under what condition (if any) do life events result in (a) an adjustment disorder, (b) dysthymia, (c) major depression and (d) dysthymia and major depression, or (e) a bereavement-type reaction?" This formulation of the research issue has the advantage that it can produce evidence speaking to the syndromic separateness (or otherwise) of these categories, and that it focuses more precisely on the conditions within which a particular association applies, rather than presupposing that the relationship between events and depression will be a unitary phenomenon.

This is not to say that these four syndromes may not represent different disorders (for instance Kovacs et al., 1984b, found that childhood adjustment disorders with depressed mood had a much better prognosis over a five-year period than major depression), but it has to be admitted that the distinctions are somewhat arbitrary, and have little foundation in the empirical literature. It also raises the point that two of these conditions are defined a priori in terms of their ostensible causes (bereavement reaction and adjustment disorder), while in the case of the other two, the effects of negative events are a matter for causal research, not the definition of the disorder itself. In the case of bereavement reactions, it is hard to doubt the existence of this syndrome, but we cannot be so sure that we are on firm ground in distinguishing between adjustment disorder and dysthymia. Even if we accept the distinction between bereavement responses and major depression, we still have an interesting problem in understanding why some individuals only manifest depressive symptoms when they are bereaved, while others do so without this stimulus. Freud (1957) regarded the bereavement response as the archetype of depressive reactions, and the theme of loss still pervades research on the causes of depression (Brown & Harris, 1978). However, recent definitions of depression have deliberately excluded one of the most significant of losses (bereavement), because the reaction to it is considered to be a normal reaction. At base, this distinction amounts to little more than the definition of abnormality being a societal agreement that some states should not be the lot of humanity. For some purposes, this approach has advantages (Angold & Costello, 1991), but such a definition may not always divide up phenomenology in the most useful way for understanding the causes of a particular disorder.

This problem has even more extensive ramifications for depression research, in that many children with psychiatric disorders live in horrible circumstances. It has been argued forcefully (e.g. Graham, 1984) that is is unreasonable to say that someone has a depressive "disorder" when they are miserable in miserable situations, and that the fact that they meet criteria for major depression is neither here nor there (just as it is irrelevant in the case of a bereavement reaction). The counter-argument here is that it is reasonable to identify a painful mental state, and then to examine its precursors and correlates, of which one may well be stressful life circumstances. Both of these positions have merit, but they spring from different conceptions of depression. In the first instance, depression is seen as being primarily a disorder of emotional regulation, with states "normally" only seen in response to life difficulties appearing in the absence of those difficulties, while the second approach involves a less selective approach to the disorder, whereby it is seen purely as an undesired phenomenological state, which may sometimes arise autonomously (i.e. in the absence of a good reason) and sometimes occur in a more "understandable" fashion. In the first case, understandable misery is excluded from the diagnosis of depression, while in the second the issue of understandability becomes a question for causal research. It is fair to say that the second approach holds sway in the research literature at present, except in the case of bereavement and adjustment disorders, but that may be more a result of difficulty in operationalizing understandability than any fault of the logic of the first argument. In fact, this issue has been struggled with for years in the adult literature under the heading of "endogenous and reactive depression", without any real resolution being arrived at, except that these two types of depression cannot be well separated phenomenologically. But since the argument revolves around differences in process, rather than differences in phenomenology, the lack of clear phenomenological differentiation is hardly the issue, and it remains quite possible that different mechanisms might underlie depressions that seem to be responsive to life difficulties, and those that appear to follow a more autonomous course, in which case, lumping them all together will hardly help in coming to an understanding of their psychopathogenesis (Carroll, 1984).

The issue of quantitative deviation also raises some obvious, but widely ignored, measurement problems. ICD-9, ICD-10, and DSM-IIIR define disorders in terms of symptoms, but they rarely define those symptoms. Consider the first criterion for depression in DSM-IIIR: "Depressed mood . . . most of the day, nearly every day, as indicated by subjective account or observation by others" (American Psychiatric Association, 1987, p. 222). How much of the day is "most of the day" and how many days is "nearly every day"? Just where these dividing lines are set will make a considerable difference to who gets into studies of depression. Some have also argued that many children with considerable depressive symptomatology do not have an unremittingly depressed mood, but present a more fluctuating picture (Poznanski et al., 1985). This is an empirical question, but no studies have yet appeared that document the amount of time that depressed children show the symptom of depressed mood. If it turns out that the other symptoms of depression are accompanied by more fluctuating depressed mood in children, then we will need to decide whether these children are (a) not depressed, (b) manifesting a specifically childhood disorder that is not related to adult depression, (c) suffering from an age-specific form of depression, or (d) suffering from a precursor of full-blown depression.

The answers to these questions will be determined by examining the correlates and outcomes of the childhood disorders. If they show continuity over time with adult-style depressions (i.e. the depressed mood becomes increasingly pervasive), and have similar risk factors, then it would be reasonable to conclude that they represent age-specific presentations of depression. If these children are not otherwise disturbed, show no impairment as a result of their symptoms, and do not go on to have typical major depressions, then it would seem most reasonable to say that they were just rather miserable for a while. If this fluctuating mood disorder were to result in impairment in normal life functions, but not to be associated with the usual risk factors for major depression of adult form, then it would be appropriate to see it as constituting a separate disorder. Finally, if transitions to adult-type depressions were to be observed, then these childhood disorders would be candidates for precursor status. It is clear from this example that risk factor research, causal analysis, and syndrome validation are not independent activities; rather each feeds into the others. This being the case, it would be most appropriate to avoid narrowing either the diagnostic groups or the possible causal factors more than absolutely necessary, since such narrowing will make it difficult to answer questions about why some children respond to stress with an adjustment reaction, while others become depressed, or why some children with dysthymia go on to major depression, but others do not.

Qualitative deviation from normality: problems with measurement imprecision and limiting the set of putative causal variables. The second type of deviation that may identify a symptom refers to states that do not normally occur at all. Delusions represent an obvious example here, in that they are defined as false beliefs that are not shared by other persons in an individual's society and social group. The identification of such qualitative deviation is easy when someone comes into the office with certain knowledge, revealed in a flash of inspiration, that they are receiving coded messages from aliens in news broadcasts. However, such qualitative abnormalities are much less clearly defined for most depressive symptoms. Consider the example of "inappropriate guilt" (American Psychiatric Association, 1987, p. 222). Where are we to draw the line between "appropriate" and "inappropriate" guilt? We have some very broad cultural conventions, so we would all recognize that feeling personally responsible for world hunger at the age of 10 was inappropriate, but beyond such obvious examples each individual diagnostician is likely to draw the line somewhat differently. In ordinary clinical practice, neither the DSM-IIIR nor the ICD-9 criteria for depression have proved to have good psychometric properties (Gould et al., 1988; Remschmidt, 1988; Cantwell, 1988), and though structured clinical interviews have improved the situation, they are far from perfect tools (Angold, 1989). Thus the diagnosis of depression has a substantial error attached to it. To make matters worse, this is true of most of our measures of potential risk factors as well. Pickles (Chapter 2 this volume) points out that we are actually modeling associations between latent independent variables and latent dependent variables, since we do not have precise measures of either. Of course, we are constantly seeking to improve our instruments, but it seems unlikely that measurement error will be eliminated in the forseeable future.

This imprecision in measurement will tend to undermine our ability to discover causal links, but it also points to another problem in the process of causal analysis—the link between measurement and cause. What we cannot measure, we tend not to ask questions about; thus causal reasoning in science tends to be closely linked to available methodologies (Feyerabend, 1975). We currently study a limited set of possible causal variables because we have measures for them. This is sensible enough, but, at the present time, it seems likely that a number of possible causal links cannot be explored adequately. For instance, we would probably understand depression much better if we could experiment on the brain of living humans as we do on that of the rat. We would probably understand the role of loss in depression better if we could randomize children to bereavement and control conditions. As it is we have to resort to less powerful methods of determining causes, with the result that we can only address a small part of the probable causal network at any one time, and then rarely under adequately controlled conditions.

(ii) *The diagnosis of depression in children and adolescents: are largely unmodified adult criteria appropriate for the diagnosis of depression in childhood?*

The position of depression in the diagnostic armamentarium of child psychopathologists has undergone several marked changes over the last 20 years or so, from a position where it was regarded as being practically nonexistent to one in which it is seen as being present in between 15 and 30% of children presenting to psychiatric clinics, and between 2 and 5% of the young people in the general population (see Angold, 1988a, b for a review; Bird et al., 1988; McGee et al., 1990). These changes have been driven by a number of factors, including the shift away from psychodynamic interpretations of psychopathology, changes in assessment procedures for disturbed children, and the increasing hegemony of the DSM-III and DSM-

IIIR nosologies (see Angold, 1988b for a brief review of this process). It would be fair to say that the standard position is now that all the symptoms of depression described in adults can be found in children, and that the presence of a syndrome that meets criteria for a major depressive episode in DSM-IIIR is regarded as indicating the presence of depressive disorders similar to those of adults. This is a good starting point, but it should be borne in mind that it represents a hypothesis, not a fact.

Phenomenological isomorphism does not necessarily represent psychopathological identity (Digdon & Gotlib, 1985; Rutter, 1986; Angold, 1988b; Kazdin, 1990)—consider crying as a symptom of depression; a 1-month-old boy who cried for 30 minutes a day would not be thought to be abnormal, but it would be worrisome if the same child were crying that much 15 years later. This need not represent a major problem if we find that there is little difference between the symptomatology manifested in those who meet DSM diagnostic criteria across most of the life-span (though the problem of how to diagnose depression in preverbal individuals will remain). However, we know that some differences do exist. Suicide is rarer in children than in adults, and many workers have described differences in the rates of symptoms reported in relation to depressed mood at different ages (Achenbach, 1978, 1980; Achenbach & Edelbrock, 1978, 1979; Achenbach et al., 1987; Verhulst, Akkerhuis & Althaus, 1985; Verhulst, Berden & Sanders-Woudstra, 1985; Ryan et al., 1987; Carlson, Asarnow & Orbach, 1987; Carlson & Kashani, 1988; Seiffer et al., 1989; Puig-Antich, 1986; McConville, Boag & Purohit, 1973; Inamdar et al., 1979; Mitchell et al., 1988; Baker et al., 1971; Weissman et al., 1987; Angold et al., 1991). It also appears that depression becomes more common in adolescence, and that the well-known preponderance of depressed females observed in adulthood only appears at this stage. In fact, there is reason to believe that depression is actually more common in prepubertal males than in prepubertal females (Rutter, Tizard & Whitmore, 1970; Rutter et al., 1976; Rutter, 1986; McGee & Williams, 1988). Data such as these may be interpreted in various ways; for instance, depression in boys might be part of a pathway that leads to an adult outcome that is not depression—such as alcoholism, which is much commoner in men than women; childhood depressions in boys might represent a transient sex-specific disorder, or girls might be subjected to some risk factor for depression only in adolescence, while boys face this risk earlier on. However, we should at least recognize that, if the base rates of symptoms in the population change with age in relation to each other, then their relative weights in contributing to the diagnosis of depression may also change, in which case such developmental progressions need to be incorporated into our diagnostic schemes (Digdon & Gotlib, 1985).

We can extend this argument a little further by noting that a number of researchers have considered that the depressive syndrome may involve a number of symptoms in childhood that are not included in the DSM-III diagnostic criteria, such as school refusal, headaches, and abdominal pain (Kolvin, Berney & Bhate, 1984; Kazdin & Petti, 1982; Ling, Oftedal & Weinberg, 1970; Weinberg et al., 1973; Pearce, 1978; Birleson, 1981; Garber, Zeman & Walker, 1990). How would one go about deciding whether or not to include items such as these or to exclude or reweigh symptoms included in the adult-derived diagnostic criteria? In the first instance one would want to show that the symptoms of interest actually clustered with one another to a greater extent than they clustered with other symptoms constituting supposedly different disorders. Analyses of this sort have supported the notion that depressed mood, anhedonia, and the cognitive symptoms of depression (such as feelings of guilt or worthlessness) cluster together quite strongly throughout the age range, but the situation with respect to other symptoms is less clear (see Angold et al., 1991, for a review). Secondly, one would expect that the symptoms of a single disorder should covary over time. In this respect, the evidence is partly reassuring, but also casts some doubts over the delineation of the diagnosis. All the studies that have looked at the issue to date have found that depressive symptoms in childhood and adolescence predict the presence of depressive symptoms and disorders years later (see Harrington et al., 1990, for a review; McGee & Williams, 1988). However, there is also cross-prediction between the diagnostic categories of dysthymia and major depression (Kovacs et al., 1984b), indicating that dysthymia may simply be a form of presentation of the depressive diathesis rather than a separate disorder. The work of Harrington et al. (1990) presents further food for thought. These workers based their 15-year follow-up study on childhood and adolescent diagnoses made according to the Pearce criteria (1978), which differ markedly from the DSM-IIIR criteria. They found that the depressive syndrome described by Pearce predicted depressive disorders in adulthood quite strongly (though more so when the original presentation had been in adolescence rather than childhood). Clearly the presence of DSM-IIIR depression in childhood and adolescence is not a necessary condition for predicting the presence of that disorder in adulthood, when depressive phenomena are present at both times.

As a third criterion for the introduction of new symptoms into the criteria for depression, one would want to show that the correlates (such as patterns of response to risk factors) of symptoms that were supposedly part of the same syndrome were themselves the same, and differed from the correlates of other syndromes. The last of these methods is important for causal analysis (and will be discussed in detail below), for it reminds us that the process of disease description goes hand in hand with the elucidation of etiology and pathogenesis. This boot-strapping approach has been typical of many advances in the medical sciences in general (for instance, in the classification of renal failure). However, in the face of uncertainty, we are in danger of foreclosing too early on the question of defining childhood depression. Most psychiatric diagnostic interviews now concentrate almost soley on the DSM-IIIR criteria for depression, and often have screening structures based on those criteria that preclude the collection of further information about depressive symptoms if that screening criterion is not met. However, these criteria are not very "robust", in that modifications of them change the rates of "depression" very markedly. Lobovits & Handal (1985) found that the DSM-III criteria resulted in lower rates of depression being diagnosed than the Weinberg criteria (Ling, Oftedal & Weinberg, 1970) which include such items as school phobia, poor school performance, and aggressive behavior, in addition to more "adult"-type depressive symptoms. The use of more stringent criteria, such as the Research Diagnostic Criteria (RDC) of Spitzer, Endicott & Robins (1978) not surprisingly results in lower overall rates of depression (see Poznanski et al., 1985, for a detailed comparison of the DSM-III, RDC, Weinberg, and Poznanski criteria). As Seiffer et al. (1989) have pointed out, exclusive reliance on one set of poorly validated a priori criteria can lead to a confirmatory bias in supporting the further use of those criteria, since one tends to find only what one looks for. Thus for both syndrome validation and causal understanding we need to remain partially agnostic about the borders of depression at this stage. Evidence other than phenomenological conformity to a particular set of criteria in cross-sectional studies is required to establish that a "disorder" defined by those criteria is the same entity as that which appears at another developmental stage.

CO-MORBIDITY BETWEEN DEPRESSION AND OTHER DISORDERS: THE "THIRD FACTOR" PROBLEM

The simultaneous presence of more than one disorder in the same individual has long been recognized as a cause of considerable problems in defining the etiology of individual diseases (Feinstein, 1970). In medical research, allocating a particular diagnosis is part of the process of obtaining relatively homogeneous groups for study; if diagnostic groups vary in their degree of homogeneity from study to study, their results may not be comparable. In determining the etiology of condition A (e.g. depression) when condition A is present in association with condition B (e.g. conduct disorder), we may identify some etiological factor (such as family psychopathology) as a cause of A, when, in fact, it is really only directly related to condition B. Furthermore, in describing the course of a disorder over time, one supposes that the course being described is related to the disorder of interest. The presence of unmeasured co-morbid conditions may invalidate this hypothesis. For instance, one might find that children referred to a child guidance clinic who received a diagnosis of depression were more frequently convicted of drug-related offenses over the following five years than those with an anxiety disorder diagnosis. In such a circumstance, a failure to measure the level of conduct problems in both groups might result in a supposition that depression leads to drug use, when, in fact, the drug-taking is related to higher levels of conduct problems in the clinic depressives than in the controls.

Phenomenological and family-genetic studies have repeatedly demonstrated that depression in adults takes many forms, and is associated with many other psychiatric diagnoses, including schizophrenia (Kasanin, 1933; Procci, 1976), anxiety disorders (Roth et al., 1972; Roth & Mountjoy, 1982; Leckman et al., 1983), personality disorders (Paykel, 1971; Guze, Woodruff & Clayton, 1971; Wood et al., 1977), and alcoholism (Roth & Mountjoy, 1982; Weissman & Myers, 1980; Rosenthal et al., 1981). The situation has proved to be very similar in childhood. The use of standardized diagnostic criteria (usually the DSM-III criteria or variants of them) applied in a nonhierarchical manner to information collected with standardized interviews or questionnaires has revealed that many clinically referred children, and a substantial number of nonreferred children, suffer from a range of symptoms of sufficient diversity to merit more than one diagnosis. In particular, it has been suggested that there are associations between depression, anxiety disorders, conduct disorders, and attention-deficit/hyperactivity disorders, and, at least for the first two co-morbid diagnoses, the association has been firmly established by several epidemiological studies (Angold & Costello, in press a,b).

This array of evidence for an association between depression and a variety of other disorders, in both childhood and adulthood, suggests that studies of the development of depression should also address the association of depression with the development of other disorders, and therefore calls for diagnostic instrumentation that covers a broad range of disorders. It also indicates that we need to ask the question, "Which risk factors are *specifically* associated with depression?" With such high rates of co-morbidity, it is highly likely that some of the identified risk factors for depression will, in fact, be related to depression only through the mediation of a second disorder (such as conduct disorder) which is itself associated with depression. In other words, co-morbid diagnoses are likely to operate as unmeasured "third factors" in studies that look at only risk factors for depression, or studies that assess the relationships with risk factors diagnosis by diagnosis without controlling for co-morbidity.

The next section briefly reviews the risk factor research in childhood and adolescent depression. If depression were to be clearly associated with a set of risk factors that are different from those for behavior or anxiety disorders, then the potential confounds just described need not worry us unduly.

NONSPECIFICITY OF RISK FACTORS: FURTHER EVIDENCE OF THE NEED TO CONTROL FOR CO-MORBIDITY

Several recent epidemiological studies from the USA, New Zealand, and Canada have reported on associations between several putative risk factors for depression and the presence of DSM-III (or similar) diagnoses of depression in children and adolescents. In summary (see Costello, 1989), these studies find that low socioeconomic status (SES), high life stress, low academic achievement, and various measures of family disruption and disharmony are associated with the presence of psychiatric disorders in general, with each study finding slightly different patterns of effect. However, no pattern of risk factors has yet appeared that is specifically associated with depression. Two fairly obvious ways out of this problem present themselves. The first is to control for associations between the co-morbid conditions and the risk factor statistically, and to try to identify variance uniquely associated with depression. The second is to search for unique predictors of depression in those without any other disorder, those with co-morbid anxiety disorders, and those with co-morbid oppositional or conduct disorders. However, the problem with both these strategies is that depression is a relatively uncommon condition, so very large studies would be required to generate sufficient cell sizes. Larger groups of depressed children may be available in clinical populations, and these analyses could equally well be applied to clinical data, but the fact that referred cases represent only about one-fifth of all cases of psychiatric disorder in childhood means that it is impossible to accept the identification of risk factors from such date uncritically, since there is every reason to assume that the referral process does not result in a random sample of cases of child psychiatric disorders. In part at least, clinical studies of risk factors are almost certain to be modeling the referral process, rather than just the disorder itself. However, analyses of clinical data would be very useful in generating hypotheses about risk that may then be tested in population samples.

The nonspecificity of risk factors may also result, in part, from the crudity of most of our measures of them. For instance, family dysfunction comes in many shapes and sizes, and an overall measure of this potential risk factor may be lumping together apples and oranges. Thus a family with an alcoholic father may have all sorts of problems (Earls et al., 1988), as may a family with a depressed mother (see below for further discussion), and two such families might score equally highly on a questionnaire about family functioning. However, the nature of the difficulties experienced by children in each of these families might be quite different, and associated with substantially different psychiatric outcomes. This suggests that there would be value in looking at family dysfunction in a more molecular fashion. Once again, however, this will increase the necessary sample size.

An alternative strategy is to focus on selecting groups who differ in family functioning, and then to measure their psychiatric status. Here, the literature on divorce provides a useful model, and one that points once again to quite substantial differences between boys and girls in their responses to risk factors (see e.g. Hetherington, Cox & Cox, 1978, 1979a, b, 1982; Wallerstein & Kelly, 1980; Wallerstein, 1983, 1984). However, this work has paid relatively little attention, as yet, to the question of the specificity of divorce as a stimulus for particular patterns of disorder, and is still grappling with the problem of how much of the later effects are attributable to the divorce itself, how much to pre-divorce marital discord, how much to post-divorce discord, and how much to the fact that children who are born into families where a divorce will occur show more pre-divorce disturbance anyway.

Let us now look at three potential risk factors for depression—the presence of a depressed parent, adverse life events, and the cognitive correlates of depression—to see where they lead us in understanding the nature of the causes of depression.

FAMILY STUDIES OF DEPRESSION: INTERGENERATIONAL NONSPECIFICITY

Numerous studies have shown that a wide range of psychiatric disorders are more common in the children of psychiatrically disturbed parents than in the children of "normal" parents (see Rutter, 1966; Rutter & Quinton, 1984; Quinton & Rutter, 1985). More recently, clear links between parental depression and child psychiatric disturbance have been established (Beardslee et al., 1983; Orvaschel, 1983; Weissman et al., 1984b, c, 1986; Strober, 1984) Having reviewed the literature, Beardslee et al. (1983) suggest that the current evidence indicates that about 40% of the children of depressives have a psychiatric disorder of some sort. Recent studies (Weissman et al., 1984a, b, c, d; Winokur et al., 1978; Tsuang, Winokur & Crowe, 1980) have found an increase in risk for depressive disorders in the relatives of depressed probands, including their children, according to both parents' and children's own reports. Perhaps the most convincing evidence with respect to childhood and adolescent depression is to be found in the work of Weissman et al. (1987), and Orvaschel et al. (1988). The former found that 37.6% of the children (aged 6–23) of a depressed parent had already experienced a depressive episode, according to the DSM-III criteria, as compared with 24.2% of the children of nondepressed proband parents. Furthermore, the children of the depressed parents had earlier onsets of their depressive disorders than the children of nondepressed parents. The average age of onset for depression for children of depressed parents was 12.6, over four years earlier than that for the children of nondepressed parents. However, it should be noted that many of these children had other problems as well; in fact, substance abuse problems in the children showed a stronger relationship with parental depression than did childhood depression itself. Orvaschel also found an increased risk for depression in the children of depressed parents (21.3% compared with 4.3% in the children of nondepressed parents), but there was also an increased risk of attention deficit disorder (19.7% vs 6.5%).

There is overwhelming evidence that disordered family functioning is involved in the etiology of a wide range of child psychiatric problems (Rutter, 1981) but the issue requires detailed exploration specifically in relation to childhood depression. There are also strong suggestions that depressed adults often exhibit poor parenting skills (Raskin et al., 1971; Weissman, Paykel & Klerman, 1972; Weissman & Paykel, 1974; Parker, 1979a, b, 1981, 1982; Zahn-Waxler et al., 1984; Gaensbauer et al., 1984; Davenport et al., 1984; Mills et al., 1984; Cox et al., 1987; Cytryn et al., 1984, 1986) as well as other defects of social functioning (John & Weissman, 1985). However, we are far from identifying specific links between each adult disorder and its childhood equivalent. Rutter & Quinton (1984) have argued that the degree of disturbance of the parent's psychosocial dysfunction is more important than the clinical diagnosis as a predictor of childhood disorder. However, even in their work, an independent effect of parental depression as a predictor of childhood disorder was found.

The mechanisms responsible for this familial patterning are not clear. Some workers postulate genetic factors, but on the other hand, several studies point to family dynamic factors as being influential in the production of psychopathology in the children of depressives. There is also little to support the idea that these factors are specific precipitants of depressive syndromes as opposed to other emotional and behavioral syndromes, such as conduct disorder.

Thus co-morbidity reappears in a transgenerational context, which suggests that we need to consider causation not just in single individuals, but in the context of transgenerational processes. If the early death of a parent and poor later care result in a susceptibility to depression, and parental depression is associated with childhood depression (at least partly because depressed people tend to have deficits in their parenting skills), then it seems reasonable to see the parent's loss as a cause of the child's depression. Many great works of fiction have struggled with this issue, and most of us have seen our parents reflected in our own thoughts and behavior. However, scientific psychology and psychiatry have tended to limit the consideration of cause to the interface between the individual and his or her own history. This may well be a practical reaction, but we should recognize that in terms of causal analysis it is an arbitrary one. Not to draw such a line leads to an infinite regress to the origin of the universe, so producing a final answer to the question, "What are the causes of depression?" is beyond the realms of possibility. However, even if we limit the study of causality to factors that have operated during the lifetime of the individual under study, we are still left without any expectation of finding a small set of simple invariant causes. Rather we must expect to face the task of examining networks or patterns of phenomena that can be expected to be differently arranged at different periods in ontogeny. At present, we have hardly begun this task, but it is already clear that we need to track the development of multiple disorders and pathways in order to describe their phenomenological relationships. Work of this sort has begun in the conduct disorder and criminology literature (see Le Blanc & Loeber, Chapter 9 this volume, for a review) and the "developmental psychopathology" of depressive disorders has some catching up to do.

LIFE EVENTS: MULTIPLE CONDITIONS FOR CAUSALITY

A further layer of complexity is added when we consider that we have no reason to suppose that depressions are precipitated by single risk factors operating addictively. It is entirely feasible that multiple conditions need to be met for depression to occur. Brown & Harris's (1978) work on life events in adults suggests just such a notion. The death of a parent is clearly an "event" in most people's lives, but these workers have also considered that events do not just occur, they are interpreted by their victims and have ramifications in their lives. Thus they find that such events only precipitate depressions when they present a threat to an individual's future life pattern. Furthermore, their data suggest that events involving loss are associated with the onset of depression, while those involving threat precipitate anxiety disorders. Thus the causal argument involves not just an event happening, but its place and meaning in the matrix of an individual's psychological and social life. Brown and Harris also found that life events were more likely to precipitate depressions in women who were also rendered vulnerable by earlier losses of certain sorts, or by current life stresses, such as the presence of three or more young children in the home (though these vulnerability factors appeared not to result in depression unless a life event also occurred).

The issue of vulnerability factors in the Brown and Harris model also offers an example of the need to consider the timing of potential risk factors in an individual's life. They found that the death of a parent before age 10 increased vulnerability to threatening life events, and this was, therefore, classified as a "vulnerability factor". However, if an adult were living with a parent, and was threatened with homelessness when his or her parent died, that could constitute a "life event". Their later work has further refined these concepts, since they have found that the loss of a parent early in life only constitutes a "vulnerability factor" when it is followed by a poor level of care after bereavement. While there is continuing debate in the literature about the nature of the relationship between these "vulnerability factors" and "life events" (see Pickles, Chapter 2 this volume, for an interpretation of some apparently disparate findings in terms of stage models), work such as this suggests that it is necessary to go beyond a simple one-to-one correspondence between risk factors and pathological outcomes, and to consider the "meaning" of those risk factors in the lives of individuals.

Adult life-events research also contains a reminder that a particular risk factor may have links to more than one sort of pathology. We have already mentioned that subtle differences in the implications of an event lead to different outcomes (anxiety disorders versus depressive disorders), but it has also been shown that life events precipitate relapses of schizophrenia. In this case, however, the time course of the association between an event and the emergence of psychopathology is different. Events occurring in the three-week period before onset appear to be capable of provoking a schizophrenic episode, whereas the period of risk for a depressive episode following a life event extends to nine weeks. Furthermore, only events with potentially negative outcomes seem to precipitate depression, whereas what would seem to be positive events (such as moving to improved accommodation) increase the risk of relapse in schizophrenia.

Overall, exploration of the simple notion that bad things happening in life is a cause of depression has revealed a more complex web of interrelated ideas and explanations than was envisioned at first. However, it also provides some encouragement that it is possible to get to grips with some of the complexities, and that doing so sharpens the causal argument. However, before we leave life events behind, we should note one further fascinating finding—that life events also appear to be familial. McGuffin, Katz & Bebbington (1988) found that depression was about twice as common in the first-degree relatives of depressives as it was in a community sample. However, recent life events were more than five times as common in the first-degree relatives. The familial aggregation of depression is usually regarded as being evidence of a genetic contribution to the causation of depression. But what is being inherited in the case of life events, since life events, by definition, are not endogenous? This association remained even when events in the relatives' lives that might have been caused by the effects of the depression in the depressed proband were discounted. Perhaps it is easiest to think that people inherit probable *lives*, not just genes. As Cairns et al. (Chapter 4 this volume), Gottlieb (1991), and others have pointed out, genes and environments are not separate entities, but part of an interactive system. This means that we cannot expect to find linear causal chains, but rather networks of reciprocal influence, and what is true at the level of the relationship between genes and environments appears to hold at many other levels of analysis as well (see Angold and Hay, Chapter 11 this volume for further discussion of this point). We have already seen that research on the causes of depression points to a wide range of factors being involved, and we are now faced with the further difficulty that these factors need not operate in unidirectional chains, but may be better represented as a network of interactions of which depressive symptomatology is a part. If this is the case, then the answer to the question, "What causes depression?" will depend upon what part of the network one decided to start from and in which direction one chooses to travel through it. In other words, the answer would be dependent, once again, upon certain arbitrary analytical decisions.

COGNITIVE THEORIES OF DEPRESSION: CIRCULAR REASONING OR PRECURSOR IDENTIFICATION?

Many studies of both children and adults have documented that high scores on depression scales, or having a depressive disorder, are associated with certain dysfunctional patterns of thinking, such as low self-esteem, the tendency to attribute negative events to stable, internal, personal, global characteristics, and overly high standards for achievement (see Rehm & Carter, 1990, for a helpful summary of this literature). The notion here is that when faced with negative events, children who think like this will be hopeless about their ability to weather the storm, and become depressed. This formulation, which finds further support in the success of cognitive therapies for depression, leads to some interesting ideas about the causation of depression. These spring from what is, in one sense, a major flaw in the argument. Negative expectations, guilt, a sense of futility or worthlessness, hopelessness, and helplessness, are all included in the criteria for the diagnosis of depression, and represent a substantial component in depression questionnaires and interviews. In fact, it has been suggested that the combination of depressed mood or anhedonia and self-depreciation represents the central core of depressive symptomatology in childhood and adolescent depression (Gittelman-Klein, 1977; Costello & Angold, 1988; Poznanski et al., 1985). Thus depressive thoughts are represented on both sides of the causal equation. Consider, for instance Kaslow, Rehm & Siegel's (1984) finding that scores on the Coopersmith Self-Esteem Inventory (Coopersmith, 1967) correlated $r = .72$ with depression scores measured with the Children's Depression Inventory (Kovacs, 1981). This degree of correlation approaches the level of the test–retest stability of the instruments involved, indicating that these two measures of supposedly different constructs are, more or less, measuring the same thing within the limits of measurement error.

While it seems foolish to say that depressive symptoms cause depression, it is not ridiculous to postulate that negative modes of thinking represent a precursor to depression. What is needed here is a demonstration that depressive thoughts continue between depressive episodes in a subgroup of individuals, and that in the face of other risk factors (such as negative life events) these individuals develop the *other* symptoms of depression more frequently than individuals without negativistic thinking. If this were to prove to be the case, it would suggest that depression represents at least a two-stage process, and we could then investigate which risk factors operated at the first stage of transition into negative thinking and which were responsible for the transition into full-blown depression. A further interesting implication of this approach is that it leads to the hypothesis that changes in the rate of occurrence of depression might occur around the age of 8, in parallel with the consolidation of concrete operational thought. On the other hand, if the negative thoughts were simply part of the depressive disorder, rather than a stage on the way to it, no such change in prevalence would be expected. To investigate these possibilities, longitudinal studies will be required, with repeated measurements of potential cognitive and environmental risk factors, and assessments of depression that exclude negative thoughts from the diagnostic criteria or scale.

THE NEED FOR A DEVELOPMENTAL APPROACH

Even if large population studies were to address these questions, we could still not be certain that a simple list of the causes of depression would emerge, because such an expectation violates one of the basic principles of development—that relationships between phenomena are often not invariant over developmental time (see Cairns et al., Chapter 4 this volume, for examples). The death of a parent provokes rather different reactions in the 1-week-old, the 1-year-old, the 10-year-old, and the 50-year-old, and it seems likely that the same will turn out to be true of risk factors for depression.

Consider age and sex as risk factors for depression. We have already observed that the sex ratio in depression reverses at some point in adolescence. The onset of puberty seems to be associated with an increase in depressive symptomatology (Rutter, 1979–1980), but why is this increase greater in girls, and does the rate of depressive disorders in boys actually fall, or merely stabilize at the level found in prepuberty? Furthermore, the presence of depression in girls cannot be due solely to hormonal changes, since there are prepubertal female depressives and most women are not depressed. Do the other risk factors for depression remain the same in girls after puberty, or does puberty establish a whole new set of causal pathways into depression? We do not know the answers to any of these questions, and longitudinal studies comparing the patterns of risk factors for depression in boys and girls before and after puberty will be required to answer them. Overall, our studies need to adopt a developmental focus in expecting differences in causal pathways at different stages of development. For the most part, the search to date has been predicated upon the assumption that we will be able to identify risk factors that will appear as main effects in our analyses and that will operate in the same way across the sexes, across groups at varying degrees of risk from other factors (e.g. those with family histories of depression, and those without), and across the whole span of development, despite the fact that there is little reason to expect this to be the case.

CONCLUSIONS

At this point it hardly seems surprising that we do not know what causes depression in children and adolescents. Much of the basic data from which we might construct a causal argument is unavailable, while certain common nosologic assumptions run counter to the needs of causal research in that they lead to truncation of the range of phenomena to be examined on both sides of the causal equation. However, in all of the areas we have discussed, strategies are available to allow us to move forward. A fairly consistent set of requirements for the next stage presents itself. First, we need to be agnostic about the phenomenology of depression in young people, and to use diagnostic instruments that will allow us to explore the borders of our diagnostic categories. Second, we should explore the development of symptoms from different diagnostic categories in relation to one another over time. Third, we can expect the impact of potential risk factors (including genetic risk factors) to vary over time. Fourth, we will have to model risks for multiple disorders simultaneously in order to identify specific causal pathways for depression. This list of requirements points to the need for longitudinal epidemiologic studies, perhaps with an emphasis on high-risk designs that will reduce the enormous burden of unstratified sampling from the general population. Such studies might start either by sampling according to depression status of the children, or according to status in relation to a variety of risk factors. There is also an important place for clinical studies in generating hypotheses and developing instrumentation, but the selection biases introduced by the use of clinical samples will always undermine confidence in the findings from such work.

If we could describe these relationships in detail, what would be the value of asking whether a particular factor or group of factors *caused* depression? The answer to this question would depend on (a) the definition of a cause in this case, and (b) the ability to rule out third factors that confounded the association between events and depression. Assuming that, to the best of our knowledge, such factors had been excluded, then the causal question would rest on nothing more than the definition of a cause—but any such definition would be bound to be arbitrary, since it would depend upon a decision as to what degree of association should be regarded as being "causal", in much the same way as "statistical significance" so often relies on Fisher's arbitrary decision to use 0.05 as the cut-off point. Thus the notion of a cause does nothing but add a further debate, without contributing any information to the description that was already available. If we were in a position to propound an empirically plausible causal theory, the question, "What causes depression?" would be meaningless.

ACKNOWLEDGEMENTS

I would like to thank Drs E. Jane Costello and Dale F. Hay for their comments on this paper, and the Faculty Scholar Program of the William T. Grant Foundation and the Leon Lowenstein Foundation for their financial support of its preparation.

REFERENCES

Achenbach, T. M. (1978). The child behavior profile i. boys aged 6–11. *Journal of Consulting and Clinical Psychology*, **46**, 478–488.

Achenbach, T. M. (1980). DSM-III in light of empirical research on the classification of child psychopathology. *Journal of the American Academy of Child Psychiatry*, **19**, 395–412.

Achenbach, T. M. & Edelbrock, C. S. (1978). The classification of child psychopathology: a review and analysis of empirical efforts. *Psychological Bulletin*, **85**, 1275–1301.

Achenbach, T. M. & Edelbrock, C. S. (1979). The child behavior profile: ii. boys aged 12–16 and girls aged 6–11 and 12–16. *Journal of Consulting and Clinical Psychology*, **47**, 223–233.

Achenbach, T. M., Verhulst, F. C., Baron, G. D. & Akkerhuis, G. W. (1987). Epidemiological comparisons of American and Dutch children: i. behavioral/emotional problems and competencies reported by parents for ages 4 to 16. *Journal of the American Academy of Child and Adolescent Psychiatry*, **26**, 317–325.

American Psychiatric Association (1980). *Diagnostic and Statistical Manual of Mental Disorders*, 3rd edn, American Psychiatric Association, Washington, DC.

American Psychiatric Association (1987). *Diagnostic and Statistical Manual of Mental Disorders*, 3rd edn, revised, American Psychiatric Association, Washington, DC.

Angold, A. (1988a). Childhood and adolescent depression i: epidemiological and aetiological aspects. *British Journal of Psychiatry*, **152**, 601–617.

Angold, A. (1988b). Childhood and adolescent depression ii: research in clinical populations. *British Journal of Psychiatry*, **153**, 476–492.

Angold, A. (1989). Structured assessments of psychopathology in children and adolescents. In C. Thompson (ed.), *The Instruments of Psychiatry Research*, John Wiley, Chichester, pp. 271–304.

Angold, A. & Costello, E. J. (1991). Developing a developmental epidemiology. In D. Ciccetti & C. Toth (eds), *Rochester Symposium on Developmental Psychopathology 3*, Erlbaum, Hillsdale, NJ, pp. 75–96.

Angold, A. & Costello, E. J. (in press a). Depressive comorbidity in children and adolescents: I. a review of research findings. *American Journal of Psychiatry*.

Angold, A. & Costello, E. J. (in press b). Depressive comorbidity in children and adolescents: II. meanings and mechanisms. *American Journal of Psychiatry*.

Angold, A., Weissman, M. M., John, K., Merikangas, K. R., Prusoff, B. A., Wickramaratne, P. & Gammon G. D. (1991). Parent and child reports of depressive symptoms. *Journal of the American Academy of Child and Adolescent Psychiatry*, **30**, 67–74.

Baker, M., Dorzab, J., Winokur, G. & Cadoret, R. J. (1971). Depressive disease: classification and clinical characteristics. *Comprehensive Psychiatry*, **12**, 354–365.

Beardslee, W. R., Bemporad, J., Keller, M. B. & Klerman, G. L. (1983). Children of parents with major affective disorder: a review. *American Journal of Psychiatry*, **140**, 825–832.

Bird, H. R., Canino, G., Rubio-Stipec, M., Gould, M. S., Ribera, J., Sesman, M., Woodbury, M., Huertas-Goldman, S., Pagan, A., Sanchez-Lacay, A. & Moscoso, M. (1988). Estimates of prevalence of childhood maladjustment in a community survey in Puerto Rico. *Archives of General Psychiatry*, **45**, 1120–1126.

Birleson, P. (1981). The validity of depressive disorder in childhood and the development of a self-rating scale: a research project. *Journal of Child Psychology and Psychiatry*, **22**, 73–88.

Brown, G. W. & Harris, T. (1978). *The Social Origins of Depression*, Tavistock, London.

Cantwell, D. P. (1988). DSM-III studies. In M. Rutter, A. H. Tuma and I. Lann (eds), *Assessment and Diagnosis in Child Psychopathology*. Guilford Press, New York, pp. 3–36.

Carlson, G. A., Asarnow, J. R. & Orbach, I. (1987). Developmental aspects of suicidal behavior in children, i. *Journal of American Academy of Child and Adolescent Psychiatry*, **26**, 186–192.

Carlson, G. A. & Kashani, J. H. (1988). Phenomenology of major depression from childhood through adulthood: analysis of three studies. *Americal Journal of Psychiatry* **145**, 1222–1225.

Carroll, B. J. (1984). Problems with diagnostic criteria for depression. *Journal of Clinical Psychiatry*, **45**, 14–18.

Coddington, R. D. (1972a). The significance of life events as etiologic factors in the diseases of children—i. a survey of professional workers. *Journal of Psychosomatic Research*, **16**, 7–18.

Coddington, R. D. (1972b). The significance of life events as etiologic factors in the diseases of children—ii. a study of a normal population. *Journal of Psychosomatic Research*, **15**, 205–213.

Coopersmith, S. (1967). *The Antecedents of Self-esteem*, Freeman, San Francisco.

Costello, E. J. (1989). Developments in child psychiatric epidemiology. *Journal of the American Academy of Child and Adolescent Psychiatry*, **28**, 836–841.

Costello, E. J. & Angold, A. (1988). Scales to assess child and adolescent depression: checklist, screens and nets. *Journal of the American Academy of Child and Adolescent Psychiatry*. **27**, 726–737.

Cox, A. D., Puckering, C., Pound, A. & Mills, M. (1987). The impact of maternal depression in young children. *Journal of Child Psychology and Psychiatry*, **28**, 917–928.

Cytryn, L., McKnew, D. H., Zahn-Waxler, C. & Gershon, E. (1986). Developmental issues in risk research: the offspring of affectively ill parents. In M. M. Rutter, C. Izard & P. Read (eds), *Depression in Young People—Issues and Perspectives*, Guilford Press, New York, pp. 163–188.

Cytryn, L., McKnew, D. H., Zahn-Waxler, C., Radke-Yarrow, M., Gaensbauer, T., Harmon, R. & Lamour, M. (1984). A developmental view of affective disturbances in the children of affectively ill parents. *American Journal of Psychiatry*, **141**, 219–222.

Davenport, Y. B., Zahn-Waxler, C., Adland, M. L. & Mayfield, A. (1984). Early child-rearing practices in families with a manic-depressive parent. *American Journal of Psychiatry*, **141**, 230–235.

Digdon, N. & Gotlib, I. H. (1985). Developmental considerations in the study of childhood depression. *Developmental Research*, **5**, 162–199.

Earls, F., Reich, W., Jung, K. & Cloniger, R. (1988). Psychopathology in children of alcoholic and antisocial parents. *Alcoholism: Clinical and Experimental Research*, **12**, 481–487.

Feinstein, A. R. (1970). The pre-therapeutic classification of comorbidity in chronic disease. *Journal of Chronic Diseases*, **23**, 455–468.

Feyerabend, P. (1975). *Against Method*, Verso, London.

Freud, A. (1966). *Normality and Pathology in Childhood*, Hogarth Press, London.

Freud, S. (1957). *Mourning and Melancholia*, standard edn, Hogarth Press, London.

Gaensbauer, M. D., Harmon, R.J., Cytryn, L. & McKnew, D. H. (1984). Social and affective development in infants with a manic depressive parent. *American Journal of Psychiatry*, **141**, 223–229.

Garber, J., Zeman, J. & Walker, L. S. (1990). Recurrent abnormal pain in children: psychiatric diagnoses and parental psychopathology. *Journal of the American Association of Child and Adolescent Psychiatry*, **29**, 648–656.

Gittelman-Klein, R. (1977). Definitional and methodological issues concerning depressive illness in children. In J. G. Schulterbrandt & A. Raskin (eds), *Depression in Childhood: Diagnosis Research Treatment and Conceptual Models*, Raven Press, New York, pp. 69–80.

Gottlieb, G. (1991). Experiential canalization of behavioral development: theory. *Developmental Psychology*, **27**, 4–13.

Gould, M. S., Rutter, M., Shaffer, D. & Sturge, C. (1988). UK/WHO study of ICD-9. In M. Rutter, A. H. Tuma & I. Lann (eds), *Assessment and Diagnosis in Child Psychopathology*, Guilford Press, New York, pp. 37–65.

Graham, P. (1974). Depression in prepubertal children. *Developmental Medicine and Child Neurology*, **16** 340–349.

Guze, S. B., Woodruff, R. A. & Clayton, P. J. (1971). "Secondary" affective disorder—a study of 95 cases. *Psychological Medicine*, **1**, 426–428.

Harrington, R., Fudge, H., Rutter, M., Pickles, A. & Hill, J. (1990). Adult outcomes of childhood and adolescent depression. *Archives of General Psychiatry*, **47**, 465–473.

Hetherington, E. M., Cox, M. & Cox R. (1978). The aftermath of divorce. In J. H. Stevens & H. Matthews (eds), *Mother–child, Father–child Relationships*, National Association for the Education of Young Children, Washington DC, pp. 149–176.

Hetherington, E. M., Cox, M. & Cox R. (1979a). Play and social interaction in children following divorce. *Journal of Social Issues*, **35**, 26–49.

Hetherington, E. M., Cox M. & Cox, R. (1979b). Family interaction and the social, emotional and cognitive development of children following divorce. In V. Vaughn & T. Brazelton (eds), *The Family—Setting Priorities*, Science and Medicine, New York, pp. 71–87.

Hetherington, E. M., Cox, M. & Cox, R. (1982). Effects of divorce on parents and children. In M. E. Lamb (ed.), *Non-traditional Families*, Erlbaum, Hillside, NJ, pp. 233–288.

Inamdar, S. C., Siomopoulos, G., Osborne, M. & Bianchi, E. C. (1979). Phenomenology associated with depressed moods in adolescents. *American Journal of Psychiatry*, **136**, 150–159.

John, K. & Weissman, M. M. (1987). The familial and psychosocial measurement of depression. in A. J. Marsella, R. M. A. Hirschfield & M. Katz (eds), *The Measurement of Depression—Clinical Biological Psychological and Psychosocial Retrospectives*, Guilford Press, New York, pp. 344–375.

Kasanin, J. (1933). The acute schizoaffective psychoses. *American Journal of Psychiatry*, **13**, 97–126.

Kaslow, N. J., Rehm, L. P. & Siegel, A. W. (1984). Social–cognitive and cognitive correlates of depression in children. *Journal of Abnormal Child Psychology*, **12** 605–620.

Kazdin, A. E. (1990). Childhood depression. *Journal of Child Psychology and Psychiatry*, **31**, 121–160.

Kazdin, A.E. & Petti, T. A. (1982). Self-report and interview measures of childhood and adolescent depression. *Journal of Child Psychology and Psychiatry*, **23**, 437–457.

Kolvin, I., Berney, T. P. & Bhate, S. R. (1984). Classification and diagnosis of depression in school phobia. *British Journal of Psychiatry*, **145**, 347–357.

Kovacs, M. (1981). Rating scales to assess depression in school-aged children. *Acta Paedopsychiatrica*, **46**, 305–315.

Kovacs, M., Feinberg, T. L., Crouse-Novak, M. A., Paulauskas, S. L. & Finkelstein, R. (1984a). Depressive disorders in childhood: i. a longitudinal prospective study of characteristics and recovery. *Archives of General Psychiatry*, **41**, 229–237.

Kovacs, M., Feinberg, T. L., Crouse-Novak, M. L., Paulauskas, S. L., Pollock, M. & Finkelstein, R. (1984b). Depressive disorders in childhood: ii. a longitudinal study of the risk for a subsequent major depression. *Archives of General Psychiatry*, **41**, 643–649.

Kraepelin, E. (1921). *Manic, Depressive Insanity and Paranoia* (trans, R. M. Barclay), Livingstone, Edinburgh.

Leckman, J. F., Weissman, M. M., Merikangas, K. R. et al. (1983). Panic disorder and major depression: increased risk of depression, alcoholism, panic and phobic disorders in families of depressed probands with panic disorder. *Archives of General Psychiatry*, **40**, 1055–1060.

Ling, W., Oftedal, G. & Weinberg, N. (1970). Depressive illness in children presenting as severe headache. *American Journal of Diseases of Children*, **120**, 122–124.

Lobovits, D. A. & Handal, P. J. (1985). Childhood depression: prevalence using DSM-III criteria and validity of parent and child depression scales. *Journal of Pediatric Psychology*, **10**, 45–54.

McConville, B. J., Boag, L. C. & Purohit, A. (1973). Three types of childhood depression. *Canadian Psychiatric Association Journal*, **18**, 133–137.

McGee, R., Feehan, M., Williams, S. Partridge, F., Silva, P. & Kelly, J. (1990). DSM-III disorders in a large sample of adolescents. *Journal of the American Academy of Child and Adolescent Psychiatry*, **29**, 611–619.

McGee, R. & Williams, S. (1988). A longitudinal study of depression in nine-year-old children. *Journal of the American Academy of Child and Adolescent Psychiatry*, **27**, 342–348.

McGuffin, P., Katz, R. & Bebbington, P. (1988). The Camberwell collaborative depression study iii. Depression and adversity in the relatives of depressed probands. *British Journal of Psychiatry*, **152**, 775–782.

Mills, M., Puckering, C., Pound, A. & Cox, A. D. (1984). What is it about depressed mothers that influence their children's functioning? In J. Stevenson (ed.), *Recent Research in Developmental Psychology*, JCPP Monograph Supplement No. 4., Pergamon, Oxford, pp. 11–17.

Mitchell, J., McCauley, E., Burke, P. M. & Moss, S. J. (1988). Phenomenology of depression in children and adolescents. *Journal of the American Academy of Child Psychiatry*, **27**, 12–20.

Orvaschel, H. (1983). Parental depression and child psychopathology. In S. B. Guze, F. J. Earls & J. E. Barrett (eds), *Childhood Psychopathology and Development*, Raven Press, New York, pp. 53–66.

Parker, G. (1979a). Parental characteristics in relation to depressive disorders. *British Journal of Psychiatry*, **134**, 138–147.

Parker, G. (1979b). Reported parental characteristics in relation to trait depression and anxiety levels in a non-clinical group. *Australian and New Zealand Journal of Psychiatry*, **13**, 260–264.

Parker, G. (1981) Parental reports of depressives: an investigation of several explanations. *Journal of Affective Disorders*, **3**, 131–140.

Parker, G. (1982). Parental representations and affective symptoms: examination for an hereditary link. *British Journal of Medical Psychology*, **55**, 57–61.

Paykel, E. S. (1971). Classification of depressed patients: a cluster analysis derived grouping. *British Journal of Psychiatry*, **118**, 275–288.

Pearce, J. (1978). The recognition of depressive disorder in children. *Journal of the Royal Society of Medicine*, **71**, 494–500.

Poznanski, E. O., Mokros, H. B., Grossman, J. & Freeman, L. N. (1985). Diagnostic criteria in childhood depression. *American Journal of Psychiatry*, **142**, 1168–1173.

Procci, W. R. (1976). Schizo-affective psychosis: fact or fiction. *Archives of General Psychiatry*, **33**, 1167–1178.

Puig-Antich, J. (1986). Psychobiological markers: effects of age and puberty. In M. Rutter, C. Izard & P. Read (eds), *Depression in Young People—Developmental and Clinical Perspectives*, Guilford Press, New York, pp. 341–381.

Quinton, D. & Rutter, M. (1985). Family pathology and child psychiatric disorder: a four year prospective study. In A. R. Nicol (ed.) *Longitudinal Studies in Child Psychology and Psychaiatry: Practical Lessons from Research Experience*, John Wiley, Chichester, pp. 91–134.

Raskin, A., Boothe, H. H., Reatig, N. A., Schulterbrandt, J. G. & Odle, D. (1971). Factor analyses of normal and depressed patients' memories of parental behavior. *Psychological Reports*, **29**, 871–879.

Rehm, L. P. & Carter, A. S. (1990). Cognitive components of depression. In M. Lewis & S. M. Miller (eds), *Handbook of Developmental Psychopathology*, Plenum Press, New York and London, pp. 341–351.

Remschmidt, H. (1988). German study of ICD-9. In M. Rutter, A. H. Tuma & I. Lann (eds), *Assessment and Diagnosis in Child Psychopathology*, Guilford Press, New York, pp. 66–86.

Rosenthal, T. L., Akiskal, H. S., Scott-Straus, A. et al. (1981). Familial and developmental factors in characterological depressions. *Journal of Affective Disorders*, **3**, 183–192.

Roth, M., Guerney, C., Garside, R. F. et al. (1972). Studies in the classification of affective disorders: the relationship between anxiety states and depressive illness. *British Journal of Psychiatry*, **121**, 147–161.

Roth, M. & Mountjoy, C. Q. (1982). The distinction between anxiety states and depressive disorders. In E. S. Paykel (ed.) *Handbook of Affective Disorders*, Churchill Livingstone, London, pp. 70–92.

Rutter, M. (1966). *Children of Sick Parents: An Environmental and Psychiatric Study*, Institute of Psychiatry Maudsley Monograph no. 16, Oxford University Press, London.

Rutter, M. (1979–1980). *Changing Youth in a Changing Society: Patterns of Adolescent Development and Disorder*, Nuffield Press, London.

Rutter, M. (1981). Epidemiological longitudinal strategies and causal research in child psychiatry. *Journal of American Academy of Child and Psychiatry*, **20**, 513–544.

Rutter, M. (1986). The developmental psychopathology of depression: issues and perspectives. In M. Rutter, C. Izard & P. Read (eds), *Depression in Young People—Issues and Perspectives*, Guilford Press, New York, pp. 3–30.

Rutter, M., Graham, P., Chadwick, O. F. D. & Yule, W. (1976). Adolescent turmoil: fact or fiction? *Journal of Child Psychology and Psychiatry*, **17**, 35–56.

Rutter, M. & Quinton, D. (1984). Parental psychiatric disorder: effects on children. *Psychological Medicine*, **14**, 853–880.

Rutter, M., Tizard, J. & Whitmore, K. (1970). *Education, Health and Behavior*, Longman, London.

Ryan, N.D., Puig-Antich, J., Ambrosini, P., Rabinovich, H., Robinson, D., Nelson, B., Iyengar, S. & Twomey, J. (1987). The clinical picture of major depression in children and adolescents. *Archives of General Psychiatry*, **44**, 854–861.

Seiffer, R., Nurcome, B., Scioli, A. & Grapentine, W. L. (1989). Is major depressive disorder in childhood a distinct diagnostic entity? *Journal of the American Academy of Child and Adolescent Psychiatry*, **28**, 935–941.

Spitzer, R. L., Endicott, J. & Robins, E. (1978). Research diagnostic criteria: rationale and reliability. *Archives of General Psychiatry*, **35**, 773–782.

Strober, M. (1984). Familial aspects od depressive disorder in early adolescence. In E. B. Weller & R. A. Weller (eds), *Current Perspectives on Major Depressive Disorders in Children*, American Psychiatric Press, Washington DC, pp. 38–48.

Tsuang, M. T., Winokur, G. & Crowe, R. R. (1980). Morbidity risk of schizophrenia and affective disorders among first degree relatives of patients wiith schizophrenia, mania, depression and surgical conditions. *British Journal of Psychiatry*, **137**, 497–504.

Verhulst, F. C., Akkerhuis, G. W. & Althaus, M. (1985). Mental health in Dutch children: I) a cross-cultural comparison. *Acta Psychiatrica Scandinavica*, Suppl. 323, **72**, –108.

Verhulst, F. C., Berden, G. F. M. G. & Sanders-Woudstra, J. A. R. (1985). Mental health in Dutch children: (II) Prevalence of psychiatric disorder and relationship between measures. *Acta Psychiatrica Scandinavica*, Suppl. 324, **72**, 1–45.

Wallerstein, J. S. (1983). Children of divorce: stress and developmental tasks. In N. Garmezy & M. Rutter (eds), *Stress, Coping and Development in Children*, McGraw-Hill, New York, pp. 265–302.

Wallerstein, J. S. (1984). Parent–child relations following divorce. In J. Anthony & C. Chiland (eds), *Clinical Parenthood*, vol. 8, John Wiley, New York, pp. 265–302.

Wallerstein, J. S. & Kelly, J. B. (1980). *Surviving the Breakup: How Children and Parents Cope With Divorce*, Basic Books, New York.

Weinberg, W. A., Rutman, J., Sullivan, L., Penick, E. C. & Dietz, S. G. (1973). Depression in children referred to an educational diagnostic center: diagnosis and treatment. *Journal of Pediatrics*, **83**, 1065–1072.

Weissman, M. M., Gammon, G. D., John, K., Merikangas, K. R., Warner, V., Prusoff, B. A. & Sholomskas, D. (1987). Children of depressed parents: increased psychopathology and early onset of major depression. *Archives of General Psychiatry*, **44**, 847–853.

Weissman, M. M., Gershon, E. S., Kidd, K. K., Prusoff, B. A., Leckman, J. F., Dibble, E., Hamovit, J., Thompson, W. D., Pauls, D. L. & Guroff, J. J. (1984a). Psychiatric disorders in the relatives of probands with affective disorders. *Archives of General Psychiatry*, **41**, 13–21.

Weissman, M. M., John, J., Merikangas, K. R., Prusoff, B. A., Wickramaratne, C. P., Gammon, G. D., Angold, A. & Warner, V. (1986). Depressed parents and their children: general health, social , and psychiatric problems. *Archives of General Psychiatry*, **40**, 801–805.

Weissman, M. M., Leckman, J. F., Merikangas, K. R., Gammon, G. D. & Prusoff, B. A. (1984b). Depression and anxiety disorders in parents and children. *Archives of General Psychiatry*, **41**, 845–851.

Weissman, M. M. & Myers, J. K. (1980). Clinical depression in alcoholism. *American Journal of Psychiatry*, **137**, 372–373.

Weissman, M. M. & Paykel, E. S. (1974). *The Depressed Woman: A Study of Social Relationships*, University of Chicago Press, Chicago.

Weissman, M. M., Paykel, E. S. & Klerman, G. L. (1972). The depressed woman as a mother. *Social Psychiatry*, **7**, 98–108.

Weissman, M. M., Prusoff, B. A., Gammon, G. D., Merikangas, K. A., Leckman, J. F. & Kidd, K. K. (1984c). Psychopathology in the children (ages 6–18) of depressed and normal parents. *Journal of the American Academy of Child Psychiatry*, **23**, 78–84.

Weissman, M. M., Wickramaratne, P., Merikangas, K. R., Leckman, J. F., Prusoff, B. A., Karuso, K. A., Kidd, K. K. & Gammon, G. D. (1984d). Onset of major depression in early adulthood: increased familial loading and specificity. *Archives of General Psychiatry*, **41**, 1136–1143.

Wood, D., Othmer, S., Reich, T., el al. (1977). Primary and secondary affective disorders: 1—past social history and current episodes in 92 depressed inpatients. *Comprehensive Psychiatry*, **18**, 201–210.

World Health Organization (1978). *Mental Disorders: Glossary and Guide to their Classification in Accordance with the Ninth Revision of the International Classification of Diseases (ICD-9)*, World Health Organization, Geneva.

Zahn-Waxler, C., McKnew, D. H., Cummings, M., Davenport, Y. B. & Radke-Yarrow, M. (1984). Problem behaviors and peer interactions of young children with a manic depressive parent. *American Journal of Psychiatry*, **141**, 236–240.

Chapter 11

Precursors and Causes in Development and Psychopathology: An Afterword

Adrian Angold and Dale F. Hay

The authors of the foregoing chapters were charged to reflect upon the concepts of precursor and cause, as applied to particular research questions. Here we ask, what sorts of conclusions did they come to? Let us first consider some ways in which the authors approached the concept of precursor.

PRECURSORS

We noted in Chapter 1 that different sorts of evidence can be used to support the claim that one state is a precursor of another. These criteria include:

(1) *Resemblance between the two states;*
(2) *Stability of individual differences from one state to the next;*
(3) *Evidence that emergence of the first state is a prerequisite for the second to occur;*
(4) *Experimental disruption or manipulation of the first state, which should have predictable consequences for the second.*

In Chapter 6 on precursors of verbal and intellectual abilities, Sigman and Mundy provided a useful consideration of how these various criteria may be applied, noting in particular the importance of the relative homogeneity or heterogeneity of a sample for the likelihood of finding stable individual differences. They also made the further assumption that precursors are "internal and stable" properties of individuals, although they note that it is sometimes conceptually difficult to separate persons from their social environments, as in the case of the infant–mother relationship. However, the attempt to restrict the concept of precursor to a property of

Precursors and Causes in Development and Psychopathology.
Edited by D. F. Hay and A. Angold © 1993 John Wiley & Son Ltd

the individual—an endogenous cause, if you will—is useful in setting reasonable limits on the phenomena to be considered. We then may ask, to what extent have any of these criteria for the detection of precursors been met in any of the domains of research surveyed in this book?

Several authors have used the simple criterion of resemblance to discover early-appearing exemplars of a phenomenon thought to emerge later in development. Thus, for example, Caplan described research in which conventional definitions of sharing, cooperation, sympathy, and the like have been used to categorize social interactions in infancy, long before the capacity for such behaviour was thought to have developed. The criterion of resemblance thus alerted researchers to the need to begin their developmental analyses of prosocial behaviour much earlier than previously thought.

Similarly, in the psychopathological domain, Angold (Chapter 10) summarized investigations of children's mental states that have focused on whether or not symptoms indicative of depression in adults are manifested in childhood. Angold noted that particular behaviours, such as crying, hold different meanings at different periods in development, and that homotypic continuity cannot be assumed in developmental analyses. Nonetheless, at a somewhat more general level, it appears that conventional diagnostic criteria can be applied in the childhood years.

It is clear that the resemblance noted between early and later occurring prosocial behaviours, or between childhood and adult depression, is similarity at a somewhat general level of analysis, rather than precise behavioural isomorphism. There are conceptual strengths to be gained by noting such resemblances. By taking a look at what is occurring in earlier phases of development, one can observe somewhat counter-intuitive findings—for example, that there may be losses as well as gains in prosocial capacities with age, and that boys, not girls, seem most at risk for depression in the childhood years. Such counter-intuitive observations in turn force different sorts of explanatory hypotheses. For example, as Caplan noted, one must pay attention to inhibitory influences on prosocial behaviour, as well as explicit efforts to socialize children into conventional ways of dealing with others.

At the same time, however, these two examples also point up some dangers in relying on the criterion of resemblance. By applying criteria invented to categorize adult behaviour to phenomena occurring in childhood, researchers may be ignoring developmentally appropriate, but on the surface dissimilar manifestations of the construct. Thus, for example, persistent enuresis or school refusal might well index depression in childhood, particularly in those children who are not predisposed to articulate their concerns and worries. As Angold noted, attempts to introduce a concept of "masked" depression in childhood have lacked conceptual clarity;

nonetheless, even if one restricts the use of the term to the same sorts of phenomena as studied in adults, quantitatively different levels of symptomatology may be required to provide developmentally appropriate research and diagnostic criteria. Tenacious insistence on precise resemblance may greatly limit the possibilities for a more complete developmental analysis of a phenomenon that changes both quantitatively and qualitatively over time. Indeed, it would be fair to say that, if precise behavioural isomorphism were observed, it would be necessary to call the earlier state a precursor, in that the mature condition would have been shown to be present. The earlier state would, therefore, be an example of homotypic continuity, not a precursor.

Stability of individual differences

Dissatisfaction with the criterion of resemblance leads investigators to move to the second criterion, the requirement of stability of individual differences over time. Stable individual differences in the absence of resemblance (e.g. the association between conduct problems in girlhood and affective disorder in young womanhood) have been described as evidence of *heterotypic* (as opposed to *homotypic*) continuity. Long-term prediction from various measures in childhood to later competencies and disorder have been described by Sigman and Mundy (Chapter 6), Le Blanc and Loeber (Chapter 8), and Angold (Chapter 10). Sigman and Mundy's review of the attempts to examine continuities in intellectual abilities from infancy to childhood provides a good example of the progress that can be made when the criterion of resemblance is dropped. Attempts to predict intelligence in childhood from standardized developmental assessments in infancy have largely proved disappointing. In contrast, experimental procedures for the assessment of visual attention in infancy appear to have much greater predictive power, particularly with respect to the rapidity of information processing in late childhood. Indeed, Sigman and Mundy make the explicit claim that "infant attention is a precursor to later information processing". It should be noted that a 3-month-old infant's gaze at one slide rather than another does not look like a 12-year-old's behaviour while being administered an IQ test; none the less, the two dissimilar activities may index the same basic cognitive processes.

This claim about the status of infant attention as a precursor of at least one aspect of later intelligence is bolstered by the fact that theories of information processing are rather highly developed. Other instances of apparent heterotypic continuity are less easily subsumed into an overarching developmental theory. It is in such instances that disregard for the criterion of resemblance poses certain problems—in the absence of resemblance, no holds are barred, and random associations might be interpreted as meaningful continuities. It is incumbent to move beyond simple tabulations of correlation coefficients in seeking evidence of such continuities. Thus, for example, Frye set out theoretical reasons why an understanding of means and goals in infancy may be a precursor to the child's later understanding of mental states. This type of theoretical analysis yields specific hypotheses about developmental continuities and suggests measures to be taken at different points in time, to assess stability of individual differences from the putative precursors to the outcomes of interest.

Prerequisites

As we noted in Chapter 1, some uses of the term "precursor" imply that a precursor must occur if the later outcome is to occur. Such an analysis could be applied to the study of children's developing theories of mind, as described by Frye, and to the progression of prosocial achievements described by Caplan. It can also be applied within the psychopathological domain, as illustrated by Le Blanc and Loeber's presentation of the "stepping-stones" model of the development of criminality. For example, Le Blanc and Loeber cited research suggesting that troublesome, risk-taking behaviour at the age of 8–10 years predicts conviction for juvenile offences at ages 10–13, which in turn predicts adolescent convictions, and so on. Le Blanc and Loeber noted some ways in which current "stepping-stone" models can be modified to provide information about mediating variables and sleeper effects; however, they stressed the importance of discovering a fixed sequence of precursor conditions leading up to an outcome of theoretical interest and practical import.

The "stepping-stone" approach outlined by Le Blanc and Loeber of course verges upon a stage theory of criminality, with all the associated conceptual issues concerning the definition of stages and sequences in any realm of development (see Hay and Angold, Chapter 1 this volume). In Chapter 2 on methodological issues in the study of precursors and causes in development, Pickles argued in general for the specification of the theory underlying an investigator's approach to the problem, and, by way of illustration, described how an underlying stage theory might provide a framework for testing causal hypotheses. Pickles moved beyond definitional issues such as those debated in the Piagetian tradition (e.g. Pinard & Laurendeau, 1969), and explored ways in which structural equation modelling techniques can be exploited to provide information about stage and sequence in development and pathogenesis.

Linking processes

Whatever the criterion used to identify possible precursors in the various domains considered, most of the authors have speculated about the underlying processes that link precursors to outcomes. For example, Nash and Hay, in considering links between relationships in infancy and adulthood, not only note resemblances (all social relationships share some common features) and evidence for the stability of individual differences (the fact that differences in early attachment relationships predict differences in later peer relationships), but also summarized evidence from a number of species concerning the representational processes that link information about one relationship to behaviour in a later one. Nash and Hay revealed that, even in birds, cognitive processes mediate continuities from one social context to another. Their analysis thus extended beyond the identification of particular precursors to a more thorough analysis of causal connections across development. Thus, attention to the processes linking precursors to outcomes brings one inexorably to another consideration of the role of causal explanation in developmental and pathogenetic studies.

CAUSAL COMPLEXITIES

The authors of the foregoing chapters confronted the concept of cause in different sorts of ways. For example, Sigman and Mundy chose to provide an exegesis of the concept of "precursor" and to eschew too much speculation about causation. In contrast, Angold posed the question why we do not know the causes of depression in childhood, and explicitly outlined some problems for causal analysis in this particular domain.

Different sorts of causal relations have been alluded to: for example, Pickles discussed how one might find evidence for synergy in developmental processes, and Caplan drew attention to the role of inhibitory, as well as facilitatory, processes in social development. Most of the authors alluded to the usefulness of different approaches to causality; for example, Le Blanc and Loeber presented a thorough consideration of what one can and cannot learn from various research designs. Nash and Hay provided a set of axioms for the developmental analysis of social relationships over time, which set directions for the types of causal theorems to be tested in that realm of development and pathogenesis. Pickles provided a clear exposition of some of the conceptual issues involved in setting out causal hypotheses about developing systems, and examined ways in which such hypotheses could be tested using structural equation models.

Perhaps the best illustrations of the causal complexities to be encountered in studying any developmental or psychopathological phenomena were provided by the chapters considering two traditional causal hypotheses, firstly, that development is controlled by genetic influences and, secondly, that psychological development mirrors the development of the central nervous system. With respect to the first question, the venerable "nature–nurture issue", Cairns and his colleagues drew attention to the "reverberating circuits" of developmental causation; genetic information does not have unique, "first cause" status but rather is itself influenced by developmental processes. With respect to the second issue, the equally hoary "mind–body problem", Goodman described how very difficult it is to test such an apparently simple proposition as the statement that psychological disorder is to some extent caused by brain damage. In both these chapters, the reader's attention is drawn to complex systems of influence, rather than single, primary causal influences.

BEYOND CAUSALITY

In reviewing the chapters that make up this volume, perhaps the most striking feature is that, though each chapter presents a great deal of information about its subject area, not one of them makes a strong claim that any single causal pathway has been identified, despite the fact that in each of the areas covered there has been an explicit desire to understand the causes of the phenomena under study. What can account for this remarkable caution spanning such a diversity of topics? The problem may lie in the notion of cause itself. Let us, therefore, look again at our common expectations about what causes should be like, in an attempt to understand the problems that arise and suggest alternative approaches that avoid them.

Causal problems

Unidirectionality

One of the most obvious implications of a causal statement is unidirectionality. When we say that X causes Y, we expect movements of time and action from left to right. In other words, the causal arrow points to the right. However, the authors in this book repeatedly have stressed the fact that development often does not work in this linear, unidirectional way. Systems tend to be "co-active" or "interactive", and by now developmental scientists are thoroughly used to feedback and feed-forward loops in biological and social systems. Most contemporary developmental theorists (e.g. Gottlieb, 1991) see the description of such circular, interactive arrangements as providing a better model for development than unidirectional lines of development. The problem with applying a causal argument to such phenomena is that it requires one to start and finish at some fixed point in the cycle, so that one can decide causal primacy between X and Y; however, the causal argument provides no *a priori* guidance as to why one should start at X rather than Y.

Levels of analysis and reductionism

Secondly, there is something inherently reductionistic implicit in the notion of cause, along with a preference for seeking for causes at the next level down in the descriptive hierarchy—hence the search for the biological "roots" of development and psychopathology. However, as Russell (1990) has reminded us, a description at another level of analysis does not constitute a causal argument. Indeed, one might argue that moving to another level of analysis makes a causal argument impossible to maintain because the constituents of the two sides of the causal equation are not comparable.

The fact that development can be studied at different levels of analysis poses a number of problems for causal reasoning. It is important to note that investigators may often try to pit two causal hypotheses against each other, even though they require evidence at two different levels of analysis, and thus might both be true simultaneously. Alternatively, evidence collected at one level of analysis is often adduced to support claims at another; a good example of this is in the realm of attachment research, where evidence of patterning of behaviour in an experimental statement and stability of attachment classifications over the childhood years is used to support claims about the biological functions of attachment behaviour (see Hay, 1980, for an extended discussion of this problem).

Infinite causal possibilities

Thirdly, it is important to recognize that the imputation of causality is always a theoretical proposition, and, as such, incapable of direct demonstration. One is usually satisfied with a causal explanation only when no plausible alternative theory exists. However, as the example of the snowball rolling down the hillside in our introduction demonstrated, even a very simple observation may result in causal statements at many levels. Given that human development involves complex interactions at numerous levels, researchers have the potential to generate numerous causal statements, all of which could be true simultaneously. This leads one to ask, what is the value of any one of these causal statements in itself? In the absence of clear decision rules, one causal statement might be accepted rather than another on aesthetic grounds—in that it is more parsimonious, more elegant, more creative, or more in line with the body of existing theory than another. We shall return to this issue of the aesthetics of causal inference.

Determinism and sufficiency

Fourthly, the common-sense idea of causality involves deterministic statements, rather than probabilistic ones. Furthermore, our preference for parsimony and simplicity in causal explanations has often led us to seek single, sufficient causes. The notion of a sufficient cause implies that the presence of that cause simply and inexorably leads to the presence of the caused. However, at any level in development we are investigating probabilistic systems, which, by definition, deny the notion of a sufficient cause. Factor X can only be said to increase the probability that Y will be observed; except in the most trivial circumstances there will always be those with X who do not have Y, and we cannot simply write such variability off as measurement error.

The very idea of cause suggests that there is a level of scientific knowledge that transcends probabilistic description. However, during the twentieth century it has been shown that, at the level of the physical laws governing our universe, only probabilistic description is possible. Bertrand Russell wrote off the concept of causality for physics in the early years of the century (Russell, 1912), and despite some objections to his position, the physical sciences show only mild interest in causal explanations at the theoretical or practical level.

Perhaps developmental science should take some route and simply stop at the point of having obtained a clear description of procedures and events. Carey (1990) presented a compelling account of the identity of description and explanation in the development of word learning in young children, which, though not case in probabilistic terms, nicely illustrates the point that a satisfying explanatory account of development need not invoke causality. She argued that perfect description, in both empirical and theoretical terms, is the goal of the developmental scientist. Invoking causality only adds an unnecessary set of theoretical and philosophical problems without a commensurate gain in understanding. This recommendation points us towards a possible boot-strapping procedure, whereby we make observations, generate working explanatory hypotheses to simplify the information before our eyes, and then attempt to test those hypotheses as a means of providing better descriptions.

Invariance of causal mechanisms

Fifthly, the notion of a cause often implies invariance over time and across individuals. Admittedly, this is not a necessary assumption, but behavioural researchers characteristically have attempted to predict long-term outcomes in diverse populations, and such endeavours suggest that long-term causal effects are to be expected. However, the chapters in this book have demonstrated that, from the level of the gene up, timing is a critical dimension for developmental analyses, and that the effects of a particular variable upon some outcome may be dramatically affected by the previous developmental history of an individual, and by the state of the individual at the time of testing. We cannot expect to find invariant causes across developmental time and individuals. In fact, the preceding chapters point to the opposite conclusion—that we should expect to find extensive variability in associations between predictor and outcome variables over time and between subjects.

It seems, then, that several implications of the notion of cause, as commonly understood, are ill adapted to the requirements of developmental analysis. However, if we gave up the usual notions of causality, what would then be the aims of developmental science? The interactionist perspective on development has been roundly criticized as seeming to suggest that everything is related to everything else in an analytically intractable sea of correlations. Are we now proposing even to sink the longed-for island of causal inference beneath the waves? The answer to this question lies in some further conceptualization of the interactionist position that is so clearly supported by the empirical evidence presented in this book.

Does the concept of cause add anything to an interactionist argument?

In the first place, in the realms of development and psychopathology, we are not in fact dealing with an unstructured sea of interrelationships, but with highly constrained relationships within the overall interaction of organism and environment that Gottlieb (1991) has called the "developmental manifold" (see also Cairns, Gariépy & Hood, 1990; Greenough, 1991; McGue, 1989; Plomin, De Fries & Loughlin, 1977; Scarr & McCartney, 1983). Three goals for developmental analysis emerge strongly from the preceding chapters. The first is the familiar one of *describing predictor–outcome relationships*, the basic task of science. The second goal is to *describe the conditions under which those relationships hold*. This means determining the constraints upon the predictor–outcome pathway indicated by the former. In other words, in Gottlieb's terminology, we are not just talking about "probabilistic epigenesis", but "conditional probabilistic epigenesis". Simple probability relations must be identified and then conditional probabilities calculated with respect to theoretically and empirically relevant constraining and facilitating conditions. Finally, the third goal is to *understand the processes whereby the predictors lead to the developmental outcome*.

Now, it could be argued that, when the three goals were met, we must have identified the causes of the phenomenon of interest, since we would know about it all there was to be known. Surely, we would have met

Aristotle's criteria. However, a question remains: If we did do all we set out to do in meeting these three goals, what would be added by talking about causality? When a complete description of these three necessary facets of any developmental analysis is available, the addition of the idea of cause will prove to be redundant.

Consider a hypothetical situation in which we were able to say with some confidence that, in post-pubertal adolescent girls, whose parents had died in childhood, and who had recently been deserted by a boyfriend, the probability of depression occurring within three months was 0.4; whereas, in deserted girls whose parents were still alive the probability of depression was 0.2; and in undeserted girls with dead parents it was 0.1. What would be added to our understanding of the phenomenon of adolescent depression by saying that desertion causes depression? Such a statement is just a crude rerendering of the data with some important details missed out. Essentially it applies a mathematical transformation to the information we have obtained, from a continuous scale of measurement (the actual probability of occurrence) to a dichotomy on a nominal scale (desertion by the boyfriend is or is not a cause). As such, it may do for ordinary conversation, but it lacks scientific precision.

Some readers might reply that causation may be approached through understanding the mechanism by which this set of probabilities is generated, as in the case of depressive cognitions, or brain amines. However, even if we understood this pathway and its constraints perfectly, we would simply have obtained a description at another level of analysis. In common with Carey (1990), we would argue that the more fundamental scientific goal is perfect description, not imperfect causal inference. To use a familiar analogy, a perfect description is the unseen parameter we are attempting to estimate; our imperfect causal hypotheses are the statistics we use to do so.

THE "NNUP" ALTERNATIVE

Our position here is similar in some ways to that of James Russell (1990) who has developed Mackie's (1974) description of causality in terms of "INUS" conditions (Insufficient, Non-redundant parts of an Unnecessary but Sufficient condition). Mackie, in dealing with the fact that multiple causes may exist for the same phenomenon, drew attention to the need to define sets of elements that form an overall condition that is sufficient to produce a particular outcome. Each element in such a condition is, in itself, insufficient to cause the outcome, but is required for the more global sufficient condition to be met, and so is non-redundant (as far as that particular condition is concerned). At the same time, the overall condition, being but one of a group of sufficient conditions, is unnecessary, but sufficient to result in the outcome.

How might this scheme aid in our understanding of causal forces in development and pathogenesis? Russell argued that the INUS scheme has an acceptable "causal flavour" when it refers to something going wrong—"For example, when asked why our car broke down we may say, 'The carburettor jets got bunged up with muck from the petrol.'" This description clearly functions as a cause because it, as it were, selects itself as an INUS condition for failure from the plethora of INUS conditions for success.

In Mackie's view, it is no accident then that we can sensibly ask, "What caused the breakdown?" because the conditions for the car working are bracketed off, and thus the holism problem avoided. However, in his view, it is either wrongheaded or mystical to ask, "What causes the car to work?" He went on to argue that most causal arguments about central psychological processes are of the "What causes the car to work?" type, and that description, rather than cause, is the proper aim of a scientific inquiry into their operations.

Clearly, we concur with this latter conclusion, but we do not agree that the situation is necessarily any different with respect to causal statements about something going wrong, at least as that concept applies to psychopathology. The acceptability of the causal argument in his "pathological" example is based upon the presumed existence of a very limited set of INUS conditions for pathology (in this case of a particular car breaking down, just one). However, we have seen throughout the book that the number of INUS conditions for psychopathology is likely to be large, with the result that the arguments that apply to the inappropriateness of causal statements for normal central processes apply equally in the realm of psychopathology.

We would also add the further modification that, in so far as we can expect to find one-to-one correspondence between predictors and outcomes only rarely, we will rarely observe truly sufficient relationships. Rather, both when studying normal development and the genesis of psychiatric disorders, we are more likely to find "probability-modifying" relationships. Our reformulation of Mackie's scheme, therefore, involves "Non-probability-modifying (since the individual parts of a probability-modifying condition do not affect the outcome variable in the absence of the other parts), Non-redundant parts of an Unnecessary but Probability-modifying condition" (NNUP). Our NNUP approach therefore represents a formalization of the descriptive task of developmental research. As a framework for causal statements, it is uninformative, simply because adding the notion of causality to a perfect description in fact adds nothing.

In our introduction, we emphasized the importance of "descriptive teleonomy" for developmental analysis, and we return to this idea here, in so far as it offers a further refinement of our critique of causality. A typical developmental causal argument takes the general form: X causes Y (where Y is some developmental outcome). However, if we adopt a teleonomic approach, this is a tautological statement, in so far as Y is defined as the end-point of the developmental process represented by X. A descriptive teleonomic argument of the sort that we are supporting takes a rather different form: "The probability of Z occurring is P when X is operating and conditions A, B & C are satisfied." This is clearly not a tautology, but a statement of the "teleonome". In other words, assuming that these terms are, as far as we can tell, all those relevant to the occurrence of Z, it is a complete developmental statement.

The concept of teleonomy as developed by Mayr (see Hay and Angold, Chapter 1 this volume) has been rightly criticized for separating the descriptive constraints on the genetic and environmental components of a teleonomic description (Gottlieb, 1991), with the result that Mayr's own form of teleonomy represents a form of genetic determinism. However, there is no logical necessity for this to be the case, in that the notion of the unfolding of a constrained sequence of events towards an eventual outcome can equally well be applied to interactions at any level of analysis. Thus a series of organismic or environmental constraints, such as those suggested in our hypothetical teenage depression example, may be seen as code in a "programme" leading to the expression of depressive symptoms just as easily as genes may be seen as constituting such a developmental programme. Similarly, as Cairns and his colleagues have pointed out in Chapter 4, the environment comprises programmes that control certain aspects of gene expression.

We have argued, in common with contemporary physical scientists, that only probabilistic relationships can be described, and that attempting to assign causal status to any of them is a mistake. Does that mean, therefore, that equal attention should be paid to all high correlations? The answer to this question must be no. The correlation between once having been alive and dying is 1.0, across all known constraints, but this fact is hardly very interesting to the developmentalist, beyond its expression of the ultimate teleonomic progression. Moving beyond the conceptually limiting notion of causality does not at all imply abandoning theory, much less common sense.

More realistically, one often does have to face the problem of high correlations between states that appear to have no obvious structural or functional relationship—the paradigmatic example here is the relationship between sales of bananas and the birth rate in post-war UK. As mentioned earlier, there is a tendency to consider any prediction manifested over a long period of time as an example of "heterotypic continuity", even if the particular association is theoretically obscure. In general, one will want to pay the most attention to correlations that contribute to the description of a developmental process (the third step in the research agenda set out above). Investigators' selective attention will be governed by their theories or models of these underlying developmental processes.

Thus we are not arguing that developmental science should be an atheoretical activity. Nor are we arguing that hypothesis testing using experimental methods should be abolished. On the contrary, we would argue that experimental designs, with their frequent emphasis on carefully controlling the constraints on the relationships between observed variables, represent a powerful descriptive tool. What we contend is that many simple causal statements, and attempts to impute causality from experimental manipulations, are unhelpful, because they introduce a wild card in the form of the indefinable notion of causality.

PRECURSORS REVISITED

What then of precursors? Is there any place for them in our agenda for developmental science? Not necessarily. An adequate developmental description need not contain descriptions of precursor states. In Chapter 1 we discussed the dictionary definition of a precursor as a harbinger of the appearance of a later state. As such, the term simply refers to the temporal ordering of states. However, as we have seen in the preceding chapters, the term contains the implication that there is some close empirical relationship between the two states. There are two possible forms of close empirical relationship within a probabilistic teleonomic statement of the sort we have described above. The first is a high probability that X state will be followed by state Y, within any particular set of constraints, while the second is that the relationship between X and Y is highly consistent across a multiplicity of constraining conditions. In fact, although the authors of the chapters in this book have tended to use one or the other criterion, the idea of a precursor probably requires that both of these conditions be met. Furthermore, as discussed earlier, the criterion of a certain resemblance between the states, short of perfect identity, cannot be completely ignored. It only seems sensible to call X a precursor of Y, when both X and Y had structural or functional similarities at the level of analysis being considered (thus it seems odd to call the streptococcus a precursor of a sore throat, but it does not seem strange to consider babbling as a possible precursor of speech).

Because the relations between early occurring and later conditions are often probabilistic, not deterministic ones, the definition of precursor is bedevilled by a good deal of vagueness. It seems utterly pointless to get into arguments about whether a situation in which X is followed by Y 80% of the time involves a sufficiently high probability for precursor status to be invoked.

Overall, it seems that deciding whether something is a precursor or not involves nothing more than a summary of the conditional probabilities of the occurrence of one state given the presence of another, followed by a series of debates over whether the other conditions have been met. In other words, the concept of precursor is not much more tractable than the concept of cause, and once again one is simply transforming information on to a new scale of measurement: from a precise description of the actual conditional probabilities of later states following upon earlier ones to a nominal scale, where we say something is either a precursor or not. Furthermore, by making this transformation, investigators are implicitly committing themselves to the assumption that the phenomenon in question develops in stages, with all the associated logic that a stage theory implies (see Pickles, Chapter 2 this volume).

Perhaps the main strength of the concept of precursor is simply in extending the range of phenomena to be included in a meaningful developmental description. In Bryant's (1990) terms, identification of possible precursors means that we begin with something rather than nothing. As such, the search for precursors is an important part of a "descriptive teleonomic" enterprise, just as much as the identification of possible end-points is. Working hypotheses about precursors and end-points concentrate the mind and parse the phenomena to be described. Precursors do not, however, hold special causal status, any more than end-points do, and they do not allow us to escape the necessity of moving beyond a single-minded quest for necessary and sufficient causes.

PRACTICAL IMPLICATIONS FOR THE STUDY OF DEVELOPMENT AND PSYCHOPATHOLOGY: PARAMETER ESTIMATION IN ADDITION TO HYPOTHESIS TESTING

If we really did stop trying to pin down causes, would that fundamentally change the way we study development and psychopathology? Our feelings are that, as scientists, we would do many of the things we have always done, but we might worry less about our choice of methods and we might waste less time. Furthermore, our efforts would be more in keeping with modern scientific strategies and statistical theory, contemporary developmental and evolutionary theories, and, most importantly, the fundamental biological and social nature of the phenomena we are trying to understand. Proper description of NNUP conditions in a developmental trajectory is a more appropriate goal than the search for linear, unidirectional, reductionist, and deterministic relationships, which, as we have seen, do not provide a good fit for many developmental phenomena. Traditional ideas about causality are, in fact, essentially inimical to the probabilistic epigenetic approach that seems best suited to the study of development and pyschopathology (Gottlieb, 1991).

In practice, setting the notion of causality to one side means that we need not always be bound by three traditional research ideals that may actually distract us from the task at hand:

(1)   *Parsimony of explanation*;
(2)   *Concern with long-term as opposed to short-term influences*;
(3)   *The superiority of experimental over non-experimental designs.*

These three ideals may often be inappropriate, because, in a probabilistic universe, important influences on development and psychopathology need not be simple, need not last for a lifetime, and may not be clearly identifiable under carefully controlled experimental conditions.

The limits of parsimony

As mentioned earlier, the requirement of parsimony is essentially an aesthetic judgement: if two explanations of a phenomenon are equally well supported by evidence, one generally prefers the simpler one. That does not mean, however, that the more complex explanation is any less true. Furthermore, in most realistic situations, the two explanations might not be equally plausible. Rather, most often one is once again dealing in probabilities. In the terminology of multiple regression equations, the added complexities of the second explanation may add somewhat to the variance accounted for and so we ask ourselves, does it do so to such an extent that we feel justified in abandoning the simpler, more attractive explanation? The chapters in this book provided a number of examples where parsimonious explanations seem inadequate, particularly with respect to the classic developmental hypotheses regarding structure–function relationships, predetermined epigenesis, and the primacy of early experience. Thus, for example, Goodman discussed the need to go beyond assessment of the role of brain damage to more complex propositions about brain abnormalities. Cairns and his colleagues provided evidence of reciprocal relationships between genetic action and developmental influences. Nash and Hay elaborated upon the simple early experience model of the relationship between early relationships and later ones by requiring information about mediating cognitive processes and constraints in adulthood. The new explanations are not as parsimonious as the ones they challenge, but probably more accurate and encompassing.

Traditionally, scientists have preferred parsimony in the phenomena they were attempting to explain, as well as in the purported causal influences. Here, too, one may not be making a proper scientific judgement but merely an aesthetic one. Thus, for example, nosologists such as Jaspers (1963) have argued for parsimony of diagnosis; if possible, a person should be assumed to be suffering from one disease rather than many (see Caron & Rutter, 1991). But, as Angold has pointed out in Chapter 10, co-morbidity of depression and other disorders in childhood is not just a methodological irritant; it is one of the most important substantive questions that the developmental psychopathologist must tackle. In general, if we refrain from seeking single cause–single outcome relationships, we can move beyond the aesthetic judgements of past scholars to a more convincing description of the available evidence.

The emphasis on long-term continuities and influences

Similar issues can be raised with respect to the quest for long-term as opposed to short-term relationships among variables. This may take several forms, including:

(1) Attempts to find long-term homotypic continuity along a particular dimension;
(2) Assumptions that early occurring influences are more important than later occurring ones;
(3) Assumptions that experimental treatments and prevention programmes have failed if they demonstrate only short-term and not long-term generalized effects.

Adoption of a probabilistic epigenetic approach to the study of development is incompatible with all of these assumptions.

Firstly, scientists need to seek mediators of whatever long-term continuities are observed, and to recognize that the factors that provoke or prevent the display of a condition early in life are probably not identical to those that provoke or prevent its occurrence later on, even if the rank order of individuals remains the same. Furthermore, as Le Blanc and Loeber have stressed, those factors that influence the onset of a trait or condition that persists over long periods of time are not necessarily the same factors as determine its offset. Thus individuals begin, maintain, and end their criminal careers for quite different reasons. Secondly, with respect to the primacy of early occurring influences, as Nash and Hay have pointed out, the early experience model requires elaboration and similar attention to mediating mechanisms. And, finally, with respect to treatment and prevention studies, there is every reason to believe that additional factors need to be examined to understand the persistence of effects, as opposed to their immediate manifestation. Lack of persistence or transfer does not negate the initial outcome.

Are experiments always to be preferred?

The latter point raises the general issue of the uses and potential abuses of experimental and quasi-experimental methods in the study of development and psychopathology. The preceding chapters have clearly demonstrated the many important contributions of experimental approaches to the topics considered. With respect to our understanding of psychopathogenesis, experiments on normal development have provided much-needed clues about proper assessment procedures and have generated important hypotheses that can be tested in other ways. Thus, for example, our understanding of the nature of the deficit in autism, and success in finding early predictors of the disorder, has been greatly furthered by the experimental work on normal children's early prosocial actions and developing theories of mind (Caplan, Chapter 7 this volume; Frye, Chapter 5 this volume; Sigman and Mundy, Chapter 6 this volume). Similarly, experimental studies of infants' attention to visual stimuli have provided important assessment tools for the study of intellectual development (Sigman and Mundy, Chapter 6 this volume).

It is clear that developmental psychopathologists are well advised to trawl through the experimental literature for new measurement strategies, and for new ideas as well. Both Cairns and his colleagues and Nash and Hay have described how the experimental literature on non-human development yields general principles that can be applied across species. A similar assumption is made by those investigators focusing on cognitive processes in depression (see Angold, Chapter 10 this volume), who have borrowed the concept of "learned helplessness" from experimental studies of dogs.

These important contributions of the experimental literature do not imply, however, that the development of psychopathology is itself always best studied by means of experimental or quasi-experimental procedures. At the outset, investigators of clinical groups need not cast their important descriptive work as if such studies were experiments. In our attempts to understand how psychopathology develops, comparison of samples from particular clinical populations is a necessary scientific activity, and thus case-control comparisons will always have a place in developmental psychopathology. However, it is important to realize that such studies provide systematic, controlled descriptions of psychopathological phenomena, but do not easily yield direct tests of causal hypotheses. This is partly because, in the absence of true experimental manipulation, perfect control is impossible; as methodologists have long pointed out, groups matched on particular variables of interest are likely to become systematically unmatched on other, unknown variables (see Everitt & Hay, 1992). For this reason, the descriptive functions of the case-control design are perhaps sharpened if more than two matched groups are compared; pairwise comparisons of groups within the overall study who differ in some respects but not others yields more precise description of the phenomena of interest.

Even if perfect matching were achieved, however, one would still have to wonder exactly what sort of causal hypothesis was being tested in a case-control design. It is perhaps easiest to see this in Aristotelian terms. In a quasi-experimental design, the investigator is borrowing the logic of inquiry used to test hypotheses about efficient causes, namely John Stuart Mill's "method of difference". The method of difference assumes that if two groups are exactly the same in every respect except for the presence or absence of the experimental manipulation, any difference in their behaviour must be due to the action of the causal variable. Because, in the evaluation of quasi-experimental designs, we often use the statistical techniques designed to test experimental hypotheses (t-tests, analysis of variance, and multivariate analysis of variance), it is tempting to think we are using the same causal logic. But, with respect to a case-control design, we are in fact testing a hypothesis about formal causation—in other words, about the emergent properties of the particular pattern of symptoms that define a clinical condition.

Consider, for example, a hypothetical study in which we ask whether depressed adolescents are less likely than other adolescents to make opposite-sex friends. Let us assume that matching of the groups has been very carefully done. The two groups then differ with respect to their psychological form—individuals in one group have been shown to exhibit a particular pattern of thoughts, feelings and behaviours that is absent in the other group. In this example, one is essentially testing whether the diagnosis of depression, so defined, is a formal cause that serves to handicap individuals' emerging social relationships. Now, depending on the particular theory of depression that investigators hold, they may believe that the psychological form in question (the depressive diagnosis) is itself a function of earlier occurring material or efficient causes (e.g. brain amines or life events respectively). But the comparison of the two groups is at best a very indirect test of earlier efficient causation, despite the illusions provided by the imitation of an experimental design.

These concerns, of course, do not prevent investigators from obtaining important descriptive information about the potentially handicapping effects of childhood depression by making such a comparison. If we side-step the issue of defining causality, we may also side-step a certain clumsiness in our own causal logic, and get on with the business at hand: estimating the true parameter of a perfect description of psychopathological development. In many cases, use of an inappropriate causal logic only delays one's efforts to estimate that perfect description.

It is important to note that our concerns about causal inference are mirrored by trends in contemporary statistical theory. The modern statistician views the use of variance-partitioning and significance-testing techniques as old-fashioned at best and misleading at worst; contemporary statistical approaches are much more concerned with parameter estimation, computer-aided graphical description, and model fitting that with the hypothesis-testing logic of Mill's method of difference (see Everitt & Hay, 1992). Note that a decision about whether a particular variable is or is not causal often relies on statistical significance-testing procedures. Once again, in the case of significance testing, we are inappropriately transforming precise information (e.g. the confidence limits for our parameter estimation) on to a simple, dichotomous scale (significant or not, and therefore causal or not). Thus the basic logic of experimental hypothesis testing provides the researcher with impoverished information, and thus a very imperfect description. In general, we recommend that developmental psychopathologists should pay more attention to parameter estimation, likelihood modelling, and graphical techniques, as supplements to, if not replacements for, conventional hypothesis testing.

CONCLUSIONS

In sum, we are proposing a research agenda for developmental psychopathology that is in line with contemporary theory in the physical and biological sciences and with contemporary developments in statistical theory. In our attempts to move beyond causality, we recognize that, for humans, the perception of causal relationships among events is probably a Gibsonian affordance (e.g. Gibson, 1982). In evolutionary terms, the characteristic human ability to deduce causal principles from diverse bits of information has no doubt conveyed advantages to individual members of our species. To paraphrase a familiar statement, if true causes do not really exist, humans in general and scientists in particular may still need to invent them. What is required, however, is a recognition of when the search for causes (and, on the way, for precursors) stimulates scientific progress and when it impedes it. We are most grateful for the careful consideration of these topics given by the contributors to this book, and for all the important findings they have so cogently presented. Even these creative scholars, however, have been unable to solve a philosophical problem that has remained unsolved for two-and-a-half-millennia. In our view, it seems unlikely to be solved in any way that would add to our understanding of development or psychopathology. We choose to remain agnostic as to whether true causes exist, and to strive for more precise descriptions.

REFERENCES

Bryant, P. (1990). Empirical evidence for causes in development. In G. Butterworth & P. Bryant (eds), *Causes of Development*, Harvester Wheatsheaf, Hemel Hempstead, pp. 33–45.
Cairns, R. B., Gairépy, J. L. & Hood, K. E. (1990). Development, microevolution, and social behavior. *Psychological Review*, **97**, 49–65.
Carey, S. (1990). On some relations between the description and the explanation of developmental change. In G. Butterworth & P. Bryant (eds), *Causes of Development*, Harvester Wheatsheaf, Hemel Hempstead, pp. 135–157.
Caron, C. & Rutter, M. (1991). Comorbidity in child psychopathology: concepts,

issues and research strategies. *Journal of Child Psychology and Psychiatry*, **32**, 1063–1080.

Everitt, B. S. & Hay, D. F. (1992). *Talking About Statistics: A Psychologist's Guide to Design and Analysis*, Edward Arnold, London.

Gibson, E. J. (1982). The concept of affordances in development: the renascence of functionalism. In W. A. Collins (ed.), *The Concept of Development. The Minnesota Symposium*, vol. 15, Erlbaum, Hillsdale, NJ, pp. 55–81.

Gottlieb, G. (1991). Experiential canalization of behavioral development: theory. *Developmental Psychology*, **27**, 4–13.

Greenough, W. T. (1991). Experience as a component of normal development: evolutionary considerations. *Developmental Psychology*, **27**, 14–17.

Hay, D. F. (1980). Multiple functions of proximity-seeking in infancy. *Child Development*, **51**, 636–645.

Jaspers, K. (1963). *General Psychopathology*, Manchester University Press, Manchester.

Lewin, K. (1939). Field theory and experiment in social psychology: concepts and methods. *American Journal of Sociology*, **44**, 868–896.

McGue, M. (1989). Nature–nurture and intelligence. *Nature*, **340**, 507–508.

Mackie, J. L. (1974). *The Cement of the Universe: A study of Causation*, Oxford University Press, Oxford.

Pinard, A. & Laurendeau, M. (1969). "Stage" in Piaget's cognitive–developmental theory: exegesis of a concept. In D. Elkind & J. Flavell (eds), *Studies in Cognitive Development: Essays in Honor of Jean Piaget*, Oxford University Press, London, pp. 121–170.

Plomin, R., DeFries, J. C. & Loehlin, J. C. (1977). Genotype interaction and correlation in the analysis of human behavior. *Psychological Bulletin*, **34**, 309–322.

Russell, B. (1912). On the notion of cause. *Proceedings of the Aristotelian Society*, **19**, 1–21.

Russell, J. (1990). Causal explanations of cognitive development. In G. Butterworth & P. Bryant (eds.), *Causes of Development*, Harvester Wheatsheaf, Hemel Hempstead, pp. 111–134.

Scarr, S. & McCartney, K. (1983). How people make their own environments: a theory of genotype → environment effects. *Child Development*, **54**, 424–435.

Index

abdominal pain 275
activation, criminal offending 236, 243, 244–6, 250–1
adaptive mechanisms 112–15
adjustment disorder 269, 270
aetiology 3–4
affect
  prosocial behavior and 173
  twin studies 92, 93
age
  behavior genetics and 89–90
  criminal offending and 237
  depression and 284
age of onset
  criminal offending 250
  distributions 32–7
aggravation, criminal offending 236, 243, 246–7, 250–1
aggressive behavior 44
  criminal offending and 245–6
  genetic influences 103, 105–6, 107–8, 109, 110, 114
alcohol consumption 103, 249
altruism, reciprocal 205
altruistic behavior 182
altruistic surrender 191
Alzheimer's disease 32
analogues 14–15
animal studies 309
  behavior genetics 99–109, 110–11
  imprinting in birds 201, 202, 206–14
anti-establishment attitude 252, 253
anticonvulsant drugs 69, 76
anxiety disorders 277
appearance–reality distinction 146, 151–2, 163–4
Aristotle 2, 9
armed forces, service in 251
arousal, state regulation, infants 127, 128–9, 136
asbestos 3, 38

assortative mating 112, 212
attachment theory 199–200, 203–5
attachments
  animal studies 105
  birds 201–2
  primary 203–6
  see also relationships
attention
  infant 128–9, 136–7, 295, 309
    childhood intelligence and 132, 134, 135
    environmental influences 137–8
  joint 129, 130, 134
attention deficits 74
  autism 134
  brain abnormalities 55, 62–3
  criminal offending and 246
  depression and 277
  Down's syndrome/mental retardation 132, 134, 135
autism 19, 45, 65, 69, 309
  infant precursors of childhood abilities 129, 133–5
  theories of mind 153–4

behavior genetics, see genetics, behavior
behavioral disorders
  birth damage and 76–9
  brain abnormalities and 54–5, 56–66
  mechanisms mediating 69
beliefs
  false, see false belief tasks
  understanding their own 149–50
Bengalese finches 207–8, 210, 211–12
bereavement reaction 268–9, 270, 281–2
birds, imprinting in 201, 202, 206–14
birth damage 55–6, 76–81
birthweight, hyperactivity and 80

Index complied by Liza Weinkove